Assessment Accommodations for Classroom Teachers of Culturally and Linguistically Diverse Students

Assessment Accommodations for Classroom Teachers of Culturally and Linguistically Diverse Students

Socorro G. Herrera

Kansas State University

Kevin G. Murry

Kansas State University

Robin Morales Cabral

Kansas State University

PEARSON

Boston ■ New York ■ San Francisco
Mexico City ■ Montreal ■ Toronto ■ London ■ Madrid ■ Munich ■ Paris
Hong Kong ■ Singapore ■ Tokyo ■ Cape Town ■ Sydney

Executive Editor: Aurora Martínez Ramos
Series Editorial Assistant: Lynda Giles
Executive Marketing Manager: Krista Clark
Production Editor: Annette Joseph
Editorial Production Service: Omegatype Typography, Inc.
Composition Buyer: Linda Cox
Manufacturing Buyer: Linda Morris
Electronic Composition: Omegatype Typography, Inc.
Cover Administrator: Kristina Mose-Libon

For related titles and support materials, visit our online catalog at www.ablongman.com.

Between the time website information is gathered and then published, it is not unusual for some sites to have closed. Also, the transcription of URLs can result in typographical errors. The publisher would appreciate notification where these errors occur so that they may be corrected in subsequent editions.

Library of Congress Cataloging-in-Publication Data

Herrera, Socorro Guadalupe.
  Assessment accommodations for classroom teachers of culturally and linguistically diverse students / Socorro G. Herrera, Kevin G. Murry, Robin Morales Cabral.
    p. cm.
  ISBN 0-205-49271-1 (alk. paper)
   1. Children of minorities—Education—United States—Evaluation. 2. Multicultural education—United States—Evaluation. 3. Linguistic minorities—Ability testing. 4. Educational tests and measurements. 5. Teachers—Training of—United States. I. Murry, Kevin G. II. Cabral, Robin Morales. III. Title.

LC3731.H475 2007
371.26—dc22

                                                                    2006046591

Printed in the United States of America

10 9 8 7 6 5 4 3 2 1   RRD-VA   10 09 08 07 06

Como el sol fuerte y lleno de vida, dedico este trabajo a mi papá, Gilberto Herrera Ramírez. Su trabajo y fuerza dio a sus hijos la fortaleza de salir adelante. Aunque mi trabajo me ha llevado lejos de él, siempre está presente en mis obras y corazón.

—Socorro

To my father, for whom the word support *has always meant lifelong persistence. For this second chance at the precipice, I am decidedly grateful. Although we have not always agreed upon our approaches to diversity, we have, nonetheless, consistently shared a common affinity for advocacy.*

—Kevin

To my mother, Edna Moody Morales, whose life of wonder, compassion, and purpose inspires her family to continually marvel at nature's gifts . . . and human possibility.

—Robin

◼brief contents

■contents

chapter 5

Assessment of Language Proficiency   118

chapter 6

Assessment of Content-Area Learning   170

chapter 7

Special Education Issues in the Assessment of CLD Students   214

chapter 8

Postinstructional Assessment   240

The trend toward increasing numbers of culturally and linguistically diverse (CLD) students in the classroom is not a new phenomenon. In border and coastal states such as Texas, California, New York, and Florida, this is a long-standing trend. What has changed is the intensity and scope of this trend, which now influences classroom, school, and district decision making and educational policy throughout the nation. This is not the first, nor is it likely to be the last, textbook to address assessment practices for diverse populations.

■ Purpose

If textbooks that address assessment practices for diverse students already exist, why is this text needed? Assessment texts have traditionally been organized around assessment types, practices, and protocols. However, the authors of this text wanted the *student* to be the driving force behind the narrative and organization and, therefore, began with a critical examination of fundamental questions about appropriate assessment practices for CLD students.

This text is written from the perspective of a *differential lens on assessment* practices for CLD students. This perspective emphasizes the following fundamental questions:

- Who should be the focus of assessment?
- Where should assessment efforts be concentrated?
- What should be the key purposes of assessment?
- When should assessments be conducted?
- How are the findings of assessment best used to improve practices for, and academic achievement among, CLD students?

The discussions in this text are designed to guide PreK–12 classroom teachers as they successfully differentiate assessment practices for diverse student populations. However, essential to these conversations is an understanding that meeting the needs of students from diverse backgrounds requires a collaborative team effort. Reading and math specialists, special education teachers, school psychologists, and other educational specialists contribute valuable expertise and assessment data to decision making about these students. The following exploration explains how answers to the aforementioned questions have guided the design and organization of this text.

Who

The question of who should be the focus of assessment (and the content of this text) can be answered by recognizing the increasing numbers of students who bring to today's classroom a complex range of cross-cultural, language, and learning needs. In many parts of the country, CLD student populations are radically changing from those whose needs were addressed even five years ago. This text, therefore, focuses on the assessment of CLD students. The changing nature of this student population is the emphasis of discussion in Chapter 1.

Where

This text also assumes a differentiating approach to the question of where assessment efforts for CLD students should be concentrated. Traditionally, this question is answered according to either the range of (primarily formal) assessments available to school educators or assessment policy perspectives. Instead, this text aligns the emphases of assessment efforts with critical dimensions of the CLD student biography (Herrera & Murry, 2005). More specifically, this text devotes three chapters to core assessments that directly relate to the four critical dimensions of the CLD student biography: the sociocultural dimension (Chapter 4), the linguistic dimension (Chapter 5), and the cognitive and academic dimensions (Chapter 6). This alignment of assessments with the CLD student biography ensures that teachers and their instructional practices are better informed by data about each dimension of the student's life.

What

What should be the key purposes of assessments for CLD students? The purposes of classroom assessments for CLD students should first encompass the need to provide the classroom teacher with the critical information necessary to adapt and refine classroom instruction and related practices for increasingly diverse populations of students. If these teachers are to prove successful with CLD students, they must determine more than what the student does not know. Today's teachers need to know what *assets* the CLD student brings to the learning environment.

Among such assets the CLD student may bring are rich socialization experiences in another country or culture (Chapters 2 and 4), unexpected cross-cultural insights (Chapter 4), prior schooling and academic experiences (Chapters 3 and 6), advanced cognitive skills (Chapter 7), strong first language knowledge and emergent capacities in a second language (Chapters 3 and 5), and real-world experiences with survival, agriculture, cooking, the marketplace, and more (Chapters 2 and 8). Thus, the purposes of assessments for CLD students are as much about informing teachers as they are related to the evaluation of learners.

When

The timing of appropriate classroom assessment practices for CLD students is the product of a teacher's reflection on student needs and assets, decisions about where to concentrate assessment efforts, and attention to the purposes of such assessments. Just as there are no recipes for successful instruction that work with all CLD student populations, there are few rules of timing for the implementation of assessments. Moreover, timing and sequence issues tend to vary according to types of assessments, including authentic versus standardized (Chapters 2–8), formative versus summative (Chapters 2, 6, and 8), informal versus formal (Chapters 2–8), and norm-referenced versus criterion-referenced (Chapters 5 and 6).

Fundamentally, successful teachers reflect on their *informed* philosophies about appropriate assessment practices for CLD students (Chapter 2). Such teachers also process and analyze data from formal and mostly informal preassessments of students (Chapter 3) to make decisions about which recurrent assessments are best for their classroom population and when such assessments should be implemented.

How

Ultimately, reflective educators are concerned with the question of how the findings of assessments with CLD students are best used. From a best-practice perspective, assessment findings may be used for at least three critical purposes: student monitoring and motivation, instructional and assessment accommodations, and stakeholder reporting. Each of these purposes is addressed throughout the text in ways that are consistent with both the complexities of the CLD student biography and the teacher's challenges in differentiating assessment practices for increasingly diverse student populations.

1. *Student Monitoring and Motivation.* Valid and purposeful assessment findings may be used to:
   - Monitor student progress in level of acculturation, first and second language acquisition, and content-area learning (Chapters 4, 5, 6, and 7)
   - Identify and document incremental gains (Chapters 3, 6, and 8)
   - Enhance student interest, engagement, and motivation (Chapters 1 and 2)
   - Enhance students' self-assessment and reflection on the quality and effectiveness of their learning efforts (Chapters 2 and 6)
2. *Instructional and Assessment Accommodations.* Valid and purposeful assessment findings may be used to:
   - Refine and improve future assessments (Chapters 2 and 8)
   - Adapt and tailor classroom instruction to accommodate CLD students' assets and needs (Chapters 3, 4, 5, 6, and 8).
   - Inform the classroom teacher's personal assessments of effectiveness in differentiating classroom practices for CLD learners and aligning his or her practices with nationally recognized standards of best practice with CLD students (Chapter 7).

3. *Stakeholder Reporting.* Valid and purposeful assessment findings may be used to inform key stakeholders, including:
   - CLD students as self-monitoring learners (Chapters 2 and 6)
   - Parents, guardians, and family members of CLD students (Chapters 1, 2, and 7)
   - School and district administration (Chapters 2 and 8)
   - State or federal monitoring (or funding) agencies (Chapters 7 and 8)

Recent educational reform initiatives have placed increased scrutiny on schools and school districts that educate CLD students. In some ways, the expectations of such measures, and the methods they recommend, fail to reflect the reality of today's increasingly diverse classrooms. In other ways, such measures remind us that the purposes of quality classroom assessment practices are numerous, multifaceted, and sometimes intimidating. This text offers a way for educators to organize their perspectives on these complexities as they seek to enhance the effectiveness of their assessment practices with CLD students.

■ Special Features

To enhance reader interest, accommodate different learning styles, and offer additional insights on topics covered, this text offers the following special features.

Chapter Outlines

By providing an outline at the beginning of each chapter, we have tried to afford our readers both an advance organizer and a fundamental understanding of the content of each chapter.

Chapter Objectives

It is our belief that every educator should have access to the purpose and idea behind a particular lesson (in this case, chapter of the text). Hence, each chapter is introduced with an inventory of objectives to be achieved as reader outcomes for that chapter.

Standards of Best Practice

These special features appear in each chapter of the text and serve as a model for professionalism in practice with diversity. Specifically, these features align the content of all lessons or chapters with nationally recognized standards for best practice—the TESOL/NCATE standards and the CEEE Guiding Principles for best practice with CLD students. In addition, these features provide teachers with a self-assessment framework as they progress through the text. Teachers can reflect on their own practices with CLD students and families and determine the extent to which they meet each noted standard of professional practice. Thus, these features provide a road map to excellence as educators continually strive to improve their differentiated assessment practices with CLD students.

Key Concepts

This feature of the text is provided in all chapters and reminds the reader of the critical content discussed in that particular chapter. Related features at the end of each chapter, especially the Questions for Review and Reflection, help ensure that the reader's study of the chapter has appropriately emphasized these key theories and concepts.

Professional Conversations on Practice

This exceptional feature, included in every chapter, suggests topics for discussion and debate among pre- and inservice educators about critical issues that have been explored or detailed in the content of the associated chapter. The feature is designed to encourage critical thinking, reflection, articulation of new knowledge, debate, metacognition, and theory-into-practice applications.

Questions for Review and Reflection

This feature recurs in each chapter of the book and provides opportunities for self-assessment of content comprehension and readiness for applications to practice. The questions included in these features are applicable to educators at all levels, including preservice teachers, paraprofessionals, inservice teachers, staff specialists, and school administrators.

Text Boxes

Four types of text boxes are variously used throughout the text to reinforce, emphasize, or expand on chapter content.

- *Accommodative Assessment Practices.* These text boxes offer the reader a glimpse of the bigger assessment picture and highlight ways in which key theories, concepts, and arguments from the narrative might be appropriately applied to professional practice with CLD students. These features are frequently structured as vignettes that identify and address assessment challenges related to the four dimensions of the student biography. These text boxes prompt school educators to reflect on various aspects of best practice for the appropriate assessment of PreK–12 CLD students. These features are provided in all textbook chapters except the introductory chapter.
- *Assessment Freeze Frames.* These enrichments offer the reader highlighted snapshots of key points from the chapter narrative. They are provided in all but the introductory chapter.

- *Assessment in Action.* These text boxes offer the reader detailed how-to information for adapting, refining, and developing accommodative assessments for CLD students. These features are provided in Chapters 2 through 6, which directly address types of assessments developed by PreK–12 classroom teachers (Chapter 8 provides specific assessment strategies embedded in the narrative).
- *Close-Ups on Assessment.* These enrichments offer the reader enlargements of perspectives on key strategies, techniques, theories, concepts, or arguments from the chapter narrative. These features are provided in all but the introductory chapter.

Figures and Tables

Every chapter of the text offers explanatory or illustrative figures or tables specifically designed to enhance the content of the chapter. Educators can capitalize on these features to more fully understand the concepts and research-based practices discussed in this book. Certain chapters also include Assessment Artifacts, which are special figures of interest to readers who already instruct or expect to teach CLD students.

- *Assessment Artifacts.* These figures are included in the core assessment chapters of the text, Chapters 4, 5, and 6. The content of these chapters emphasizes differentiated assessments and practices for each of the four dimensions of the CLD student biography (discussed in Chapter 3): the sociocultural dimension (Chapter 4), the linguistic dimension (Chapter 5), and the cognitive and academic dimensions (Chapter 6). These artifacts, from the actual field experiences of classroom teachers, typically highlight examples of assessments used with CLD students. Assessment artifacts are included to provide exemplars of teachers' creative resolutions of the many challenges involved in the development of equitable assessments for diverse student populations.

Appendix

This feature provides teachers with ready-to-use resources for their assessment practices with CLD students. The resources are drawn from chapter content that addresses types of assessments developed by PreK–12 classroom teachers.

Glossary

This feature serves as an auxiliary resource for current readers and for applications of content to practice in the future. Particular attention has been given to those terms likely to seem unfamiliar to current and future educators who have had few educational experiences with CLD students.

Reference List

Assembled in the American Psychological Association's bibliography style, this feature documents the theory, research, and analyses that support the discussions, content, conclusions, and recommendations of the authors in this text. Additionally, the feature serves as a resource for preservice and inservice educators of CLD students.

■ Acknowledgments

Assessment that does not highlight the accomplishments and further the potential of the student is like productive efficiency without a valuable product outcome. Similarly, the value of this text to the field and to the practitioners who find it useful will be a function of the accomplishments of those who contributed to it and who collaborated to maximize its potential. Therefore, the three of us wish to acknowledge the many contributions of others who have collaborated with us to make this text possible.

We would like to extend special thanks to and acknowledge Sheri Meredith. Her patience, diligence, sacrifice, and persistence have proved integral to the organization, quality, and accuracy of this product outcome. We are infinitely grateful for her collaboration.

Likewise, we extend a very special acknowledgment to Melissa Holmes for her conscientiousness, tolerance, and caring. Melissa brought many valuable qualities to this effort, not the least of which were editorial expertise, organizational awareness, attention to readability, and steadfast determination. We would also like to recognize Chris Ostrom for his assistance in revising and refining the text for readability and accuracy.

Special thanks are also in order for Shabina Kavimandan who, despite many other pressing obligations, took time to provide insightful perspectives, refinements, and reviews. Her willingness to brainstorm, discuss, and review was extremely valuable.

We wish to acknowledge the significant people in our lives, Esteban Cabral, Dr. Gilbert Davila, and Dr. Nancy Kole, as well as our students, faculty, and staff, whose varied contributions from prior experience with (or as) CLD students in public schools and with diverse school practice have made this work possible. To these people we each owe our heart and soul.

A number of classroom teachers who serve the differential learning and transition needs of CLD students have provided insights from their professional practices. These are greatly appreciated and have been primarily included in the Assessment Artifacts and Accommodative Assessment Practices features. We especially wish to acknowledge the insightful contributions of the teachers of Hillcrest Elementary School, Lawrence, Kansas, and their school administrator, Tammy Becker. The many experiences of these educators highlight the ways professional practice can effectively and mutually accommodate both the assets and needs of the CLD student.

Finally, we would like to thank the following reviewers for their comments on the manuscript: Zohreh Eslami, Texas A&M University; Janet Medina, McDaniel College; Dr. Fay Roseman, Barry University; and Sam Worley, Arkansas Tech University.

Dr. Socorro G. Herrera currently serves as professor of elementary education at Kansas State University and is director of the Center for Intercultural and Multilingual Advocacy (CIMA). Certified in elementary education, bilingual education, and school counseling, Dr. Herrera's recent publications have appeared in *Bilingual Research Journal, Journal of Latinos and Education,* and *Journal of Latinos in Rural Education.* Her recent research and teaching in education have emphasized emergent literacy, reading strategies, the differential learning needs of second language learners, and mutual accommodation for language learning students.

Dr. Kevin G. Murry is currently associate professor of secondary education at Kansas State University and is director of research and development for the CIMA Center. His work in research and development has focused on ESL/dual language programming in secondary public schools and teachers' accommodation readiness for transnational students. Dr. Murry's recent research has emphasized advocacy frameworks for culturally and linguistically diverse students, the linguistic and cross-cultural dynamics of ESL instruction, portfolio-based practicum experiences, and school restructuring for linguistic diversity. His recent publications have appeared in *Journal of Continuing Higher Education, AACTE Briefs,* and *Bilingual Research Journal.*

Robin Morales Cabral currently serves as instructional coordinator for the CIMA Center at Kansas State University. Ms. Cabral prepares school educators to professionally address the social, emotional, and learning needs of students in highly diverse K–12 schools. She has a background in communicative disorders and sciences, school leadership, bilingual special education, and assessment for culturally and linguistically diverse students. Ms. Cabral's years of experience as a bilingual speech language pathologist, parent–teacher liaison, intervention coordinator, and assessment specialist have led to advisory roles with classroom teachers, special educators, and school administrators dedicated to implementing best school and classroom practices for CLD students.

Assessment Accommodations for Classroom Teachers of Culturally and Linguistically Diverse Students

Classroom Assessment amidst Cultural and Linguistic Diversity

I have a student that has a very difficult time taking multiple-choice exams. But, if I verbally give him the test, he has a much easier time completing the test. . . . I also have a student that is an incredible artist. I have asked her to take several vocabulary words and create pictures that portray these words, and I then ask her to explain the term and the picture. . . . If I fail to unveil [my students'] capabilities and strengths, then I am just . . . well, failing them, and shutting doors on a bright future. I do not want to be responsible for turning away from their right to a great education and having them leave my room feeling insignificant and discouraged. In concern for the ELL [CLD] student, my challenge is intensified!

Michael Berndt
Fourth-Grade Teacher

critical standards *Guiding Chapter Content*

TESOL/NCATE teacher standards reflect professional consensus on standards for the quality teaching of PreK–12 CLD students. Additionally, the CEEE Guiding Principles and their accompanying indicators serve as a framework to assist practitioners, policymakers, and clients as they collaborate to enhance academic enrichment and language acquisition among CLD students. Therefore, to help educators understand how they might appropriately target and address national professional teaching standards in practice, we have designed the content of this chapter to reflect the following standards.

TESOL/NCATE Standards for P–12 Teacher Education Programs

Domain 4: Assessment. Candidates understand issues of assessment and use standards-based assessment measures with ESOL students.

- **Standard 4.c. Classroom-Based Assessment for ESL.** Candidates know and use a variety of performance-based assessment tools and techniques to inform instruction.
  - **4.c.2.** Use various instruments and techniques to assess content-area learning (e.g., math, science, social studies) for ESOL learners at varying levels of language and literacy development.

Domain 5: Professionalism. Candidates demonstrate knowledge of the history of ESL teaching. Candidates keep current with new instructional techniques, research results, advances in the ESL field, and public policy issues. Candidates use such information to reflect upon and improve their instructional practices. Candidates provide support and advocate for ESOL students and their families and work collaboratively to improve the learning environment.

- **Standard 5.c. Professional Development and Collaboration.** Candidates collaborate with and are prepared to serve as a resource to all staff, including paraprofessionals, to improve learning for all ESOL students.
  - **5.c.2.** Work with other teachers and staff to provide comprehensive, challenging educational opportunities for ESOL students in the school.

Note: All TESOL/NCATE standards are cited from TESOL (2003). All Guiding Principles are cited from Center for Equity and Excellence in Education (CEEE) (2005). Reprinted by permission.

CEEE Guiding Principles

Principle #4: English language learners receive instruction that builds on their prior knowledge and cognitive abilities and is responsive to their language proficiency levels and cultural backgrounds.

4.11 **Understand** and value the linguistic backgrounds and cultural heritages of their English language learners' families and use this information to enrich classroom instruction and to support their students' learning of academic content.

Principle #5: English language learners are evaluated with appropriate and valid assessments that are aligned to state and local standards and that take into account the language development stages and cultural backgrounds of the students.

5.45 **Employ** culturally and developmentally appropriate, authentic, criterion-referenced, and other alternative assessment instruments that are capable of measuring gains in content-area academic knowledge and English language proficiency.

The following problem was given to a classroom of urban middle school students from diverse cultural and linguistic backgrounds as part of a criterion-referenced classroom assessment (Glaser & Silver, 1994, p. 22).

Busy Bus Company Problem

Yvonne is trying to decide whether she should buy a weekly bus pass. On Monday, Wednesday, and Friday, she rides the bus to and from work. On Tuesday and Thursday, she rides the bus to work but gets a ride home with her friends. Should Yvonne buy a weekly bus pass?

Busy Bus Company Fares
One Way: $1.00
Weekly Pass: $9.00

The classroom teacher was surprised to find that many of these culturally and linguistically diverse (CLD) students concluded that Yvonne should purchase the weekly pass instead of paying the daily fare. The teacher considered the daily fare to be more economical.

Anxious to explore the reasoning behind students' decisions, the teacher decided to discuss the problem with the class. This discussion revealed surprising but reasonable applications of out-of-school knowledge and problem-solving strategies to this mathematical problem (Glaser & Silver, 1994). Basically, students who selected the weekly pass argued it was a better choice because it would allow several family members to use it, especially after work and in the evenings, but also on weekends. In effect, these insightful students had reasoned beyond the decontextualized statement of the problem to apply their background knowledge gained from urban living. Moreover, they applied this knowledge in a way that demonstrated a cost-effective use of public transportation. The teacher became convinced that more than one correct answer existed for the problem. In fact, she concluded that future assessments should more thoroughly explore what CLD and other students knew and were able to do. That is, students needed opportunities not only to provide answers but also to explain their reasoning and their applications of knowledge gained.

This example illustrates several of the rewards and challenges of differential assessment discussions, adaptations, and teaching practices for CLD students. These students bring to the classroom background knowledge and experiences that are often different from those of other students yet powerfully connected to real-world challenges, problems, dilemmas, and living. Unfortunately, traditional assessments may fail to capture the knowledge that CLD students bring to content-area learning. Classroom teachers are often in the best position to appropriately create, adapt, and modify assessments and assessment practices for CLD students so that these measures reflect the authentic, real-world knowledge and abilities of these students. *Assessment*, in this sense, can be purposefully defined as a range of procedures used to gather information about what students or other individuals know and are able to demonstrate.

Given the diversity of CLD students' experiences and prior knowledge, it is not surprising that classroom teachers of increasing numbers of CLD students are searching for resources to help them appropriately create, adapt, and apply differentiated assessment practices for CLD students. This text provides just such a resource, as well as a variety of useful guidelines for PreK–12 classroom teachers of CLD students.

Among the sorts of questions this text addresses are those that surface among classroom teachers as their numbers of CLD students increase on an annual and sometimes weekly basis. These questions include, but are not limited to, the following:

- How do I know that Jessie's difficulties with reading, language arts, and social studies don't indicate a disability?
- Thao has been in my room for six weeks. Why doesn't she respond to my questions during the lesson? Why doesn't she speak during group work? How can I evaluate what she comprehends and what she does not?
- I think that Marleny has already learned what we are studying in math right now. How do I find out what she learned while she was in El Salvador?
- We even used the Spanish version of the test! I know that Madai learned this material in Mexico. Why didn't she excel on this assessment?
- I know that my students from Bosnia are improving. But their six- and nine-week tests don't show it. What's wrong?

The concern of these teachers is evident in their queries. Yet such questions also tend to illustrate why differentiating classroom assessments and assessment practices is so critical to teacher and student success in today's classroom.

Nonetheless, these observations beg the question: What is so different about today's classroom that such differentiation of tools and practices has become essential? In the real world of today's classroom teacher, from elementary schools to high schools, from rural communities to large cities, these changes have begun with the students in the classroom.

What's Different about Today's Classroom?

What has changed and is constantly changing in today's public school classroom is the diversity of the student population. Most radically changing is the number of students that we refer to in this text as culturally and linguistically diverse (CLD). In the literature of education, these students are sometimes referred to as minority students. Additionally, this literature has variously referred to CLD students whose first or native language is not English as English language learners (ELL) or limited English proficient (LEP) students.

However, the term *culturally and linguistically diverse* is the most inclusive and cross-culturally sensitive description of a student whose culture or language differs from the dominant culture or language. The use of this term and its associated acronym are increasingly prevalent in educational literature (Buxton, 1999; Chamot & O'Malley, 1996; Escamilla, 1999; Herrera & Murry, 2005; New York State Education Department, 2002; Rodriguez, Parmar, & Signer, 2001). CLD students are those who bring diverse cultural heritages and assets to the school (Baca & Cervantes, 1998; Escamilla, 1999; Murry & Herrera, 2005a, 2005b). Yet, because diversity does not imply a level playing field, the acronym CLD most appropriately and affirmatively describes students who will require classroom assessments and assessment practices that are appropriately differentiated.

Immigration Fallacies and Facts

So, who are these CLD students? Where did they come from? Like virtually all Americans (Lurie, 1991; Cushner, McClelland, & Safford, 2006), CLD students are immigrants from another country. Some are recently immigrated; others are second- or third-generation Americans. Therefore, it becomes increasingly valuable for classroom teachers to know something about immigration trends and dynamics in the United States. One reason for this is that a number of myths and fallacies surround the subject of immigration in the twenty-first-century United States. Table 1.1 summarizes the top ten myths, as well as associated facts, as researched by the National Immigration Forum (2003). This table reminds us that CLD students and their family members, like immigrants of the past, come to this country for rational, valid, and compelling reasons. Moreover, like immigrants in the past, they not only contribute to the creativity and productivity of the nation, but they also want to learn English and become productive members of our society.

Similarly, a practical understanding of current immigration trends and associated dynamics is often crucial to the classroom teacher's appropriate preparation for CLD students, as well as the teacher's ability to meet student assessment needs.

■ **table 1.1**   Top Ten Immigration Myths and Facts

Myth	Fact	Source
1. Immigrants don't pay taxes.	All immigrants pay taxes, whether income, property, sales, or other. As far as income tax payments go, sources vary in their accounts, but a range of studies find that immigrants pay between $90 and $140 billion a year in federal, state, and local taxes. Even undocumented immigrants pay income taxes, as evidenced by the Social Security Administration's "suspense file" (taxes that cannot be matched to workers' names and social security numbers), which grew $20 billion between 1990 and 1998.	National Academy of Sciences, Cato Institute, Urban Institute, Social Security Administration
2. Immigrants come here to take welfare.[1]	Immigrants come to work and reunite with family members. Immigrant labor force participation is consistently higher than native-born, and immigrant workers make up a larger share of the U.S. labor force (12.4%) than they do the U.S. population (11.5%). Moreover, the ratio between immigrant use of public benefits and the amount of taxes they pay is consistently favorable to the U.S., unless the "study" was undertaken by an anti-immigrant group. In one estimate, immigrants earn about $240 billion a year, pay about $90 billion a year in taxes, and use about $5 billion in public benefits. In another cut of the data, immigrant tax payments total $20 to $30 billion more than the amount of government services they use.	American Immigration Lawyers Association, Urban Institute
3. Immigrants send all their money back to their home countries.	In addition to the consumer spending of immigrant households, immigrants and their businesses contribute $162 billion in tax revenue to U.S. federal, state, and local governments. Although it is true that immigrants remit billions of dollars a year to their home countries, this is one of the most targeted and effective forms of direct foreign investment.	Cato Institute, Inter-American Development Bank
4. Immigrants take jobs and opportunity away from Americans.	The largest wave of immigration to the U.S. since the early 1900s coincided with our lowest national unemployment rate and fastest economic growth. Immigrant entrepreneurs create jobs for U.S. and foreign workers, and foreign-born students allow many U.S. graduate programs to keep their doors open. Although there has been no comprehensive study done of immigrant-owned businesses, we have countless examples: in Silicon Valley, companies begun by Chinese and Indian immigrants generated more than $19.5 billion in sales and nearly 73,000 jobs in 2000.	Brookings Institution
5. Immigrants are a drain on the U.S. economy.	During the 1990s, half of all new workers were foreign-born, filling gaps left by native-born workers in both the high- and low-skill ends of the spectrum. Immigrants fill jobs in key sectors, start their own businesses, and contribute to a thriving economy. The net benefit of immigration to the U.S. is nearly $10 billion annually. As Alan Greenspan points out, 70% of immigrants arrive in prime working age. That means we haven't spent a penny on their education, yet they are transplanted into our workforce and will contribute $500 billion toward our social security system over the next 20 years.	National Academy of Sciences, Center for Labor Market Studies at Northeastern University, Federal Reserve

(continued)

■ **table 1.1**   Continued

Myth	Fact	Source
6. Immigrants don't want to learn English or become Americans.	Within ten years of arrival, more than 75% of immigrants speak English well; moreover, demand for English classes at the adult level far exceeds supply. More than 33% of immigrants are naturalized citizens; given increased immigration in the 1990s, this figure will rise as more legal permanent residents become eligible for naturalization in the coming years. The number of immigrants naturalizing spiked sharply after two events: enactment of immigration and welfare reform laws in 1996 and the terrorist attacks in 2001.	U.S. Census Bureau, U.S. Department of Homeland Security (Bureau of Citizenship and Immigration Services)
7. Today's immigrants are different than those of 100 years ago.	The percentage of the U.S. population that is foreign-born now stands at 11.5%; in the early twentieth century it was approximately 15%. Similar to accusations about today's immigrants, those of 100 years ago initially often settled in mono-ethnic neighborhoods, spoke their native languages, and built up newspapers and businesses that catered to their fellow émigrés. They also experienced the same types of discrimination that today's immigrants face and integrated within American culture at a similar rate. If we view history objectively, we remember that every new wave of immigrants has been met with suspicion and doubt and yet, ultimately, every past wave of immigrants has been vindicated and saluted.	U.S. Census Bureau
8. Most immigrants cross the border illegally.	Around 75% have legal permanent (immigrant) visas; of the 25% that are undocumented, 40% overstayed temporary (nonimmigrant) visas.	INS Statistical Yearbook
9. Weak U.S. border enforcement has led to high undocumented immigration.	From 1986 to 1998, the border patrol's budget increased sixfold, and the number of agents stationed on our southwest border doubled to 8,500. The border patrol also toughened its enforcement strategy, heavily fortifying typical urban entry points and pushing migrants into dangerous desert areas, in hopes of deterring crossings. Instead, the undocumented immigrant population doubled in that time frame, to 8 million—despite the legalization of nearly 3 million immigrants after the enactment of the Immigration Reform and Control Act in 1986. Insufficient legal avenues for immigrants to enter the U.S., compared with the number of jobs available to them, have created this current conundrum.	Cato Institute
10. The war on terrorism can be won through immigration restrictions.	No security expert since September 11, 2001, has said that restrictive immigration measures would have prevented the terrorist attacks—instead, the key is good use of good intelligence. Most of the 9/11 hijackers were here on legal visas. Since 9/11, the myriad measures targeting immigrants in the name of national security have netted no terrorism prosecutions. In fact, several of these measures could have the opposite effect and actually make us less safe, as targeted communities of immigrants are afraid to come forward with information.	Newspaper articles, various security experts, and think tanks

1. Due to welfare reform, legal immigrants are severely restricted from accessing public benefits, and undocumented immigrants are even further precluded from anything other than emergency services. Anti-immigrant groups skew these figures by including programs used by U.S. citizen children of immigrants in their definition of immigrant welfare use, among other tactics.

Source: National Immigration Forum (2003).

Immigration Trends and Dynamics in the United States

Researchers at the Urban Institute and the Hewlett Foundation have summarized the most salient immigration trends and dynamics in the United States for use by policymakers, administrators, and classroom teachers (Fix, Passel, & Ruiz-de-Velasco, 2004). These researchers have argued that classroom teachers of CLD students should understand and adapt their practices to align with four major trends in immigration.

The first of these trends is high-sustained flows (Fix et al., 2004). That is, the population of foreign-born individuals in the United States has more than tripled from 10.0 million in 1970 to 32.5 million in 2002. By the year 2010, Fix and colleagues further project, this immigrant population will make up 13 percent of the total population. However, it is essential to note that this projection continues to fall below the 15 percent figure that represented foreign-born individuals in the United States in the 1880s, during the height of European immigration to the United States.

The second major trend in immigration to the United States is dispersal to nontraditional receiving communities (Fix et al., 2004). This trend reflects a rapid dispersal of immigrant populations to communities that have not experienced significant influxes of immigrants for almost a century. In fact, recent immigration has shifted from traditional receiving states, such as California, Texas, and Florida, to twenty-two new growth states, most of which are located in the Midwest, Southeast, and Rocky Mountain regions. During the 1990s, the immigrant population in these states grew at a rate that was three times faster than that of the nation as a whole.

Fix and colleagues (2004) have asserted that this trend is especially important for schools and classroom teachers for two reasons. First, this new population is more recently immigrated, younger, more likely to exhibit limited English skills, and less likely to draw significant income from employment. Second, schools and other institutions in these new receiving states are less apt to have the necessary infrastructures in place to meet the needs of these families and their school-age children (e.g., bilingual teachers and paraprofessionals, adult ESL programs, quality second language programming, and differential assessment instruments).

Not surprisingly, the third trend in U.S. immigration suggests growth in the population of CLD students and families whose first language is not English (Fix et al., 2004). From 1990 to 2000, this population grew by 52 percent, from 14.0 to 21.3 million. Once again, the twenty-two growth states received the lion's share of these increases.

The fourth and final immigration trend noted by Fix and colleagues (2004) is the rising number of CLD students who are themselves citizens but whose parents are undocumented. The population of undocumented immigrants in the United States is estimated to be 9.3 million. However, three-quarters of children with undocumented parents are themselves U.S citizens.

Necessarily, these trends mean changing demographics among children of immigrants. These demographics, in turn, are at the core of changing student dynamics in the PreK–12 classroom, as well as of assessment challenges for classroom teachers.

■ **figure 1.1**
Immigrant
Children
Constitute a
Rising Share
of Students
(1 in 5)

Source: Van Hook
& Fix (2000); Urban
Institute tabulations
from C2SS PUMS.
Excludes Puerto Rico.

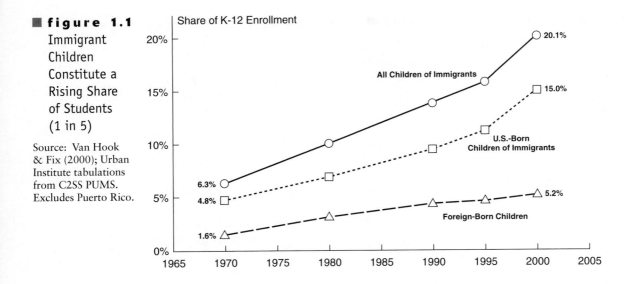

Changing Classroom Demographics, PreK–12

With changing immigration trends come redefined classroom demographics, which by necessity require public school teachers at all levels to embrace adaptive practices and assessment approaches. Among the changing classroom demographics, which have been the subject of recent research (Alcala, 2000; Cortez, 2003; Fix et al., 2004; Thompson, 2004), several are of special significance to teachers of CLD students.

Increasing Classroom Populations of CLD Students As illustrated in Figure 1.1, between 1970 and 2000 the number of children from immigrant families tripled from 6 to 20 percent. However, as this figure illustrates, the highest percentage of these students were born in the United States, not in foreign countries. Moreover, while the rate of population growth for U.S.-born children of immigrants has increased markedly from 1995 to 2000, the rate of growth for the foreign-born population has remained comparatively stable from 1970 through the year 2000.

Variations in the National Origins of CLD Students The national origin of most children of immigrant families has, over the past generation, been Canadian or European (Fix et al., 2004). However, that pattern is changing to one of significant immigration from Asia, Mexico, and Latin America. In 1970, children of Canadians and Europeans made up 60 percent of the school-age immigrant population. However, by the year 2000, that population had declined to 16 percent of the total. The remaining population of immigrant children claimed a range of countries as their nation of origin. The population of children from Mexico was by far the fastest growing immigrant population (from 15 percent in 1970 to 38 percent in 2000) during this period.

Cortez (2003) has referred to the consequential trend of increasing Hispanic student enrollments as the "emerging majority" (p. 1). Cortez (p. 3) also notes the following percentage increases (between 1990 and 2000) in Hispanic populations in states not traditionally associated with such immigration:

- North Carolina: 394 percent
- Arkansas: 337 percent
- Georgia: 300 percent
- Tennessee: 278 percent
- Nevada: 217 percent
- South Carolina: 211 percent
- Alabama: 208 percent
- Kentucky: 173 percent
- Minnesota: 166 percent
- Nebraska: 155 percent

Furthermore, in contrast to non-Hispanic populations, in which only 25 percent of individuals are age 18 or younger, over 35 percent of Hispanics in the United States are under the age of 18. Not surprisingly, one in every six students enrolled in public schools is of Hispanic origin (Cortez, 2003). It is projected that one in every four children will be of Hispanic origin by the year 2025. Murdock (2002) has forecasted that Hispanic students will constitute the majority population (53.1 percent) in Texas by the year 2030.

High Poverty Levels among CLD Students CLD students are far more likely to live in a home that is at or below the poverty line. Much of this trend can be traced to the changing national origins of these students. Since 1970 the percentage of immigrant families living below the poverty line had risen from 12 percent to about 50 percent by 1995 (Fix et al., 2004). Since 2000 the percentage of CLD families living below the poverty line has increased from about 25 percent to approximately 29 percent.

Marzano (2004) has synthesized the findings of a comprehensive body of research to support his argument that poverty among students and families has negative influences on academic achievement. Based on his analyses, Marzano argues that students who are socialized at or near the poverty line are 70 percent less likely to pass an academic achievement test than their counterparts who do not experience poverty. Furthermore, Marzano demonstrates that poverty is associated with a variety of other factors detrimental to student success, including:

- An increase in home and family conflicts
- Decreased levels of self-esteem
- Family isolation
- Frequent and disruptive moves from one living unit to another
- Reduced exposure to language (especially academic language) interactions

Marzano's (2004) analyses also revealed a disconcertingly strong relationship between poverty and ethnicity. In the United States, about 12 in every 100 persons (12.0 percent) live at or below the poverty line. Among whites, the figure drops to 9.9 percent. However, for Hispanics the figure is 21.4 percent. And for African Americans, this likelihood increases to 22.7 percent. Fundamentally, these figures indicate that children of color differ considerably from white children in access to material resources during childhood and school-age years.

For Marzano these analyses indicate that students of color are far more likely to enter school with disproportionately low levels of academic vocabulary and the kinds of background knowledge that have traditionally been valued in U.S. classrooms. However, even more problematic are the ways in which many educators currently assess the vocabulary knowledge and vocabulary-building processes these students *do* possess. Many of the assets that CLD students bring to the educational setting continue to be unexplored avenues to academic success.

Increasing Incidence of Secondary-Level CLD Students CLD students who are foreign-born and recently immigrated are also more likely to be taught in secondary (6.4 percent) rather than elementary (3.8 percent) schools. This trend is a virtual reversal of patterns typical among immigrant students since the late 1970s (Fix et al., 2004). Alcala (2000) has found that this reversal is also accompanied by a pattern of slight increases in the number of secondary-level students with limited formal schooling (LFS). These students are sometimes referred to in the literature as *preliterates*. LFS or preliterate students do not know how to read and write but will eventually obtain these skills with accommodative instruction, assessment practices, and support (Alcala, 2000). These students, who are typically from 12 to 21 years of age, exhibit limited literacy skills in their native language because of limited formal education (i.e., less than two years).

The sharp increases in the numbers of recently immigrated CLD students who are educated in secondary rather than elementary schools suggest noteworthy implications for classroom teachers. First, these students are far less likely to have received language-programming support services during their elementary school years. Consequently, these students are less likely to demonstrate high levels of English language proficiency, especially the cognitive academic language proficiency (CALP) skills necessary for success in content-area classrooms. Second, the incidence and history of language-programming services in secondary schools is typically more limited than for elementary schools (Ruiz-de-Velasco & Fix, 2000). Third, secondary schools are less likely to have in place the necessary infrastructure, as well as the differentiated programming, instructional, and assessment practices CLD students require to be successful (Ruiz-de-Velasco & Fix, 2000). Finally, Title III funds have historically been more regularly allocated to elementary-level programs, instruction, and assessment.

Languages Spoken by CLD Students Today's classroom is also increasingly characterized by the native languages spoken by CLD students. First, sustained levels of immigration from nontraditional countries have doubled the number of children from homes where the first language is not English (Alcala, 2000; Fix et al., 2004; Thompson, 2004). Second, the number of children from Spanish-dominant home environments is increasing and already represents over 66 percent of CLD students whose first language is not English. Third, the number of school-age children from homes where families speak Asian languages is also increasing, from 0.4 million children in 1980 to 1.5 million in 2000 (Fix et al., 2004).

Among these CLD students whose first language is not English, Hispanic students are more likely to be identified as limited English proficient (a government-related designation) within the first and successive generations than are Asian students or the K–12 population as a whole (Fix et al., 2004). Furthermore, second-generation CLD students of Mexican origin who are enrolled K–12 are more than twice as likely to be designated as LEP (28 percent) as Asian children (14 percent). Increasingly, CLD students who have been classified as LEP have also lived in the United States for many years (Fix et al., 2004). For students of this group who are enrolled in grades K–5, more than 43 percent are native-born. Among those enrolled in grades 6–12, 22 percent are native-born.

CLD students who have been classified as LEP are also increasingly educated in schools in which the overwhelming majority of students are also classified as LEP. In fact, using 1999–2000 *Schools and Staffing Survey* (SASS) data, Fix and colleagues (2004) found that more than half of all students classified as LEP are concentrated in schools where roughly one-third or more of their classmates are also designated LEP. This trend is even more evident when examined in terms of student ethnicity. For example, according to Fix and colleagues (2004):

> The "average" Hispanic student attends a school that is 24 percent LEP; for Asians the share is 14 percent. The "average" African American student attends schools that have a larger share of LEPs than does his or her white, non-Hispanic counterpart (5 versus 3 percent for the nation, and 11 versus 6 percent within the traditional receiving states). (pp. 29–30)

The trends associated with CLD students whose first language is not English suggest emerging implications for public schools and classroom teachers. For example, academic achievement and adequate yearly progress will be major emphases of classroom-based instructional and assessment practices for CLD students, tomorrow and for the foreseeable future. Yet the ways in which the aforementioned factors are frequently addressed have already served to significantly lower academic achievement levels among these students, especially CLD students whose first language is not English. For example, Goldman's (2003) analyses of data from the 2003 National Assessment of Educational Progress (NAEP) indicated that achievement levels among fourth- and eighth-grade LEP students were approximately two to three years lower than those of other students tested at the same grade level.

Among other implications, effective, classroom-based instructional and assessment practices will have to reflect the CLD student's country of origin, first and second language proficiencies, issues of acculturation, and prior schooling and academic experiences (both inside and outside the United States). In a nutshell, schools will be challenged to maintain high standards of educational quality in an era of educational reform and amidst an increasing scale and pace of changing student and family dynamics.

In effect, the demands on the capacities and readiness levels of classroom teachers for the radically changing tapestry of the classroom are evolving in ways that reflect recent and shifting trends in national, state, and local demographics. So, to what extent do inservice teachers demonstrate readiness for a rapidly changing classroom population? This question is the focus of discussion to follow.

■ What's Changed about the Readiness of Classroom Teachers for Student Diversity?

Although many states and school districts are responding to the changing demographics of the U.S. classroom, these efforts have often failed to match the pace of change (Hakuta, 2001; Murry & Herrera, 2005b; Thompson, 2004). This is especially true with respect to the long-term professional development of classroom teachers for the appropriate accommodation of CLD student needs (Hakuta, 2001; Herrera, Perez, & Murry, in press; Murry & Herrera, 2005a, 2005b; Murry, Herrera, & Perez, 2005). In fact, although most CLD students are educated in grade-level classrooms for the greatest portion of the school day, the majority of teachers in these classrooms have had little or no professional development for meeting the differential needs of these students (Herrera & Murry, 2005; Thompson, 2004).

Specifically, a recent estimate indicates that about 42.0 percent of teachers in the United States have in their classroom at least one CLD student whose first language is not English (Hakuta, 2001). Yet only 12.5 percent of classroom teachers who instruct these students have been provided eight or more hours of professional development specific to the needs of this student population (National Center for Education Statistics, 2002). For example, in California, 101,000 teachers instruct and assess CLD students. About 16,000 of these teachers report that they use the students' native language to offer content-based instruction. But fewer than 11,000 of these teachers have the appropriate professional development and certification to conduct this type of instruction (Hakuta, 2001).

Regrettably, too much of the instruction and assessment that occurs in today's classroom has become the responsibility of classroom aides and bilingual paraprofessionals. At the national level, Moss and Puma (1995) report that 58 percent of CLD students whose first language is not English receive their English and reading instruction from a teacher aide or paraprofessional. At the same time, less than 21 percent of these students receive instruction from aides who possess any educational preparation beyond high school (Moss & Puma, 1995). The results of a recent national survey indicate that less than 30 percent of the forty-four responding states have funds available to cover the necessary professional development costs for paraprofessionals who work with LEP students (Cosentino de Cohen, 2005). Consequently, two of the primary purposes of this text are to inform teachers about the range of assessment alternatives for diverse students and to help them use differentiated assessment strategies in the classroom. To this end, it is appropriate to explore what is different about assessment in today's culturally and linguistically diverse classroom.

■ What's Evolved about Appropriate Assessment Practices for CLD Students?

From the standpoint of schoolwide achievement testing, at least one answer to this question is, very little! In fact, most prevailing practices used in assessing achievement have changed little in the past fifty years (Firestone & Mayrowetz, 2000; Glaser & Silver, 1994). On the whole, if any significant change has taken place, it is that the assessment of achievement has become increasingly standardized, norm referenced, and institutionalized.

What is also changing is the emergent body of criticism regarding these assessments and the consequences of building national school reform initiatives around them (Firestone & Mayrowetz, 2000; Glaser & Silver, 1994; Hakuta, 2001; Uriarte, 2002). Especially criticized are the negative effects these tests have on classroom climate, instructional practices, and classroom assessment routines. An analysis of research (Glaser & Silver, 1994) on such consequences has concluded that these standardized, norm-referenced, high-stakes tests:

- Limit and negatively affect the quality of content-area instruction
- Prompt teachers to narrow the curriculum taught in classrooms
- Encourage so-called teaching to the test
- Push students out of the system
- Divert classroom instruction to an emphasis on low-level content and basic skills
- Increase the redundancy of instruction

Research has shown that these consequences are especially exacerbated for CLD students (Firestone & Mayrowetz, 2000; Glaser & Silver, 1994; Hakuta, 2001; Uriarte, 2002). For example, one study found that 74 percent of the teachers studied who taught in classrooms with large CLD populations reported starting test preparation activities at least one month before the administration of mandated assessments (Madaus, West, Harmon, Lomax, & Viator, 1992), whereas only 32 percent of teachers in classes with small CLD populations reported this pattern of test preparation. Similarly, more than 30 percent of teachers with large CLD populations reported spending at least 20 hours of class time in test preparation.

As a result of these and other critiques of assessment practices in schools, the emphasis of best-practice literature on the assessment of CLD students in diverse classrooms is on finding alternatives to these and similar types of tests (Chappuis & Stiggins, 2002; Roskos & Christie, 2002; Wiliam, 2004). This trend toward more authentic assessment practices for CLD students tends to emphasize classroom-based assessments in more inclusive areas such as level of acculturation, language proficiencies, and content-area learning.

Accordingly, this text has been designed specifically as a resource for classroom teachers of CLD students (PreK–12). The chapters reflect the latest trends in appropriate and authentic assessment for the differential needs and assets that CLD students bring to the classroom. This book not only examines what is novel about differentiated practices, but also offers background information, details on assessments used in today's classrooms, examples of assessment in practice, and an exploration of concerns teachers must address in critical areas of assessment for CLD students.

Specifically, this text has been divided into eight chapters. Chapter 1 has summarized (a) what is different about today's classroom, (b) what has changed about the readiness of teachers for classroom diversity, and (c) what has evolved about appropriate assessment practices for CLD students.

Chapter 2 discusses and justifies cutting-edge trends toward the alternative and authentic assessment of CLD students in the classroom. Among types of authentic assessment explored are performance-based, portfolio, student-initiated, interview-based, and cooperative group assessments. Classroom teachers will also benefit from discussions of (a) the steps for creating a high-quality rubric for authentic assessment and (b) ways to maximize dialogue journals and scaffolded essays in classroom assessments. Among the relevant questions Chapter 2 addresses are the following:

- Why are alternative and authentic assessments increasing in popularity with classroom teachers of CLD students?
- How have teachers used rubrics, checklists, and questionnaires for scoring authentic assessments of CLD students?
- Why is it critical to assess and document incremental gains among CLD students?

Secondary and elementary teachers will also find the discussions in Chapter 3 both interesting and useful. In this chapter, we discuss how teachers can use the biographies of the CLD student to better target, adapt, and refine instruction. Of particular interest are teachers' preassessments of three histories that the student brings to the learning environment: (a) the biopsychosocial history, (b) the education or content-area learning history, and (c) the language history (L1 and L2). Among practical questions Chapter 3 addresses are the following:

- What are the advantages for classroom teachers who conduct preinstructional assessments of their CLD students?

- Why should teachers be concerned with both the level and rate of acculturation (the process of adjusting to a new culture) of CLD students, and what potential pitfalls should teachers be aware of when assessing these?
- What are "Wh" questions, and how can they be used for preassessing language proficiencies of CLD students?

Classroom teachers of recently arrived CLD students will find the discussions of Chapter 4 especially helpful. The challenges and processes that CLD students confront in a new country, which are formidable and sometimes frightening, have remarkable impacts on the students' abilities to learn and benefit from instruction. This chapter explores in depth the acculturation issues for students adjusting to a new country, a new culture, a new school system, a new language, and more. Teachers learn how to gain a holistic assessment picture of the CLD student's adjustment processes and become aware of the influences this portrait can have on classroom performance. Chapter 4 addresses questions such as the following:

- What is the role of cultural identity in self-esteem and motivation among CLD students?
- What does brain-based learning have to do with acculturation?
- How often should the student's level and rate of acculturation be assessed?

The assessment of language proficiency is a familiar topic for teachers. But why should teachers want to know about assessment of first or native language proficiency? Chapter 5 explores this issue and many others of practical importance. For example, language assessment is usually undertaken in formal ways (e.g., the LAS or the IPT). Nonetheless, there are many useful ways for teachers to informally assess language proficiencies in the classroom. Such assessments powerfully inform and help the teacher refine the nature and effectiveness of classroom instruction. Among these informal ways to assess language proficiency are anecdotal logs, narrative assessment, and cloze assessments. This chapter also explores the implications of language proficiency assessment for programming-related decisions involving student identification, placement, monitoring, and exit (programming-related issues are also addressed for assessments of acculturation and content-area learning in Chapters 4 and 6 respectively). Among the questions that Chapter 5 addresses are:

- How do primary language skills affect second language acquisition in the areas of content, form, and use?
- What are the difficulties with relying solely on formal language assessments (e.g., IPT, Woodcock–Munoz) to provide appropriate placement and instruction for CLD students whose first language is not English?
- What are the strengths and weaknesses of home language surveys?
- What factors might prompt a classroom teacher to overestimate the second language abilities of CLD students whose first language is not English?

Content-area assessment is a challenging aspect of teaching and is the subject of assessment discussions in Chapter 6. This facet of assessment of CLD students is one of the most complex. A broad range of both informal and formal tools is available to classroom teachers of CLD students. Yet the question of which tools are most appropriate with a given population of students is seldom self-explanatory. Additionally, there is always the need to both formatively and summatively assess content-area learning. This chapter seeks to unravel some of the challenges of content-area assessment for CLD students. Among the questions Chapter 6 explores are:

- For what reasons are content-area assessments sometimes underemphasized with CLD students?
- Content-area assessments for CLD students are best aligned with what two indicators?
- How does limited wait time in inquiry assessment negatively affect the content-area learning potential of CLD students?
- How can educators ensure that teacher-made tests for the informal content-area assessment of CLD students are appropriate and purposeful?
- What are the steps a classroom teacher should follow in developing curriculum-based measures for the content-area assessment of CLD students?

Unique among texts that address the assessment of CLD students in the classroom, Chapter 7 explores potentially problematic relationships between classroom assessment practices and referrals to special education. This best-practice issue is among the most important for classroom teachers of CLD students because CLD students continue to be disproportionately represented in special education programs. Significant anecdotal and research evidence suggests that basic misunderstandings about the impact of language and culture on student behavior and academic performance remain primary contributors to this problem. Unfortunately, these misunderstandings can be erroneously validated through inappropriate assessments or the uninformed interpretation of assessment results. Chapter 7 guides teachers through the primary considerations of exceptionality and the critical role that appropriate classroom assessments play in distinguishing between a genuine disability and (a) cultural/linguistic difference, (b) opportunity to learn, or (c) an instructional mismatch. Chapter 7 addresses a variety of related and pertinent questions, including:

- What is disproportionality and why does it matter?
- Which characteristics of learning disabilities are also shared with CLD students who do not possess a learning disability?
- Why is low achievement (even very low achievement) an insufficient rationale for the special education placement of a CLD student?
- Why is it essential to involve parents or guardians in every step of the referral, intervention, and placement processes relating to a CLD student?

The use of postinstructional assessment to gauge learning outcomes and refine classroom practices for CLD students is the emphasis of discussions in Chapter 8. Teachers at all levels will appreciate the valuable insights gained by assessing student skills after an activity, presentation, or unit of study. Besides describing the rationale for, types of, and useful information gained from postinstructional assessment, Chapter 8 provides specific examples of ways these data can be used to inform and refine instruction. The capacity to continually reflect on student learning as well as on our own instructional practices is essential for meeting the needs of diverse students in today's schools. Also addressed in Chapter 8 are questions such as the following:

- In what informal ways can teachers postinstructionally assess the skills students gained during instruction?
- How can postinstructional assessment results be used to better understand a CLD student's language development or acculturation progress?
- How can information from postinstructional assessments be used to increase a student's success with subsequent lessons?

■ key concepts

Assessment

Background knowledge

Culturally and linguistically diverse (CLD) students

Differential learning needs and assets of CLD students

Educational reform initiatives

Evolving immigration patterns

Immigration myths

Nontraditional receiving communities

Poverty-related influences on assessments

Real-world applications in assessment

Schoolwide achievement testing practices

■ professional conversations on practice

1. Defend the use of the term *culturally and linguistically diverse (CLD) student* versus alternative terms, including *minority student* and *LEP student*. Why is it important to consider such distinctions in serving the needs of CLD students and families?

2. Discuss and debate the origins and persistence of at least three myths surrounding immigrant CLD students and families. What sociopoliti-

cal agendas are served by the perpetuation of such myths?

3. Discuss the most significant implications of increased classroom diversity in nontraditional receiving communities. What are at least two implications of these increases for teachers' classroom assessment practices?

4. Between the years 1970 and 2000, the highest percentage of CLD students in public school

classrooms were born in the United States, not in foreign countries. Explore ideas about at least two factors that may have contributed to this trend.

5. Most immigrant CLD students no longer arrive from Canada or Europe. From what countries or continents are they most likely to have emigrated? Discuss and analyze the implications of this change for classroom teachers and classroom assessment practices. Explore at least three implications.

6. Discuss the practical realities of recent increases in the number of CLD students in secondary versus elementary classrooms. What are the implications for the assessment practices of secondary-level classroom teachers?

7. Discuss factors that might account for the limited access of classroom teachers to professional development specific to the dynamics of CLD students, especially students whose first language is not English. Given recent demographic trends, what are the implications of this pattern of teacher readiness to accommodate student diversity?

8. Reflect on factors that might account for the number of CLD students who receive much of their classroom instruction and assessments from classroom aides and bilingual paraprofessionals. Discuss in detail possible solutions to this dilemma of classroom practice.

■ questions for review and reflection

1. How would you define the term *assessment*?

2. In what ways are classroom teachers in the best position to appropriately create, adapt, modify, and accommodate classroom assessments for the differential learning needs and assets of CLD students?

3. In what ways might an informal interview with a student yield more valuable and useful assessment information than a paper-and-pencil test?

4. Why should classroom teachers value the student's capacity to demonstrate real-world applications of knowledge?

5. The demographics of the grade-level classroom are changing. Some of this change is the result of recent immigration. However, much of this change is not. What factors, other than immigration, might account for these changes?

6. What are four major trends in immigration discussed in this chapter?

7. What is a nontraditional receiving community? What should teachers know about such communities in relation to classroom diversity and assessment?

8. According to year 2000 census data, which five states witnessed the highest percentage increases in their populations of Hispanic CLD families? What should classroom teachers know about this trend?

9. Increasingly, CLD students arrive at school from homes that are at or below the poverty line. What are at least three implications of this trend for classroom teachers and classroom assessment practices?

10. What relationships exist between students from poverty and their levels of background knowledge? What are at least two implications of these relationships for classroom teachers and classroom assessment practices?

11. What deterrents to student success in the classroom have been associated with poverty (list at least four)?

12. What pattern has tended to accompany recent increases in the number of secondary-level CLD students?

13. What group of CLD students is more likely than others to be identified as LEP? What fac-

tors in the student's home may contribute to this trend?

14. In what ways have schoolwide achievement testing practices changed in today's classrooms? What are the implications of this pattern?

15. What are at least five problematic consequences of an increasing emphasis on standardized, norm-referenced high-stakes tests in recent educational reform initiatives? Briefly discuss each.

Authentic Assessment

I feel that we have to know much more about the cultural backgrounds of our students before creating instruments to assess their knowledge. . . . When trying to assess a student's knowledge, I feel that authentic assessments make the most sense. I am interested in what my students know . . . not if they know how to take a test. . . . The authentic assessments that we use to assess the grasp of academic concepts range from projects to portfolios. Sometimes students work and present as a collaborative group, other times they present their information solo.

Tamara Bucher
K–5 ESL Teacher

critical standards *Guiding Chapter Content*

TESOL/NCATE teacher standards reflect professional consensus on standards for the quality teaching of PreK–12 CLD students. Additionally, the CEEE Guiding Principles and their accompanying indicators serve as a framework to assist practitioners, policymakers, and clients as they collaborate to enhance academic enrichment and language acquisition among CLD students. Therefore, to help educators understand how they might appropriately target and address national professional teaching standards in practice, we have designed the content of this chapter to reflect the following standards.

TESOL/NCATE Standards for P–12 Teacher Education Programs

Domain 4: Assessment. Candidates understand issues of assessment and use standards-based assessment measures with ESOL students.

- **Standard 4.c. Classroom-Based Assessment for ESL.** Candidates know and use a variety of performance-based assessment tools and techniques to inform instruction.

    4.c.1.   Use performance-based assessment tools and tasks that measure ESOL learners' progress toward state and national standards.

    4.c.2.   Use various instruments and techniques to assess content-area learning (e.g., math, science, social studies) for ESOL learners at varying levels of language and literacy development.

    4.c.3.   Prepare ESOL students to use self- and peer-assessment techniques when appropriate.

Note: All TESOL/NCATE Standards are cited from TESOL (2003). All Guiding Principles are cited from Center for Equity and Excellence in Education (CEEE) (2005). Reprinted by permission.

In classrooms, CLD students are encouraged to use their language skills, cognitive development, and academic knowledge to listen, read, comprehend, synthesize, analyze, compare, contrast, relate, articulate, write, evaluate, and more. Yet attaining these capacities is a long-term process, the success of which cannot be adequately measured through traditional, standardized, or even norm-referenced student assessments. In fact, the ability of an assessment to measure incremental gains is especially critical for CLD students, who are often struggling to simultaneously (a) acculturate to new living and school environments, (b) acquire a second and unfamiliar language, and (c) perform according to grade-level standards in the content areas.

Not surprisingly, then, there is an increasingly salient recognition that *alternative* forms of assessment are essential to best practices among classroom teachers of CLD and other students. Especially needed are assessments that are authentic, process as well as product focused, and capable of measuring incremental gains. Such assessments are the focus of this chapter.

■ Rationale for the Use of Authentic Assessments

One of the primary purposes of this text is to explore the range of ways to gather and interpret information about CLD student learning in order to inform instruction. For years, standardized and teacher-made tests (e.g., multiple choice, fill-in-the-blank) have dominated our views and practices about measuring student learning. However, the results of such assessments have not always yielded information useful to classroom teachers for creating instructional accommodations for CLD students. Although the data generated by traditional tests are certainly helpful in comparing students, programs, and schools on quantitative bases, what the data actually mean for each individual student is often much more obscure.

close-up *on Assessment* **2.1**

Authentic assessments:

- Are generally developed directly from classroom instruction, group work, and related classroom activities and provide an alternative to traditional assessments
- Can be considered valid and reliable in that they genuinely and consistently assess a student's classroom performance
- Facilitate the student's participation in the evaluation process
- Include measurements and evaluations relevant to both the teacher and the student
- Emphasize *real-world* problems, tasks, or applications that are relevant to the student and his or her community

Therefore, it is not surprising to find that many classroom teachers are seeking or have already developed their own forms of assessment, which provide more usable information about how well their students are learning what is actually being taught in class. These instruments are sometimes referred to as *alternative assessments* because they can supplement formal assessments and may also help refine or enhance current assessment practices. Because alternative assessments usually represent nontraditional or accommodated approaches to measuring student learning, they are often considered more authentic than the formal assessments they replace. Although the literature of assessment has employed a variety of criteria to define *authentic assessment,* such definitions tend to share certain commonalities (Crawford & Impara, 2001; Cooper, 1999; Diaz-Rico & Weed, 2006; Hancock, 1994; Linn & Miller, 2005). Among these commonalities, authentic assessments:

- Are generally developed directly from classroom instruction, group work, and related classroom activities and provide an alternative to traditional assessments
- Can be considered valid and reliable in that they genuinely and consistently assess a student's classroom performance
- Facilitate the student's participation in evaluation processes
- Include measurements and evaluations relevant to both the teacher and the student
- Emphasize *real-world* problems, tasks, or applications that are relevant to the student and his or her community

Because well-designed alternative assessments are also authentic, we simply refer to these as *authentic* assessments throughout the remainder of this text.

Across the nation, many classroom teachers have already embraced authentic assessment techniques as useful for gathering information that helps them plan, adapt, and individualize instruction. These techniques, however, may prove even more valuable for CLD students because, with careful planning and implementation, teachers can avoid a number of cultural or linguistic biases inherent in traditional assessments. When assessing CLD students, it is particularly important to design tasks that help us distinguish what we are in fact actually testing (e.g., language, content knowledge, acculturation). We must also assess CLD students in ways that allow them to demonstrate how they understand, access, and apply their knowledge in novel or real-life contexts. Authentic assessments need not be restricted to use as add-on or follow-up components of a lesson. They can often be embedded within the actual contexts of instruction.

Because we create and employ authentic assessment strategies to sample what students can actually do as well as what they know, most assessments, regardless of format, include a focus on individual growth and learning over time. Authentic assessments identify and build on student strengths such as language, prior experiences, interests, and funds of knowledge (Moll, Armanti, Neff, & Gonzalez, 1992) to facilitate learning. They emphasize student-constructed (rather than prescribed or regurgitated) responses and center on activities that challenge and engage students while encouraging them to integrate knowledge and skills. Well-designed authentic assessments promote higher-order thinking and learner self-evaluation to monitor growth and progress.

As previously discussed, authentic assessments typically invite CLD students to become much more engaged in their own learning than do traditional or dipstick testing approaches. In addition to providing high-quality and in-depth information, student involvement in the assessment process can facilitate learning by increasing motivation and lowering anxiety levels (Chappuis & Stiggins, 2002).

---

assessment *FREEZE FRAME* 2.1

Authentic assessments identify and build on student strengths such as language, prior experiences, interests, and funds of knowledge to facilitate learning.

---

close-up *on Assessment* 2.2

When creating authentic assessments, it is important to keep in mind:

- *Why* they are used
- *What* information can be obtained from them
- *How* this information can help improve instruction and learning

Reliability and Validity of Authentic Assessments

When creating authentic assessments, it is important to keep in mind:

- *Why* they are used
- *What* information can be obtained from them
- *How* this information can help improve instruction and learning

As with other forms of measurement, we judge authentic assessments by their reliability and validity as indicators of student learning.

Reliability is best understood as the power of an assessment to gather consistent evidence of skills, regardless of the examiner, time, place, or other variables related to its administration. One measure of reliability is inter-rater reliability. This is the degree to which a student's product or performance is rated the same by different raters or evaluators. Ensuring inter-rater reliability is especially important for authentic assessments, which generally lack the discrete point scales of more objective forms of assessment such as multiple-choice and true/false tests. Inter-rater reliability for authentic assessments is often achieved through well-defined criteria and thorough training for teachers and students in how to rate works according to the criteria. Not only does this practice help enhance rater reliability, but also the resulting focus on key criteria sharpens the teacher's attention to those skills during other teaching and learning activities.

Validity refers to the ability of an assessment, process, or product to measure the knowledge or skills it is intended to measure. Teachers of CLD students are particularly concerned with content validity, which is the extent to which the assessment tasks and items represent the domain of knowledge and skills to be measured (especially regarding the most critical content). For example, we might question the content validity of a test that purports to measure only computational skills but includes problems such as the following:

> The players on Morgan's baseball team take turns bringing water bottles for their teammates. Last week, Tyler brought 12 bottles, and one player was absent. The coach decided to save the extra bottles and just have Morgan bring the remaining number needed the following week. How many bottles does Morgan need to bring next week so there are just enough for each player on the field?

Teachers should consider the level of knowledge and skills needed to answer this question, as well as language cues a CLD student might misinterpret. Although

---

assessment *FREEZE FRAME* 2.2

Reliability is best understood as the power of an assessment to gather consistent evidence of skills, regardless of the examiner, time, place, or other variables of its administration.

assessment *FREEZE FRAME* 2.3

Inter-rater reliability for authentic assessments is often achieved through well-defined criteria and thorough training for teachers and students in how to rate works according to the criteria.

seemingly simple, this problem requires much more of students than basic computational skills. The question also requires:

- Knowledge of baseball (number of players on the field and on a team)
- An understanding that water bottles come in individual sizes
- The cultural assumption that bottles are not shared
- The linguistic savvy to understand that *just enough* implies exactly the right amount (a one-to-one correspondence), whereas *enough* may signify at least enough for everyone, but more may be fine

Much cultural knowledge is implicit in questions of this sort. Because the goal of assessment is to provide information about student learning in a specific content area, assessments must be meaningful indicators of whether—and how—that learning occurs. Therefore, it is crucial that we take validity and reliability into consideration when choosing and administering all forms of assessment, including those considered authentic, to ensure they are consistently measuring what they are supposed to measure.

> ### assessment *FREEZE FRAME* 2.4
>
> Teachers of CLD students are particularly concerned with *content validity*, which is the extent to which the assessment tasks and items represent the domain of knowledge and skills to be measured (especially regarding the most critical content).

■ Types of Authentic Assessment

We can authentically tap into our CLD students' formative (along-the-way) learning processes and summative (end point) grasp of curricular material through many different forms of authentic assessment (see Chapter 6 for in-depth discussion of formative and summative assessment). Some are popular for the ease with which teachers can adjust them for their own class of diverse learners. Authentic assessments include experiments, projects, observations, interviews, and student narratives. However, these are only a representative sample of the many ways academic skills can be assessed relative to their uses in the real world. Although a variety of authentic assessments are suitable for use with all students in the classroom, the following discussion explores some of the types most useful with CLD students. Many of these authentic assessments can be adapted for multiple purposes and for virtually any content area.

Performance-Based Assessments

If we think of assessments as snapshots of student learning in time, performance-based assessments provide a longer exposure with a panoramic lens, or real-time video. Performance-based assessments (PBAs) typically involve the "actual doing of a task" (Linn & Miller, 2005, p. 7). PBAs encompass a variety of ways to observe and monitor student learning over various spans of time and involve much more authentic applications than do traditional paper-and-pencil tests. Figure 2.1 provides an example of a science-related PBA.

■ **figure 2.1** Science PBA

Preparation of a Dry Mount Microscope Slide

This performance-based assessment is designed to document the student's ability to independently prepare a dry mount microscope slide.

The following materials must be among those available to the student:

- Microscope with which the student has familiarity
- Slides
- Cover slips
- Object to be examined

The following steps are considered essential elements of this procedure. Circle each as it is completed by the student. Add observational notes as desired.

1. Place slide on a flat surface.
2. Lay specimen on top of slide.
3. Attend to thickness of specimen (does student seek thinnest sample?).
4. Place cover slip slowly on top of specimen.

If a student has been exposed to the creation of and rationale for both wet and dry slides, this PBA can be modified to require the student to determine and execute the appropriate procedure for one or more objects or organisms.

Grade-level teachers who use PBAs generally embrace the idea that knowledge is constructed during learning—that students *discover* knowledge for themselves rather than *receive* knowledge from the teacher. Applying this constructivist perspective to learning and assessment facilitates not only how students take in information but also how they store and retrieve this information and apply new thinking to novel situations. For constructivist teachers, PBAs provide an effective way to direct content learning through the two-dimensional curriculum. However, that content learning comes to three-dimensional life in the individual minds and experiences of the students (Wangsatorntanakhun, 1997). Besides eliciting constructed responses, performance-based assessments incorporate authentic tasks that prompt higher-order thinking and the integration of skills.

In his article on brain-based classrooms, Holloway (2000) espouses the power of environments in which students track their own progress and relate this progress to their personal efforts and experiences. He suggests that brain-compatible learning environments include thematic units; opportunities for extended language use; long-term, constructivist learning projects; and multidimensional assessment tools.

Some educators think about brain-based learning as teaching students to scuba dive rather than water ski. Because water skiers are able to stay upright and cover a relatively large amount of territory, their skills are easier to see and may, at first glance, be more impressive. Unfortunately, this ability to skim the surface does not speak to the knowledge of what lies underneath or the necessary skills to swim in deep or unfamiliar waters. By contrast, scuba divers intentionally learn to investigate more deeply and propel themselves to areas of further interest. This can result in far greater knowledge at ever-deeper levels, as well as an ongoing desire and ability to continue the learning process.

As with scuba diving, much of the learning that takes place in constructivist contexts occurs at these deeper levels and may be neither obvious on the surface nor measurable by traditional means. Performance-based assessments are designed to create situations that tap into the depth as well as the breadth of student learning. Instead of asking students to reiterate static facts or volumes of superficial content, PBAs allow students to demonstrate how deeply they understand and can navigate the waters of novel concepts, as well as the degree to which they can make new discoveries through self-directed learning.

Although it is relatively common for classroom teachers to acknowledge hands-on activities, such as performance-based assessments, as appropriate and beneficial for young children, these activities are equally powerful for older students. For example, secondary students whose teachers incorporate hands-on learning activities outperform their peers by 40 to 70 percent in studies of science and math learning (Wenglingsky, 2000). Activities such as science applications are wonderful tools for both content instruction and assessment because they generally lend themselves to the storage of information as a procedural memory (information on the steps or sequences involved in a process). This efficient type of storage tends to make information easier to retrieve at a later time (Holloway, 2000).

> **assessment FREEZE FRAME 2.5**
>
> Performance-based assessments are designed to create situations that tap into the depth as well as the breadth of student learning.

> **assessment FREEZE FRAME 2.6**
>
> Secondary students whose teachers incorporate hands-on learning activities outperform their peers by 40 to 70 percent in studies of science and math learning.

Because PBAs help to naturally and sequentially scaffold student learning, performance-based assessments are particularly appropriate for CLD students, who may have little prior exposure to the information, language, or process involved. For these students, the classroom teacher might scaffold assessment processes by (Sprenger, 1999):

- Providing the tools or equipment used in past procedures
- Permitting students to engage in their own discovery processes
- Noting each step students perform

Such a format also encourages CLD students to create their own scaffolds to help them answer higher-order thinking questions that appear on more traditional assessments.

PBAs are also especially useful for assessing the learning of CLD students whose prior experiences and knowledge may differ dramatically from those of students from the dominant culture. Although some CLD students will not share the same background with or have the same cultural knowledge as other students, this does not mean they have a deficit of experience. Rather, they have *differences* of experience. When teachers from the dominant culture explore student backgrounds, they are often astonished at the variety and depth of abilities CLD students are able to demonstrate through accommodative and authentic assessments.

Portfolios

Portfolios in various forms have been in use for some time. However, early versions often amounted to undifferentiated compilations of student work, sometimes judged merely by overall heftiness or mass. Although portfolios were appreciated as indicators of student (and teacher) effort, many parents felt that this abundance of academic memorabilia provided little information about the actual progress of their children in school.

Over time, portfolios have become more organized, purposeful, and indicative of student learning. Although there are many ways to use them, portfolios generally include:

- Samples of student work
- Some indication of how the student rated himself or herself on the processes and products included
- Evidence of how those products met established criteria

The criteria for judging portfolio pieces should describe outcomes that align with curricular standards. In many cases, school districts align these standards with relevant state and/or national benchmarks.

A student portfolio might also include such things as writing samples, drawings, reading logs, student self-evaluation or progress notes, and audio- or

close-up *on Assessment* 2.3

Over time, portfolios have generally become more organized, purposeful, and indicative of student learning. Although there are many ways to use them, portfolios generally include:

- Samples of student work
- Some indication of how the student rated himself or herself on the process and products included
- Evidence of how those products met established criteria

The criteria for judging portfolio pieces should describe outcomes that align with curricular standards. In many cases, school districts align these standards with relevant state or national benchmarks.

videotapes, to name a few. The most common forms of portfolios contain either highlighted or showcased examples of a student's best work or work samples that depict learning in progress. In many cases, as in the following scenario, portfolios can actually prompt teachers to provide students greater opportunities for more authentic learning.

Mrs. Carpenter was a first-grade teacher who once believed that her instructional time was best spent directly teaching to curricular goals. She would follow up her lessons with quick objective quizzes to assess student mastery of content. However, the addition to her class of students who spoke English as a second language inspired her to adopt a host of new teaching and assessment practices. A case in point was how she altered her methods to incorporate the portfolio assessment of language arts objectives related to story skills.

The first year, Mrs. Carpenter began by leading her class in discussions of books she read aloud, in terms of the main characters, setting, possible solutions, and so forth. Together they discovered and discussed the essential components of a "good story" and formulated a simple class rubric (see Figure 2.2) for judging future storytime selections. Over the next few weeks, Mrs. Carpenter intentionally chose stories she knew would be rated either exemplary or poor, according to the class criteria. Such exercises built the students' skills in applying the criteria and reinforced their understanding of the useful-ness of the criteria. These skills would be needed when students later assessed their own story-writing efforts.

One day, after a particularly disappointing selection, Mrs. Carpenter guided the group in revising the lower scoring elements of the story. As she wrote the new version on poster paper, she also modeled the use of rebus cue drawings (e.g., I was riding my 🚲 and a 🚗 drove by.) for words that were unfamiliar or "hard to spell."

The next day, students were anxious to write their own original stories. Although all the students were excited about this, Mrs. Carpenter's experience told her that many students would not know where or how to start. As she reviewed the story elements featured in the rubric, she focused first on the importance of setting. To graphically demonstrate the vital importance of the setting to a story, Mrs. Carpenter told all the

■ **f i g u r e 2 . 2** Story Rubric

STORY ELEMENTS

	The Main Character?	**The Setting?**	**The Problem?**	**The Solution?**	**Score (add here)**
Does this story describe . . .	Yes = 2 A Little= 1 No = 0	Yes = 2 A Little = 1 No = 0	Yes = 2 A Little = 1 No = 0	Yes = 2 A Little = 1 No = 0	

students to line up, and, with digital camera in hand, she led them on a walk around the school building and grounds. As they talked about different settings, Mrs. Carpenter took photos of students in settings they had chosen. Once they returned to class and printed these photos, the students took turns talking about the various settings each classmate had chosen (e.g., "James is on the bench in front of the school." "Ana is under the big slide near the swings.").

Mrs. Carpenter hoped these visuals would trigger experiences and memories students could use as scaffolds for writing their first stories. These stories were drafted with an emphasis on content, so Mrs. Carpenter encouraged students to use invented spellings and rebus pictures for words they could not spell. Students would search for these words in the dictionary and correct them later.

She then recorded students as they read their short stories aloud in groups. No one interrupted the readings with comments. However, when the tape was replayed, group partners listened for and commented on the simple elements of the story rubric that the class had devised earlier. Group members also attended to key curricular objectives and practiced the important skills of explaining and supporting their opinions.

The primary purpose of the tapes was to document students' developing narrative skills. However, the tapes also documented other parameters of language acquisition such as vocabulary, word order, sentence length, and pronunciation. Because the students, including the CLD students, were allowed to use rebus pictures for words they could not spell, vocabulary gaps were less of an issue. Students could still demonstrate their knowledge of the concept of setting. At this point, the students were able to add the written story (to be revised later) and the recorded narrative to their portfolios. Both would be strong benchmarks by which to measure future progress. Mrs. Carpenter then planned an extension of the lesson to build on this new learning and stimulate students' imaginative thinking skills.

As she carried out the photo-taking activity with her class the following year, Mrs. Carpenter remembered observing a CLD student who was not following directions–and yet she *loved* what he was doing. This year she deliberately incorporated that student's "detour into fun" as an extension of the lesson. After writing and recording their first stories, the students cut themselves out of the photos they took during the "setting" exercise. Then came the really fun part. Students were encouraged to place a picture of themselves anywhere and any way (such as upside down) on a blank piece of drawing paper. Through this activity, they began to create an entirely new setting and story for their main character, an exciting way to introduce the second element of the rubric. Mrs. Carpenter always marveled at how these new stories reflected the relevant interests and background experiences of the students.

For example, Joel (who was swinging on the monkey bars in his original setting) was suddenly transported to a locale in which he hung precariously from the lower lip of a *Tyrannosaurus rex*. Tuyen, no longer poised at the water fountain, was now bending over to smell the abundant flowers in her grandmother's garden. Mrs. Carpenter noticed how the stories that evolved from this activity were more personal and animated than those elicited by her typical story starters. Moreover, the students were eager to share these new stories with peers. When the drawings were finished, they were laminated and added to each student's portfolio.

Throughout the year, students had other opportunities to practice and build narrative skills, such as reporting the news (e.g., family, community, world) and retelling events or stories from different perspectives (e.g., the wolf's perspective from "The Three Little Pigs" or the perspective of one of their favorite action figures). As the year progressed and Mrs. Carpenter conferenced with students about their portfolio entries, she was amazed at how often students spontaneously commented on how their earlier stories could have been better. Some students even contrasted them to more recent selections. For instance, Magda said, "That story didn't have a very good ending. This one has a better problem and solution. I tell you more about my characters now too."

By the end of the year, Mrs. Carpenter felt that she, her students, and their parents had a much better grasp of student progress than they ever could have gained through traditional indicators of achievement.

In summary, portfolio assessments authentically connect classroom instruction and the assessment of its impact on students. They are *alternative* in the sense that:

- They incorporate both teacher and student perspectives on learning and the assessment of learning.
- They offer a longitudinal perspective on academic and language development.
- They measure incremental gains in knowledge, skills, and proficiencies.

Portfolio assessments are *authentic* in that:

- They derive directly from classroom activities.
- They effectively assess student performance.
- They reflect in-process adaptations to instructional methods and assessment.
- They assess learning in a way that is relevant to and motivating for the student.

Self-Assessment and Peer Assessment

Whenever practical, student self-assessment can be an extremely valuable tool for learning as well as measurement. When CLD students are engaged in assessing their own work, they more thoroughly and purposefully understand the criteria for high-quality products and performance—and experience greater motivation for meeting those criteria. Rather than simply attempting to produce work that will satisfy the teacher, students involved in effective self-assessment work toward a positive vision of the instructional goals. This vision is enhanced and authenticated by their own perspectives and interpretations. In addition, many teachers report notable improvements in students' ability to regulate their own behaviors related to time and task management. Figure 2.3 (and the related appendix resource) depicts a self-assessment rubric that can be used to supplement a content scoring rubric. This rubric requires students to assess not only their overall achievement but also the *effort* they actually put into the task.

■ **figure 2.3** Effort and Achievement Comparison Rubric

Name: _____   Date: _____

Assignment/Project: _____

Effort & Achievement Comparison Rubric	
Effort	**Achievement**
5 = I put maximum effort into this task. I stretched myself to complete this task despite its difficulty. I approached task difficulties as challenges to be overcome. I built new capacities as a result of confronting these challenges.	5 = I exceeded the objectives of this task. 4 = I met all of the objectives of this task. 3 = I met at least half of the objectives of this task. 2 = I met less than half of the objectives of this task. 1 = I did not meet the objectives of this task.
4 = I put exceptional effort into this task. I stretched myself to complete this task despite its difficulty. I approached task difficulties as challenges to be overcome.	
3 = I put moderate effort into this task. I stretched myself to complete this task despite its difficulty. I approached task difficulties as challenges to be overcome.	
2 = I put average effort into this task. I stretched myself to complete this task despite its difficulty.	
1 = I put limited effort into this task.	
Scale: 5 = Excellent 4 = Outstanding 3 = Good 2 = Improvement Needed 1 = Unacceptable	

Peer assessment is equally beneficial because it provides students additional opportunities to identify and evaluate targeted skills related to established criteria. Peer assessment requires students to consider how examples of other students' work meet the criteria. Such comparisons enable students to discern outstanding elements of both their own and their classmates' performances and prod-

close-up *on Assessment* **2.4**

Portfolio assessments are *authentic* in that:

- They derive directly from classroom activities.
- They effectively assess student performance.
- They reflect in-process adaptations to instructional methods and assessment.
- They assess learning in a way that is relevant to and motivating for the student.

ucts, as well as those components in need of improvement. This type of critical consideration often prompts students to refine their own concept of a quality product.

Another advantage of peer assessment is that many students are more apt to engage in dialogue with and accept criticism from peers than from teachers, and are more likely to do so using language that is uniquely comprehensible to them. This is particularly important for CLD students for whom bilingual peers (or peers who share the same dialect in the native language) may more effectively mediate and clarify the concepts of instruction. Figure 2.4 depicts one type of peer assessment that can provide CLD students a lifeline to deeper understanding (see also related appendix resource).

assessment *FREEZE FRAME* **2.7**

Peer assessment requires students to consider how examples of other students' work meet the criteria. Such comparisons enable students to discern outstanding elements of both their own and their classmates' performances and products, as well as those components in need of improvement.

Interview-Based Assessment

Teacher–student interviews are yet another way of gathering pertinent information to authenticate instruction and assessment. These interviews can vary from casual to highly structured. Informal interviews are a long-standing aspect of professional practice for many classroom teachers. However, most teachers do not consider them a valid form of assessment. This is unfortunate because interviews can be an accurate and effective means of obtaining information crucial to accommodative instruction for CLD students.

Whether through informal conversation or a more detailed interview process, the teacher who maximizes interviews can learn a great deal about students' interests, backgrounds, experiences, activities, and beliefs. The teacher can then use these data to appropriately adapt instruction for the students' benefit. For example, a math teacher may realize that particular students enjoy cooking. She may find that connecting mixed fractions to measurement conversion during a lesson on baking greatly facilitates comprehension of the math concept. In fact, through the interview process, teachers and students may also discover unexpected

■ **figure 2.4** Peer Assessment

Lifeline Hook: A Peer Assessment

Content Area: 🖊 Writing   📖 Reading   🔬 Science   🖩 Math

❏ Other Content Area

(Peer 1 Name) _____. I like the way (Peer 2 Name) _____ ❏ thought out,
❏ reasoned, ❏ worked, ❏ explored, ❏ documented, ❏ visualized, ❏ described, _____
(another word you could use to give your peer feedback) _____
(e.g., problem, challenge, assignment).

I can tell that you (my peer) understood the objective(s) by:
1.
2.
3.

I have questions about:
1.
2.
3.

What questions do you (my peer) have?
1.
2.
3.

Questions and comments **WE** (as peers) have for the teacher.
1.
2.
3.

Comments:

A summary of what we learned from each other:

commonalities. For example, in the scenario to follow, a teacher who conducts a student interview realizes that linguistic differences can interfere with the development of deeper connections with her students, connections that may prove more profound than she thought possible:

> Mrs. Bontrager had always felt that the bilingual paraprofessional, Mrs. Silva, shared more common experiences with and could therefore better relate to the Spanish-speaking CLD students in her fourth-grade class. Over time, Mrs. Silva assumed a more and more significant role in their instruction while Mrs. Bontrager concentrated her efforts on the native English speakers. This seemed to be a reasonable approach given that Mrs. Silva, a Puerto Rican–born New Yorker, was able to communicate with the students in their native language.
>
> Mrs. Bontrager felt confident that, because of this shared language, Mrs. Silva's instruction would foster the students' engagement in a farm simulation the class conducted. She eagerly anticipated listening to the students' accounts of choices they had made during postproject interviews. However, she got a big surprise when she interviewed Abel. He began with a wonderful explanation for his group's decision to raise cattle instead of sheep. Abel stated: "Sheeps eat the whole grass and it might not grow back. But cows eat just the top, and it keeps growing so you've always got food for them."
>
> Mrs. Bontrager was impressed and, thinking Abel would credit Mrs. Silva or the school library as sources, asked how his group had learned this important piece of information. "We already knew it," Abel replied. "My uncle has cows in Mexico, and Hector's seen sheeps eat grass 'til it's all gone. Mrs. Silva told us sheeps might be better 'cause you can make a sweater, but we decided that doesn't matter because if there's nothing left for them to eat, they die." Of course, this made perfect sense to Mrs. Bontrager, who grew up on a farm.
>
> Suddenly, Mrs. Bontrager felt a sense of loss for what her CLD students could have gained, or for the deeper levels of application they could have achieved, had she been a more active mentor. After all, Abel, Hector, Rosa, and several others were farm kids just as she had been. Imagine what could have happened if their knowledge had surfaced and been valued as a resource to enrich cooperative groups of mixed-language students. So often their backgrounds had been viewed as a deficit to be overcome. Mrs. Bontrager decided to continue to use summative interviews but also resolved to conduct a preproject interview that would allow her to discover the knowledge and skills her students already possessed. This interview strategy would also provide an opportunity to talk about what students were learning as the lesson moved along. Mrs. Bontrager concluded that both she and the students had missed valuable opportunities.

Such an example vividly illustrates the assessment value of informal interviews with CLD students. Interview discussions often provide the classroom teacher with invaluable insights about the CLD students' prior experiences, cultural backgrounds, language use at home, level of adjustment to a new culture and school, academic history, and more.

Play-Based Assessment

One often-overlooked source of valuable information on student knowledge and skills is play-based assessment. Such assessments are especially suitable for evaluating young children and CLD students acquiring English. Children as young as preschool age are often able to use toys or "pretend" objects in ways that signify an understanding of their actual use and function in the real world. Such representational play is a fundamental precursor to comprehending the similar nature of oral and written words. Other ways to promote literacy instruction and assessment during play, as described by Roskos and Christie (2002), include:

- Creating literacy-rich play settings ("housekeeping centers" with shopping lists, newspapers, magazines, and cookbooks, in addition to the typical pots, pans, and ironing board)
- Encouraging children to playact roles and scenarios that require literacy activities (ticket pads for police officers, waiters, and waitresses, prescription pads for doctors, small dry-erase boards or chalkboards for teachers)
- Promoting social interaction and including literacy-related challenges during play.

When provided with props, tools, and opportunity, CLD students often demonstrate procedural or conceptual knowledge they would not otherwise be able to demonstrate on written or verbal tests. An example of this is the CLD student who cannot verbally explain or understand the words for concepts of relative weight, size, or amount (e.g., *heavy, light, equal, more,* or *less*) but who is amazingly skillful in a game that calls for adding or subtracting just the right number of plastic beans to counterweight a classmate's wooden pegs so that neither pile on the balance falls to the floor. Although this student definitely possesses conceptual knowledge of weight, amount, and equivalence, he would fail virtually any traditional test that exclusively examines the acquisition of words we use to describe this knowledge, rather than evidence of the knowledge itself.

Astute teachers at higher grade levels tap into the power of play by having students role-play or dramatize events and concepts from history, literature, or even the sciences; after all, who wouldn't want to be a germ-fighting white corpuscle? Other highly engaging forms of role-play, such as teacher- or technology-facilitated simulations, can also provide alternative ways for CLD students to demonstrate acquired skills and concepts.

Whether conducted in a play-based manner or in some other way, authentic assessment is not merely about evaluating students in nontraditional ways. As noted by Goodwin (2000), "Authentic assessment begins with teachers making it their business to purposefully watch, listen to, talk with, and think about the children in their classrooms" (p. 6). Reflective teachers observe and value student play as evidence of who these children are, what they know, and how they learn. Such teachers then use this information to construct more potent instructional contexts.

Cooperative Group Assessment

The Western perspective on what constitutes success places priority on individual effort and achievement, to the exclusion of group collaborations and products (Cushner et al., 2006). This is particularly evident in sports and entertainment in which individual success usually commands more attention than the arguably superior accomplishments of collaborative (e.g., team) endeavors. In fact, people in the United States are more often inclined to identify and empathize with the "stars" in activities that *do* require ensembles or teams. Similarly, educational institutions are most apt to grade, rank, and reward students based primarily on measures of individual achievement.

However, schools and educators are increasingly recognizing that many students are better able to demonstrate their genuine skills, knowledge, and proficiencies through cooperative learning and assessment activities. This reality is not surprising when we consider how most children learn the noncurricular, and potentially more critical, lessons of life. In everyday situations across many cultures, children have been taught to work cooperatively and collectively (as a family or tribe) and to reflect on what they have learned from life's daily "lessons." This experiential, hands-on, real-world education features the most authentic assessment system possible—the continuous challenges of life itself. Performance on these "assessments" has determined whether people live or die, or whether a tribe's culture survives (Nelson-Barber, 1999). Although the stakes in the typical classroom may not be quite that high, there is great power and potential in drawing on those natural patterns of cooperative behavior to design and conduct learning and assessment environments.

> **assessment *FREEZE FRAME* 2.8**
>
> Schools and educators are increasingly recognizing that many students are better able to demonstrate their genuine skills, knowledge, and proficiencies through cooperative learning and assessment activities.

Insightful teachers who recognize the value of authentic assessment to highlight a CLD student's individual growth also consider how this type of assessment can be used with cooperative groups. Peer assessment can be effectively used within the context of cooperative groups to enhance each student's experience with and interpretation of personal processes and products. Group or collaborative activities often culminate in projects or experiments that may or may not require oral or written reporting. As with other forms of authentic assessment, the group's understanding of outcome criteria will guide the creation of these products. Opportunities for ongoing refinement enable the group to improve the quality of their product.

Planning for cooperative group assessment requires us to consider both group rewards and individual accountability (Slavin, 2006). However, teachers sometimes have difficulty discerning individual student learning and contributions when projects are carried out collectively. In the following example, Mr. Martinez, a high school science teacher, has overcome this problem by having students create reflection journals to document individual progress:

Mr. Martinez told his sophomore biology students that their reflection journals would enable him to understand what they were really learning. He also planned to rely on their journals to document where students were struggling so that he could reteach material in a different way that might enhance their learning efforts. He showed his students some exemplary journal samples, as well as a rubric, so they would clearly understand his expectations for this new responsibility. After the next group project, Mr. Martinez's students used their journals to reflect on individual learning. In these journals, the students:

- Provided written or pictorial demonstrations of how they understood the material presented during the project
- Noted questions, concerns, or misunderstandings for follow-up with the group or Mr. Martinez
- Logged or revised new learning
- Cited related commentary and information from outside resources
- Described and reflected on their own contributions to the progress of the group
- Detailed personal feelings, thoughts, hypotheses, and conclusions even if different from the group's consensus

Because maintaining scientific logs was an identified objective for this course, Mr. Martinez gave students direct feedback about the grammar and organization of their written notes. Beyond that, the information available in these journals provided Mr. Martinez a wealth of ongoing (formative) insights about how his students comprehended the subject material. As a scientific person himself, he found the process of discovering *how* his students understood the material—as well as *what* in their lives they connected it to—much more interesting than discrete information about whether they had learned the material.

When reflection journals of this type are used as authentic assessment tools, they document the thought and action processes of individual students as they learn from cooperative classroom activities.

Dialogue Journals and Scaffolded Essays

Teachers also gather valuable information about student learning through carefully accommodated and scaffolded assignments. CLD students in particular are often better able to demonstrate learning through tasks that incorporate supportive structures than through all-or-none applications. Because one goal of authentic assessment is to find out what students *can do* with what they know, focusing on what they *cannot do* is often of limited value. Fortunately, some of the most salient information about student learning is readily available to teachers who observe and read student responses to accommodated instruction.

Dialogue journals constitute one tool that classroom teachers can use to meld assessment with

> **assessment** *FREEZE FRAME* **2.9**
>
> Because one goal of authentic assessment is to find out what students *can do* with what they know, focusing on what they *cannot do* is often of limited value.

Accommodative Assessment Practices 2.1

In the following example, Mrs. Spencer, a fifth-grade teacher, assessed Carmen's writing and scaffolded her response to it while maintaining an encouraging, enthusiastic, and nurturing perspective that focused on the content of Carmen's journal entries. Such accommodation and scaffolding ensured that Mrs. Spencer was able to authentically assess the learning efforts of this CLD student while engaging her in authentic writing tasks.

Carmen: *Last nite my dad came home with a big sprise. He say close yur eyes and then he say open them. Ther was a cat baby under his chert. I can wate to go home and play with the cat baby.*

Mrs. Spencer: *What a surprise! What did you think when Dad said, "Close your eyes"? Were you happy there was a kitten under his shirt? I used to have a grey kitten named Tom. What color is your kitten? I can't wait to hear more about your new kitten.*

Carmen (the next day's entry): *When my Dad said close your eyes I thot the surprise was candy. I like the kitten better than candy. It's a gril and hes white all over. I tol my Dad about your kit-ten and he said he used to have a grey cat to.*

Mrs. Spencer was pleased by the insights she gained from these first few exchanges. Carmen quickly recognized that she spelled words differently than Mrs. Spencer had in her entry and corrected her spellings accordingly and consistently (*sprise/surprise, yur/your*). Carmen was able to recognize the new spellings that should replace hers from the context of Mrs. Spencer's reply. Carmen also adopted the word *kitten* over her own quite serviceable *cat baby*, understanding that this was the more commonly used term in English. Carmen added several other new spellings to her English vocabulary, including *grey, shirt,* and *wait.*

■ *Why might Mrs. Spencer's indirect corrections be more effective than simple use of a red pencil to mark Carmen's errors? What more might be learned from Mrs. Spencer's technique than from the traditional red pencil?*

accommodative teaching in authentic contexts. Although they may take many forms, dialogue journals require students to use written language in an ongoing dialogue with the teacher about events, thoughts, feelings, stories, and more. The teacher then responds to the content of the interaction by intentionally modeling grammar, spelling, or vocabulary that would improve the student's communications. When CLD students are genuinely engaged in conversation with someone else, they are more highly motivated to communicate effectively.

Another example of accommodated teaching as a means of assessment is the scaffolded essay. With this method of authentic assessment, a more complex essay question is reduced to a variety of prompts that require only short answers. This accommodation ensures that students are being assessed on their knowledge of content-area material and not on their capacity to answer the question in the essay format (Berkowitz, Desmarais, Hogan, & Moorcroft, 2000). If the teacher wants to ascertain what the student knows about a given subject, a scaffolded essay is an excellent option. Likewise, if the purpose of the assessment is purely to gauge the student's ability to construct an essay, this approach helps the teacher

■ **figure 2.5** Scaffolded Essay

Essay Question: Who do you think was the most important president of the United States?

1. **Who do you think was the most important president?**

   (e.g., I think _____ was the most important president of the United States.)

2. **Why do you think he was the most important president?**

   (e.g., I think _____ was the most important president because _____
   _____.)

3. **What other characteristics made this person a great leader?**

   (e.g., _____ was also very knowledgeable about _____
   _____ and skilled at _____.)

4. **How do you know this?**

   (e.g., I learned these facts about _____ by reading the book
   _____ written by _____.)

5. **What else did you learn about this president?**

   (e.g., I was surprised to learn _____.)

6. **Summarize or restate what you have learned or believe about the topic.**

   (e.g., In summary, _____ was a very good leader whose
   ability to _____ and _____ made him my choice for the
   most important president of the United States.)

determine whether the student can do so with accommodations. Figure 2.5 depicts a scaffolded essay question that could be used with a history class. As with all assessments, it is the teacher's responsibility to first decide what a given tool will actually assess before engaging in the assessment and drawing conclusions from it.

In general, authentic assessment approaches, such as dialogue journals and scaffolded essays, benefit teachers and students because these assessment tools:

- Provide more precise information about the student's learning and skills than traditional assessments
- Identify the levels and types of support needed for students to demonstrate what they know or can do
- Embed assessment within an instructional process that helps students acquire targeted skills

- Increase students' awareness of their own need for scaffolds and supports to facilitate learning

Although they may not be aware of it, many classroom teachers already incorporate authentic assessment into their accommodated instruction for CLD students. Continual daily assessment helps teachers know when to modify instruction and strengthen (or reduce) supports or scaffolds to keep students challenged, engaged, and learning. When teachers recognize the power of ongoing classroom assessment to document student progress, they are embracing one of the richest methods for gathering meaningful assessment information.

■ Scoring and Related Issues of Authentic Assessment

One of the most commonly cited reasons teachers express hesitancy about using authentic assessments is that the assessments rarely provide information in the numerical format traditionally associated with tests. This has left intuitive and reflective teachers in the awkward position of recognizing that traditional tests often fail to measure actual student achievement, yet feeling somehow unprofessional—or even guilty—about switching to more authentic methods. Fortunately, these concerns can be allayed by awareness of the many ways authentic learning can indeed be measured and quantified—along with the knowledge that authentic assessment can also foster unexpected gains in learning. The following are examples of effective methods for ensuring equitable and accurate scoring of authentic assessments.

Rubrics

Rubrics, as discussed elsewhere in this text, are a frequent component of performance-based assessment but are also valuable in other contexts. The reason for this is that rubrics can be used to engage CLD students in the details of their own learning. CLD students can, in fact, become quite proficient with rubrics at almost any developmental level. For example, even preschool-age children can match the face they have drawn with a rubric that depicts a list of faces (i.e., faces with eyes only; eyes and mouth; eyes, nose, and mouth; and eyes, nose, mouth, and ears). When "eyes only" earns a smaller sticker than "eyes, nose, mouth, and ears," young learners quickly begin to adapt their work.

In the upper grades, teachers can either provide students with examples of work on which to model their efforts or help them select appropriate examples for themselves. Comprehensible discussion about how to identify key attributes of these examples increases the likelihood that students will attend to these when creating their own products. When used as self-assessment tools, rubrics guide student compilations of ongoing work (such as portfolios) or help students prepare for more summative events (such as written or oral presentations).

Involving CLD students in rubric creation is particularly worthwhile, as the ensuing discussion typically provides multiple opportunities to focus on the key features of the targeted criteria and helps build content-area vocabulary. When creating rubrics or other sets of criteria for authentic assessments, teachers must be clear about the skills being targeted. Even though the activity might afford opportunities to measure other skills, a narrower focus helps students thoroughly attend to the target skills. For example, the rubric (see Figure 2.2) developed in Mrs. Carpenter's class was designed to focus on grade-level narrative skills. However, the resulting voice recordings and written products also provided a wealth of information and evidence about student growth in other areas, such as spelling, vocabulary, sentence structure, and pronunciation. Although it would be beneficial for Mrs. Carpenter to make notes on these additional areas of student progress, such skills would not be included in the rubric.

When creating a rubric, the first step is to determine the desired outcome. In a given content area, what do you want your students to be able to do? This step requires familiarity with the academic standards to which the curriculum is aligned. Some secondary teachers may choose additional outcomes that reflect skills more relevant to potential employers or institutions of higher education.

Bear in mind that the behaviors or skills you choose as features of assessment should be measurable. For example, although "pays attention in class" is an important objective, it is comparatively difficult to measure because some students may appear to be attentive when they actually aren't, and vice versa. In this case, the teacher may want to identify a more quantifiable behavior associated with paying attention, such as "responds appropriately when called on" or "follows directions in class." However, when CLD students are involved, it is important to ensure that their ability to demonstrate the identified skill is not compromised by their level of English language proficiency. Teachers should consider alternative skills or behaviors for determining whether a CLD student is attending to instruction.

■ Assessment in Action 2.1

The following are a few general steps to follow when creating a rubric:

- Determine the desired outcome.
- Develop or identify within your current classroom practices a task that will create opportunities for students to demonstrate the targeted skill.

- Determine what a good or high-quality performance on this task might look like.
- Complete the rubric by describing the requirements that must be met to attain each quantified level of performance.

Let's explore a specific curricular example, such as the way a teacher might create a rubric to address the following sixth-grade social studies standard:

Economics Standard: The student uses a working knowledge and understanding of major economic concepts, issues, and systems of the United States and other nations—and applies decision-making skills as a consumer, producer, saver, investor, and citizen in the interdependent world.

Mr. Bryant is a sixth-grade teacher of a class in which about 50 percent of the students are CLD and are acquiring English as a second language. In targeting the stated economics standard, he focused on the need for students to understand basic principles of market forces. Based on this target knowledge, he stated the desired outcome as follows:

"The student will demonstrate an understanding of how the scarcity of resources requires communities and nations to make choices about goods and services (e.g., what food to eat, where to locate food, how to use land)."

The second step for teachers in creating a rubric is to develop or identify within their current classroom practices a task that will create opportunities for students to demonstrate the target skill.

Because the notion of planning and designing authentic learning opportunities was new to Mr. Bryant, he consulted with teaching peers for ideas. His colleagues told him that many such tasks could be found on Internet teaching and lesson planning sites, as well as on discussion lists.

Mr. Bryant decided to do a simulation that required students to weigh the economic, environmental, and sociological impacts of either preserving a specific area of forested land for recreational use or converting it to commercial use. He chose their town for the setting and selected a wooded tract of land just beyond the school's outermost attendance zone. The students were required to examine the issue from a variety of perspectives and to rely on multiple resources to determine whether this piece of land should remain natural (for recreational use) or be developed commercially as a site for a discount superstore. Although Mr. Bryant recognized there might be disadvantages to portraying a fictitious development opportunity, he hoped local relevance would increase student interest, motivation, access to authentic resources, and opportunities to learn more about the politics and priorities of their own community. As a result, students would be compelled to construct their own meaning and apply the targeted skills in a real-world context.

The third step in creating a rubric is for the classroom teacher to determine what a good or high-quality performance on this task might look like. The teacher can later revise this vision to reflect the highest-quality responses or products actually produced. A new rubric usually remains a draft, pending its proven capacity to accurately describe and guide student work.

Because half of his students are culturally and linguistically diverse, Mr. Bryant decided they would be allowed to present their final decisions and defend their choices by means of any format that met the rubric criteria of providing "a well-stated and supported decision based on evidence of the financial, environmental, and sociological impact of each option at two or more levels (local, state, national, global) ." Whether students chose to demonstrate their knowledge through a written report, an oral presentation, a graphic display (e.g., local polling results on the issue), an object representation (e.g., a model or diorama), a drama (e.g., a re-creation of a city hall meeting or a news exposé), or any other appropriate means, they were required to support their decisions by addressing each element in the criteria to meet the highest rating on the rubric.

The fourth step in creating a rubric requires teachers to complete the rubric by describing the requirements that must be met to attain each quantified level of performance. In our example, once the target level was operationally defined, Mr. Bryant described the elements that had to be present at each successive level of performance. He continued until all levels of the rubric criteria had been detailed and quantified in a way that could describe virtually any type of product or outcome. The lowest levels of achievement included descriptors of unmet criteria such as "student presents few concepts and details related to the assigned situation" or "little evidence of peer collaboration or discussion." In the end, the pragmatic value of a rubric will depend not only on how much time and detail goes into its development but also, as with all forms of assessment, the degree to which the information is used to improve teaching and learning for each individual student.

Checklists and Questionnaires

Authentic assessments can also take the form of checklists or questionnaires as a means of teacher, peer, or self-evaluation. Although the format of these assessments varies, the instruments themselves can be developed the same way as rubrics, starting with the identification of skills, knowledge, and competencies necessary to perform tasks associated with the activity. Once those skills and competencies are clearly defined, a series of questions or statements can effectively describe varying levels of expected performance or product development. For instance, an assessment checklist of narrative skills might include the following:

The setting of the story is:
0 = Unclear
1 = Named
2 = Named and described

This checklist can stand alone or be included in a student's portfolio along with other components of teacher and student assessment.

Checklists can also be used for student self-assessment. The value of self-assessment to student learning and capacity-building efforts, especially those of

■ Assessment in Action 2.2

Using a checklist such as the following, students can perform and mark off each task sequentially to ensure they have included all information necessary to meet the teacher's criteria:

____ Selected character of interest from California's history.

____ Found three sources of information on this person (list to follow).

____ Highlighted or noted the most important points from each source.

____ Developed a chronological outline of the subject's life.

CLD students, is well documented (Chamot & O'Malley, 1994; Herrera & Murry, 2005; Marzano, 2004; Paris & Ayers, 1994). Using a checklist to note or quantitatively rate the steps to task completion helps students recognize and monitor their own progress toward a goal. Students soon understand that each level of the task is built on the knowledge gained at previous steps. Authentic assessment tools of this sort help students recognize their own areas of difficulty and encourage them to seek assistance with specific issues. Creating such a checklist also requires the teacher to analyze tasks in ways that enhance his or her awareness of subskills with which the CLD student may need additional supports or accommodations.

Questionnaires also serve as a form of authentic assessment because they help the teacher elicit information about a range of learning behaviors. Some teachers use questionnaires to gather information about what students know prior to the lesson. This helps them avoid redundancy in instruction and provides them with insights about the prior or background knowledge students bring to the classroom. Such connections to background knowledge can greatly enhance student understanding of new concepts. Figure 2.6 (and related appendix resource) illustrates one questionnaire teachers can use to gather information about students' prior knowledge and experiences.

■ Additional Considerations

Although authentic assessments are usually developed and used in ways that increase CLD students' abilities to demonstrate academic learning, such assessments are not immune to bias. A teacher may inadvertently provide more feedback to some students than to others. The teacher may view a performance or product only in terms of his or her own perspective, rather than in terms of what it actually means to the student. Moreover, when assessing any aspect of the educational experience (e.g., student growth), a teacher must consider whether the lens he or she uses to view outcomes is different from the one that was used to develop the assessment. Occasionally, a mismatch can lead to misperceptions (which are not necessarily obvious) and can distort or limit the teacher's ability to accurately interpret

■ **figure 2.6** Student Self-Assessment of Content Concepts and Vocabulary

Content Area: ❑ Reading ❑ Writing ❑ Science ❑ Math ❑ Social Studies
❑ Other: _____

Content Objectives:

Language Objectives:

Key Vocabulary:

I have knowledge of the concept from the last school or classroom I attended:
❑ Not at all ❑ Some ❑ A lot

What I remember includes:

I have knowledge of the key vocabulary from the last school or classroom I attended:
❑ Not at all ❑ Some ❑ A lot

I used the key vocabulary for:
❑ Reading ❑ Discussion ❑ Writing

To better understand the vocabulary, it would help me if:
1.
2.
3.

My home experiences support my understanding of the vocabulary/concept in the following ways.
1.
2.
3.

For this topic, I can contribute the following:

what he or she sees. Although a teacher's perceptual lens may have "worked just fine" in the past, without correction or the addition of another perspective, it may prevent the teacher from recognizing, interpreting, and responding to nonstandard evidence of student learning.

Fortunately, a great deal of insight and perspective can be gained when teachers involve CLD students in their own assessment. Information that teachers garner from performance-based assessments or portfolios also illuminates areas previously beyond their scope of attention. Such new insights allow teachers to bring the entire picture of student learning into greater contextual focus. Authentic assessments enable students to demonstrate what they know and become more familiar with themselves as learners in the real world.

■ key concepts

Alternative assessments	Inter-rater reliability	Reliability
Authentic assessments	Interview-based assessment	Representational play
Brain-based learning	Peer assessment	Rubrics
Checklists	Performance-based assessments (PBAs)	Scaffolded essays
Constructivist perspective		Self-assessment
Content validity	Play-based assessment	Validity
Cooperative group assessment	Portfolios	
Dialogue journals	Questionnaires	

■ professional conversations on practice

1. Explain the use of authentic assessments with CLD and other students. What sorts of information do such assessments gather that traditional assessments do not?

2. Discuss factors that classroom teachers should bear in mind as they create authentic assessments.

3. Explore how performance-based assessments may draw on the prior experiences and knowledge that CLD students bring to the classroom in ways that traditional assessments may not.

4. Discuss the advantages of capacity building for self-assessment among CLD students. How might self-assessments play a role in the portfolio-based assessment of these students?

5. Discuss how scaffolded essays, as a means of authentic assessment, benefit both the CLD student and the teacher.

■ questions for review and reflection

1. What reasons account for the increasing popularity of alternative and authentic assessments with teachers of CLD students? List at least three.

2. What factors should classroom teachers consider as they create authentic assessments?

3. Why is the content validity of an assessment of particular concern to classroom teachers of CLD students?

4. How would you compare and contrast the use of performance-based assessments and portfolio assessments with CLD students?

5. What are the specific advantages of capacity building for self-assessment among CLD students?

6. How have teachers used play-based and cooperative group assessments in the authentic assessment of CLD students?

7. In what ways would you justify the use of dialogue journals and scaffolded essays in the authentic classroom assessment of CLD students?

8. What are at least three key characteristics of authentic assessments?

9. What are the steps for creating a high-quality rubric for the authentic assessment of CLD students?

10. What is peer assessment, and why is it useful in the authentic assessment of CLD students?

11. How can interviews be used to monitor the progress of CLD students?

12. In what ways have teachers used rubrics, checklists, and questionnaires in the scoring of authentic classroom assessments of CLD students?

13. What reasons might account for the fact that authentic assessments are not immune to assessment bias?

14. Why is it critical to assess and document incremental gains among CLD students?

15. How can a teacher of CLD students discern individual student learning and contributions while using cooperative group assessment?

- Describe the advantages of preinstructional assessments of CLD students for classroom teachers.

- Discuss three critical aspects of the CLD student's biopsychosocial history that teachers should explore with preinstructional assessments.

- Explain why the degree of similarity between a CLD student's home culture and the school culture is an essential aspect of preinstructional assessment.

- Explain why classroom teachers should be concerned with both the level and rate of acculturation of their CLD students.

- Discuss informal assessments teachers can use to preassess the content-area knowledge, level of acculturation, and language proficiencies of their CLD students.

- Describe how the notion of an *affective filter* might complicate the use of formal tools in the preassessment of CLD students.

- Explain why CLD students who arrive from the same country, speak the same primary language, and have similar schooling biographies may, nonetheless, demonstrate different levels and rates of acculturation.

Preinstructional Assessment and the CLD Student

To help students respond to our efforts, teachers must first acknowledge students as persons, legitimize their knowledge and experiences, and engage with them personally and intellectually. In doing so, educators recognize students as whole people and show them that they are valued, thereby relaying a message of hope.

Louie Rodriguez, "Yo Mister!"

critical standards *Guiding Chapter Content*

TESOL/NCATE teacher standards reflect professional consensus on standards for the quality teaching of PreK–12 CLD students. Additionally, the CEEE Guiding Principles and their accompanying indicators serve as a framework to assist practitioners, policymakers, and clients as they collaborate to enhance academic enrichment and language acquisition among CLD students. Therefore, to help educators understand how they might appropriately target and address national professional teaching standards in practice, we have designed the content of this chapter to reflect the following standards.

TESOL/NCATE Standards for P–12 Teacher Education Programs

Domain 3: Planning, Implementing, and Managing Instruction. Candidates know, understand, and use standards-based practices and strategies related to planning, implementing, and managing ESL and content instruction, including classroom organization, teaching strategies for developing and integrating language skills, and choosing and adapting classroom resources.

- **Standard 3.a. Planning for Standards-Based ESL and Content Instruction.** Candidates know, understand, and apply concepts, research, and best practices to plan classroom instruction in a supportive learning environment for ESOL students. Candidates serve as effective English-language models, as they plan for multilevel classrooms with learners from diverse backgrounds using standards-based ESL and content curriculum.

  3.a.3. Plan students' learning experiences based on assessment of language proficiency and prior knowledge.

CEEE Guiding Principles

Principle #1: English language learners are held to the same high expectations of learning established for all students.

1.9 **Create** classroom environments in which the efforts and contributions of all students are respected and encouraged.

Note: All TESOL/NCATE Standards are cited from TESOL (2003). All Guiding Principles are cited from Center for Equity and Excellence in Education (CEEE) (2005). Reprinted by permission.

Principle #3: English language learners are taught academic content that enables them to meet challenging performance standards in all content areas, consistent with those for all students.

3.7 Use appropriate multiple assessment tools and techniques to measure English language learners' progress in achieving academic standards and in acquiring English proficiency; use assessment results to inform classroom teaching and learning, and communicate these results to families in a meaningful and accessible manner.

Principle #4: English language learners receive instruction that builds on their prior knowledge and cognitive abilities and is responsive to their language proficiency levels and cultural backgrounds.

4.11 Understand and value the linguistic backgrounds and cultural heritages of their English language learners' families and use this information to enrich classroom instruction and to support their students' learning of academic content.

Principle #5: English language learners are evaluated with appropriate and valid assessments that are aligned to state and local standards and that take into account the language development stages and cultural backgrounds of the students.

5.8 Develop student profiles that include English language proficiency level, native language literacy level, language/cultural background, educational history, courses and programs taken, and appropriate and valid student assessment data to monitor the progress of English language learners and evaluate the efficacy of their instructional programs.

5.10 Use a variety of formal and authentic assessment techniques to enhance classroom knowledge of English language learners and to evaluate their academic and linguistic progress.

5.11 Maintain records of student work and performance across time and grade levels to communicate progress over time for individual English language learners.

Preinstructional assessment, generally referred to as *preassessment,* is essential for effectively teaching diverse students in today's schools. Although the term correctly suggests assessment that occurs *before* instruction, in more dynamic classrooms preassessment activities are embedded in and revisited throughout the teaching and learning processes. Preassessment involves gathering information about the knowledge, skills, and capacities of students prior to participation in a new lesson or course of instruction. This information can be gathered with measures such as subject-area pretests, or it can be gleaned from observations, home visits, informal conversations, classroom discussions, and more.

An inclusive and professional perspective on preassessment further acknowledges that students bring various funds of knowledge to the classroom (Moll et al., 1992). As with many other students, much of what CLD students know and many of the skills they possess were not learned exclusively at school. Therefore, the most effective preassessment practices help us better understand the knowledge, skills, and background experiences students have gained through prior socialization in a particular culture.

> **assessment *FREEZE FRAME* 3.1**
>
> The most effective preassessment practices help us better understand the knowledge, skills, and background experiences students have gained through prior socialization in a particular culture.

close-up *on Assessment* **3.1**

The classroom teacher's awareness of the needs and assets CLD students bring to each lesson will enable her or him to:

- Maximize instructional time by avoiding redundancy
- Connect new learning to prior knowledge and frames of reference
- Directly address misconceptions and gaps in conceptual understanding
- Adapt lessons to enhance authenticity and meaning for students

Information gathered from preinstructional assessments is critical for appropriately accommodating CLD students in the classroom. This is especially true for students whose backgrounds contain a particular gap in or wealth of knowledge related to targeted concepts and skills. The classroom teacher's awareness of the needs and assets CLD students bring to each lesson will enable her or him to:

- Maximize instructional time by avoiding redundancy
- Connect new learning to prior knowledge and frames of reference
- Directly address misconceptions and gaps in conceptual understanding
- Adapt lessons to enhance authenticity and meaning for students

Unless teachers understand and account for what students already know (i.e., baseline data), student responses to instruction and performance on post-instructional assessments may not clearly distinguish new learning from old knowledge. These distinctions are necessary for evaluating both the effectiveness of instruction and the learning outcomes of students.

Insightful teachers effectively use both formal and informal assessment tools. Accordingly, this chapter discusses both formal and informal ways to preassess CLD students in order to develop a better understanding of their prior experiences with acculturation, language, and content-area learning.

assessment *FREEZE FRAME* **3.2**

Unless teachers understand and account for what students already know (i.e., baseline data), student responses to instruction and performance on postinstructional assessments may not clearly distinguish new learning from old knowledge. These distinctions are necessary for evaluating both the effectiveness of instruction and the learning outcomes of students.

Formal and Informal Preassessment

Educational preassessments can take many forms and be used for a variety of purposes. Currently in the spotlight are the types of tests used to meet federal or state accountability mandates. These high-stakes tests are typically formal and generate numerical data used to compare students, schools, and districts regarding specific areas of student achievement. Such standardized assessments are usually administered to all students under similar conditions (although assessment accommodations may be possible for some CLD and special education students). Data from these tests not only serve to measure learning to date, but also commonly provide an index of preinstructional skills and knowledge for the coming year. However, teachers who rely exclusively on the results of high-stakes tests for preassessment information often receive an incomplete, if not misleading, picture of what each student actually knows and is capable of demonstrating in the classroom.

Other formal methods of preassessment are screening tests, benchmark assessments, and so forth. However, the vast majority of preinstructional assessment that takes place in the classroom is informal. Informal assessment is especially beneficial with CLD students because formal preassessments often cause higher levels of anxiety and raise students' *affective filter*. The affective filter has been compared to a defense mechanism that controls the extent to which an individual internalizes input by converting it into learning. Krashen (1982, 2000) has argued that raising the student's affective filter can significantly and adversely affect his or her ability to benefit from instruction and other forms of classroom input. Informal preassessment encompasses a continuum of strategies that range from structured teacher-made pretests to unobtrusive observations conducted in natural contexts.

> **assessment *FREEZE FRAME* 3.3**
>
> Teachers who rely exclusively on the results of high-stakes tests for preassessment information often receive an incomplete, if not misleading, picture of what each student actually knows and is capable of demonstrating in the classroom.

Effective preinstructional assessment begins with an understanding of factors that influence the CLD student's success in the classroom. Student histories are some of the richest and most illuminating sources of preinstructional information. Educators who attempt to teach without these insights often miss the mark in their efforts to appropriately instruct, accommodate, motivate, and challenge CLD students.

■ History/Herstory: What the CLD Student Brings to the Classroom

Oftentimes, information that can prove crucial to instruction shows up where it's least expected. At other times, such information results from a teacher's purposeful efforts to explore the student's background. Keep in mind that each student arrives with *a story* (be it his-story or her-story). This history or biography is too often ignored amidst the many challenges of teaching a student with atypical needs and circumstances. Yet it is often this history of prior experiences, prior schooling, and prior learning that unlocks classroom adaptations and instructional accommodations necessary for ensuring student success. Simply put, the classroom teacher's diligence in exploring student histories with preinstructional assessments is often the key to success with CLD students. The following phone conversation illustrates how Mrs. Pham, a classroom teacher, obtained historical information about her student Aida:

Mrs. Pham: Hello, I'm a science teacher at Champion Middle School. We have a new student here named Aida Galvan, and our records indicate she was in your school and class last year.

Mr. Dansby: Oh yes, I remember her. How can I help you?

Mrs. Pham: I notice that she received an "L" in all content areas, including science, on her last report card. According to your system, "L" stands for "learning in progress." As we're not familiar with this type of grading, I was wondering what else you could tell me about Aida's knowledge and performance that might be helpful.

Mr. Dansby: To be honest, I didn't determine her grade. Although Aida was assigned to my class, most of the kids like Aida actually got their content-area instruction from the ESL teacher.

Mrs. Pham: Was Aida with grade-level classroom peers for any academic subjects?

Mr. Dansby: Well, the ESL students always returned to class during the last part of the block when we performed experiments but, since I never knew what they were learning on any given day in ESL, I just had them do worksheets, like word searches, while the rest of the class finished their projects and experiments.

On the surface, this conversation may seem rather uninformative, but it was actually enlightening to Mrs. Pham, who could now better understand Aida's current knowledge and skills in terms of her previously restricted opportunities to learn. This interaction shed light on gaps in Aida's grade-level skills that could be effectively addressed by providing highly contextualized, sheltered opportunities to participate in a rich and challenging curriculum.

> **assessment *FREEZE FRAME* 3.4**
>
> The classroom teacher's diligence in exploring student histories with preinstructional assessments is often the key to success with CLD students.

Biopsychosocial History of the CLD Student

Much of a classroom teacher's success with CLD students depends on his or her understanding of the biopsychosocial histories of these students. Although the term *biopsychosocial* sounds complex and intimidating, it is basically just an adopted descriptor for the core aspects of human experience (Engel, 1977; Gates & Hutchinson, 2005; Saleebey, 2001).

For example, if we examine the *bio* portion of a CLD student's biopsychosocial history, we are concerned with his or her health, as well as physical and mental readiness for schooling. More specifically, educators are concerned with questions such as the following:

- In the home country and in the United States, has the student received (and is the student currently receiving):
  —Adequate nutrition
  —Opportunities for medical, dental, and vision checkups, as well as intervention as needed

—Periodic assessments of hearing and speech capacities
—Immunizations as recommended
—Appropriate opportunities for rest and sleep
—Periodic assessments of physical and mental stressors that may compromise the student's well-being (e.g., after-school work, living conditions)

Related factors that may affect the answers to questions such as these include the socioeconomic status of the family, the English proficiency of family members, the health and responsibilities of parents or guardians, family awareness of and access to appropriate services, the number of persons living at home, family immigration status, and the degree of family isolation from others of the same ethnic or cultural heritage. Without physical and mental readiness for instruction, CLD students are unlikely to achieve their full academic potential.

Equally important and useful to teachers is the *psych* aspect of the biopsychosocial history of the CLD student. For example, teachers benefit from the pre-assessment information gained from answers to the following sorts of questions:

- Has the CLD student recently emigrated from a country that has experienced any of the following problems?
  —Violence or war
  —Weather or environmental calamities (e.g., earthquakes, floods, famine, hurricanes)
  —Oppressive governmental or political regimes
- What measures have been taken to reduce the student's anxieties and concerns about such stressors as moving to a new country, attending a new school, or acquiring a foreign language?
- Does the student show any symptoms that might indicate persistent homesickness, excessive stress, withdrawal, depression, or anger?

Answers to such questions may reveal a variety of previously hidden factors that can powerfully influence student performance. Such factors include (a) psychological disorders (e.g., sleeplessness, nightmares, hysteria) arising from traumatic experiences with violence, war, and weather or environmental calamities; (b) psychological trauma arising from the arrest, incarceration, or torture of family members at the hands of oppressive regimes; and (c) psychological reactions related to transition or school-related adjustments (e.g., homesickness, lashing out, withdrawal, depression).

Last, teachers who preassess the readiness of students are concerned with the *social* aspect of the CLD student's biopsychosocial history. For instance, teachers who capitalize on the many advantages of home visits gain useful information from the following sorts of social (sociocultural) questions:

- Did the CLD student emigrate from another country and if so, how recently?
- What role did the student have in the decision to come to the United States?
- How is the student adjusting to a new country, a new language, a new educational system, a new community, or a new school?

- How stable and how stressful are employment opportunities and work schedules for family members?
- What access does the family have to other families of the same ethnicity or home culture?
- How dissimilar are the home culture and the school culture?

Answers to such questions offer classroom teachers valuable insights into the challenges and processes family members face at the sociocultural level (Gates & Hutchinson, 2005).

Elsewhere, we have referred to this biopsychosocial aspect of the CLD student's history as the *sociocultural* dimension of the CLD student biography (Herrera & Murry, 2005). This dimension involves some of the most critical precursors to academic success, including self-concept, self-esteem, social identity, cultural identity, and student motivation. Accordingly, successful teachers of CLD students are notably careful to preassess essential challenges and processes of this dimension, especially the process of acculturation.

Preassessment of Level of Acculturation

As previously discussed, students enter our schools with a wealth of information and experience they have accrued throughout their lives. This knowledge is acquired in the context of their *culture,* which has been defined as "[t]he totality of socially transmitted behavior patterns, arts, beliefs, institutions, and all other products of human work and thought typical of a population or community at a given time" (Berube et al., 2001, p. 102). Finding oneself immersed in a new culture can be disorienting because one's normal ways of thinking and interacting are suddenly out of sync with those of others. Such challenges are part of what we refer to as *acculturation*—the process of adjusting to a culture different from one's home culture.

close-up *on Assessment* 3.2

Teachers who capitalize on the many advantages of home visits gain useful information from the following sorts of social (sociocultural) questions:

- Did the CLD student emigrate from another country and if so, how recently?
- What role did the student have in the decision to come to the United States?
- How is the student adjusting to a new country, a new language, a new educational system, a new community, or a new school?
- How stable and how stressful are employment opportunities and work schedules for family members?
- What access does the family have to other families of the same ethnicity or home culture?
- How dissimilar are the home culture and the school culture?

■ **figure 3.1**

Stages of the U–Curve Hypothesis

Source: K. Cushner, A. McClelland, and P. Safford (2000), *Human Diversity in Education: An Integrative Approach,* 3rd ed. (Boston: McGraw-Hill). Page 97. Reprinted by permission of the McGraw-Hill Companies.

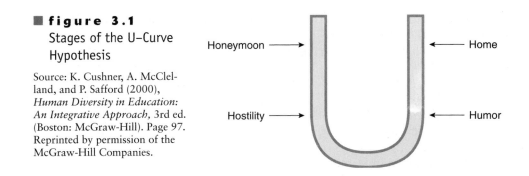

The U-Curve hypothesis (Cushner et al., 2006; Trifonovitch, 1977) has been used to describe the process of acculturation. At first, there is often a sense of novelty to the unfamiliar situation and culture. This *honeymoon* stage is frequently followed by one of *hostility,* as reality dampens idealized dreams. During this stage, the behavior patterns of students either are misinterpreted by others or are ineffective for interacting within the norms of the new culture. CLD students in the hostility stage often feel overwhelmed and disheartened and, as a result, are more likely to drop out of school. However, with adequate support and understanding, students can progress through the hostility stage to one in which they see the *humor* of cross-cultural experiences from both sides. In the best of circumstances (especially circumstances of accommodation), the student transitions to a new sense of home. In this *home* stage of acculturation, he or she feels equally at home with both the old and the new cultures. Figure 3.1 illustrates these stages of the acculturation process.

As an individual becomes involved in the process of acculturation, the clash of cultures that occurs may result in "extreme resistance to adaptation" or "a series of small maladjustments that are overcome one by one" (Lewis & Jungman, 1986, p. 4). How a teacher interprets and responds to the behaviors and reactions of students in various stages of acculturation can profoundly impact both the ability of students to benefit from instruction and their positive adaptation to the new cultural environment. Therefore, preassessing the CLD student's level of acculturation is crucial to the classroom teacher's ability to accommodate student needs and assets effectively.

One of the easiest ways to discover more about a student's acculturation experiences is through an informal conversational interview, using a bilingual interpreter when necessary and feasible. The value of preassessing students in this manner goes well beyond the immediate information acquired. Teachers can develop an invaluable foundation for ongoing communication and reflection when they periodically converse with students about what the students already know and would like to know, as well as what they currently feel and think about themselves, school, and the learning process. This type of informal, communicative

assessment *FREEZE FRAME* 3.5

How a teacher interprets and responds to the behaviors and reactions of students in various stages of acculturation can profoundly impact both the ability of students to benefit from instruction and their positive adaptation to the new cultural environment.

relationship empowers teachers and students to understand and respond to each other's teaching and learning needs.

In addition, teachers who converse with students are better able to recognize and respond to actions that signal student disengagement from or rebellion against the new culture. Such behaviors and reactions include (Herrera & Murry, 2005, p. 22) but are not limited to:

- A sense of alienation
- Actions that are interpreted as hostile
- Patterns of indecision
- Feelings of frustration and sadness
- An intense desire to withdraw from situations
- Symptoms of physical illness
- Exhibitions of anger, grounded in resentment

Many students who are dealing with issues of acculturation or even culture shock (see Chapter 4) struggle to function in an environment that limits their effective use of communication. More than just a pedagogical tool, language is the means by which we establish, mediate, and maintain relationships. It allows us to hear and be heard. Teachers can help students deal with acculturation stress by providing sheltered or translator-assisted opportunities to discuss feelings, thoughts, and experiences.

The details of formally assessing a student's acculturation level is thoroughly explored in Chapter 4. Nevertheless, the Acculturation Quick Screen (AQS) is worth mentioning here because it is a well-recognized formal assessment of acculturation that is widely used as a preassessment tool by classroom teachers and is being strongly recommended by an increasing number of school districts throughout the nation.

> **assessment FREEZE FRAME 3.6**
>
> Teachers can develop an invaluable foundation for ongoing communication and reflection when they periodically converse with students about what the students already know and would like to know, as well as what they currently feel and think about themselves, school, and the learning process.

The AQS is a commercially available, research-based tool that is designed to measure a CLD student's level and rate of acculturation to grade-level school culture (Collier, 2004). The AQS is grounded in research conducted in both rural and urban school districts and is helpful for placing and monitoring CLD students from migrant, refugee, and immigrant families whose first language is not English. Although the original research base for the AQS was established with Hispanic CLD students, the AQS has been effectively used to monitor and plan assistance for students from Native American, Asian American, African American, and other culturally and linguistically diverse populations throughout the United States and Canada (Collier, 2004).

Among the many uses of the AQS are the following (Collier, 2004):

- To inform instructional decision making and development of appropriate interventions during prereferral processes and follow-up

- To inform instructional decision making for prevention (of culture shock) or intervention (for difficulties with acculturation) activities in the classroom or the school
- To aid in the collection of data needed to separate difference from disability concerns when CLD learners exhibit problems with learning or behavior

The findings from preinstructional use of the AQS are especially valuable for establishing a baseline for monitoring the CLD student's progress in acculturation and adaptation. Such formal monitoring is typically conducted on an annual or semiannual basis (compared with informal monitoring, which is ongoing). When used to gather baseline data, the AQS should be administered no later than four weeks after the student begins classes at the new school. (For additional information on the AQS, see Chapter 4.)

Education History of the CLD Student

In addition to preassessing the student's level of acculturation and other relevant aspects of the sociocultural dimension, effective teachers are concerned with the CLD student's prior education history. The process of gathering information about a student's educational history often begins with a review of available school records. Generally, these provide basic details of enrollment, attendance, and achievement for each year of education. Among other data that can be obtained from this cumulative file are evidence of basic health assurances (e.g., inoculations, vision and hearing screenings), enrollment in special language or special education programs, and indications of whether the student has ever been referred to a teacher assistance or student intervention team.

Although this is a great place to start, by itself the cumulative folder is a rather skeletal source. Once basic details of student achievement are located, teachers need to gain an understanding of the conditions in which that achievement (or lack thereof) occurred. In essence, educators need to determine the degree to which the curriculum was presented appropriately for the CLD student at each level. If, for example, records indicate a student was classified as a limited English speaker in grades K–3, the type of instruction the student received during those years will have significantly affected his or her ability to participate in and gain from the academic experiences teachers assume to be prerequisite for a given grade level. When a review of the educational history suggests a student's language skills were not at the level needed to benefit from past instruction as provided—or the supports were insufficient to ensure fair access to the curriculum—the student will often lack the skills necessary to function at grade level.

Aligning language and academic experiences is useful for native language instruction as well. In the following vignette, neither teachers nor parents initially recognized the variables affecting the student's academic achievement in his primary language:

Jorge's parents were pleased and excited to learn that his new school offered language arts instruction in Spanish as well as English. Learning to read in English had been dif-

Accommodative Assessment Practices 3.1

Yassir is starting middle school in a new town. His parents report that he began school in the first grade speaking no English. Available records indicate that Yassir was enrolled in the ESL program at his previous school, but he was exited during the third grade. Although Yassir appears quite fluent in conversational English, a preassessment of his academic skills indicates that he is performing far below grade level and is having much greater academic difficulty than his CLD peers in the classroom.

Contacts with Yassir's elementary school reveal that the ESL program in which he participated consisted of thirty minutes of pull-out service each day and focused on the students' acquisition of *survival English*, with an emphasis on developing a core vocabulary (e.g., food, clothes, colors) and basic grammar structures. When he met these limited criteria by third grade, Yassir was considered no longer in need of special language support, and he returned to the unaccommodative classroom. In contrast, the second language learners at Yassir's new school come from schools where the majority of grade-level teachers have received training in the use of strategies and supports for CLD students, with equal emphasis on language and content-area achievement.

Yassir's history suggests that the minimal amount of language support provided in elementary school and his premature exit from language services may be factors in his current lack of academic success. If Yassir's new teachers had not looked carefully into the differences between the ESL programs in question, they might have arrived at inaccurate conclusions about why Yassir is struggling more than the other CLD students.

■ *In what ways do past program differences account for the current achievement discrepancy between Yassir and his new ESL peers? Without knowing this aspect of Yassir's history and the corresponding implications, how might the achievement differences between him and his ESL peers have been perceived by teachers at the new school?*

ficult for Jorge, and he remained about a year behind his English-speaking peers. The teacher last year had told Jorge's parents this was "normal" for students learning to read in their second language. However, Jorge's parents thought he could do much more if given the chance to do schoolwork in his primary language. On learning about the bilingual offerings at the new school, they were thrilled and assumed Jorge would now have the opportunity to catch up.

Nonetheless, within a few weeks, Jorge was complaining that he didn't like Spanish and didn't want to be with the other Spanish-speaking students. His parents found these comments surprising and somewhat hurtful. They wondered if his years with mostly native-English-speaking peers had fostered this negativity. They were confused and distressed. Perhaps it had to do with the teacher. By the first parent–teacher conferences, Jorge was still performing a little below grade level in the English-speaking teacher's class but was continuing to demonstrate progress. Unfortunately, the Spanish language arts teacher could not offer similarly positive news. Although she acknowledged that Jorge was better able to communicate his ideas verbally in Spanish than in English, he was not completing assignments and had begun to irritate other students during independent work times.

In many ways, the process of reviewing academic records of students such as Jorge puts teachers in the role of an educational anthropologist or investigator.

Enrollment staff at Jorge's new school could have made better decisions about Jorge's educational placement if they had given greater consideration to his academic history. Such consideration would have suggested that, despite his Spanish dominance, Jorge had no prior literacy instruction in that language. As a result, many aspects of the Spanish language arts curriculum were beyond his abilities.

Although some schools and districts provide more detailed academic records, it is not uncommon for student files to provide few clues about actual instructional levels, types of accommodations (and the degree to which they have been used), or even the language(s) of instruction. In addition, parents may not be aware that the phrase "ESL services" can mean very different programs from state to state and school to school. Parents and the students themselves are, however, often the best and most immediate sources for potential data. Even when a particular program cannot be named, a parent's or student's description of the program can often provide enough information for staff to make an educated guess.

Parent and student descriptions of prior development and schooling experiences are aspects of the cognitive and academic dimensions of the CLD student biography (Herrera & Murry, 2005). Among the many challenges for CLD students associated with the *cognitive* dimension (Herrera & Murry, 2005) are:

- Cognitively demanding, decontextualized classroom environments and learning tasks
- Instructional approaches that fail to access the deep prior knowledge these students bring to learning tasks and problem solving
- Reductionist (i.e., basic skills-based and memorization-intensive) curricula and programming that involve few opportunities for higher-order thinking

Challenges associated with the *academic* dimension of the CLD student biography (Herrera & Murry, 2005) include:

- Academic presentation and textbook formats that involve content-area-specific terminology, unfamiliar grammatical structures, and inordinate assumptions about prior knowledge
- Limited classroom interactions that promote meaningful vocabulary development and familiarity with content-area-specific language
- Classroom curricula focused on preparing for high-stakes assessments
- Lack of reward structures for process learning and incremental gains in academic performance

Elaborating on prior academic knowledge and skills is critical to the ongoing cognitive development of CLD students. Successful classroom instruction focuses on the construction of meaning and helps students develop lasting connections between new learning and existing knowledge. Ultimately, this type of instruction depends on the effective preassessment of students' content-area knowledge, skills, and capacities.

Preassessment of Content-Area Knowledge, Skills, and Capacities

The student's knowledge of content-area material, as well as related skills and capacities, are among the most vital areas for teachers to preassess. Sometimes this information is gathered through written pretests, but there are many other ways to begin identifying and tapping into what students already know. One of the most easily incorporated techniques for drawing on prior experience is used by Mr. Carlson in the following scenario:

> Mr. Carlson begins his unit on predators and prey with a simple question: "How many of you have ever seen an animal or bug eat another animal or bug?" Hands fly into the air. For nearly thirty minutes, the class is fascinated by student tales of what they have seen eaten by *what, where,* and their guesses as to *why*. Sometimes, as with the praying mantis and grasshopper on Samuel's porch, these descriptions also include a rather detailed *how*.
>
> Mr. Carlson is thrilled by the excitement of his students as he draws on their experiences to introduce new vocabulary and concepts.
>
> **Mr. Carlson:** What makes a predator successful, Sasha? (After a long pause) Think about the cat you observed. What made him a good hunter?
>
> **Sasha:** I couldn't see him in the tree at first, because he's grey like the grey part of the tree . . . the trunk. He moved real slow and was quiet, but when he got close to the bird, he was fast!
>
> Many hands are raised as Sasha finishes, and other students discuss the traits of predators they have seen in real life or on TV. Mr. Carlson marvels at the way their prior experiences enhance their understanding of the curricular objectives regarding physical adaptations, prey–predator relationships, and human and environmental influences on that balance.

Preassessment information can also help identify sources of family knowledge from which the student and class can all benefit (Moll et al., 1992). The following example describes how Ms. Engelken draws on content-related knowledge from the parents of her students:

> Every time the class prepares to begin a new theme or unit of study, Ms. Engelken sends a note home about the upcoming topic. Even though the notes are translated into the native languages of parents, she ensures that there is at least one content-related picture for those with limited literacy skills. The notes are designed not only to inform parents about the lesson topics but also to encourage them to share any of their own related stories, knowledge, and experiences.
>
> Last month the class began a unit on volcanoes by listening to Kita tell the Hawaiian tale of how the Goddess Pele came to be responsible for the eruptions of Kilauea. In addition, Arturo had seen Popocatepetl puff steam while visiting family in Mexico City. Rick's mom had downloaded pictures of Mt. St. Helens from the Internet, and Andre's grandmother actually visited the classroom and told the whole class about how her cousin's house had been buried by ash in Montserrat. Listening to these tales and

experiences validated the parents' knowledge and involvement and fueled the students' interest in, and ability to relate to, the topic.

Although they gather information in different ways, Mr. Carlson and Ms. Engelken both dynamically use what they learn through preassessment to help students make connections between their background knowledge and new content-area concepts. The teachers in these scenarios understand that the pooled knowledge and experiences of students and families offer a library of resources. Some teachers never realize the value of such resources, and others fear to venture beyond their predetermined curriculum. Those who do take advantage of these funds of knowledge access a wealth of ideas and approaches to enhance the instructional experience for everyone involved.

There are quite a number of different methods teachers can use to probe students' current understandings of targeted curricular concepts. Examples include:

- Traditional subject-matter pretests (written and oral)
- Class discussions that focus on related experience or knowledge (which may include fictional references)
- Questionnaires
- Student interviews
- Creative student work (e.g., drawings or stories related to the content)
- K-W-L and K-W-L-H charts (see Assessment in Action 3.1)

Although critical preassessment information can usually be gathered easily, sometimes it is revealed only by chance. As illustrated in the following scenario, unexpected details can significantly enhance the academic achievement of students:

Marisa was referred to the counselor's office early in the second semester at Northfield High. She had begun the school year unremarkably. She always attended class and met the expectations of her teachers. However, she had already accumulated five unexcused tardies and three absences since the new semester began.

On review of Marisa's file, Ms. Lujano, the counselor, discovered that Marisa entered school in August as a newcomer from Guadalajara, Mexico. Because she had no prior English instruction, Marisa was assigned to Mr. Campbell's ESL class every morning. There she received most of her content-area instruction. Given her age and limited English proficiency, this seemed an ideal placement.

At the start of the scheduled counseling visit, Marisa appeared apprehensive about the session. However, she spontaneously returned Ms. Lujano's smile when greeted in Spanish. Ms. Lujano kept the tone informal and allowed social discourse to precede "business." As she listened to Marisa discuss her family and recent changes, Ms. Lujano identified many issues pertaining to acculturation and related adjustments. These seemed to be compounded of late by Marisa's sense that she had been identified as "dumb" (*una burra*). Marisa further explained that school here was boring and that she would rather be helping her mother at home than "wasting time" at school. When asked if she had felt that way in Mexico, Marisa replied, "No, I liked school there." Realizing there were a multitude of issues involved, Ms. Lujano decided to temporarily focus on school, and the following conversation ensued in Spanish:

■ Assessment in Action 3.1

K-W-L charts also provide a framework for tying prior knowledge and student motivation to new learning. Briefly, students begin a K-W-L chart before a new lesson by listing what they already **k**now about the topic and what they **w**ant to know. This serves to engage both interest and prior learning as students construct new knowledge during the course of instruction. After the lesson, students list what they have **l**earned and compare that with what they already knew or desired to learn. Some teachers add an "h" component to create K-W-L-H charts, which require students to think about **h**ow they learned and what strategies or resources worked best for them. This adds a dimension of metacognition (thinking about one's own thinking) to the students' self-assessment efforts. The Assessment Artifact below illustrates a completed K-W-L-H chart about the monarch butterfly.

■ Assessment Artifact: K-W-L-H Chart

Monarch Butterfly

K	W	L	H
• Has wings • Has antennae • Is black and orange • Comes from a cocoon • Is only here for part of the year	• What does it eat? • Where does it live? • Where is it flying?	• Life cycle: egg, caterpillar, pupa, adult butterfly • Caterpillar eats milkweed leaves • Butterfly eats flower nectar • Found all around the world • Migrates in the winter to warm places like California and Mexico	• Internet • Personal observation

Ms. Lujano: What is different about school here?

Marisa: They think we're dumb. We color pictures and copy sentences and learn how to say things in English.

Ms. Lujano: Like what?

Marisa: We learned the names of the continents and some of the countries. We learned that Egypt has pyramids, but that's all. I already know that and a lot more . . . in Spanish.

Ms. Lujano: You have already learned about the pyramids?

Marisa: Yes! I know how the pyramids were built.... It took more than twenty years and 20,000 people to make just one! They worshipped these different gods and put things in the sarcophagus with the mummy. I know why they did that too... so the dead person had what he needed for the next life. They have pyramids in Mexico too, but my family left before I got a chance to study them.

Ms. Lujano was amazed at the enthusiasm, detail, and vocabulary of Marisa's response. Without context, even she herself would not have understood the word *sarcophagus* in Spanish. They ended the visit by agreeing to meet later that day with Mr. Campbell, the ESL teacher.

Mr. Campbell was also surprised by Marisa's depth of knowledge in many areas. As he thought about ways they might better address her academic needs, he suddenly realized what had never occurred to him—that Marisa's Spanish skills and knowledge could be an asset to her learning *in* English. Perhaps instruction for Marisa had focused too excessively on English acquisition.

Over the next several weeks, Marisa led a team that searched Spanish Internet resources, downloaded pictures, and conversed with grade-level peers in Mexico (via email) to develop a comprehensive report that compared the pyramids of Giza in Egypt with Mexico's pyramids at Teotihuacán. The team was encouraged to involve more proficient ESL and native-English-speaking peers from Spanish class in the process of developing Spanish and English versions of the report. Not surprisingly, the outcome was tremendous... and Marisa stopped skipping school.

Although identifying the crux of an issue is not always this easy, conversations like these can yield key information. When educators focus on practices that connect the prior learning, experiences, and relevant interests of students with current academic goals and opportunities, students continue learning at multiple levels.

The details of formally assessing content-area knowledge and skills are thoroughly explored in Chapter 6. Nevertheless, the Snapshot Assessment System is worth mentioning here because it is a well-recognized assessment that has been widely used as a preassessment tool by classroom teachers throughout the United States. Moreover, the relative ease of its implementation facilitates its use for both formal and informal preassessment of content-area learning.

The Snapshot Assessment System (Rangel & Bansberg, 1999) is used to identify the knowledge and skill levels of CLD students in core curriculum areas. The degree of formality associated with the system is low because it can be quickly and easily administered. The Snapshot prompts CLD students to perform a series of tasks that are keyed to content standards in mathematics, science, and language arts. The standards and benchmarks targeted by the system are grade-level appropriate and considered fundamental to understanding future content. Teacher researchers helped develop the system, and content-area experts identified critical, overarching concepts essential to each content area assessed. The assessment tasks in the Snapshot are designed to be as free from cultural bias as possible and are especially valuable for CLD students whose primary language is not English.

Accommodative Assessment Practices 3.2

The preinstructional assessment of a CLD student's education history can reveal significant prior schooling experiences outside the United States. Yet some teachers tend to hold unverified assumptions about the prior schooling of CLD students. Specifically, some tend to assume that most schooling experiences undertaken outside the country are necessarily inferior to those undertaken by students in the United States.

In reality, this is often not the case. For example, middle- and high school–age students who emigrate from Mexico have often pursued studies in mathematics that are equivalent to, or frequently above, the grade level to which they are assigned in U.S. schools. This is especially the case for students who have attended private schools in Mexico. The fact that a CLD student is struggling to acculturate to a new country and school and may be wrestling with the many nuances of comprehending a new language does not necessarily indicate that she or he is unable to perform at grade level in any given content area, including mathematics. It is important to keep in mind that the validity of such assumptions is easily tested with even a limited number of informal, content-area preassessments. For example, an informal conversation/interview with the CLD student will often suggest the genuine extent of his or her background knowledge and skills in a particular subject area.

■ *What type of questions might be asked of a student at your grade level to gain insights into their prior knowledge and current skills in specific content areas?*

Language History of the CLD Student

In addition to preassessing biopsychosocial and education histories, successful teachers also preassess CLD students' language histories. Although language histories have always been important for placing students in language programs (e.g., ESL), they also have powerful implications for classroom instruction.

The process used to identify CLD students who qualify for special language programs usually provides the first level of information about their individual language histories. Student information is often gathered via home language surveys that ask specific questions about current language used by students and their family members in the home. Such surveys may yield an adequate picture of the present situation but often do not gather critical information about the student's prior language acquisition experiences. (See Chapter 5 for an in-depth discussion of home language surveys.)

In general, students with stronger first language skills have greater linguistic resources to draw on as they acquire a second language. These funds of knowledge are an important resource for the teacher as well. An immigrant student with substantial literacy skills in the primary language may initially communicate only in the primary language. However, such a student can often acquire academic English faster than some U.S.-born CLD students who either (a) began learning one language at home but shifted to learning English before fully developing the primary language or (b) are socialized in a family in which English is not the dominant language of parents or siblings but is the language they use most when addressing the student.

Language use patterns can also provide clues to social, emotional, and academic issues that may arise during adolescence. It is not uncommon for parents of CLD students whose first language is not English to report frustration that they can no longer communicate well with their teenage children. Although this is a sentiment shared by many parents regardless of culture or language, it is particularly distressing for non- or limited-English-speaking parents, who quite literally cannot help with homework or talk about crucial feelings, thoughts, values, problems, and aspirations with their now English-dominant children. Although parents may continue to speak the home language, students can easily become English-dominant through the influences of peers, school, and society. A language barrier between parents and students during this critical developmental time can have significant social and educational implications for many CLD students.

Elsewhere, we refer to this language aspect of the student's history as the *linguistic* dimension of the CLD student biography (Herrera & Murry, 2005). Regrettably, teachers often pay so much attention to this dimension that they sometimes overlook the student's acculturation and academic needs. This is especially true among teachers who believe the student is incapable of significant content-area learning until he or she has mastered the English language. In reality, no single dimension of the CLD student biography is typically any more or less crucial than any other to the life and academic successes of CLD students. These dimensions are interrelated and demand classroom instruction and assessment approaches that target the needs of the whole student.

Nonetheless, student challenges associated with the linguistic dimension (Herrera & Murry, 2005) include:

- Limited exposure to authentic literacy development activities
- Instructional emphasis on isolated basic skills of the target language (English)
- Fragmented literacy instruction, including postponed exposure to writing in English
- Widespread reliance on ineffective language-programming models (e.g., ESL pull-out)
- Lack of understanding among educators about the time actually required for second language (English) acquisition (e.g., seven to nine years for some students)
- An inordinate focus on basic decoding skills in reading

Many of these challenges are less about innate student abilities than about the range and types of language development approaches (and especially instructional approaches) used in the classroom.

Language assessment approaches used with CLD students in the classroom should be well grounded in research and best practices. Schools and districts have typically based their language assessment practices on the pre- and sometimes postinstructional use of formal language proficiency assessments (e.g., LAS, IPT, Woodcock–Munoz). However, informal language assessment tools are increasingly used by classroom teachers for constructing a more in-depth, inclusive picture

It is not uncommon for parents of CLD students whose first language is not English to report frustration that they can no longer communicate well with their teenage children. Although this is a sentiment shared by many parents regardless of culture or language, it is particularly distressing for non- or limited-English-speaking parents who quite literally cannot help with homework or talk about crucial feelings, thoughts, values, problems, and aspirations with their now English-dominant children.

of the language assets and literacy needs of CLD students—as well as for making appropriate instructional and curricular modifications based on this emerging picture.

Preassessment of L1 and L2 Language Proficiencies

CLD students who have been identified for language-programming services will usually be given a formal assessment to measure their preexisting or baseline skills in the target instructional language (L2) and sometimes the primary language (L1) as well. Formal tests used for this purpose are discussed in Chapter 5. However, there are numerous other ways of learning about the linguistic knowledge of CLD students. A multidimensional look at language is inevitably more valid and informative because it takes into account the many ways that the student actually uses language in varied academic and social contexts.

As we detail in subsequent chapters, it is not unusual for students to reveal skills in real-world situations that they fail to demonstrate on static tests. For this reason and others, effective teachers seek and share ideas about how to better understand the language skills of their students before, in addition to, and between periods of formal test administration. These teachers:

- Preassess the CLD student's knowledge of curricular vocabulary and concepts and are aware that activities requiring verbal or written responses may not allow students to demonstrate as much of their linguistic knowledge as those that also permit alternative responses (e.g., picture selection, demonstration).
- Observe the student's ability to nonverbally respond to written or verbal directions (one-step as well as multilevel) with and without visual cues.
- Note the CLD student's ability to answer concrete "Wh" questions about a curricular topic with and without visual cues (e.g., *Who discovered radium?*).
- Note the student's ability to answer more complex (e.g., inferential) questions with and without visual cues (e.g., *Why is it important for a firefighter to be strong?*).
- Assess the student's use of language to seek assistance with tasks or ask for clarification of ideas and information. This is an area rarely addressed by

Accommodative Assessment Practices 3.3

The most effective preinstructional assessments of L1 proficiency are informal and may involve the classroom teacher's collaboration with a bilingual paraprofessional. Yet classroom teachers should be aware that even informal and collaborative preassessments of L1 proficiency may yield problematic results.

For example, many highly assimilated parents or guardians of CLD students convince their children that the only way to adequately acquire English for schooling is to discontinue any use of the native language (English immersion). Therefore, these students come to believe they should no longer acknowledge comprehension of their L1 or engage in language production that reflects a comprehension of that language. Classroom teachers should be aware that this belief could profoundly influence the findings of even informal preassessments of L1 proficiency. Specifically, these findings may errone-ously indicate very limited L1 proficiency.

Although CLD students are typically not very willing to discuss this perspective on native language use, their parents or guardians are often so convinced they are doing the right thing that they are more than willing to discuss prohibitions on native language use. Therefore, this potential problem may be identified during a home visit or through the preassessment of the sociocultural dimension.

■ *As part of a home visit with a student's family or guardian(s), what specific questions might an insightful teacher ask to uncover perspectives on native language use at school or in the home?*

formal assessments but one that can profoundly influence the academic success of CLD students.

- Observe whether the student is better able to communicate knowledge or ideas when given access to, or allowed to create her or his own, visual supports.
- Observe the CLD student's ability to use language to convey higher-order thinking through explanation, comparison, synthesis, and analysis of information. These skills are often first observed in nonacademic contexts as students describe and discuss movies, games, sports, peer or sibling conflicts, and so forth.

By observing language skills used in daily contexts, teachers can learn much about what their CLD students already know and can do. In many cases, teachers also discover how these students will best be able to demonstrate knowledge and skills during instruction. Because this information can significantly inform a teacher's use of particular instructional approaches, the benefits of preassessing language proficiency far outweigh any initial expenditures of time.

■ Preassessment Resources: Home Visits and School Conferences

Teachers of CLD students who conduct home visits not only create opportunities for observing language use in context but also gain valuable information for preassessing the student's level of acculturation, content-area capacities, academic background, and more. Although parent conferences at the school offer considerably less contextualized information about the student's home environment, these conferences also provide helpful preassessment information. During these interactions, teachers often find that their initial impressions gave them few or misleading insights into a student's talents and skills.

When talking with parents of CLD students, it is helpful to remember that the majority of these parents regard teachers as extremely knowledgeable and worthy of their utmost respect. In fact, some parents may defer entirely to the teacher on academic issues, placing their complete trust in the teacher's ability to do what is right for the child. This level of trust may compel some parents to respond in ways that signal agreement with a teacher's comments rather than offering contrary opinions or evidence on the child's abilities and difficulties. Therefore, when visiting with parents, it is essential for teachers to look for and ask about evidence of student skills and knowledge in multiple contexts, as the following scenario demonstrates:

> Mrs. Adams was somewhat nervous about her home visit to meet Tamara's family. In addition to getting acquainted, they would be discussing the kindergarten placement test that demonstrated Tamara's lack of academic readiness. As Mrs. Adams talked about Tamara's inability to do basic tasks such as sorting and matching blocks by color, Tamara's mother nodded. Not having blocks at home, she had never seen her daughter use that skill either. Tamara's mother appreciated the teacher's concern and agreed to purchase blocks if that would help Tamara learn to match.
>
> Although this response initially pleased Mrs. Adams, she noticed that while they had been discussing Tamara's skills, the girl had dutifully sorted a large pile of family socks by size and color, laying them in perfectly coordinated sets of two. Laughing aloud, Mrs. Adams explained her observation to Tamara's mother and said, "Never mind the blocks . . . unless she wants them for play." From that point on, Mrs. Adams eagerly asked parents for alternative evidence of skills at home and, over time, became quite an advocate for the many ways that curricular skills can be taught and assessed through home routines.

Parents such as Tamara's, who do not feel that their own observations and ideas are relevant to academic learning, will often not volunteer potentially critical information. Therefore, cross-culturally sensitive teachers encourage parents to share related perceptions and experiences about their children. Figure 3.2 depicts an informal assessment tool that can be used with parents to gather evidence of a student's curricular skills (see also appendix resources).

Educators can do a number of things to lay the groundwork for an informative home visit. Because communication is often an issue, following up with verbal confirmation of written communication (and vice versa) ensures that the family is aware of the time, place, and purpose of the visit. Some teachers also use such contact opportunities to ask a few questions ahead of time so that family members can think over the related issues or confer with a partner who will not be present.

■ **figure 3.2** Home Skills Survey

Academic Skills Demonstrated with Clothes/Laundry

Can your child:

Yes	No	Unsure	Sort laundry by *color*?
Yes	No	Unsure	Locate items that *match* (e.g., socks)?
Yes	No	Unsure	Tell you which shirt or sock is *bigger/smaller*?

Academic Skills Demonstrated in the Kitchen

Can your child:

Yes	No	Unsure	Sort items by *color* or *shape*?
Yes	No	Unsure	Sort boxes or cans by *size* (e.g., large cans/small cans)?
Yes	No	Unsure	Sort items *in order* from smallest to largest?
Yes	No	Unsure	Show you which cup is *empty* and which is *full*?
Yes	No	Unsure	Identify items from the same *group* (e.g., fruits, vegetables, desserts)?
Yes	No	Unsure	Pick out foods having a particular *characteristic* (e.g., sweet, smooth)?
Yes	No	Unsure	Tell you which bowl has *more* (e.g., ice cream, beans)?
Yes	No	Unsure	Tell you which container has the *most* or *least* (e.g., grapes, chips)?
Yes	No	Unsure	Tell you which foods he or she *does* or *does not* like?
Yes	No	Unsure	Demonstrate that he or she knows *where* to find or put things in the kitchen?
Yes	No	Unsure	Demonstrate that he or she understands that the refrigerator is *cold* and the stove is *hot*?
Yes	No	Unsure	Select the correct *number* of spoons/napkins to help set the table for a family meal?

For example, a teacher might inform family members that the following questions will be asked during the upcoming visit:

- What would you like me to know about your child?
- What do you think she or he does particularly well?
- Do you have any concerns?
- What would you like to see your child accomplish this month, semester, or year?

Open-ended questions such as these invite parents and others to share knowledge and insights about the student that the teacher might otherwise miss. In addition, if family members are able to provide responses before the scheduled visit, this input can help the teacher more personally frame the conference objectives in terms of the family's concerns and wishes for their child.

When necessary, the teacher should bring a trained interpreter who, ideally, is also familiar with the community and particular culture of the student. Before the visit, the educator should brief the interpreter on the goals for the meeting and expectations for the interpreter's involvement. Although time constraints and norms of their primary culture may compel some educators to get right to business during the visit, many parents feel more comfortable if a little time is allowed for general social niceties in accordance with the community norm.

After the visit, teachers should document observations and insights gathered about the sociocultural, cognitive, academic, and linguistic dimensions of the student's biography. Thorough reflection on the home visit often illuminates details that can significantly inform instruction and assessment practices. In addition, teachers can easily complete a brief write-up of key information to be added to the student's cumulative folder. Figure 3.3 (and the related appendix resource) illustrates one way of summarizing a student's cultural profile. A profile sheet of this kind serves as a quick reference for the current teacher as well as the student's future teachers.

close-up *on Assessment* 3.4

Some teachers also use contact opportunities prior to a home visit to ask a few questions ahead of time so that family members can think over the related issues or confer with a partner who will not be present. For example, a teacher might inform family members that the following questions will be asked during the upcoming visit:

- What would you like me to know about your child?
- What do you think she or he does particularly well?
- Do you have any concerns?
- What would you like to see your child accomplish this month, semester, or year?

Open-ended questions such as these invite parents and others to share knowledge and insights about the student that the teacher might otherwise miss. In addition, if family members are able to provide responses before the scheduled visit, this input can help the teacher more personally frame the conference objectives in terms of the family's concerns and wishes for their child.

■ **figure 3.3** Cultural Profile Sheet

Cultural Profile from Home Visit

Student Name:

_____

Ethnicity:

_____

Country of Birth:

_____

Native Language/Other Languages Spoken at Home:

_____

Second Language Proficiency (LAS score/Information on parent questionnaire or survey):

_____

Family Specifics:

_____

Cultural Characteristics:

_____

_____

_____

_____

Other Information:

_____

_____

_____

_____

close-up *on Assessment 3.5*

When regular home visits are not undertaken, parent participation in school conferences can be increased by:

- Holding CLD parent conferences at alternate times (e.g., evenings and weekends) or places (e.g., a community center)
- Designating a school area as a resource room for CLD parents and families—an area where they can confer with one another and school personnel
- Inviting community resource representatives from medical and dental clinics, social services, and police and fire departments to familiarize parents with available services and answer general questions
- Providing childcare for parents during conference times

By taking interpersonal and cultural variables into consideration during parent conferences—and by respecting parents as valued educational partners—teachers can form a solid basis for collaborative parent–teacher relationships.

Most of the aforementioned considerations for home visits with CLD families are equally applicable to school-based conferences. Although such meetings are typically less informative and take place outside the context of the home, they do provide opportunities for collecting useful preassessment data. Schools or teachers who report lower participation by CLD parents in such conferences may want to examine the cultural and linguistic climate of the setting, as well as the supports available to parents and family members. When regular home visits are not undertaken, parent participation in school conferences can be increased by:

- Holding CLD parent conferences at alternate times (e.g., evenings and weekends) or places (e.g., a community center)
- Designating a school area as a resource room for CLD parents and families—an area where they can confer with one another and school personnel
- Inviting community resource representatives from medical and dental clinics, social services, and police and fire departments to familiarize parents with available services and answer general questions
- Providing childcare for parents during conference times

By taking interpersonal and cultural variables into consideration during parent conferences—and by respecting parents as valued educational partners—teachers can form a solid basis for collaborative parent–teacher relationships.

■ key concepts

Academic dimension of the CLD
  student biography

Acculturation Quick Screen
  (AQS)

Affective filter

Biopsychosocial history of the
  CLD student

Cognitive dimension of the CLD
  student biography

Culture

Education history of the CLD
  student

Language history of the CLD
  student

Level of acculturation

Linguistic dimension of the CLD
  student biography

Preassessment

Preinstructional assessment

Sociocultural dimension of the
  CLD student biography

Student history

■ professional conversations on practice

1. Discuss why teachers benefit from preinstructionally assessing each dimension of the CLD
   student biography—the sociocultural, cognitive, academic, and linguistic.

2. Discuss the range of benefits associated with
   home visits as a venue for preinstructional assessment. Relate each of these benefits to each
   of the four dimensions of the CLD student
   biography.

3. Discuss the difficulties associated with relying
   too heavily on tools designed for formal, as opposed to informal, preinstructional assessment
   of CLD students.

4. Discuss reasons why educators often tend to
   discount the value of prior schooling experiences of CLD students outside the United States.
   How can the validity of this practice be tested
   through formal and informal preassessments?

5. Discuss how formal or informal preassessments
   of L1 proficiency might yield problematic or erroneous findings. What is the appropriate role
   of the classroom teacher in such assessments?

■ questions for review and reflection

1. What are the advantages to classroom teachers
   who conduct preinstructional assessments of
   CLD students? Specify at least three.

2. As teachers preassess the sociocultural biography or biopsychosocial history of a CLD
   student, what three critical aspects of the
   student's history are assessed? Briefly explain
   each.

3. Why should teachers be concerned with events
   or circumstances that prompted the family of a
   CLD student to immigrate?

4. Why is the degree of similarity between
   the home culture of a CLD student and the
   school culture important to the classroom
   teacher?

5. What characteristics of the *bio* aspect of the
   CLD student's biopsychosocial history are important when preassessing CLD students?

6. Cross-culturally sensitive teachers often informally preassess the CLD student's level of acculturation through conversational interviews.
   How do the benefits of this sort of preassessment transcend the value of the immediate information acquired?

7. Why should classroom teachers be concerned
   with both the level and rate of acculturation of
   CLD students?

8. What sorts of informal assessments can teachers use to preassess the content-area knowledge,
   skills, and capacities of their CLD students?

9. What sorts of informal assessments can teachers use to preassess the L1 and L2 proficiencies of CLD students?

10. Why should a classroom teacher allow a student who is acquiring English to offer nonverbal responses (e.g., picture selection and demonstrations) during preassesments of curricular vocabulary and concepts?

11. How does the notion of an *affective filter* complicate the use of formal tools when preassessing CLD students?

12. CLD students who arrive from the same country, speak the same primary language, and have similar schooling biographies may, nonetheless, demonstrate different levels and rates of acculturation. What factors might account for these differences and why? Explore at least five.

- Define acculturation and explain how it differs from enculturation.
- Explain what is meant by a cultural lens and defend why teachers must learn to recognize its influence on their perceptions of, expectations for, and pedagogical actions with CLD students.
- Discuss symptoms or behaviors associated with culture shock.
- Describe the situation of anomie, which a CLD student may experience as one aspect of the acculturation process.
- Explain the key differences between assimilation and adaptation as outcomes of the acculturation process.
- Discuss how gatekeeping staff of a school may contribute to the acculturation difficulties of CLD students.
- Discuss how a school's approach to second language acquisition with CLD students may actually promote deculturation.
- Explain how emotions, especially those associated with the challenges of acculturation, may affect CLD student performance and achievement.
- Explain why research has tended to support a strong correlation between proficiency in the first language and acculturation progress for CLD students.
- Analyze how a CLD student's ethnicity or nation of origin may influence his or her acculturation pattern.
- Summarize specific advantages of a home visit for informally assessing the acculturation level of CLD students.
- Discuss how adaptation, as a product of the acculturation process, often contributes to the achievement of CLD students.
- Summarize effective actions that schools can take to reduce acculturative stress for CLD students.
- Discuss the relationship between familism and the acculturation challenges confronted by CLD students.

Assessment of Acculturation

My sensitivity to my students and their families has been heightened. I think that the first step to take involves getting to know my ELL [CLD] students' parents, their attitude and beliefs about education, and their goals for their children. I need to emphasize the parents' role in their child's education and suggest ways that I can be of assistance. I can provide appropriate materials written in their native language so that they can work with their children at home. Throughout the school year, I will continue to communicate "good news" to parents through notes, phone calls, and newsletters. During conferences it is important that I explain carefully their child's progress in the school curriculum, always emphasizing their strengths. I will continue to showcase student work and progress in the curriculum through a portfolio collection of their student's work and assessments.

Karen Burkholder
Third-Grade Teacher

critical standards *Guiding Chapter Content*

TESOL/NCATE teacher standards reflect professional consensus on standards for the quality teaching of PreK–12 CLD students. Additionally, the CEEE Guiding Principles and their accompanying indicators serve as a framework to assist practitioners, policymakers, and clients as they collaborate to enhance academic enrichment and language acquisition among CLD students. Therefore, to help educators understand how they might appropriately target and address national professional teaching standards in practice, we have designed the content of this chapter to reflect the following standards.

TESOL/NCATE Standards for P–12 Teacher Education Programs

Domain 2: Culture. Candidates know, understand, and use the major concepts, principles, theories, and research related to the nature and role of culture and cultural groups to construct learning environments that support ESOL students' cultural identities, language and literacy development, and content-area achievement.

- **Standard 2.b. Cultural Groups and Identity.** Candidates know, understand, and use knowledge of how cultural groups and students' cultural identities affect language learning and school achievement.

  2.b.2. Understand and apply knowledge about how an individual's cultural identity affects their ESL learning and how levels of cultural identity will vary widely among students.

  2.b.3. Understand and apply knowledge about cultural conflicts and home-area events that can have an impact on ESOL students' learning.

Note: All TESOL/NCATE Standards are cited from TESOL (2003). All Guiding Principles are cited from Center for Equity and Excellence in Education (CEEE) (2005). Reprinted by permission.

Domain 4: Assessment. Candidates understand issues of assessment and use standards-based assessment measures with ESOL students.

- **Standard 4.a. Issues of Assessment for ESL.** Candidates understand various issues of assessment (e.g., cultural and linguistic bias; political, social, and psychological factors) in assessment, IQ, and special education testing (including gifted and talented); the importance of standards; and the difference between language proficiency and other types of assessment (e.g., standardized achievement tests of overall mastery) as they affect ESOL student learning.

  4.a.3. Demonstrate understanding of the limitations of assessment situations and make accommodations for ESOL students.

CEEE Guiding Principles

Principle #5: English language learners are evaluated with appropriate and valid assessments that are aligned to state and local standards and that take into account the language development stages and cultural backgrounds of the students.

5.8 Develop student profiles that include English language proficiency level, native language literacy level, language/cultural background, educational history, courses and programs taken, and appropriate and valid student assessment data to monitor the progress of English language learners and evaluate the efficacy of their instructional programs.

5.10 Use a variety of formal and authentic assessment techniques to enhance classroom knowledge of English language learners and to evaluate their academic and linguistic progress.

Families and students come to this country for different reasons. Some arrive in search of opportunity, some come to escape the problems of a war-torn country, and many are recruited by industries to work in high-need areas. Very seldom does the child, adolescent, or young adult arrive in this country by his or her own choice. For newly arrived CLD students, stress related to changes in environment, language, and schooling places a strain on their capacity to learn. Educators often overlook these stressors as they scramble to plan for these new arrivals. Consider the following case:

> Isamari arrived midyear in a small midwestern town as a fifth-grade student. A very short biography provided by the school stated he had received schooling in Mexico up to the second grade. His score on the LAS (Language Assessment Scale) indicated that he was a non-English speaker. Informal assessments indicated he did not know the majority of his letter sounds in English or Spanish and that he struggled to read at a first-grade level.

Given such information, we educators often focus on what the student knows or does not know academically, without exploring the acculturation stressors he or she may have experienced since arriving in the United States. Not surprisingly, this student was on the prereferral road soon after his arrival.

Fortunately, one of the members of the special education (SPED) prereferral team took it upon herself to further explore the sociocultural background of the student. What she learned was that Isamari had been sent to the United States by his mother to learn English (by himself) at the age of 7. He had moved in with his aunt, who enrolled him in school a few months later. After attending school for six months, the family began to have financial difficulties and decided they could no longer keep him. He was then sent to live with another family member and was enrolled in a new school. However, it was not long before this family suffered a financial setback as well and, again, Isamari was sent away, this time out of state. On arrival in his current school district, he was again enrolled in school and (as previously discussed) was found to be lagging behind grade level, as assessed through both formal and informal measures. This situation raises a few key questions:

- How might this additional background information cast new light on the ability of assessments to provide critical information about the student?
- How might stressors associated with the acculturation process affect learning for this student?
- In what way do the student's acculturation process and the teacher's own culture interact to accelerate or hinder learning?

■ Acculturation and Enculturation Processes

"*Acculturation* [italics added] is the type of culture change that occurs when an enculturated individual comes into proximity with a new or different culture" (Collier, 2004, p. 6). By contrast, *enculturation* refers to an individual's *initial* socialization to the norms of his or her own culture or group. This is the process by which children acquire the foundational values, behaviors, and language appropriate for the contexts in which they will physically, cognitively, and socially develop. Therefore, acculturation results when a person who is already socialized to a particular set of norms comes into contact with those of another culture, whose norms or ways may be markedly different.

This new culture may be that of a faraway land, people, and language. However, acculturation can also be experienced by individuals who move within their own country, who join a new group (e.g., religious, military), or who are exposed to alternative ideas and experiences via the media, entertainment, literature, and education. The behavioral and psychological adjustments that individuals undergo in the process of acculturation arise from the need to cope or the desire to thrive in the new environment. Consequently, important questions for educators to consider include:

assessment *FREEZE FRAME* 4.1

Acculturation results when a person who is already socialized to a particular set of norms comes into contact with those of another culture, whose norms or ways may be markedly different.

- Why must classroom teachers and other educators understand the values and beliefs to which they themselves have been enculturated?

- How can these values and beliefs influence educators' responses to, and relationships with, their students?

When What Used to Work No Longer Works

The process of enculturation leaves the individual with a sort of filter through which he or she interprets the behaviors and interactions of others. We become accustomed to our own patterns of response because they generally work effectively with people who have been socialized in the same, or a very similar, culture. However, when we try to read situations and behaviors that result from different cultural norms and experiences, inaccurate assumptions and misunderstandings often follow. Reflecting on one's own enculturation can be an eye-opening experience. Teachers who are able to identify their own cultural lens (or way of viewing the world) are generally much better able to recognize how that lens colors or distorts their perceptions of other people and events. The culturally reflective teacher also understands that the CLD student has often been thrust into an environment in which her or his own lens is suddenly an unreliable guide for social interaction. This can lead to confusing (and inadvertently punishing) situations in which previously appropriate behaviors garner unpredictably negative reactions. In the case to follow, Fadi's experience is a prime example of these compounding misperceptions:

> assessment *FREEZE FRAME 4.2*
>
> The process of enculturation leaves the individual with a sort of filter through which he or she interprets the behaviors and interactions of others.

Fadi is a very bright Palestinian student. He seems to be doing well with sheltered instruction but is frequently involved in playground conflicts. Although it's not unusual for fourth graders to prefer same-sex playmates, Fadi's constant touching of the other boys has led to many problems. Fadi disregards the looks and body language warning him to stop but becomes overly upset and cries when his actions result in name-calling, hitting, and alienation from those he considers his friends. Mr. Tennyson has seen this type of inappropriate behavior before and refers Fadi to the social worker as a possible victim of sexual abuse. The conversation that follows is both un-

close-up *on Assessment 4.1*

We become accustomed to our own patterns of response because they generally work effectively with people who have been socialized in the same, or a very similar, culture. However, when we try to read situations and behaviors that result from different cultural norms and experiences, inaccurate assumptions and misunderstandings often follow. Reflecting on one's own enculturation can be an eye-opening experience.

comfortable and confusing to Fadi. School, which he has always enjoyed, has now become an unpleasant place. His increasing visits to the nurse and number of days home sick only add to the teacher's concerns that something negative is happening to Fadi.

Although Fadi is experiencing stress from problems he is having at school, Mr. Tennyson is fortunately wrong in his conclusion that Fadi may be a victim of abuse. Fadi is, in fact, just behaving as expected of a boy with his background. He has been socialized in a culture that does not stigmatize males for platonic physical contact. Touching is common during play as a means to communicate camaraderie. Interestingly, Mr. Tennyson has himself become acculturated to accept these very same behaviors among professional athletes but remains enculturated to view them as abnormal in young boys.

In this situation, Fadi and the other boys perceived and responded to one another's behaviors according to their own socialization or frameworks of thinking. Mr. Tennyson's interpretation, similar to that of the boys, was enhanced by professional training about the potential significance of Fadi's actions. Unfortunately, these ways of thinking led to a web of assumptions and reactions that initially interfered with appropriate resolution of the conflict.

The relationship between enculturation and acculturation is fascinating but not always easy to understand for those who have not experienced it firsthand. In an unrelated but helpful analogy, imagine the frustration you would feel if suddenly the function keys on the familiar television remote were randomly reassigned. Now, pressing any of the automatically understood keys (those to which you are enculturated to use) results in a completely undesired response. How might you feel and react? This is exactly what Mr. Gabriel does in the following scenario with his high school students. He uses this scenario to help his students understand the frustration their current and future peers often feel while trying to interact in an unfamiliar culture.

> **assessment *FREEZE FRAME* 4.3**
>
> Teachers who are able to identify their own cultural lens (or way of viewing the world) are generally much better able to recognize how that lens colors or distorts their perceptions of other people and events.

Mr. Gabriel begins by giving his students an authentic assignment that involves identifying two of the day's top news stories, the weather forecast for Atlanta, scores from any of the previous days' national sporting events, and a music video being played at a given time during the activity (e.g., 11:17 A.M.). Without exception, the students feel this is an easy task that should require no more than five to seven minutes. Mr. Gabriel has discovered it takes only one or two students attempting the activity as others watch to make a very valuable point.

At first there is shock when the power button on the television remote has no effect. Once Mr. Gabriel assures students that the television is not broken, the realization sets in that this remote is somehow programmed differently. Random efforts eventually result in turning on the set, but the familiar channels are all wrong. Keying the sports channel brings up a shopping network. The volume is too low to hear, but the up arrow turns the screen blue. Even channel surfing is impossible because the channel buttons won't change the television to higher or lower stations.

Students write down what they are feeling as the activity progresses. Interestingly, many start with words such as *amused, surprised,* and *challenged.* Within minutes, however, the majority are adding words such as *stupid, frustrated,* and *angry* to the list. This is followed among some students by feelings of resignation, rejection, or a desire to give up (e.g., "Who cares?" "This is dumb." "I quit."). Some, however, are able to maintain an understanding of their own innate competencies and realize the numerous missteps resulted from a reprogrammed remote control, not anything personal about themselves. Mr. Gabriel has observed that these students stay with the activity longer and are more likely to decipher and successfully adapt to the differences.

Feelings like those expressed by Mr. Gabriel's students are common among individuals who experience acculturation simulations. However, the major difference with actual acculturation is that stress and feelings of isolation, frustration, and anger may continue for long periods of time and frequently erode the student's self-esteem or self-efficacy as a learner.

Hidden scars of acculturative stress may even remain in otherwise fully acculturated and successful individuals. Esteban Piña, a medical professional, reflected on his own acculturation experience:

For a long time I believed "Mexican" was something that was considered to be a bad thing.... I tried to make sense out of why it was important to speak only English and try to look like and fit in with my Anglo peers. We were punished for speaking Spanish so many of us stopped, but then we could no longer talk to our *abuelos* and *tios.* It felt bad that even after complying with these expected changes, we were still more or less confined to an area south of the railroad tracks. Most of my friends are still in that area or nearby. Through the military, I had opportunities to pursue an education beyond anything I'd ever imagined, but feelings of inadequacy persisted. When I think about my career, I realize that for years no matter how confident I was in my work with patients, I could never get to the point of feeling equal to my professional peers. I carry that around in other ways too that have affected my personal life. Sometimes I wonder if I will ever stop reconciling what I gave up, what I gained, and where I fit.

Although the impact of Piña's acculturation profile was outwardly subtle, his thoughts show that it had and still has a compelling influence on his life.

Acculturation can affect people in many different ways. The types and degrees of difference between cultures are also factors in acculturation. As the degree of difference between the cultures increases, so does the likelihood that the norms of one will violate the norms of the other—and that the process of acculturation will also be accompanied by culture shock.

Culture shock commonly occurs as the novelty of the unfamiliar evolves into a frustrating reality for which there is no quick or easy remedy. In addition to sudden changes in language, recently immigrated students are often dealing with issues of loss associated with the friends, family, and community left behind. De-

Students who experience culture shock may demonstrate anger, irritability, disorderly behavior, signs of depression, emotionality (e.g., crying), increased somatic complaints (e.g., headache, upset stomach), homesickness, excessive sleeping, overeating or loss of appetite, social withdrawal, or loss of interest in previously enjoyed activities.

pending on the reasons for immigration, there may be increased family tensions and insecurities. Language barriers, social isolation, finances, and work schedules can leave some parents less able to provide the emotional support their children need during this critically stressful time.

Students who experience culture shock may demonstrate anger, irritability, disorderly behavior, signs of depression, emotionality (e.g., crying), increased somatic complaints (e.g., headache, upset stomach), homesickness, excessive sleeping, overeating or loss of appetite, social withdrawal, or loss of interest in previously enjoyed activities. These symptoms are significant areas of concern for educators because they not only impair a student's ability to learn but also are serious indicators of psychological and physical distress. Because "the effects of acculturation are similar to and may be confused with some of the behaviors for which children are referred to special education" (Collier, 2004, p. 2) and because erroneous placements only compound the problems, it is essential for teachers to understand and be able to assess as much as possible their students' levels of acculturation. An understanding of the multiple factors contributing to a student's behavior enables teachers and other educators to make informed decisions about appropriate programming, instruction, and assessment.

Culture shock commonly occurs as the novelty of the unfamiliar evolves into a frustrating reality for which there is no quick or easy remedy. In addition to sudden changes in language, recently immigrated students are often dealing with issues of loss associated with the friends, family, and community left behind.

■ Acculturation Dynamics

Acculturation does not necessarily occur at the same rate or to the same degree among individuals, even among members of the same immigrant group or family. Most models of acculturation recognize that students often go through a variety of phrases characterized by:

1. *Euphoria.* There is a curiosity and enthusiasm about the host culture.
2. *Culture Shock.* Novelty gives way to reality. Irritability, anger, grief, and sometimes depression ensue.

3. *Anomie.* The individual begins to understand and sort out his or her role in each culture. Frequently, however, the individual feels he or she is in a cultural "no man's land," estranged from the home culture but not yet accepted into the mainstream of the host culture. This period can be short-lived or persist throughout an individual's lifetime. Anomie is often associated with negative overall socialization. By contrast, the ability to adapt to the norms of the new culture while retaining affiliation with the old correlates with much more positive acculturation.

4. *Adoption/Adaptation.* The individual may fully adopt the new culture as a replacement for the primary culture (assimilation) or adapt to it in a manner that allows him or her to function authentically within both (integration).

Common to the various models for describing how people adjust to acculturation experiences (Berry, Kim, Power, Young, & Bujaki, 1989) are the psychological, linguistic, and cultural changes related to assimilation, integration, rejection, and deculturation. It is extremely helpful for teachers to understand what each means for CLD students in their classroom.

As discussed, assimilation occurs when a student (or individual) replaces his or her native cultural patterns and language with those of the new (or host) community. Among overt indicators are style of dress, customs, religious practices, and espoused beliefs. Assimilation represents a sacrifice rather than integration of or adaptation to new cultural and linguistic norms. Not all students want to look and act like everyone else, yet the need to feel accepted often forces CLD students to replace their previous ways with those of their host culture peers. Rapid assimilation to a new culture or language may result in a disconnection between CLD students and parents or family members that undermines family cohesiveness and strength (e.g., the ability to guide, support, solve problems, and communicate values).

Integration or adaptation reflects the degree to which the CLD student is capable of and comfortable participating differentially in the norms and customary routines of different groups. Some indications of integration include situationally appropriate language, style of dress, and food preferences, but other signs are more subtle. It is important to note that behavioral (e.g., language, social skills, customs) acculturation and psychological (e.g., values, belief systems, attitudes) acculturation often do not occur in a parallel manner. Therefore, it may not be appropriate to infer acculturation levels based on single indicators, such as language or style of dress.

Rejection reflects the conscious choice an individual makes to shun either the host or the home culture. The former situation is sometimes prevalent among

> **assessment *FREEZE FRAME* 4.5**
>
> Acculturation does not necessarily occur at the same rate or to the same degree among individuals, even among members of the same immigrant group or family.

> **assessment *FREEZE FRAME* 4.6**
>
> Assimilation occurs when a student (or individual) replaces his or her native cultural patterns and language with those of the host (or new) community. Among overt indicators are style of dress, customs, religious practices, and espoused beliefs. Assimilation represents a sacrifice rather than integration of or adaptation to new cultural and linguistic norms.

immigrants who choose to isolate themselves from and reject nearly everything about the new culture. In the latter case, individuals may come to believe that customs and behaviors associated with the old culture are undesirable or a threat to their security. Unfortunately, there is little evidence that directing such negative emotions toward one's own group eases conflicts of the acculturation process. Instead, it is far more often associated with enduring psychological conflict (Padilla, 1980).

Deculturation describes the cultural anomie or "no man's land" that some immigrants experience as a result of the disconnection from the home culture and language that occurred before, or in absence of, positive acculturation to the new community, culture, and language. According to Durkheim (1951), anomie occurs when cultural norms break down as a result of rapid change. When a CLD

Accommodative Assessment Practices 4.1

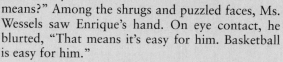

As Ms. Wessels prepared notice letters for the year's first conferences, she recalled that Enrique's enrollment listed Spanish as the home language. To verify this, she asked, "Your parents speak Spanish, right?" "No," Enrique said, with noticeable irritation. "We speak only English." Because the enrollment form could certainly be in error, Ms. Wessels asked the school's bilingual aide to be on the extension as she called home to make arrangements for the conference.

"*Bueno?*" on the other end of the line cued the aide to ask Enrique's mom her preferred language. She replied that although she was trying to learn English, she would not be able to communicate well without an interpreter. When Ms. Wessels shared her confusion about Enrique's comments, there was a long sigh. "Yes," said his mother. "He tells me to only speak English, but I can't. Then he says he wants hot dogs and macaroni and cheese . . . no more *taquitos*. That upsets us and we don't know what to do." Ms. Wessels agreed that these were important issues they would follow up on during their conference.

By the time she hung up the phone, Ms. Wessels decided to add a new word to this week's vocabulary list. As the class reviewed the list of words later that day, nearly all the students knew each word until they got to *facile*. Enrique looked up but remained silent. The others shook their heads or frowned when Ms. Wessels asked if anyone had ever heard that word before. Then she put the word in a sentence: *Michael is a facile basketball player.* "What do you think that means?" Among the shrugs and puzzled faces, Ms. Wessels saw Enrique's hand. On eye contact, he blurted, "That means it's easy for him. Basketball is easy for him."

"Wow!" she exclaimed. "You're right! How did you know what *facile* means?"

Without hesitation, he answered, "Because I know *fácil*, and that means "easy" in Spanish."

"So you have two languages' worth of vocabulary words?"

"Yes," he smiled.

To the class, she asked, "How many of you would like to learn some of the extra vocabulary words Enrique knows?" Of course, hands flew in the air, and Ms. Wessels had the perfect opportunity to begin her "Double Value" word wall, which Enrique assisted with every week thereafter.

■ *In what other ways might Ms. Wessels have turned Enrique's self-perceived deficit into a group-accepted asset? How might continued communication between Ms. Wessels and Enrique's parents positively affect his acculturation?*

student's ties to her or his primary culture are weakened or broken due to factors such as language loss or societal negativity, the social norms of that home and culture may no longer influence his or her behavior. Unless positively integrated into the host culture, deculturated individuals may experience dissatisfaction and conflict for years as they struggle to find their place in society.

The process of acculturation is unique to each individual student. Many factors, including those related to the home, school, and larger society, influence a student's ability to adapt positively to the new culture. Although educators cannot control the myriad complexities of a student's acculturation process, they *can* work to ensure that the school environment both values students from diverse cultural and language backgrounds and encourages their successful integration. For example, school gatekeeping staff (e.g., secretaries, administrative assistants, office aides, administrative specialists, school–community liaisons, social workers) can significantly contribute to the acculturation difficulties CLD students and families face at school. Without recurrent professional development in cross-cultural and cross-linguistic sensitivity, these staff members are often unaware of the influences they have on family perspectives about the school, its mission, and its faculty. Accordingly, successful classroom teachers of CLD students are persistent advocates for appropriate and progressive professional development for school staff, faculty, and administrators. Table 4.1 details ways a school environment either encourages or discourages each form of cultural adjustment.

Relationship between Cultural Identity and Acculturation

How well CLD students acculturate—and the attitudes about self and others that are formed during this process—can profoundly affect the students, their families, and their communities. Recent studies on the relationship between cultural identity and student wellness (and achievement) have yielded the following findings:

- Ethnic identity is the strongest predictor of overall wellness for CLD students (Dixon Rayle & Myers, 2004).
- Higher levels of positive socioemotional development are consistent with a student's positive identification with both his or her own and the majority group's culture (Shrake & Rhee, 2004).
- Low levels of ethnic identity, characterized by negative attitudes toward one's own group, can result in psychological distress, including feelings of marginality, low self-esteem, and depression (Phinney, 1993).

Ethnic or cultural identities are particularly significant components of a CLD student's self-identity. Research suggests that CLD students who have a positive association and affiliation with their own cultural group are less likely to experience internal or external conflicts in their own identity development and are more likely to develop positive relations with members of other groups (Phinney, 1993; Shrake & Rhee, 2004). Students with a strong sense of ethnic or cultural identity also rate higher on measures of emotional wellness that correlate with higher

■ **table 4.1**   Acculturation Environments

Acculturation Experience	Encouraging School Setting	Discouraging School Setting
Assimilation	• Requires that only English be spoken • Mandates strict adherence to a single school uniform • Celebrates only Christian holidays • Forbids prayer • Allows only specific types of responses during classroom instruction and activities • Maintains and promotes only Western views on issues (e.g., medicine, the meaning of life, legitimate sources of knowledge)	• Supports and incorporates use of the native language • Allows for variation within the school dress code • Encourages students to learn about and celebrate the holidays of multiple cultures • Allows private prayer (appropriate to the religion of the student) • Encourages multiple forms of response during classroom instruction and activities • Views open-mindedness as an asset to the construction of knowledge
Integration	• Investigates discrepancies between student behavior and expected behavior to determine the crux of the matter as well as the most appropriate course of action • Recognizes the value of communication in the native language, even if the speakers are able to communicate in English • Encourages students to see themselves as capable of understanding, appreciating, and working from multiple perspectives	• Punishes all deviances from behavior that is expected in academic situations • Expects CLD students to speak only in English, especially if monolingual English speakers are present • Encourages the perspective that there is only one right way to think, speak, and behave
Rejection	• Allows discrimination based on language, religion, or culture to persist • Encourages students to view differences in customs, behaviors, and so forth as either good or bad	• Prohibits all forms of discrimination and promotes a climate that embraces difference • Views differences in customs, behaviors, and so forth as simply differences, with no inherent values attached
Deculturation	• Encourages CLD parents to speak only English with their children • Makes few attempts to involve parents in the learning process • Continues to use a curriculum that offers limited connections to the experiences of CLD students • Puts forth little, if any, effort to ensure that students maintain ties to their primary culture	• Encourages CLD parents to speak the native language with their children • Promotes parent involvement both at home and within the classroom • Incorporates into the curriculum the cultures and languages of the students • Encourages students to research and celebrate their primary culture

student achievement (Caldwell & Siwatu, 2003; Dixon Rayle & Myers, 2004). In essence, students who are able to maintain a positive ethnic identity throughout the acculturation process demonstrate:

- Better overall mental health (Dixon Rayle & Myers, 2004)
- Fewer somatic symptoms (Wright & Littleford, 2002)
- Improved academic achievement (Caldwell & Siwatu, 2003)
- Lower teen pregnancy rates (Goodyear, Newcomb, & Locke, 2002)
- Less drug and alcohol use (Kulis, Napoli, & Marsiglia, 2002; Hendershot, MacPherson, Myers, Carr, & Wall, 2005)

As a result, teachers who encourage CLD students to maintain their cultural or ethnic ties promote their personal and academic success.

Tools such as the one depicted in Figure 4.1 help teachers gather useful information for understanding cultural aspects of a student's identity. This identity survey is an informal assessment in that it is teacher created and serves classroom purposes. It is also authentic in that it uses information about what is relevant to the CLD student and his or her real-world experiences. The responses of one CLD student to this secondary-level survey are included. Questions 1 through 11 assess the student's perspectives on family, home culture, and ethnic heritage. Questions 12 through 18 assess level of acculturation, as well as how the CLD student is responding to a variety of acculturation challenges.

Ethnic identity perspective may be a particularly significant issue for adolescents who are also dealing with developmental issues of identity formation. For this reason, acculturation models based on adults may not be as appropriate for children and adolescents because they do not take into account many variables that distinguish acculturative and developmental phenomena (Sam & Oppedal, 2002). Other factors contributing to the differing acculturation experiences of CLD students include the extent of their primary language development; second language acquisition experiences; and access to, interest in, and acceptance by the host community.

close-up *on Assessment 4.3*

Ethnic or cultural identities are particularly significant components of a CLD student's self-identity. Research suggests that CLD students who have a positive association and affiliation with their own cultural group are less likely to experience internal or external conflicts in their own identity development and are more likely to develop positive relations with members of other groups. Students with a strong sense of ethnic or cultural identity also rate higher on measures of emotional wellness that correlate with higher student achievement.

■ **figure 4.1** Assessment Artifact: Identity Survey

IDENTITY   Name _____   Block ____I____

Make a list of ideas that are important to you personally or culturally.

1. **What roles do you play within your family?** *Im the baby of the family*
   at school? *the student*
   at work? *Dont have a job*
   among your friends? *Im the joker I make them laugh.*

2. **How do you change your appearance for different roles?**
   I don't change my roles I act the same in front of any body

3. **What ancestor from your family tree came to the United States most recently?**
   How many generations have lived in the United States? *2*
   What would one of your ancestors be well-known or famous for?

4. **What did your ancestors do for a living?** *Work hard, + made us understand things*
   Where did they come from? If not another country, then another area of the U.S.
         Mexico

5. **What celebrations are unique to your culture?**
   The day of the dead

6. **Does your native culture wear any special clothing or folk costumes?**
   Cowboy stuff, and sometimes ponchos.

7. **What animals or plants carry special meaning in your culture? What do they**
   symbolize? *Catuses they carry water for us in the*
   desert.

8. **Photocopy, Print from the internet or Sketch a piece of artwork from your native**
   culture. Explain why it was made or how it was used.

9. **Briefly describe a tale or folklore story from your native culture.**
   Bloody mary killed her kids and at night you here calling for her kids

10. **List some cultural beliefs that are important to you.**
    Jesus, virgen Mary, working hard, living a good life

11. **Describe some music instruments or songs that are unique to your heritage.**
    Trumpet, acordian, mariacies.

12. **What personal qualities do you strive for? What are your outstanding personality**
    traits or character strengths? How do others see you?

13. **What have been some of the most important events in your own life?**
    My tia died, when I saw my grandma + grandpa, when my consin got married.

14. **How do imagine yourself in the future? In your dreams? Goals?**
    Working hard, having my own house, and passing.

15. **What is your proudest moment in life so far?**
    When I made varsity in long Jump for track.

16. **Do you identify with a group of friends at the high school? Would you refer to them**
    in any general term such as Brains? Jocks? Nerds? Slackers? Movers and Shakers?
    Rebellious trouble makers? Good students? Loners?

17. **What one event or person influenced you most in life? why and how?**
    My uncle he more like a father to me telling me to finish school + always be there for me.

18. **What activity or hobby would you like to spend more time doing?**
    Playing baseball + working more harder for track.

The Role of Acculturation and Emotions in Learning

Recent research on brain-based learning (Jensen, 2000) suggests that issues related to acculturative stress and culture shock may only be the tip of the iceberg regarding the impact emotions can have on CLD student learning. As with an iceberg, certain signs of culture shock and stress can be easily observed, but intuitive teachers realize how much more is happening below the surface. Jensen makes the point that learning occurs interdependently with an individual's emotional state. Consequently, the emotional climate of a learning situation can either hinder or facilitate a student's ability to make authentic and enduring meaning from learning experiences. To be effective with CLD students, teachers must consider and build on the emotional states and experiences of their students.

Among his observations, Jensen (2000) notes: "Events . . . and learning that tap into our emotions will be remembered . . . [and] how you feel about a topic or subject is critical" (p. 346). This notion underscores the importance of assessing a student's affect (feelings) in addition to his or her concrete knowledge and skills. Translated into action, this means teachers need to provide "learners the opportunity to discuss what is personally meaningful to them and how the subjects they're studying connect to their own lives" (p. 347). Teachers can provide such opportunities quite naturally by regularly preassessing and incorporating students' existing knowledge into instructional practice.

In Chapter 3, Mr. Carlson began a lesson on predators and prey by tapping into his students' emotionally charged prior experiences. As LeDoux (1996) has argued, these emotions are important in all mental functioning because the states of arousal they cause are significant factors in memory, attention, problem solving, and perception. In fact, there is increasing evidence that emotions are tied to everything from cortical (thinking) functions to neurological events at the cellular level (Pert, 1997). Therefore, when emotions are involved, it is a powerful whole-body experience that significantly influences our ability to learn. At their most basic level, emotions can boost, imprint, delay, or short-circuit almost any transmission of meaning. Stressed or disconnected students are unlikely to learn as well as those who feel secure and engaged. Because of the difficulties CLD students experience during acculturation, it is critical for teachers to determine the emotional readiness of students and create positive learning experiences for them.

> **assessment *FREEZE FRAME 4.7***
>
> The emotional climate of a learning situation can either hinder or facilitate a student's ability to make authentic and enduring meaning from learning experiences.

◼ Assessing Level of Acculturation

Acculturation is generally understood to develop along two continua: behavioral and psychological (Berry, 1992; Searle & Ward, 1990). Behavioral aspects include areas such as language, social skills, and customs, whereas the psychological aspects have more to do with values, belief systems, attitudes, and preferences. This is important to bear in mind because assessment perspectives that emphasize

■ Assessment in Action 4.1

This student survey represents one way teachers can gather information about a student's attitude toward school, perceived areas of academic strength and weakness, and affective response to content areas. Although this is a simple survey designed for use with elementary students, teachers can easily modify the tool to assess the feelings and perceptions of older students.

■ Survey of Student Affect

Student Interview

Student Name: _____

Date: _____

1. Write or draw a picture about your old school.

   (Attitude toward learning and school)

2. Write or draw a picture about what you are good at in school.

   (Strengths)

3. Write or draw a picture of what is hard for you at school.

   (Weaknesses)

4. Circle the face that shows how you feel about reading.

   Very Happy   Happy   Sad   Worried   Angry

5. Circle the face that shows how you feel about math.

   Very Happy   Happy   Sad   Worried   Angry

close-up *on Assessment 4.4*

Acculturation is generally understood to develop along two continua: behavioral and psychological. Behavioral aspects include areas such as language, social skills, and customs, whereas the psychological aspects have more to do with values, belief systems, attitudes, and preferences. This is important to bear in mind because assessment perspectives that emphasize primarily the behavioral or observable aspects of acculturation (e.g., customs) can lead to inappropriate assumptions and erroneous educational decisions for CLD students.

primarily the behavioral or observable aspects of acculturation (e.g., customs) can lead to inappropriate assumptions and erroneous educational decisions for CLD students. The following case illustrates this phenomenon:

Ms. Cantu considered herself an experienced teacher of CLD students and an adept observer of their acculturation. However, last year she learned a lot more about one particular student and herself.

Ms. Cantu was concerned from the outset about the austerely veiled new girl in her class. Although Nashida was from Michigan and spoke English with virtually no accent, her style of dress suggested that she was far less acculturated than her classmates who struggled with language but had adopted much more "American" ways. Ms. Cantu worried that Nashida would be uncomfortable with the informality and levity common among the eleventh graders in this history class and wondered if she should revert to more of a lecture approach to reduce the possibility of unintentional offense.

Admittedly, Ms. Cantu was apprehensive about her upcoming visit to the home of Nashida. She knew that inadvertent disrespect could get any relationship off to a poor start. So Ms. Cantu did some reading and contacted the local Islamic center for help. Although these efforts provided valuable insights, her anxiety rose as she approached Nashida's door. She was already slipping off her shoes as planned when a young woman in jeans, T-shirt, and flowing hair answered the door. For a second, Ms. Cantu thought it was the wrong house. Then she recognized Nashida, who excitedly welcomed her in and proceeded with introductions. Nashida's mom noticed immediately that the teacher had removed her shoes before entering, and she smiled.

Ms. Cantu could hardly take her eyes off Nashida. She looked so … so *American* in her trendy T-shirt and jeans. Nashida's mom asked for a few moments before they started, so Ms. Cantu quietly observed as they all sat together on the couch. Nashida's mom read aloud from a list she was writing. Ms. Cantu guessed it was a grocery list because several of the words, such as *sucar* and *roz*, were similar to food words used in her childhood home. Glances at the muted television revealed an oddly familiar picture. Other than a few unrecognizable printed words, it looked exactly like the sort of variety show her parents still watched every Saturday night. Suddenly, two little boys, powered by sound effects and dishtowel capes, sped through the room. Nashida's mom said something softly, and they answered in English, "Okay, but can we go out back?" She nodded.

During the conversation about her daughter's education, Nashida's mom smiled and nodded frequently as Ms. Cantu discussed Nashida's performance and opportunities at school. Nashida beamed and giggled at her mother's periodic and obviously humorous quips in their native language. As the visit ended, the group headed toward the door. Nashida's mom handed Nashida the list, and when they neared the door, Nashida reached behind it, quickly cloaking herself to leave. Car keys jingling, she bid Ms. Cantu a cheerful good-bye and bounded over to the family's Buick. Ms. Cantu was struck by her own surprise. Why had she just assumed Nashida didn't, couldn't, or wouldn't be allowed to drive? Why did Nashida seem so different to her now? Why had she assumed so many things based on Nashida's style of dress? Ms. Cantu realized that for all her cultural sensitivity, the limitations of her own experiences had led to a very limited perception of this student.

As this case illustrates, it is important to avoid making assumptions and drawing conclusions about a student's level of acculturation based only on a single source of information. Rather, educators need to use multiple types of assessment to gather information for making informed educational decisions. Such measures include both informal and formal assessments of acculturation.

> **assessment FREEZE FRAME 4.8**
>
> It is important to avoid making assumptions and drawing conclusions about a student's level of acculturation based only on a single source of information. Rather, educators need to use multiple types of assessment to gather information for making informed educational decisions. Such measures include both informal and formal assessments of acculturation.

Informal Assessment of Acculturation

The informal assessment of acculturation can take many forms. Sometimes it is merely the impressions one gathers through classroom observation. However, relying on impressions can prove problematic, as in the case of Ms. Cantu and Nashida. Ms. Cantu drew a number of inferences about Nashida's level of acculturation based on a single parameter about which she had little actual understanding.

One of the most powerful methods of informal assessment is the home visit. When teachers visit the homes of students, they create opportunities to observe students, caregivers, and other family members in the home environment. As a result, these educators are better able to sense the stressors and challenges students and their families face on a daily basis. Although teachers may initially be apprehensive about conducting home visits due to potential language and cultural differences, such obstacles can be easily overcome with the help of a linguistically and culturally competent translator. For a more detailed discussion of home visits, see Chapter 3.

Additional ways to informally gather acculturation information include:

- Reviewing school records
- Using surveys that gather information about (a) student connectedness with school and home, (b) preferred language of the student within the home and community, and (c) preferred learning styles
- Conferencing or conversing with the student and parent (via a culturally and linguistically competent translator, if necessary)

- Collecting data through observational checklists or rubrics (see Figure 4.2 and related appendix resource), which assess behaviors such as:
  —Communicative effectiveness with native-English-speaking peers
  —Choice of language when addressing bilingual peers or those who speak English as a second language
  —Large-group participation (e.g., calling out or hesitation to volunteer in large groups)
  —Small-group participation (e.g., willingness to serve as group leader or offer suggestions)
  —Miscommunications with culturally dissimilar peers
  —Learner preferences (e.g., individual vs. collective, demonstration vs. recitation)

Furthermore, the astute teacher will recognize signs that a CLD student may be experiencing acculturative stress or shock by noting such objective physical indicators as absenteeism, health room visits, and somatic complaints. Indicators of social or psychological stress may be observed in school, during home visits, or as reports from a parent or guardian. Such indicators include personality changes; withdrawal; over- or undereating; behavioral incidents or referrals; conflicts with siblings or parents; and rejection of home language, customs, and foods. Teachers familiar with these issues are much better able to reduce the impact of acculturative stress on CLD students.

To gain a more thorough understanding of a student's level of acculturation, as well as of her or his cultural assets and background experiences, teachers can also incorporate or develop any number of creative activities. The following are a few examples:

- *School Puzzle.* Each student receives a poster board puzzle piece on which to illustrate any aspect(s) of her or his identity. The student can include interests, hobbies, academic strengths, favorite foods, cultural traditions, and so forth. After the students have finished decorating their individual puzzle pieces, the pieces are combined to create the finished puzzle. The final puzzle picture illustrates the idea that the students bring unique cultural and linguistic perspectives, as well as other attributes, talents, and international (in some cases multinational) experiences that combine to create a diverse whole. Figure 4.3 (page 98) depicts portions of one school's puzzle.
- *Place of Origin Map.* CLD and other students write personal information such as their name and city of origin on a sticky note. The students then place their sticky notes next to their countries or states of origin. The finished map is hung in a prominent place in the classroom to remind students of their unique backgrounds and experiences. CLD students are then given opportunities to discuss their countries of origin, ethnicity, home culture, and more with the teacher and in groups throughout the school year.
- *Heritage Paper.* Each student researches his or her personal family background. The student works with parents, guardians, or extended family

■ **figure 4.2** Level of Acculturation Observation Rubric

LOA* Observation Rubric

Student:			
Date of Observation:		Time of Observation:	

Criterion	Range & Rating	Anecdotal Notes	Monitor Status**
Level of affect	5 Upbeat 0 Sullen and/or Angry		
Data:	5 - 4 - 3 - 2 - 1 - 0		
Level of interaction with peers of a similar culture and/or language	5 Highly Interactive 0 Withdrawn		
Data:	5 - 4 - 3 - 2 - 1 - 0		
Level of interaction with peers of a different culture and/or language	5 Highly Interactive 0 Withdrawn		
Data:	5 - 4 - 3 - 2 - 1 - 0		
Communication effectiveness with peers of a different culture and/or language	5 Highly Effective 0 Ineffective		
Data:	5 - 4 - 3 - 2 - 1 - 0		
Level of participation in group learning	5 Highly Participative 0 Nonparticipative		
Data:	5 - 4 - 3 - 2 - 1 - 0		
Level of student engagement with classroom learning activities	5 Highly Engaged 0 Not Engaged		
Data:	5 - 4 - 3 - 2 - 1 - 0		
Legend:	* LOA = Level of Acculturation ** Status Range = Enhance, Maintain, or Reduce Monitoring of LOA		

■ **figure 4.3** Assessment Artifact:
School Puzzle

members to gather and record information that is then used to create a bound keepsake book. Possible types of information to incorporate include:

—Personal student information (e.g., variations of name, contact information, physical description, personal goals)

—Family members and relatives (e.g., age, location, occupation, activities in which the student also participates)

—Ancestral ties (e.g., oldest known relative to come to the United States, immigration experiences)

—Places of residence (e.g., birthplace of student, other places in which the student has lived)

—Family customs (e.g., languages, holidays, celebrations, special meals, traditional clothing)

—Favorite recipes

—Challenges of adjustment (e.g., to a new country, region, city or town, school, neighborhood)

- *Cultural Quilt.* The teacher begins the two- to three-day project by reading *The Josefina Story Quilt* (Coerr, 1986). In the story, the protagonist creates a quilt of her journey to California. To help newcomer students apply the concept to their own lives, the teacher asks students to create their own cultural quilts. Students first create a time line of their life or journey to the United States. They write important facts from their life and might, for example, include country of origin, modes of transportation, struggles in their journey, and acculturation challenges. This time line is considered the first draft. Students then create a picture for each entry in the time line. After they have finished their illustrations, students create quilts of their life story or journey to the United States, using yarn to sew together the quilt pieces. Figure 4.4 depicts two examples of finished student quilts.

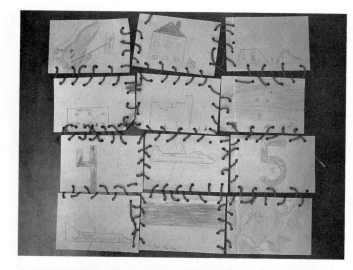

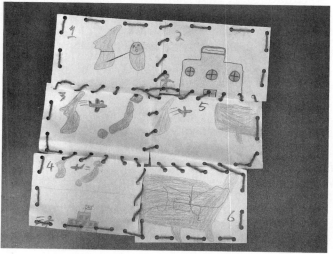

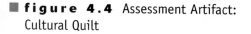
■ **figure 4.4** Assessment Artifact: Cultural Quilt

- **The Essentials Book:** Students illustrate and record their written responses to prompts such as the following:

  —The most important thing about me is _____.

  —The most important thing about my name is _____.

  —The most important thing about my family is _____.

  —The most important thing about my language is _____.

  —The most important thing about my culture is _____.

  —The most important thing about my school is _____.

  —The most difficult adjustments for me have been _____.

  The illustrated pages are then collected and bound to create a book. CLD students share their books with the teacher and others in the class, especially during the first few weeks of the school year or semester.

- *Cultural Mosaic.* Students create illustrated mosaics about themselves. Possible ideas to incorporate include perceptions of self, personal goals, academic interests, career goals, friendships, family, and cultural or language transition experiences. Students then write explanations for the various components of their mosaics. Figure 4.5 depicts one example of a CLD student's cultural mosaic and includes an explanation, which was derived from a discussion of the mosaic that the teacher had with the student.

- *Sociocultural Mind Map.* Mind mapping is a strategy that incorporates visual images to help students recognize relationships among concepts and ideas (Buzan, 1983). Mind maps are increasingly being used for both instruction and assessment in both elementary and secondary classrooms (see Figure 4.6 on page 102). Although similar to webbing or clustering graphic organizers, mind maps rely on symbols to depict main ideas and related organization. Specific vocabulary terms or concepts are then added to the map to clarify connections. Students can simply create mind maps, or they can transition to mind mapping from activities such as the cultural mosaic.

The potential contributions of mind maps to assessing and especially pre-assessing CLD students are multifaceted. A mind map often brings to the surface information relating not only to acculturation and the sociocultural dimension of the CLD student biography but also to the cognitive, academic, and linguistic dimensions as well. The following vignette illustrates these potentials:

Julianna, an eleventh-grade student who arrived six months ago from Mexico, developed a mind map (see Figure 4.6) from the cultural mosaic (see Figure 4.5) she was asked to create in Mrs. Villareal's language arts class. In an informal interview, Julianna discussed her mind map with Mrs. Villarreal. Their discussion revealed details of Julianna's prior socialization patterns, as well as her new acculturation experiences in the United States.

From this conversation, Mrs. Villarreal learned that the rose in the center of the mind map portrays Julianna's love for nature. Julianna was born in a rural community of Mexico and has found the transition to urban living difficult. She misses the time, access, and friends with whom she used to enjoy nature and the outdoors. The rings, on the other hand, depict Julianna's desire to someday have a family.

■ figure 4.5 Assessment Artifact: Cultural Mosaic

Legend:

The center:
The eyes reflect my soul, and if you pay attention, you can see what's inside me
The rose portrays my love for nature
The rings my desire for a family

Top right hand corner:
The buildings signify the city in which I'm in
The light bulb shows my knowledge about Science and Mathematics
My face depicts sadness because no one knows about my knowledge and my desire to have new friends

Bottom right hand corner:
My goal is to become a fashion designer and also a secondary teacher

Bottom left hand corner:
I have to go to an institution where I feel out of place
I long for my friend back home

Top left hand corner:
I find myself spending time with my little brother
The Bible on the table shows our closeness as a family
The picture shows we are a proud family

■ **figure 4.6** Assessment Artifact: Sociocultural Mind Map

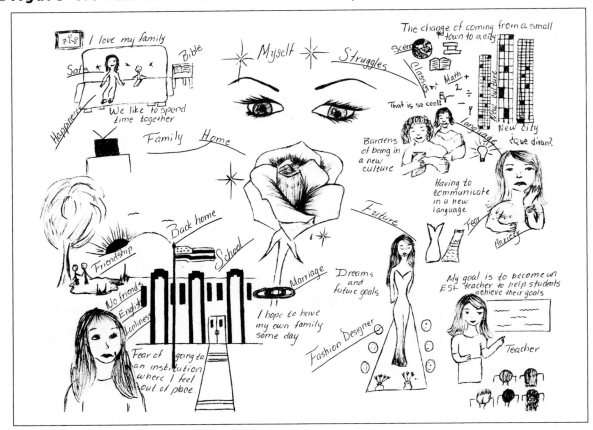

The illustrations in the upper left-hand corner of Julianna's mind map portray the relative safety, comfort, and pride she recalls about living in Mexico. Her drawings indicate that family and religion were of particular comfort to her, despite the poverty in which she and her family lived.

To the right of this point in the mind map, the illustration of the eyes represents Julianna's soul. She told Mrs. Villarreal, "If you pay attention [to these eyes], you can see what's inside me [e.g., the tears that have fallen upon the rose]." Like many other CLD students, Julianna often feels ignored and sometimes lost in many of her classes.

In the upper right-hand corner, the buildings characterize the new city in which Julianna lives. For Julianna, the many sociocultural transitions from rural small-town life to urban living have been challenging. Note the illustrations and passages below and to the left of the buildings. The phrase "*Que diran*?" expresses her concerns about what other adults and fellow students will think and say about her appearance, her culture, and her language.

The lightbulb and associated passages represent the knowledge Julianna feels she brings to the classroom—knowledge she believes is little recognized by her new teachers, especially her prior knowledge of science and mathematics. Julianna considers herself a good student in science and very much enjoys studying this subject. According to Julianna, the illustration below the buildings further depicts her sadness about the fact that no one knows about her knowledge, her aspirations, and her desire to make new friends like those she had in Mexico. For Julianna, friends have always been the source of her strength and her motivators in school. Now that she lives in a new city and has few friends to turn to, she increasingly struggles to cope with the many challenges of immigration and academics in a new school system.

The illustrations and passages in the lower left-hand corner of Julianna's mind map show the difficulties she faces trying to succeed in a new school system. Her lack of friends, difficulties with the English language, and increasing loneliness each further complicates the fears she already has of "feeling out of place." In fact, the illustrations that surround the tree indicate that Julianna, amidst her many struggles, is often drawn to memories from her prior socialization, especially memories of nature and fun with her friends.

Finally, the illustrations and passages in the lower right-hand corner portray her dreams, goals, and aspirations for the future, including her future beyond school. Along with her desire to have a family, Julianna's mind map suggests that she envisions herself as a career woman. She considers both a career in fashion design and a career as an ESL teacher to be within reach.

In summary, Julianna's mind map reflects the powerful potential of this tool to (a) prompt CLD students to explore and discuss difficult issues they might not otherwise talk about; (b) reveal student interests and academic potentials; (c) assess student struggles with acculturation issues; and (d) serve as a focal point of discussions for assessing sociocultural, academic, cognitive, and linguistic challenges experienced by CLD students.

The aforementioned activities constitute but a sample of the many informal classroom assessments teachers can use to gather information about CLD students and their acculturation experiences. Activities and projects that involve parents and other family members are especially helpful for promoting family ties that support students through the acculturation process. Informal assessments that incorporate multiple forms of communication (e.g., written, pictorial) enable maximum participation of CLD students who are in the beginning stages of acquiring English and transitioning to a new culture. Moreover, opportunities to illustrate their unique perspectives help students express themselves in multiple, and oftentimes surprising, ways.

Formal Assessment of Acculturation

It is important to avoid misperceptions and to assess acculturation in a standardized way, and there are a number of tools available for this purpose. Each assesses somewhat different parameters or characteristics. Therefore, an informed review of such tools is recommended to determine which assessment tool best fits the community and targets the desired acculturation information. One of the most popular formal assessments of acculturation is the Acculturation Quick Screen (AQS).

The AQS is often used as a preinstructional assessment tool and is capable of measuring the level and rate of acculturation to grade-level school culture. In addition to the uses described in Chapter 3, the AQS (Collier, 2004) is often used (a) to make decisions about the modification of testing, evaluation, and other assessment procedures and (b) to provide an early warning system to alert that placements, services, assessments, and other aspects of schooling may be compounding the student's acculturation challenges. When the AQS is used preinstructionally, the findings are especially valuable for establishing a baseline from which to monitor the CLD student's acculturation and adaptation progress. In fact, the AQS is recommended for routine use among CLD students in newcomer programs (Collier, 2004).

For purposes of monitoring, students should be reassessed (i.e., postinstructionally assessed) using the AQS at the same time each year. The findings of the AQS provide a map of acculturation patterns from less acculturated to more acculturated, according to a 48-point scale. Five levels of acculturation are measured by the AQS, ranging from "significantly less acculturated" to "in transition" to "significantly more acculturated." Long-term results have indicated the average rate of acculturation falls between 10 percent and 12 percent each school year and varies according to the type of assistance offered the student (Collier, 2004).

The cultural and environmental factors identified as significant by the AQS can serve as an index of important areas to preassess, regardless of the particular tool or method used. Most acculturation assessments require the school to gather information related to:

1. *Number of years in the school district.* In most cases, students who have been in a new country a relatively short time are less acculturated than those who have lived there many years. The number of years in a given school district may suggest greater or lesser acculturation, given the time in the country, due to the transitions and acculturation adjustments associated with mobility.

2. *Number of years in ESL/bilingual education.* Knowledge of a student's educational history is essential to making decisions about appropriate placement and programming.

3. *Native language proficiency.* The strength of a CLD student's proficiency in the first language (Cummins, 1984; Szapocznik & Kurtines, 1980) is positively correlated with acculturation because students are able to draw on first language knowledge to facilitate second language understandings and skills.

4. *English language proficiency.* An understanding of a student's second language proficiency is needed for teachers to be able to appropriately accommodate the student's instructional and assessment needs.

5. *Bilingual proficiency.* Proficiency in both the first and second languages correlates with indicators of mental health (e.g., lower incidence of social and emotional problems) as evidence of bilingualism and biculturalism increases (Szapocznik & Kurtines, 1980).

6. *Ethnicity/nation of origin.* A CLD student's ethnicity and nation of origin play an important role in acculturation because of the degree of similarity or difference between the new culture and the native culture (for example, those coming to the United States from western European countries vs. eastern European countries or Pacific Islands).

7. *Percentage of students in the school who speak the CLD student's language or dialect.* The percentage of others in a particular school who speak the CLD student's language or dialect can also affect acculturation (Juffer, 1983). The more interaction students have with the host population, the more likely they are to acculturate to that population.

In addition to the AQS, a number of other instruments are available to formally assess student acculturation. A representative sample can be found in Table 4.2. Because no two students will experience acculturation the same way, it is important to preassess the acculturation of each individual student rather than draw broad comparisons between potentially dissimilar peers.

Impact of Acculturation on Appropriate Methods of Assessment

Although a primary emphasis of this chapter is on the assessment of acculturation, it is also important to understand the impact of acculturation on assessment in general. CLD students often arrive with cultural values and behaviors that differ from the Western cultural perspective on which so much of our educational system is based. Traditional assessment practices typically value individual achievement, competition (ranking), speed, verbal prowess, and recitation of knowledge. Therefore, many traditional approaches to assessment favor students who enroll each year with strong, existing competencies in the expectations and mores of the dominant culture. By contrast, the CLD student may not:

- Understand the cultural assumptions of assessment prompts that are grounded in the dominant culture (e.g., that pizza slices are cut into even proportions)

Acculturation Assessment	Development/Key Characteristics
Acculturation Rating Scale for Mexican Americans-II (Cuéllar, Arnold, & Maldonado, 1995)	A revision of the Acculturation Rating Scale for Mexican Americans (ARSMA) that found a strong link between communication and acculturation. This tool assesses a student's cultural orientation toward Mexican and European American cultures. Results can be generated that describe multidimensional acculturation types.
Acculturation Scale for Southeast Asians (Anderson et al., 1993)	The responses of 381 Cambodian, 359 Laotian, and 395 Vietnamese research participants (age 18–89) living in the United States were analyzed in the areas of language proficiencies and language, social, and food preferences. Interitem reliability and construct validity were demonstrated. Among the sample population, males tended to show higher scores for the proficiency in language subscale, with Laotian and Vietnamese females scoring higher than males on language, social, and food preferences.
African American Acculturation Scale (Landrine & Klonoff, 1994)	The African American Acculturation Scale is a 74-item scale that has been demonstrated to have good internal construct and validity (Landrine & Klonoff, 1994). This scale examines acculturation in terms of eight dimensions of African American culture: (a) traditional African American religious beliefs and practices; (b) traditional African American family structure and practices; (c) traditional African American socialization; (d) preparation and consumption of traditional foods; (e) preference for African American things; (f) interracial attitudes; (g) superstitions; and (h) traditional African American health beliefs and practices.
Children's Acculturation Scale (Franco, 1983)	Developed for use with Mexican American children, this Likert-type scale can be completed by anyone who knows the child well. Data from 141 Mexican American and 34 European American first-, third-, and sixth-grade subjects have demonstrated the reliability and validity of the scale. Results obtained support the hypothesis that variables such as peer associations, ethnic identification, and language issues (preference, usage, and proficiency) are important for the measurement of student acculturation.
Mexican American Acculturation Scale (Montgomery, 1992)	This scale looks at student perceptions about acculturation status. Developed with students in South Texas, this 28-item rating scale measures Mexican vs. European American cultural information and their comfort levels with each of these identities. The items in the scale focus on 5 factors: (a) comfort with Mexican traditions and the Spanish media; (b) English media and European American tradition; (c) preferred EI (ethnic identity); (d) self-rated EI; and (e) comfort with speaking English. Initial results included findings that acculturative stress was evidenced by high numbers of students who rated themselves as culturally alienated.
Short Acculturation Scale for Hispanic Youth (Barona, & Miller, 1994)	This brief self-report tool identifies extra-familial language use, familial language use, and ethnic social relations as significant factors of acculturation.
Suinn-Lew Asian Self-Identity Acculturation Scale (Suinn, Richard-Figueroa, Lew, & Vigil, 1987)	The Suinn-Lew Asian Self-Identity Acculturation Scale (SL-ASIA), modeled after the Hispanic acculturation scale (ARMSA), was designed to assess the acculturation of Asian-heritage students. The SL-ASIA measures similar factors to the Hispanic ARSMA and is sensitive to determining Western acculturation among Asian individuals.

Callslip Request   1/25/2016 7:30:38 AM

Item Location: stx
Call Number: 371.26 H5656
Enumeration:
Copy Number: 1
Chronology:
Year:
Item Barcode:

Title: Assessment accommodations for
      classroom teachers of culturally and
      linguistically diverse students / Socorro
      G. Herrera, Kevin G. Murry, Robin
      Morales Cabral.
Author: Herrera, Socorro Guadalupe.

Patron Name: OZGE EVCEN
Patron Group: UBReg
Patron Barcode:

Reason if item is not available:
__At Bindery: Seeking next available
__Item Charged Out: Seeking next available
__Damaged: Seeking next available
__Local Circulation Only: Seeking next availab
__Missing/Not on Shelf: Seeking next available
__Noncirculation item: Seeking next available

Reassignment History:
None

Patron comment:

Request date: 1/22/2016 05:02 PM
Request number: 52573

ck Up Location if Local Request:

- Be comfortable demonstrating knowledge in ways that are perceived as condescending or cause others to lose face (e.g., provide the answer to a question another student missed)
- Be motivated by competition, speed (faster is better), or nonsocial reinforcers (e.g., grades)

Because the goal of assessment is to determine *what* and *how* the student learns in order to inform instruction, assessment methods that do not account for acculturation only serve to cloud the teacher's ability to gain anything valuable from their results.

Understanding how acculturation affects student performance is key to recognizing how inadequate traditional assessments are for measuring what we really need to know: *Is this student learning?* Furthermore, the tendency to think "that students should all be learning the same thing at the same time is based on a model that disregards the importance of personal relevance and normal differences in the developmental process" (Jensen, 2000, p. 347). Each CLD student, by the very nature of age and cultural difference, develops along multiple physical, emotional, linguistic, cognitive, and acculturative continua. Testing students according to static, predetermined points of learning "before they are ready creates frustration, disillusionment, and a distrust of the system" (Jensen, 2000, p. 343). As many of us have experienced on a personal level, being subjected to assessment practices that emphasize what we *don't* know rather than what we *do* know—along with those that result in negative consequences (e.g., failure, overt/covert comparison to others)—can significantly undermine our attitudes about education . . . and ourselves.

close-up *on Assessment 4.6*

Many traditional approaches to assessment favor students who enroll each year with strong, existing competencies in the expectations and mores of the dominant culture. By contrast, the CLD student may not:

- Understand the cultural assumptions of assessment prompts that are grounded in the dominant culture (e.g., that pizza slices are cut into even proportions)
- Be comfortable demonstrating knowledge in ways that are perceived as condescending or cause others to lose face (e.g, provide the answer to a question another student missed)
- Be motivated by competition, speed (faster is better), or nonsocial reinforcers (e.g., grades)

Because the goal of assessment is to determine *what* and *how* the student learns in order to inform instruction, assessment methods that do not account for acculturation only serve to cloud the teacher's ability to gain anything valuable from their results.

■ Using Acculturation Information to Inform Instruction

A growing number of schools, districts, and states are recognizing the relationship between acculturative adaptation (which does not negate the student's primary cultural and language identity) and student academic success. "Knowing that many ELLs [CLD students whose first language is not English] define their 'cultural identity' by the *language* and *ethnicity* of the sociocultural group to which they feel connected supports the necessity to include students' native language during instructional and non-instructional time" (Indiana Department of Education, 2005, p. 2). Policies that value native language use stand in stark contrast to past policies, which often promoted academic environments in which students were humiliated, punished, or forbidden from using their home language at school.

Knowledgeable educators recognize that there are many ways to incorporate and affirm the strengths and cultural assets of CLD students. Among these are the instructional use and validation of the student's primary language. Depending on available resources and student languages represented, schools may provide native language support by using bilingual staff or trained parent volunteers to:

- Provide linguistically adapted instruction. For example, staff or volunteers can:
  —Do "read-alouds" with students in their native language
  —Preteach/review content-area vocabulary or concepts
  —Facilitate higher-order thinking skills related to the class topic
- Manage a language-specific calling tree to keep parents informed about school events
- Translate pertinent notes about student progress, school news, and conferences (both *to* and *from* parents)

When resources do not exist for direct primary language support, the following can aid in accommodating the needs of CLD students and families:

- Informed teachers who:
  —Emphasize second language acquisition in the context of academic content
  —Facilitate critical thinking and problem-solving skills in ways that adapt to, yet stimulate, the student's emergent language proficiency
  —Encourage students to take notes or write journals in their primary language
  —Pair peers who share the same culture or language in cooperative groups that include native English speakers as well
  —Provide native language materials (e.g., books, computer activities, magazines) for all to use and explore
- Progressive schools that:
  —Convey a climate of affirmation and celebration for the languages and cultures represented

—Provide staff with rich professional development opportunities in the areas of acculturation and second language acquisition
—Regard CLD student cultures and languages as enriching assets
—Adopt curricula that reflect the cultures and values of the student populations represented
—Encourage home–school connections, which:
  • Promote parent involvement
  • Use home visits
  • Value the unique ability of families to support and guide students toward success

Keep in mind that effective student instruction and accommodation require the combined efforts of students, parents, and the community. Community members represent an extraordinary source of knowledge, insight, and experience. Unfortunately, the community often remains an untapped resource. Table 4.3 examines educator perspectives regarding the assets that students, parents, and communities bring to the education process.

Cultural Differences as Learning Assets

Many teachers of CLD students have discovered that acculturation can prove a mutual (and mutually beneficial) process. Increased contacts with diverse students often result in the type of reflection that fosters significant personal and professional growth among education personnel. The ability to identify cultural assets to which one is not accustomed and view them from an alternate perspective is similar to experiences with optical illusions. Many of us have looked at a picture, certain of the *one thing* it depicts . . . only to have someone else point out a completely different image or way of perceiving the work. Suddenly, those things our minds did not allow us to see before become glaringly obvious. One such "ah hah" moment occurred as a group of midwestern teachers reviewed the following dilemma:

Mrs. Bingham is concerned because Joel rarely completes his math homework. The homework usually consists of twenty to twenty-five practice problems involving computation skills he has learned and has been able to perform in class. Joel's mother is single, and her evening attentions are split between cooking, cleaning, laundry, and bathing the little ones. However, she tries her best to help Joel in whatever ways she can. Joel has several older and younger siblings, so Mrs. Bingham is concerned that the home environment is interfering with his ability to do homework. She suggests to his mother that Joel be provided a quiet place to work without distraction for a certain period every night. Joel's mother agrees to keep his siblings out of their shared bedroom, but they continue to play at the door. The teacher then advises her to "shut the door for half an hour . . . or until Joel gets the work done." After several weeks, there is little improvement in Joel's homework.

(text continues on page 113)

table 4.3 Sociocultural Environment: Educator Views of Student, Family, and Community Assets

Level of Performance

Component	Meets Criteria	Basic	Needs Improvement	Unsatisfactory
Culture	The student's culture is respected and valued as a source of knowledge and experiences that advance learning and enhance the cultural climate of the school. Issues and behaviors related to acculturation processes are identified and mediated with sensitivity and knowledge of research-based approaches that are appropriate for the CLD student/family/community involved.	The student's culture is respected and valued on principle. General implications and stages of acculturation are understood as influencing student learning and behavior. Recognizes but is unable to comfortably mediate cultural misperceptions and conflicts between families and self or other staff.	Behaviors that arise from cultural differences or acculturation are viewed as interfering with student achievement and long-range success. Instructional strategies and interventions emphasize acculturation to the dominant culture.	The CLD student's culture is viewed as a negative influence on the student and school. Cultural considerations are rejected as irrelevant to the development of appropriate instructional practices and intervention.
Language	Supports L1 use at home and school. Understands, models, and is able to explain the rationale for L1 and sheltered instructional strategies. Is knowledgeable about language acquisition phenomena, including language loss and implications of language support, or lack thereof, on student achievement.	Supports L1 use at home. Understands basic language acquisition stages and time lines. Can explain the benefits of sheltered instruction. Considers CLD student's language as potentially affecting behavior and/or achievement.	Regards continued use of home language as an obstacle to English acquisition and school success. Is supportive of, but cannot describe or model, instructional strategies that benefit CLD students.	Regards the student's home language as a deficit to be overcome. Is unsupportive of ongoing adaptations and instructional modifications for CLD students.

table 4.3 (continued)

Level of Performance

Component	Meets Criteria	Basic	Needs Improvement	Unsatisfactory
Academics	Is able to articulate the relationship between L1 and L2 learning and analyze classroom tasks in terms of prerequisite language, academic, or social experiences. Makes specific recommendations regarding instructional modifications and assessment of CLD student progress.	Understands the impact of language and acculturation on CLD student academic progress. Identifies general instructional strategies that benefit CLD students.	Provides strategies to meet the academic needs of general students performing below grade level but does not understand or provide strategies particular to the needs of CLD students.	Considers the academic difficulties of CLD students to be either environmental or innate and therefore is resistant to long-range change regardless of interventions.
Families	Exemplifies a respect for CLD families that is evident through greetings, verbal and nonverbal communication, and overall accessibility. Advocates for programs, events, and activities that engage families. Demonstrates an understanding of, and respect for, culturally different family dynamics. Respectfully mediates cultural issues and behaviors that conflict with a student's positive school participation.	Expresses respect and value for CLD families. Encourages CLD family involvement but has little direct contact with parents beyond those required by policy or events. Recognizes when cultural issues affect school–family communications but does not initiate or engage in actions to address potential conflicts or concerns.	Feels that truly interested families are already involved. Communication with CLD families is limited to required procedural or behavioral matters.	Regards CLD families as unsupportive of education. Is opposed to initiatives or incentives to increase CLD family involvement. Avoids communicating with CLD families.

(continued)

table 4.3 (continued)

Level of Performance

Component	Meets Criteria	Basic	Needs Improvement	Unsatisfactory
Community	Is knowledgeable about, and communicates with, community resources that can provide or assist CLD students and families. Regards community resources as potential assets and partners in the educational, linguistic, and social-emotional learning of CLD students. Involves members of the local neighborhood and CLD community in schoolwide events and celebrations.	Is knowledgeable about and appreciates, but does not personally communicate with, community resources that can provide or assist CLD students and families. Recognizes selected organizations (e.g., religious, fraternal) as valuable to the positive overall development of CLD students.	Provides CLD students/families with referrals only to school-based professionals such as social workers, nurses, and counselors. Does not communicate with community or seek additional resources for meeting the essential and/or enrichment needs of CLD students and families.	Speaks in generalities about community support but feels resources and influences in the student's community conflict with school ideals of what "is best" for the student. Is unable or unwilling to provide resources or contacts appropriate to the needs of CLD students and families.

When the group of experienced teachers was presented this scenario, their comments and observations included:

- "I feel sorry for the mom."
- "That's the problem with so many of our students."
- "Clearly, there is no way he can study in *that* home."
- "Perhaps there is an after-school program where Joel could do his homework."

Although their comments reflect empathy for Joel and his mother, this empathy is inadequately rooted in preconceived ideas about what constitutes study and the notion that large families are distractions rather than resources. Interestingly, the teachers' comments were in response to the following question, which had been crafted to inspire insights about cultural assets: "Given Joel's collectivist culture, what other kinds of solutions may have been generated if Joel and his mother were involved in identifying their own resources and solutions?" Despite this prompt and the teachers' previous exposure to professional development (which included the cultural concepts of individualism and collectivism—see Table 4.4), only one teacher made a comment that reflected the desired consideration: "Maybe Joel isn't comfortable being alone . . . isolated. Is there a way the kids

■ **table 4.4**   Key Features of Individualism and Collectivism

Individualism	Collectivism
Home cultures that value and promote individualism:	*Home cultures that value and promote collectivism:*
Encourage the understanding of the physical world as knowable or manipulable, irrespective of its meaning for the members of the culture	Encourage the understanding of the physical world in the context of its meaning to the members of the culture
Promote independence across members of the culture and individual achievement	Promote interdependence among members of the culture and group success
Value egalitarianism, role flexibility, and upward mobility	Value stable, hierarchical roles associated with gender, family background, age, etc.
Foster self expression, self-directedness, and personal choice	Foster adherence to cultural norms, respect for authority, deference to elders, and group consensus
Favor individual ownership and private property	Favor group ownership and shared property

could do their homework together?" This particular teacher was from a CLD family herself, and she more readily saw that the family might be more comfortable working together.

Another term that describes this characteristic is *familism*, the tendency to value family and family goals above those of the individual. When this trait is studied in CLD families, high degrees of familism correlate with positive interpersonal relationships, strong family unity, the ability to work with others toward shared goals, and close ties to extended family (Gaines et al., 1997; Buriel & Rueschenberg, 1989). Higher levels of familism are also associated with significant indicators of mental health, including lower rates of substance use, juvenile delinquency, and child abuse (Coohey, 2001; Unger et al., 2002).

Indeed, many in the education and health care fields are beginning to agree with Romero, Robinson, Haydel, Mendoza, and Killen (2004) that "the maintenance of culture of origin values such as familism may decelerate the rate of acculturation [assimilation] within families, leading to less intergenerational strife and better health outcomes" for CLD students (p. 34). These findings appear consistent with the observed relationship between a student's deculturation and higher risks of academic, social, and behavior problems. Given that rapid assimilation and deculturation may pose a threat to healthy development and positive adaptation, it is important for educators to realize that cultural assets enhance the student's acculturation process—not detract from it. One need not sever ties nor abandon values to build new relationships within, and learn the alternate norms of, a new society.

Once the educators discussing Joel were allowed to benefit from one another's perspective, they were able to see how the dynamics of his home situation could facilitate his learning in a variety of ways. While generating ideas about interactive games and activities to practice skills, one teacher commented that such interactions would also be suited to her own child's preferred learning style. Another, who had characterized the original situation as "a mess," suddenly realized the inconsistency of her own views. After all, she was a strong proponent of cooperative education as a way to authenticate, differentiate, and provide natural models for learning. Why had she not seen before the benefits of bringing these practices home where they could be made even more powerful by involving parents or siblings? As a result of this scenario, several teachers added optional forms of home practice (e.g., games) that resulted in more actual opportunities to practice the concepts and skills than the old worksheets. Although many students preferred the interactive formats, some continued to choose traditional formats as the best fit for their own style of learning.

CLD students are likely to experience a number of dramatic and pervasive emotions associated with acculturation to a new setting or group. These feelings and the reactions they evoke can interfere with learning, identity development, personal wellness, and societal success. An improved understanding of each student's

> **assessment FREEZE FRAME 4.11**
>
> Given that rapid assimilation and deculturation may pose a threat to healthy development and positive adaptation, it is important for educators to realize that cultural assets enhance the student's acculturation process—not detract from it.

acculturation pattern helps teachers create authentic instructional opportunities that enhance CLD student learning and personal success.

Programming-Related Issues: Assessment of Acculturation

Necessarily, issues of placement and programming for CLD students who are acquiring English as a second language are topics beyond the scope of this text. Nonetheless, the results of assessing acculturation, content-area skills and knowledge, and, in particular, language proficiency can aid decision making associated with these issues. Therefore, the following discussion highlights salient, grade-level issues of acculturation assessment that are relevant to the identification, placement, monitoring, and exit of CLD students. This discussion is by no means exhaustive but provides a synopsis of issues that should be considered.

Identification

Acculturation status is an essential component of the larger body of information collected when identifying CLD students for alternative language programs. Students with lower levels of English language proficiency may experience concurrent issues of acculturative stress or, in some cases, culture shock. Such stress can affect the ability of a student to demonstrate his or her actual abilities through language and content-area assessments. Therefore, it is important to allay student fears during the formal assessment process and emphasize informal assessment information, which is generally obtained in less anxiety-provoking contexts.

Placement

Levels of acculturation and the degrees of difference between the home and host culture can help determine the most appropriate instructional placement and approaches for CLD students. An unaccommodative classroom can greatly hinder the academic success of students in early stages of acculturation. Such students may benefit from extensive opportunities to draw on their native language and culture as learning assets.

Monitoring

CLD student acculturation, along with language acquisition, should be monitored across settings. Negative acculturative phenomena, such as deculturation or rejection, will require attention to both individual student needs and the educational environment. Home visits and conversations with parents can provide critical insights into how students can best be assisted through their acculturation journeys.

Exit

It is important to realize that CLD students who have met the language and achievement criteria to exit alternative language programs may continue to require supports and affirmation. Even after students exit a program, such support is often necessary for positive cultural identity development and acculturation processes that lead to integration or adaptation. Students who integrate aspects of the host culture to form a bicultural identity are able to draw on the strengths of both cultures to overcome personal and academic challenges. Such individuals are also better able to help fellow students facing similar acculturation challenges.

■ key concepts

Acculturation

Acculturation surveys

Acculturative stress

Adaptation

Anomie

Behavioral continuum of acculturation

Collectivism

Cultural assets

Cultural identity

Cultural lens

Culture shock

Deculturation

Enculturation

Familism

Individualism

Integration

Objective indicators

Observational checklists

Observational rubrics

Psychological continuum of acculturation

Rejection

■ professional conversations on practice

1. Discuss the role that prior socialization in a particular culture plays in developing the lens through which a teacher views the abilities, behaviors, and performance of a CLD student. Why is it critical for teachers of CLD students to recognize, understand, and monitor this lens? Why should teachers want to know about the origins of that lens?

2. Assimilating the CLD student to so-called American culture has long been the overarching goal of the schooling institution. Discuss why adaptation or integration is a superior goal of schooling and a more appropriate outcome of the acculturation process. What factors may have prompted the original goal of assimilation? Is there an American culture? Why or why not?

3. Discuss the research that has sought to establish the relationship between cultural identity and student wellness. What are the implications of this research for achievement among CLD students? How can teachers' perspectives on classroom assessment affirm or demean a student's sense of cultural identity? What are the implications for best practice in assessing CLD students?

4. Review the case of Nashida discussed in this chapter. Discuss the pitfalls of informally assessing level of acculturation according to a single continuum of acculturation development or progress (i.e., behavioral or psychological). How can relying on a single source of assessment information foster inappropriate assumptions about CLD students?

5. Discuss how assessing acculturation of CLD students can encourage the teacher to use appropriate instructional and other classroom accommodations with these students. How can classroom teachers better identify and reduce acculturative stress with CLD students?

6. Discuss the influence of Western cultural norms on traditional assessment practices. Dis-

cuss how such practices are problematic for CLD students, especially those whose first language is not English. What should the goal of assessment be, and how do traditional assessments detract from that goal, especially in the case of the CLD student?

7. Reflect on and debate the role of familism in the acculturation of CLD students in your school or district. How can home visits promote or detract from the CLD student's sense of familism and the school's cultural perspective on familism?

questions for review and reflection

1. What is acculturation, and how does it differ from enculturation?

2. What does the phrase *cultural lens* mean, and why must teachers learn to recognize its influence on their perceptions of, expectations for, and pedagogical actions with CLD students?

3. Name at least five symptoms or behaviors a student may exhibit as a result of culture shock.

4. How would you describe the anomie a CLD student may experience as one aspect of the acculturation process?

5. What are key differences between assimilation and adaptation or integration as potential outcomes of the acculturation process?

6. Who are the gatekeeping staff of a school, and how might they contribute to the acculturation difficulties of CLD students? What can classroom teachers do about this potential problem?

7. In what ways can a school's approach to second language acquisition with CLD students actually promote deculturation?

8. How can emotions, especially emotions associated with the challenges of acculturation, affect CLD student performance and achievement?

9. Along what two continua is acculturation generally understood to develop?

10. How has research supported a strong correlation between strength of proficiency in the first language and acculturation progress among CLD students?

11. In what ways does a CLD student's ethnicity or nation of origin influence his or her acculturation pattern?

12. What are specific advantages of a home visit for informally assessing the level of acculturation of CLD students?

13. Describe at least two informal assessments of acculturation a classroom teacher might use with CLD students.

14. What are at least three effective actions schools can take to reduce acculturative stress with CLD students?

15. Define *familism*. What is the relationship between familism and the acculturation challenges confronted by CLD students?

- Explain why the primary language proficiency assessment of CLD students (whose first language is not English) is necessary for accommodating their differential assets and needs.

- Discuss the English language proficiency assessment of CLD students whose first language is not English.

- Describe five language subsystems.

- Compare and contrast language competence and language performance.

- Explain style shifting and the influences it may have on language proficiency assessment.

- Defend the informal assessment of language proficiency for CLD students whose first language is not English.

- Explain why classroom teachers of CLD students should build cross-cultural competencies while building capacities to appropriately assess language proficiency.

- Describe special considerations for using home language survey results to place students and plan instruction.

- Describe at least three types of informal assessments of language proficiency and the advantages of each type.

- Describe at least three types of formal assessments of language proficiency and the advantages of each type.

- Discuss how one's common underlying proficiency (CUP) contributes to the transfer of knowledge and language skills for CLD students whose first language is not English.

- Summarize the difficulties of interpreting results of language proficiency assessments used with CLD students whose first language is not English.

Assessment of Language Proficiency

In my class, I recently gave a vocabulary aptitude assessment. It was not an assessment that I created, but one supplied by our text materials. The words on the test were difficult for native English speakers, but the ELL [CLD] students had a particularly difficult time with it. To reduce the affective filter in future assessments, I gave points only for taking the assessment, not on the results. It's important with my ELL students to have some assessments that are scored and some that are not. Also, it is sometimes more appropriate for the ELL students to take the same type of self-assessment in Spanish to gain a more realistic score for themselves.

Dana DeMarco
Secondary Education Teacher

chapter outline

critical standards *Guiding Chapter Content*

TESOL/NCATE teacher standards reflect professional consensus on standards for the quality teaching of PreK–12 CLD students. Additionally, the CEEE Guiding Principles and their accompanying indicators serve as a framework to assist practitioners, policymakers, and clients as they collaborate to enhance academic enrichment and language acquisition among CLD students. Therefore, to help educators understand how they might appropriately target and address national professional teaching standards in practice, we have designed the content of this chapter to reflect the following standards.

TESOL/NCATE Standards for P–12 Teacher Education Programs

Domain 3: Planning, Implementing, and Managing Instruction. Candidates know, understand, and use standards-based practices and strategies related to planning, implementing, and managing ESL and content instruction, including classroom organization, teaching strategies for developing and integrating language skills, and choosing and adapting classroom resources.

- **Standard 3.a. Planning for Standards-Based ESL and Content Instruction.** Candidates know, understand, and apply concepts, research, and best practices to plan classroom instruction in a supportive learning environment for ESOL students. Candidates serve as effective English-language models, as they plan for multilevel classrooms with learners from diverse backgrounds using standards-based ESL and content curriculum.
  - **3.a.3.** Plan students' learning experiences based on assessment of language proficiency and prior knowledge.

Note: All TESOL/NCATE Standards are cited from TESOL (2003). All Guiding Principles are cited from Center for Equity and Excellence in Education (CEEE) (2005). Reprinted by permission.

Domain 4: Assessment. Candidates understand issues of assessment and use standards-based assessment measures with ESOL students.

- **Standard 4.b. Language Proficiency Assessment.** Candidates know and use a variety of standards-based language proficiency instruments to inform their instruction and understand their uses for identification, placement, and demonstration of language growth of ESOL students.

  4.b.1. Understand and implement national and state requirements for identification, reclassification, and exit of ESOL students from language support programs.

  4.b.4. Understand, construct, and use assessment measures for a variety of purposes for ESOL students.

- **Standard 4.c. Classroom-Based Assessment for ESL.** Candidates know and use a variety of performance-based assessment tools and techniques to inform instruction.

  4.c.2. Use various instruments and techniques to assess content-area learning (e.g. math, science, social studies) for ESOL learners at varying levels of language and literacy development.

CEEE Guiding Principles

Principle #1: English language learners are held to the same high expectations of learning established for all students.

1.1 **Believe** that English language learners can achieve the same high standards and meet the same academic expectations as all students.

Principle #3: English language learners are taught academic content that enables them to meet challenging performance standards in all content areas, consistent with those for all students.

3.7 **Use** appropriate multiple assessment tools and techniques to measure English language learners' progress in achieving academic standards and in acquiring English proficiency; use assessment results to inform classroom teaching and learning, and communicate these results to families in a meaningful and accessible manner.

Principle #4: English language learners receive instruction that builds on their prior knowledge and cognitive abilities and is responsive to their language proficiency levels and cultural backgrounds.

4.1 **Consider** the whole student, including English language proficiency, language/cultural background, native language literacy, and appropriate and valid student assessment data when making decisions about placement and provision of services for English language learners.

4.6 **Identify** and design instruction that is responsive to the English language learners' developmental levels, stages of English and native language development, dominant learning styles and individual strengths (e.g., spatial, musical, interpersonal, verbal, and logical-mathematical abilities).

Principle #5: English language learners are evaluated with appropriate and valid assessments that are aligned to state and local standards and that take into account the language development stages and cultural backgrounds of the students.

5.11 **Maintain** records of student work and performance across time and grade levels to communicate progress over time for individual English language learners.

5.10 **Use** a variety of formal and authentic assessment techniques to enhance classroom knowledge of English language learners and to evaluate their academic and linguistic progress.

For CLD students whose primary or home language is not English, language proficiency assessments are an ever-present reality beginning from their first month in a U.S. school. Although they may not be directly involved in the formal language assessment of these students, the teachers' capacity to use both informal and formal assessment results to plan appropriate and effective classroom instruction is pivotal to student success.

Rationale for Language Proficiency Assessment

If CLD students are to succeed in the grade-level classroom, they must acquire cognitive academic language proficiency (CALP) skills in English. For those CLD students whose home language is not English, they must draw on their common underlying proficiency (which is discussed later) in order to make language and knowledge transfers from L1 to L2 (Cummins, 1981; Herrera & Murry, 2005; Thomas & Collier, 2002). Therefore, it is critical to explore the L1 and L2 proficiencies of these students.

Rationale for Assessing Primary Language Proficiency

English acquisition and English achievement are the primary focuses of accountability assessments. However, some schools and districts also choose to measure the learning and maintenance of skills in a student's primary language. There are a number of compelling reasons why districts or schools may choose to assess both first and second languages. Sometimes such assessment is necessary because the first language is a purposeful component of academic instruction, as in bilingual or dual language programs. The assessment of first language proficiency can also be important in understanding issues related to second language acquisition and student achievement. Research and analyses support the idea that skills and knowledge from the primary language are transferable and can be used to support secondary language acquisition (Cummins, 1981, 2001; Kameenui & Carnine, 1998; Krashen, 1996; Thomas & Collier, 2002).

Cummins (1984) suggests that once cognitive linguistic knowledge is acquired in one language, those concepts become part of a common underlying proficiency (CUP) the speaker can access and apply to other languages. This concept is supported by research that demonstrates how students' mastery, continued use, and academic development of their first language correlates with higher levels of proficiency in English as a second language (Hakuta, 1987; Thomas & Collier, 2002). Information gathered through informal or formal first language assessment can aid in monitoring first language development, as well as provide instructional insights into skills mastered in that language, versus those skills for which the student lacks preexisting knowledge.

By assessing the knowledge and skills students possess in their primary language, teachers can plan for optimal levels of academic challenge and support in the classroom. For example, by knowing that a student is already familiar with targeted academic concepts in the primary language, a teacher is able to support instruction differently for that student than for one who lacks a basis for understanding the concept in either language. For the first student (who has preexisting knowledge), presenting new vocabulary with pictures, graphics, or L1 translations may be sufficient to promote the transfer of a concept to the student's new language. However, for the second student (who lacks preexisting conceptual knowledge), the foundational referent does not exist. Therefore, the teacher may be more successful teaching the new concepts through demonstration, hands-on experiences, or other activities that help the student learn the *meaning* associated with the new word. Consideration of primary language skills is not always required, but it can greatly enhance teaching and learning.

Rationale for Assessing English as a Second Language

Chief among the reasons for assessing the English language skills of CLD students is that, in most educational settings in the United States, English is the primary vehicle of instruction, the language in which curricular material is taught. The ability of a CLD student to benefit from and participate in the general curriculum depends greatly on his or her proficiency in the language in which that curriculum is presented—that is, English. Therefore, the more classroom teachers know about a student's ability to function in the instructional language, the better they can plan lessons that minimize potential language barriers while providing students maximum opportunities to learn content-area material.

Periodic formal and informal assessment of the second language enables educators to assess and reflect on the effectiveness of the alternative language programs and supports offered within the school or district. Figure 5.1 depicts one example of an informal, longitudinal writing assessment from a first-grade classroom. The CLD student is originally from Korea and, at the time of the first sample, had been in the United States for six months. An analysis of the writing samples reveals the student's growth in L2 literacy skills.

Accounting for English acquisition among CLD students is often an important component of federally funded programs. Examples of this are federal initiatives that specifically require states to approve evaluation measures for assessing students' English language proficiency, attainment of state academic achievement standards, and progress toward meeting the annual objectives specified in the law. The purpose of these assessments is essentially to measure student acquisition of English and to evaluate school and program effectiveness in guiding students to full participation in English language classrooms. Such mandates and initiatives are the result of a series of laws and rulings, starting with *Lau v. Nichols* (1974), which protect students from being denied access to the curriculum based on language.

In summary, English language proficiency is assessed to determine the appropriate educational placement for each student so she or he can receive the language

■ figure 5.1 Assessment Artifact: Longitudinal Writing Analysis

support necessary to benefit from content-area instruction. In this chapter, we discuss the characteristics of language proficiency and explore informal and formal standardized measures of language proficiency.

■ Key Elements of Language Acquisition and Proficiency

Although different theories exist to explain the phenomenon, it is apparent that normally developing children are able to associate abstract features of a language they hear with inherent rules about the content, form, and use of that language (Bloom & Lahey, 1978). *Content* is the meaning of the message; this is also called semantics. *Form* is the structural aspect that involves attaching some symbol to the

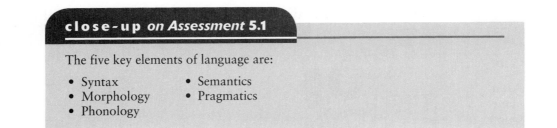

close-up *on Assessment 5.1*

The five key elements of language are:

- Syntax
- Morphology
- Phonology
- Semantics
- Pragmatics

meaning. The symbol can include the spoken word, a picture, or a gestured sign. Form also refers to the structures we create by combining symbols such as words (syntax) and additive forms such as suffixes (morphology) to refine the meaning of our message. *Use* refers to the purpose of our message and how it is conveyed (pragmatics). As illustrated in the following examples, the acquisition of an additional set of language-specific rules can affect the language performance of second language learners.

Syntax

Syntax basically refers to language-appropriate word order. As with all skills, this ability is acquired developmentally over time. For example, young native English speakers, as well as new-to-English speakers who have yet to distinguish between subject and object pronouns, commonly produce sentences such as "Her went to the store." CLD students who are acquiring a second language may initially combine L2 words and L1 syntax patterns. For example, the Spanish sentence "Yo tengo un perro *chiquito*" ("I have a *little* dog") is structured with the modifier following, rather than preceding, the noun. For this reason, many native Spanish speakers initially produce sentences such as "I have a dog *little*." With time and experience, most CLD students can automatically differentiate these patterns as specific to only one or the other language.

Morphology

Morphology refers to the rules and patterns for changing words to alter meaning by way of tense, person, number, and so forth. For instance, the addition of *-ed* to most verbs tells us we are referring to a past event ("I walked"), but the addition of *-s* to many verbs usually indicates a present-tense action by a third person ("She walks"). It violates the commonly accepted rules of English—and therefore sounds awkward—to say "I walks" or "She walk." Chomsky (1968) has argued that all languages and dialects share a universal grammar. This point is significant to the argument that no language or dialect is *higher* (more complex or sophisticated) than another (Edwards, 1989; Thanasoulas, 2001). Yet the conventions of "standard" English are among the benchmarks by which a person is deemed proficient in the United States. As with syntax, CLD students must not only master English morphological conventions but also differentiate those from the conventions of their first language.

Phonology

Phonology refers to the sound system of a language, the manner in which phonemes (distinct sounds) can be combined to create meaning. Phonemes in one language may not be phonemes in another. If a sound is phonemic, it may change the meaning of a word. For example, the sound /z/ (as in *zip*) is not a phoneme in Spanish. The Spanish language does spell words with the letter *z*, but the sound produced is like the English language *s*. For example, *taza* (cup) sounds like *tasa*. There are no sounds in Spanish like the one English speakers associate with the letter *z*. Consequently, native Spanish speakers are not as attuned to distinctions between /s/ and /z/ as are native English speakers, for whom *zip* and *sip* are very different words with very different meanings. Occasionally, minor phonemic distinctions can lead to interesting results. For example:

> Ms. Murillo presented Ezequiel with a quick set of prompts to check his knowledge of opposites.
>
> **Ms. Murillo:** What is the opposite of *up?*
> **Ezequiel:** Down.
> **Ms. Murillo:** Empty?
> **Ezequiel:** Full.
> **Ms. Murillo:** Dead?
> **Ezequiel:** Mom.
> **Ms. Murillo:** (pause) . . . Um, not Daaaaaad . . . *dead.*
> **Ezequiel:** Oh, alive!
> **Ms. Murillo:** Heavy?
> **Ezequiel:** Not heavy.
> **Ms. Murillo:** False?
> **Ezequiel:** Stands.

Ms. Murillo noted four out of five correct on Ezequiel's chart. Which response did she consider incorrect? Ezequiel realized that *heavy* is an adjective with which it is appropriate to use the modifier *not*. Ms. Murillo knows this realization demonstrates an important element of linguistic comprehension but does not demonstrate Ezequiel's ability to provide an appropriate opposite. By contrast, his most blatant "error" came when he heard Ms. Murillo say *falls* (because he did not distinguish between /s/ and /z/) instead of the word *false*. Seemingly incorrect, Ezequiel's response of *stands* is actually an appropriate opposite for the word he believed Ms. Murillo to have said—*falls.*

This example demonstrates that, although language production "errors" are usually recognizable as features of a person's accent, experienced teachers such as Ms. Murillo learn more about their students by considering the ways phonological perception may influence what they hear and how they answer.

■ Assessment in Action 5.1

One area of preassessment that is growing in importance and relevance is the practice of measuring phonological ability. This refers to the student's ability to recognize, discriminate, and manipulate the sounds or sound units of language. Research on English speakers has shown that phonemic awareness skills are strongly predictive of literacy development (Anthony & Lonigan, 2004; Kirby, Parrila, & Pfeiffer, 2003; O'Connor & Jenkins, 1999; Schatschneider, Fletcher, Francis, Carlson, & Foorman, 2004). For CLD students acquiring English, phonological skills in the primary language have been found highly predictive of literacy success in both L1 and L2 (August & Hakuta, 1997; Durgunoglu, Nagy, & Hancin-Bhatt, 1993; Gottardo, 2002; Quiroga, Lemos-Britton, Mostafapour, Abbott, & Berninger, 2001). Because a child's brain has had more exposure to the sounds and patterns of his or her primary language, the child will often initially be more adept at demonstrating and learning these skills in that language (Anthony & Lonigan, 2004), but transfer of skills from one language to another (Cisero & Royer, 1995; Gottardo, 2002) suggests there is value in measuring and teaching these skills in whatever languages possible in that setting.

Assessment of Phonemic Awareness for Pre- and Nonreaders

I.   Imitation of Auditory Patterns*

Instructions: Tap or knock *X* number of times. Encourage the child to imitate by saying, "Do this," by using the equivalent saying in the child's native language (e.g., "Haz esto" for Spanish speakers), or by using gestures to convey the instruction. Note the child's response by recording the number of times he or she tapped.

Student Taps

1. X   _____
2. XXX   _____
3. XXXX   _____
4. XX   _____
5. X   _____
6. XXX   _____
7. XX   _____
8. XXXXX   _____

II. Syllable Segmentation with Physical Cues

This may be done using native language words, English words, nonsense words, or a combination of these. (Please circle stimuli types used for this task.)

Instructions: Say a word with the targeted number of syllables. Say it again slowly, clapping or jumping once to each syllable count (e.g., Clap/jump two times as you say "ca-sa" [Spanish for *house*] and three times as you say "bas-ket-ball"). Ask the child to join you. Once he or she can perform this task well in unison, have him or her imitate your performance with new words, clapping on each of the syllables. If this is easy, give the child words to segment independently. Use two to three words comprising the different numbers of syllables, and note the child's responses. (A "+" can be used to indicate a correct response, and a "–" can be used to indicate an incorrect response.) These data can then be used to inform instruction of readiness skills.

(imitation)	L1	L2	Nonsense
1 syllable			
2 syllable			
3 syllable			
4 syllable			

(independent)	L1	L2	Nonsense
1 syllable			
2 syllable			
3 syllable			
4 syllable			

III. Auditory Discrimination

Instructions: The student will need to understand the concept of sameness. If the student is young, point to his or her shoes, nod, and say, "Same" ("*iguales*," etc). Then put your shoe next to one of the child's, shake your head, and say, "No, not same." Do this several times with environmental objects (e.g., pencils, blocks).

Using two identical objects such as blocks or pennies, touch each as you repeat the same word "car–car." Do this several times and model a "thumbs up" or nod as you affirm their sameness. Then take two dissimilar objects (e.g., a block and an eraser) and touch each for dissimilar words "car–milk." Shake your head and model "No, not same." It is not necessary for the student to use words such as *same, different,* or *not same* to perform this task. Any reliable gesture (head shake/nod, thumbs up/down) will do. Encourage the student to watch your mouth as you say the words, and note if he or she can determine whether the following pairs of words are the same (head nod) or not (head shake).

		L1 words:
car – car	spoon – spoon	_____
milk – milk	spoon – soon	_____
candy – candy	chair – chair	_____
apple – dog	made – mad	_____
apple – apple	eat – eat	_____
banana – spoon	cup – come	_____

IV. Structured Rhyming

An example of how to elicit structured and independent rhyming is included in a subsequent section of this chapter. Although it is not necessary to probe the student's skills using all stimuli types mentioned below, the distinction of language used will inform instructional planning for this student.

	L1	L2	Nonsense
Recognizes rhyme	yes/no	yes/no	yes/no
Selects rhyming word	yes/no	yes/no	yes/no
Offers rhyming word	yes/no	yes/no	yes/no

V. Sound–Syllable Blending

Instructions: To determine the level(s) at which the student is able to blend sound segments into words, you may need to begin by using something visual or tangible to demonstrate the desired behavior. For example, ask the student to guess your word as you lay a token down for each syllable and say "back-pack" or "wa-ter-fall." The student's familiarity with the vocabulary will be a factor in his or her ability to understand the purpose of this task. Familiar words from the child's L1 and L2 as well as nonsense words can be used for this assessment. Children who are shy or not yet comfortable speaking the target language can demonstrate skills by pointing to the appropriate picture among a set provided by the teacher. Present several words for each of the following three levels to discover the student's instructional readiness. Note the student's responses.

	L1	L2	Nonsense
1. By syllable ("bu-tter-fly")			
2. Initial sound + remainder of word ("r-ock")			
3. By sound ("d-e-s-k")			

(continued)

■ Assessment in Action 5.1 *(continued)*

VI. Phoneme/Syllable Deletion**

Instructions: This skill is often not evident in the preschool years but becomes very relevant for previously unschooled students or struggling early readers. This skill can also be demonstrated with colored blocks or other items to represent the sound or syllable segments being manipulated. To assess elision, tell the student:

1. Say "hot dog."   Student: "hot dog"
   Now say it again,
   but don't say "hot."   "dog"
2. Say "hamburger."   "hamburger"
   Say it again,
   but don't say "ham."   "burger"
3. Say "baloney."   "baloney"
   Say it again,
   but don't say "low."   "bunny"
4. Say "bake."   "bake"
   Now say it again,
   but don't say "b."   "ache"

(Be sure to pronounce sounds rather than say letter names.)

5. Say "meat."   "meat"
   Now say it again,
   but don't say "t."   "me"
6. Say "cloud."   "cloud"
   Now say it again,
   but don't say "k."   "loud"

Feel free to substitute words with similar patterns and expand on this list. Note below words and responses generated while assessing elision in the student's primary language:

_____

_____

_____

Source: Selected items adapted from the *Spanish/English Preschool Screening Test* (Kayser, 1995) and the **Test of Auditory Analysis Skills* (TAAS) (Rosner, 1979).

Semantics

The study of semantics involves the meanings of words, phrases, and sentences. Meaning can be expressed by our choices of words, their endings or prefixes, and the order in which we arrange them. Therefore, most of us choose our words rather carefully based on the meanings we believe they hold or the context in which we wish to use them. The ability to understand the concepts and relationships conveyed by language is semantic knowledge.

Although most of us master the syntax, morphology, and phonology of our primary languages as children, semantic knowledge is the area that continues to develop and grow the most throughout our lives. Semantic knowledge is also, for many, the most readily transferred aspect of language because so much of a person's semantic knowledge is related to her or his understanding of vocabulary. When one has a rich primary language vocabulary, it is much easier to connect the new form with an already understood concept than it is to learn a concept one has never been exposed to (in a language

assessment *FREEZE FRAME 5.2*

The ability to understand the concepts and relationships conveyed by language is semantic knowledge.

not yet fully understood). Figure 5.2 (page 130) illustrates a strategy that helps students make connections to their primary language in order to enhance their English vocabulary skills. Students whose primary language development is supported with opportunities for cognitive enrichment and application have a far more substantial foundation on which to map English than those whose cognitive linguistic foundation is disconnected from the educational process and content.

assessment *FREEZE FRAME* 5.3

When one has a rich primary language vocabulary, it is much easier to connect the new form with an already understood concept than it is to learn a concept one has never been exposed to (in a language not yet fully understood).

Pragmatics

Pragmatics refers to ways in which context can influence the interpretation of language. Such influences depend on the speaker, listener, context, and intent rather than on just the static meaning of the spoken words. For example, depending on the people and their relationship, interaction style, situation, and nonverbal cues, the word *great* can be used as a sincerely positive or a sarcastically negative comment. Let's consider a simple (and unpunctuated) exchange:

Jack: It's starting to rain
Saul: Oh great

This simple dialogue is difficult to interpret unless the author provides us with some context, along with descriptive or stylistic cues such as punctuation or italics to inform us about the pragmatic aspects of the message. The study of pragmatics encompasses a variety of both blatant and subtle, as well as verbal and nonverbal, features of language that influence how a message is delivered and perceived. Most people generally understand language pragmatics as the appropriateness of the communication action or intent in context.

The pragmatics of a situation should be considered an influence on a student's generated response. For example, in many languages—including English—it can be considered pragmatically redundant to repeat the subject of a question in the response. For most of us, "What is the boy doing?" will elicit an acceptable response that directly answers the question, such as "Riding a bike," without the additional phrase "The boy is . . ." Unfortunately, it is common to find prompts requiring an artificial construction (e.g., repetition of the subject when the subject is already understood) on tests intended to measure a child's ability to construct complete sentences. Such prompts may penalize students who provide the more natural fragmented response.

Language is complex, and mere knowledge of its structure is insufficient. Language is also acquired at the level of communicative competence. Effective communication demands that we know what to say, when to say it, to whom to say it, and under what circumstances. The answers to such questions typically lie in the dynamic norms of varying linguistic and social groups.

■ **figure 5.2**

Assessment
Artifact: Bilingual
Vocabulary Book

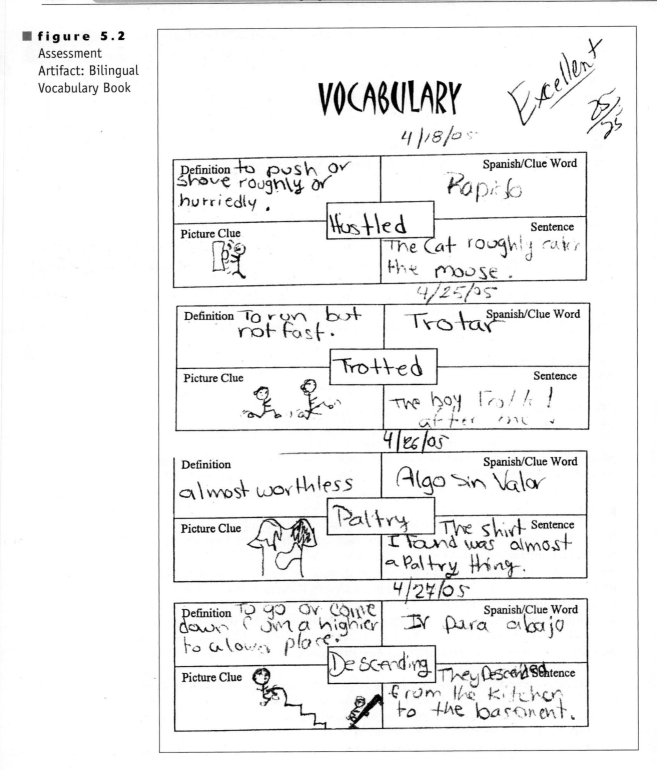

In addition, most speakers, regardless of background, shift their manner of speaking or style depending on the situation. To illustrate, depending on the formality of a workplace, it may seem unusual to hear someone speak to a boss in the same manner he or she would use with close friends or family. In addition to tone of voice, speakers also unconsciously adjust vocabulary, syntax, intonation, and grammar to fit the discourse style necessary for that particular setting or purpose. Style shifting is a sophisticated skill, and weaknesses in this area can be socially awkward. CLD students who demonstrate communicative competence are able to communicate effectively in a variety of social groups.

Informal Assessment of Language Proficiency

Language is a rich and complex system of sounds, words, sentences, nuances, and gestures that is, by its very nature, reciprocal and spontaneous. Other than for distinct purposes, such as formal speeches, language is incredibly interactive and socially dynamic. For example, it is quite natural for teachers to adapt their style and pace or stop for clarification when reading to students who appear confused or inatten-

> **assessment FREEZE FRAME 5.4**
>
> Any time we seek to assess language, we must understand not only what our tests can tell us but also, more significantly, what they *cannot*.

tive. These subtleties, which make replicating language with technology so difficult, also hamper our use of formal assessments to measure a student's grasp of a language's multidimensional, interdependent components. Therefore, any time we seek to assess language, we must understand not only what our tests can tell us but also, more significantly, what they *cannot*. In this section, we discuss a variety of informal assessment techniques for developing a clearer picture of a CLD student's language profile and proficiency level.

Key Issues in Informal Assessment

Before we explore specific informal assessments, it is important to note that the value of informal assessment data frequently depends on the types and numbers of settings in which we observe the student's use of language—as well as the perspectives through which we interpret that language usage. For example, because language can be so situation specific, it is unwise to assume that a single sample of a CLD student's language is fully representative of her or his broader linguistic abilities. What a CLD student may not be able to properly express in one language or manner of speaking, she or he may be perfectly capable of expressing in another.

In addition, we can observe language performances that do not match our contextual expectations but that are still quite appropriate from the perspective of a different cultural norm. For instance, some children may feel that to answer questions with obvious answers is disrespectful, or they may avoid eye contact as a sign of respect, despite the teacher's insistence to "look at me when I'm talking to you." Other children may call out agreement or commentary as the teacher

close-up *on Assessment 5.2*

Speakers may adjust these elements of language when style switching:

- Tone of voice
- Vocabulary
- Syntax
- Intonation
- Grammar

speaks. We all attend to different cultural norms that affect our communication style in various settings. How might we be judged if, while in church, we respond to the sermon in a manner appropriate for a football game? How many of us find "table talk" quite different at our own house than it is at the homes of our in-laws or neighbors? Just as it takes any child time to learn the subtleties of when and what to say where, CLD students will, if not demeaned for their culture's rules, learn additional cultural norms for effectively communicating with multiple groups in multiple settings.

At times, some children also seem to have trouble getting to the point. This may reflect differences in discourse patterns, the patterns through which a person expresses his or her thoughts on a subject (Herrera, 2001). English speakers of the dominant culture in the United States tend to use a linear discourse pattern, one that is highly sequential and focused on succinct resolution. Speakers from other cultures often follow very different discourse patterns in which narratives, by contrast, may seem circular, repetitious, or digressive (Herrera, 2001). However, virtually every language exhibits particular syntactic and lexical structures that are generally comprehensible to speakers from that culture. Figure 5.3 illustrates one perspective on the directionality of discourse patterns that may be associated with various languages. Considerable debate persists about the patterns illustrated for specific languages (Kaplan, 2005). For example, Kaplan notes that "every speaker

assessment *FREEZE FRAME 5.5*

Because language can be so situation specific, it is unwise to assume that a single sample of a CLD student's language is fully representative of her or his broader linguistic abilities. What a CLD student may not be able to properly express in one language or manner of speaking, she or he may be perfectly capable of expressing in another.

■ **figure 5.3**
Directionality of
Discourse Patterns

Source: Adapted by permission from R. B. Kaplan (1966). Cultural thought patterns in intercultural education. *Language Learning, 16*(1), 1–20; and C. Collier (2004). PowerPoint image. Ferndale, WA: CrossCultural Developmental Education Services.

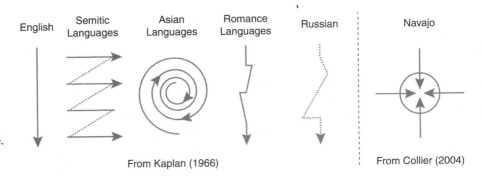

English   Semitic Languages   Asian Languages   Romance Languages   Russian   Navajo

From Kaplan (1966)   From Collier (2004)

close-up *on Assessment 5.3*

Different cultural norms may prompt CLD students to:

- Feel that it is rude to respond to questions that call for obvious answers
- Attempt to "save the face" of their peers by avoiding responses that might be interpreted as superior to that of their peers
- Avoid eye contact as a sign of respect
- Have trouble getting to the point
- Shout out agreement or commentary as the teacher speaks

perceives his/her language as linear and all others as non-linear" (p. 388). Nonetheless, Figure 5.3 does convey the less controversial notion that there are perceptible differences in rhetorical preferences across languages to which teachers should attend as they assess their CLD students' content-area writing attempts in English.

For these reasons and others, many classroom teachers choose to broaden their own sociocultural competencies by learning about the interaction styles of other cultures and how these styles may influence personal and academic communication in diverse classrooms. Besides appealing to parents for information on home language skills and dynamics, teachers of CLD students also have opportunities to observe these students in less formal settings, such as in the lunchroom or gym, with family during school-sponsored events, on the playground, or just conversing in the hall. Intuitive teachers recognize and seize these opportunities to engage students in conversations about their interests and experiences. If structured appropriately, such practices provide not only information about student language proficiencies but also, more important, insights about students as people. Home language surveys and parent interviews are two of the most valuable avenues for gaining insights about a student's performance in another setting and as seen through the parents' eyes.

Home Language Surveys

Home language surveys, such as the one depicted in Figure 5.4, are one of the most common ways that schools and districts gather information about the language(s) used in a student's home. As such, these informal assessments of language proficiency help teachers understand more about the student's level of exposure to English and his or her linguistic foundations in the primary language. Although these surveys can serve a variety of additional purposes, they are generally the first and broadest step toward identifying students who may qualify for alternative language services. When the home language survey indicates a primary language other than English is spoken in the home, the student is often referred. Postreferral assessments help determine whether a student is proficient enough

■ figure 5.4 Home Language Survey

Elementary Home Language Survey

Date: _____   Grade: _____

Student's Name: _____   Phone: _____

Parent/Guardian's Name: _____

Current address: _____

What is student's country of origin? _____

What is student's native language? _____

How long has the child been in the United States? _____

What brought your family to the United States? _____

Student Info

How proficient is he/she in using their native language?

Scale (circle)

Speaking/Listening	Proficient (fluent)	Intermediate-High	Intermediate-Mid	Intermediate-Low	Beginner
Reading	Proficient (fluent)	Intermediate-High	Intermediate-Mid	Intermediate-Low	Beginner
Writing	Proficient (fluent)	Intermediate-High	Intermediate-Mid	Intermediate-Low	Beginner

Has your child had academic instruction in their native language?

❏ Yes ❏ No   How long? _____   School/Place _____

Has your child had trouble learning in his/her native language?   ❏ Yes ❏ No

What were areas of concern? _____

What are your child's areas of strength? _____

Has your child had formal academic instruction in English?

❏ Yes ❏ No   What grades? _____   How many minutes of English per day? _____

Describe school in your native country

_____

If child has been in US, has child been in an ESL/Bilingual program?

❏ Yes ❏ No   What grades? _____   How many minutes of ESL per day? _____

How proficient is your child in using English?

Scale (circle)

Speaking/Listening	Proficient (fluent)	Intermediate-High	Intermediate-Mid	Intermediate-Low	Beginner
Reading	Proficient (fluent)	Intermediate-High	Intermediate-Mid	Intermediate-Low	Beginner
Writing	Proficient (fluent)	Intermediate-High	Intermediate-Mid	Intermediate-Low	Beginner

Elementary Home Language Survey

Parent Info

Do you and your child have access to children's books in your language?   ❏ Yes   ❏ No

If you have pictures or other materials from your country would you be interested in sharing with our school/classrooms?   ❏ Yes   ❏ No

Do you and your child have access to children's books in English?   ❏ Yes   ❏ No

Who is the primary caregiver? _____ Language Spoken? _____

How will your child get to and from school? _____

Where will your child go before/after school? _____

Contact info: _____

Mother's native language? _____ Father's native language? _____

Can mother read and write fluently in native language?   ❏ Yes   ❏ No   Can father read and write fluently in native language?   ❏ Yes   ❏ No

When **listening** to others in English do you understand?   Mother: ❏ Yes   ❏ No   Father: ❏ Yes   ❏ No

Can you **speak** to others in English?   Mother: ❏ Yes   ❏ No   Father: ❏ Yes   ❏ No

Can you **read** in English?   Mother: ❏ Yes   ❏ No   Father: ❏ Yes   ❏ No

Can you **write** in English?   Mother: ❏ Yes   ❏ No   Father: ❏ Yes   ❏ No

Are you fluent enough with English to help your child with regular homework?   ❏ Yes   ❏ No

Family Info

If available, would you be interested in additional tutoring?   Before school? ❏ Yes ❏ No   After school? ❏ Yes ❏ No   Home based? ❏ Yes ❏ No

Does your child have brothers/sisters?   Do they live in same household?   Speak English?

Name/age _____   ❏ Yes   ❏ No   ❏ Yes   ❏ No

Name/age _____   ❏ Yes   ❏ No   ❏ Yes   ❏ No

Name/age _____   ❏ Yes   ❏ No   ❏ Yes   ❏ No

Are there extended family members living in your home?   ❏ Yes   ❏ No

Who? _____

Do you have a support system in Lawrence?   ❏ Yes   ❏ No

Are there cultural opportunities for you and your family in Lawrence?   ❏ Yes   ❏ No

Contact in home country: _____

(continued)

■ figure 5.4 (continued)

Elementary Home Language Survey

Are there resources we can connect you with?   ❏ Yes   ❏ No

❏ Transportation	❏ Housing	❏ Mental Health
❏ Health care	❏ Utilities	❏ Parenting Skills
❏ Dental care	❏ Food	❏ Support system within their cultural community
❏ Child care	❏ Clothing	
❏ Nutrition Info.	❏ Adult English Classes	_____

If available, in what language would you prefer to receive school communications? _____

Would you like an interpreter for school meetings? (i.e., parent/teacher conferences?)   ❏ Yes   ❏ No

Do you have someone you use regularly?   ❏ Yes   ❏ No

Contact Info. (Name, phone number) _____

Would you like for us to find an appropriate interpreter?   ❏ Yes   ❏ No

Other Interview Information: _____
_____
_____
_____
_____

Follow-up Phone Interview:

Date _____

I am just calling to check in on how things are going. In your perspective, how is your child doing in school?
_____
_____
_____

What are they enjoying most in school? _____

Have they reported any problems? _____

Based on resource needs from our initial contact, have you been able to find. . .

Are there any additional ways that we can support your child or family?

Source: Reprinted with the permission of Tammy Becker and Hillcrest Elementary School, USD 497, Lawrence, Kansas. Please note: The quality of a home language survey depends on the extent to which it reflects the cultural and linguistic student dynamics at the school where it is used. Although this example is a high-quality home language survey for Hillcrest Elementary School, its utility for another school or school system may be limited without appropriate, site-specific adaptation.

in English to participate fully in classrooms where instruction is delivered only in English.

Whether home language surveys are simple or complex, school personnel who review them should bear in mind that some parents will lack the literacy skills (in either English or the first language) or the trust in school officials necessary to complete these forms without additional support and information. Efforts to explain the survey's purpose and ensure privacy, as well as provide assistance to parents in completing the survey, can greatly increase the quality and reliability of the data gathered.

Because there are so many variables regarding language dialects, translation quality, and parent literacy levels, some parents misinterpret the meaning or intention of survey questions. Such misinterpretations can lead to inappropriate educational decisions or actions. Therefore, some schools require teachers to verify the parents' interpretation of provided information during translator-assisted conferences. This effort provides valuable opportunities for teachers as they establish lines of communication with parents or guardians and seek additional information about the funds of knowledge students bring to the classroom.

With conscientious use and interpretation, home language surveys such as the Bilingual Language Proficiency Questionnaire (Mattes & Santiago, 1985; Mattes & Nguyen, 1996) can also elicit critical information about primary language development. Such information can allay the teacher's concerns about students who exhibit longer-than-expected silent periods. A silent period is part of the preproduction stage of the second language acquisition process. During this period, CLD students may communicate in only nonverbal ways as they primarily listen to the new language and try to understand its patterns and rules before attempting production in that language. In the following situation, a misunderstanding about language acquisition processes almost resulted in an inappropriate assessment of the student's actual communicative competence.

close-up on Assessment 5.4

When asking CLD parents, guardians, or extended family members to complete home language surveys:

- Clearly explain the purpose of the survey.
- Attempt to allay any respondent concerns about immigration issues.
- Ensure respondent confidentiality.
- Provide any survey completion assistance that the respondent may require.
- Provide bilingual translators or translated surveys, as appropriate.

Lily's kindergarten teacher referred her to the student intervention team because she was "still not speaking English in class." The teacher felt something was very wrong, because other teachers noted that Lily's brother began speaking with peers "nearly right away" and their father was reportedly able to convey basic information in English to staff. The teacher was concerned that Lily might be developmentally delayed.

In reviewing the home language survey, the intervention team quickly noted that although the father had some English proficiency, Vietnamese was reported as the only language spoken in the home. This was logical as Lily's mother did not speak English at all. Despite the initial impressions of the teacher, the team concluded that Lily probably was not developmentally delayed, but rather had had very limited exposure to English prior to her first preschool year. The survey used in this school also asked about the dominant language of the child at home (in this case, Vietnamese) but did not ask for any information about the child's perceived proficiency with that language. To effectively meet Lily's needs and help her achieve in school, it was decided that the team needed more information about her first language proficiency and use.

Parent Interviews

Data gathered from observational assessments such as home visits can greatly enrich and validate findings from other types of language proficiency measures or surveys. Observing language use in context allows educators to see how students actually use the relatively compartmentalized skills measured by formal tests. Seeking this kind of additional data was essential in Lily's case, in which the teachers concluded they simply did not have enough information to make the appropriate decisions about her instruction. Because a genuine developmental delay or learning concern would be evident in Lily's home environment as well, the team followed up the standard survey with a home visit interview.

During a home visit interview, teachers asked a few more detailed questions about Lily's use of language in the home. The team was able to assess Lily's interactions with her family, who of course shared the same cultural and linguistic knowledge base. Because these assessments were conducted in Lily's language of comfort, they were more likely to yield genuine information about her true linguistic abilities.

The responses the teachers received and the language performance they observed indicated the following: Lily actually began speaking at an early age, was able to speak in complete sentences, and used language effectively to tell her parents about her day at school. These findings reassured the team that Lily possessed a strong language base rather than an innate problem. The home visit also provided additional information her teacher could use to enhance the home–school connection. Aided by a translator, the teacher encouraged the parents to talk about and build on school topics they could glean from translated newsletters, notes, and Lily herself. The parents were reassured that doing so in the home language would not only facilitate Lily's classroom learning and confidence but also enhance her ability to transfer her primary language skills to the new language.

The next month, during a class discussion on weather, Lily raised her hand excitedly to share, "My dad say Vietnam so much rain." "Yes," the teacher replied, "Some places like Vietnam get much more rain than we do." Along with other class members, Lily walked over to the globe to find Vietnam and, together, they talked about the weather in Vietnam, Mexico, Israel, and even Chicago, where Jason said his grandmother calls wind "the hawk." It was amazing how a few simple strategies for helping Lily's parents enrich her learning had such an impact on the learning experiences of others.

Informal parent interviews are forms of observational assessment in that they provide valuable information based on a parent's observations of the child's language use in the home and with family. Ideally, teachers will have the opportunity to meet with parents at home and will benefit from both the parents' increased comfort levels and the opportunity to observe in a setting that is comfortable and nonthreatening for the student. Translators involved in this process should know the teacher's agenda for the meeting and should be trained (in both linguistic and cultural competencies) to provide both parent and teacher a reliable interpretation of the messages exchanged.

A guide or prepared list of questions may be helpful, but the astute interviewer also invites parents to "tell me more" or to "think of a time when" the student demonstrated the skill being discussed. This manner of asking questions to gain information about the family's perspective or experiences is referred to as *ethnographic interviewing* (Spradley, 1979).

Checklists of communication functions (i.e., how the student uses language in context) are also useful for obtaining information about a student's overall communication proficiencies. Such checklists allow teachers to note the child's use of L2 at school and then probe parental perceptions about how the child uses language in the home or community. When a teacher has more clues about a student's particular language strengths and preferences, he or she can more appropriately accommodate that student's learning and second language acquisition needs. The following vignette illustrates Mrs. Holmes's use of this type of informal assessment:

Mrs. Holmes used a simple checklist of communication functions (see Figure 5.5 and related appendix resource) to quickly note language skills she had observed with CLD students in various classroom contexts. Although Jean, a CLD student, was demonstrating several important skills, such as describing experiences well and expressing imagination, he continued to struggle with sequential directions in class. Mrs. Holmes doubted that language was a factor, because Jean understood each step perfectly when instructions were broken down into smaller units. Therefore, she decided to explore other issues that might be involved.

During conference week, Mrs. Holmes met first with the French interpreter to discuss Jean's progress and her concerns before they met with Jean and his mother in the home. Mrs. Holmes also discussed the communication inventory with the interpreter so they were both aware of particular language skills to ask about in the home language setting.

■ **figure 5.5** Communication Functions Checklist

Please indicate whether the following communicative behaviors are:

Observed (+)   Reported (R)   Not Observed (−)

Student Name: _____Jean_____

	L1	L2
1. Student comments on actions of self or others.	+	
2. Student initiates conversations.	+	
3. Student maintains a topic in conversation.	+	
4. Student follows multipart directions.	−	
5. Student uses language to request (action/object, assistance, information, clarification, etc.).	+	
6. Student uses language to tell (needs, feelings, thoughts, answers to questions).	+	
7. Student describes experiences (retells events).	+	
8. Student predicts outcomes or describes solutions.	+	
9. Student expresses and supports opinions.	−	
10. Student uses language to express imaginative and creative thinking.	+	

Jean's mother was expecting them and left her supper to simmer while visiting with the guests from school—she was so pleased to meet them! After exchanging greetings with the teacher, Jean's mother turned to her son with several comments, and he headed over to the open kitchen. Mrs. Holmes noticed the interpreter watching him as she and Jean's mother resumed the conference. After a minute or two, Mrs. Holmes cleared her throat ever so slightly to regain the translator's attention. The translator smiled and told the teacher that Jean had just carried out every one of the four things his mother told him to do in the kitchen, precisely as directed. Momentarily putting the agenda aside, Mrs. Holmes commented on the interpreter's observation.

Mrs. Holmes: Some children have trouble following directions even when they try. Does Jean usually follow directions this well?

Mom: Oh, yes. Back in Port-au-Prince, I could send him to my sister's apartment or to the market, and he always remembered all the things I said to do and get. He's a good boy.

Mrs. Holmes: That's great! I always forget things on my grocery list. How do you remember everything, Jean?

Jean: Sometimes my mother sings while she's doing her chores, so when she tells me lots of things to do, I make a song in my head too. Hey, that rhymes!

Mrs. Holmes gained many valuable insights about how to more effectively work with Jean, such as using music and rhyme in the classroom as mnemonic devices. Classroom teachers should always keep in mind that CLD student performance may be affected by variables other than language. Students of all cultures and linguistic backgrounds can benefit from the careful differentiation of instruction to meet their particular needs.

Informal Assessment of Academic Language Proficiency

In addition to developing social language—or basic interpersonal communication skills (BICS)—CLD students must acquire the academic language skills necessary for classroom success. These include but are not limited to inquiring, classifying, describing, comparing, contrasting, explaining, analyzing, inferring, supporting one's opinions, persuading, synthesizing, and evaluating. The checklist depicted in Figure 5.6 provides examples of skills related to BICS and CALP development (see also related appendix resource).

It is often easier and more authentic for a teacher to evaluate how students demonstrate academic language skills with activities and materials he or she already uses than it is to create unrelated or isolated assessments to measure the skills. As illustrated in the following example, sometimes an awareness of the language skills necessary to support the curriculum enables a teacher to make the most of unplanned classroom events:

Mrs. Adelaja knew it was important to stimulate the higher-order thinking skills of her CLD students. She was also aware the students would need such skills to demonstrate their abilities to meet grade-level standards. Recently, she returned from an inservice workshop thinking about opportunities to practice and assess these skills in ways she had never before imagined.

One day early in the school year, Manny, a native Spanish speaker, had to forfeit his recess. He was, once again, out of his seat at an inappropriate time. He responded somewhat indignantly, arguing that last year's teacher, Mr. Viega, "was nicer" and that he wished he could still be in Mr. Viega's class. Previously, Mrs. Adelaja might have responded negatively to his comment and the way it made her feel, but this time she chose to use it as a teaching and learning opportunity.

The class was transfixed as Mrs. Adelaja wrote her name above one of two large, intersecting circles on the board. She wrote Mr. Viega's name above the other. This would

Basic Interpersonal Communication Skill (BICS)

L1	L2	Listening
○	○	Understands school/classroom routines
○	○	Responds, with little hesitation, when asked to perform a nonverbal task
○	○	Follows oral directions at the end of lesson (with familiarity and modeling)
○	○	Listens to peers when process is provided
○	○	Becomes distracted when lesson is not differentiated
○	○	Distinguishes sameness or difference between English sounds

L1	L2	Speaking
○	○	Is comfortable with groups speaking English
○	○	Communicates with peers in social settings
○	○	Responds to questions in class when the question is context embedded or the teacher provides scaffolding
○	○	Is able to retell a pictured, cued, or scaffolded story
○	○	Can describe the topic of the lesson using limited vocabulary
○	○	Struggles with concept retelling when topic is not contextualized
○	○	Withdraws when group discussions go beyond known vocabulary
○	○	Is eager to participate when language demands are supported

L1	L2	Reading
○	○	Recognizes common language of school
○	○	Recognizes environmental print (e.g., signs, logos, McDonald's)
○	○	Can match or read basic sight words
○	○	Reads best when material is contextualized
○	○	Demonstrates limited use of reading strategies
○	○	Volunteers to read when material is known

L1	L2	Writing
○	○	Writes personal information (e.g., name, address, phone number)
○	○	Writes with contextual and/or instructional scaffolding
○	○	Writes with some spelling errors
○	○	Writes with many spelling errors
○	○	Writes with moderate to high levels of syntax errors

Cognitive Academic Language Proficiency (CALP)

L1	L2	Listening
○	○	Is able to carry out academic tasks without language support
○	○	Understands vocabulary in different content areas (e.g., *sum* in math vs. *some* in science)
○	○	Understands process/sequence across content areas
○	○	Uses selective attention when taking notes
○	○	Understands teacher idioms and humor
○	○	Understands English language functions
○	○	Comprehends teacher lecture, movies, and audiovisual presentations

L1	L2	Speaking
○	○	Asks/answers specific questions about topic of discussion
○	○	Uses temporal concepts (e.g., first, next, after) appropriately
○	○	Recognizes the need for, and seeks, clarification of academic tasks or discussion
○	○	Expresses rationale for opinion
○	○	Poses thoughtful questions
○	○	Actively participates in class activities and discussions
○	○	Volunteers to answer subject-matter questions of varying difficulty

L1	L2	Reading
○	○	Demonstrates knowledge and application of sound–symbol association
○	○	Demonstrates phonemic awareness skills such as sound blending, elision, and rhyming
○	○	Regards print with appropriate spatial skills and orientation (e.g., left to right, top to bottom)
○	○	Interprets written words and text as the print representation of speech
○	○	Understands differential use of text components (e.g., table of contents, glossary)
○	○	Reads for information and understanding
○	○	Reads independently to gather information of interest

L1	L2	Writing
○	○	Performs written tasks at levels required by the curriculum
○	○	Uses complex sentences appropriate for grade level
○	○	Writes from dictation
○	○	Writes for audience and purpose
○	○	Understands purposes and application of writing conventions
○	○	Uses writing as a tool for personal means (e.g., correspondence, notation, journaling)
○	○	Writes compellingly or creatively (e.g., editorials, poetry, lyrics, stories)

Source: Adapted from B. Bernhard & B. Loera (1992). Checklist of language skills for use with limited English proficient students. *Word of Mouth Newsletter,* 4(1). San Antonio, TX: Lauren Newton.

later prove to be one of the year's most memorable and powerful Venn diagrams. With her guidance, the class described the differences and similarities between the teachers (Mrs. Adelaja and Mr. Viega) and their classrooms. Mr. Viega's class was, after all, first grade, and they were now in second grade. Javier commented, "Little kids get up more than big kids, but bigger kids are supposed to know how to sit." The class agreed that growing older meant sitting "better" at the table, at church, and in school. Mrs. Adelaja was impressed by Javier's effective use of his L2 to justify and persuade. Manny, however, still felt that losing his recess time was "unfair." Yet he could neither explain nor support this opinion, even as bilingual peers in the group tried to help him. Mrs. Adelaja noted that as well.

According to the curriculum sequence for her grade level, comparing, contrasting, and explaining skills would not be covered in Mrs. Adelaja's lesson plans for several months. Nevertheless, because Mrs. Adelaja knew her curriculum and seized the unanticipated opportunity, she gained new insights about her CLD students, their language skills, and their perspectives. For example, some students like Manny might require greater support in the future to develop and explain ideas. This activity fostered a rich and revealing discussion that also prompted Mrs. Adelaja to rethink some of her classroom structures that might have been barriers to this type of engagement in the past.

Mrs. Adelaja's experience demonstrates the ability of informal assessment to illuminate instructional issues that may influence student participation or achievement.

When teachers assess academic language proficiency, they should keep in mind that, at times, it may be beneficial to allow students to use their native language to demonstrate content-area knowledge and skills. For example, by informally assessing student work, one first-grade teacher was able to determine whether her student, a newcomer to the school in the earliest stages of English language acquisition, could construct a nonfiction text. Students in the class worked in small groups to produce books about whales (*ballenas*), and this student participated fully by writing her page in Spanish (see Figure 5.7).

Anecdotal Logs

Much can also be learned about the academic language proficiencies of students through anecdotal logs. These are important components of observational assessment. Although it is certainly easier to set aside distinct times and situations to observe specific students, those moments are unlikely to yield the quantity and richness of results one can achieve by also noting incidents that arise naturally during the school day. The possibilities for this sort of observation are unlimited, and the various systems that creative teachers have developed to record and manage such data truly are awe-inspiring.

One example of an anecdotal log is a flip file, created by taping the top edge of overlapping index cards onto a clipboard (see Figure 5.8 on page 146). Each card lists a student's name and specific goals, if desired. As language-related or

assessment *FREEZE FRAME 5.7*

Anecdotal logs provide the classroom teacher with real-time, authentic information about CLD students.

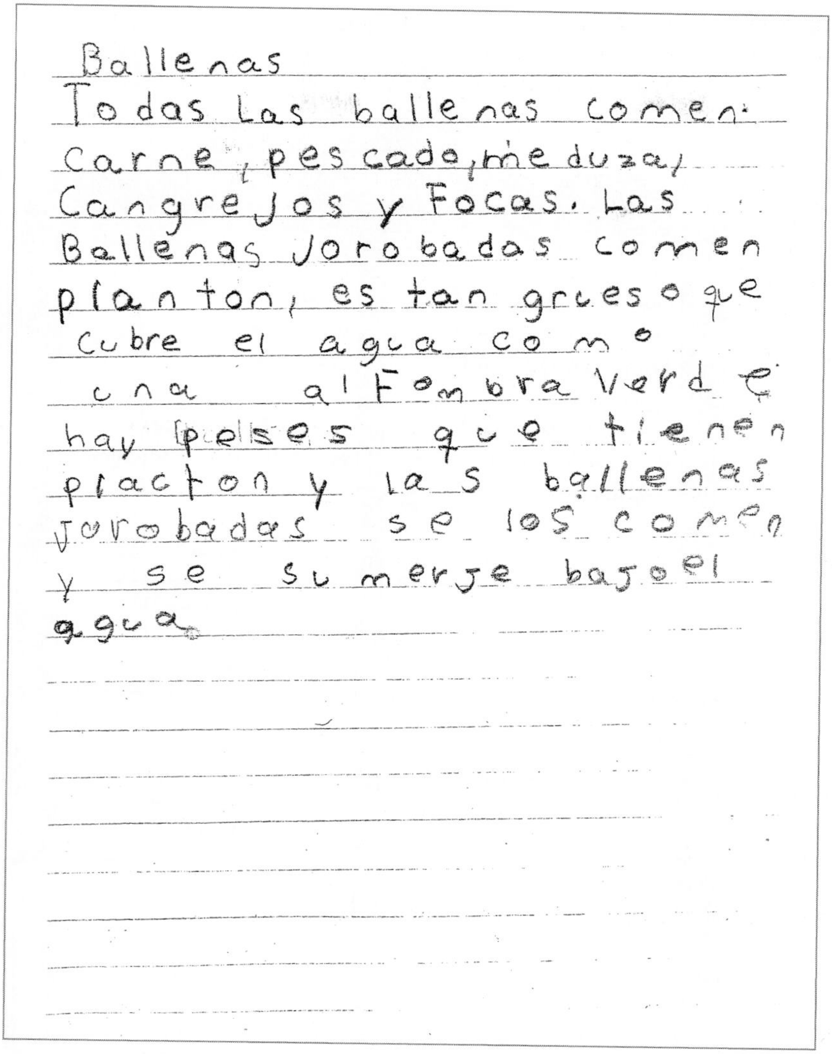

> Ballenas
> Todas Las ballenas comen
> carne, pescado, meduza, y
> Cangrejos y Focas. Las
> Ballenas Jorobadas comen
> planton, es tan grueso que
> cubre el agua como
> una alfombra verde
> hay peses que tienen
> placton y las ballenas
> Jorobadas se los comen
> y se sumerje bajo el
> agua.

■ **figure 5.7**
Assessment Artifact:
Primary Language CALP

other significant actions are observed, the teacher need only write a date and a short comment on that student's card. The cumulative assessment information from these cards can then be used to inform decisions about classroom settings, support rubric assessment, and share authentic evidence with parents or other evaluators.

Another type of anecdotal log calls for the teacher to write the class roster or targeted students' names on sheets of removable labels (either on computer or by hand). These can be positioned or transported on a handy clipboard. As interesting language behaviors occur—or do *not* occur (lack of expected behavior is also noteworthy)—the teacher jots the date and comment on that student's label. At the end of the day or week, these labels are moved to a page in the student's folder.

■ figure 5.8
Assessment
Artifact:
Flip File

Goal 1: Works with L1 peers to understand target L2 vocabulary

Goal 2: Shares orally in L1 during group discussions

Benjamin
Zoe
Jorge
Mario
Amanda
Miki
Rachel
Arun
Victoria
Suzanne

Goal 1: Uses target L2 vocabulary in conversation

Goal 2: Summarizes main points of group discussion

Sheri
Shabina
Susan
Carol
Gabriela
Tonnie
Gisela
Christian
Cristina
Seong

This strategy builds a chronological and reproducible account of language acquisition in progress.

Matrices and Rubrics

Effective classroom teachers use matrices and rubrics to plot observed academic language performance according to established criteria. The Student Oral Language Observational Matrix (SOLOM) (California State Department of Education, n.d.) is one example of a matrix teachers can use as a general diagnostic

close-up *on Assessment 5.5*

Stages of second language acquisition:

- Preproduction
- Early production
- Speech emergence
- Intermediate fluency
- Advanced fluency

tool or screening instrument. It can serve as a valuable resource in CLD student placement decisions or can be used to plot language acquisition over time. The matrix (see Figure 5.9 on page 148) is based on the premise that the most authentic environments for sampling language occur in natural contexts in which the student uses language to understand or communicate for academic or social purposes.

Matrices and rubrics can provide added benefits for the classroom teacher by heightening her or his awareness of key criteria throughout the instructional day. For example, a teacher who is familiar with the language acquisition rubric for the school district is often much more aware of the need to develop descriptive vocabulary among CLD students. This teacher might then purposefully elicit words such as *crunchy, gooey, delicious, crisp*, or *sweet* during nonacademic periods of the day, such as snack time.

Rubrics based on the stages of language acquisition (preproduction, early production, speech emergence, intermediate fluency, advanced fluency) are also a popular means of quantifying student progress. They may be used with either naturally occurring language samples or with those drawn out through story retelling or other more standardized contexts. Because pragmatics and context influence the student's response, the teacher should note how the sample was obtained. This information assists reviewers as they interpret the results and compare them with other student work.

Because the teacher can make more accurate and revealing observations once the student is more familiar with the teacher and setting, language observation rubrics may not be as informative for initial placement decisions as they are for monitoring ongoing growth and readiness for reclassification. Teachers who gather observational data frequently find it a powerful tool for measuring learning over time. This ability to aid ongoing instructional planning is a distinct advantage over most formal measures.

There are many ways in which teachers can adapt rubrics to gather the type of assessment information they need. Although some classroom teachers prefer to use multiple forms to note behaviors on different dates, others like to plot skills observed over time (by date) on the same page. Figure 5.10 (and related appendix resource) illustrates one way of recording ongoing observations. Teachers who plot skills over time may then color-code data by setting (playground, large group,

assessment *FREEZE FRAME 5.8*

Teachers who gather observational data frequently find it a powerful tool for measuring learning over time. This ability to aid ongoing instructional planning is a distinct advantage over most formal measures.

■ **figure 5.9** Student Oral Language Observation Matrix: SOLOM

Student Name _____ Grade _____ School _____

Language of Student _____ Rater Name _____ Total Score _____ Date _____

	1	2	3	4	5	Score
Comprehension	Cannot understand even simple conversation.	Has great difficulty following everyday social conversation, even when words are spoken slowly and repeated.	Understands most of what is said at slower than normal speed with some repetitions.	Understands nearly everything at normal speed, although occasional repetition may be necessary.	Understands everyday conversation and normal classroom discussion without difficulty.	
Fluency	Speech is so halting and fragmentary that conversation is virtually impossible.	Usually hesitant, often forced into silence because of language limitations.	Everyday conversation and classroom discussion frequently disrupted by student's search for correct manner of expression.	Everyday conversation and classroom discussion generally fluent, with occasional lapses while student searches for the correct manner of expression.	Everyday conversation and classroom discussion fluent and effortless; approximately those of a native speaker.	
Vocabulary	Vocabulary limitations so severe that conversation is virtually impossible.	Difficult to understand because of misuse of words and very limited vocabulary.	Frequent use of wrong words; conversation somewhat limited because of inadequate vocabulary.	Occasional use of inappropriate terms and/or rephrasing of the ideas because of limited vocabulary.	Vocabulary and idioms approximately those of a native speaker.	
Pronunciation	Pronunciation problems so severe that speech is virtually unintelligible.	Difficult to understand because of pronunciation problems; must frequently repeat in order to be understood.	Concentration required of listener; occasional misunderstandings caused by pronunciation problems.	Always intelligible, although listener conscious of a definite accent and occasional inappropriate intonation pattern.	Pronunciation and intonation approximately those of a native speaker.	
Grammar	Errors in grammar and word order so severe that speech is virtually unintelligible.	Difficult to understand because of errors in grammar and word order; must often rephrase or restrict speech to basic patterns.	Frequent errors in grammar and word order; meaning occasionally obscured.	Occasional errors in grammar or word order; meaning not obscured.	Grammar and word order approximately those of a native speaker.	

individual) or register (academic, social, with peer, or with adult) for a more holistic view of the student's language acquisition progress.

Observational matrices and rubrics such as the Student Written Language Observation Matrix (SWLOM) (California Department of Education, n.d.) are also helpful tools for assessing writing to inform placement decisions and track student progress. Teachers using such approaches may wish to identify representative yet varied samples of writing for different audiences, such as narratives or journals, before rating skills according to the matrix. Inconsistencies in performance, such as improved voice or sentence variety in journal or letter writing—as compared to essay attempts—can give teachers ideas for bridging strengths from one format to

■ **figure 5.10** Plotted Skills

Expressive Communication Rubric

Student Name **Karina T.**

Date(s) Completed: X above **9/22/05**   X below **2/28/06**

	Level 1	**Level 2**	**Level 3**	**Level 4**
Message effectiveness	Unable to understand intent/ meaning.	**X** Difficult to understand.	Able to understand most but not all of message. **X**	Message is easily understood.
Language structure	**X** Multiple errors with word order and grammar.	Noticeable errors but student able to convey aspects of the message. **X**	Uses mostly correct structures with some errors.	Use of language structures is similar to that of a native speaker.
Vocabulary	Incorrect word choices and/or limited vocabulary hinder social and academic communication.	**X** Relies on a limited range of vocabulary to communicate. **X**	Vocabulary is not usually conspicuous but is rarely specific or elaborate.	Varied types of words, including idioms, are used with facility.
Pronunciation	Speech is often unintelligible.	Speech is understandable with careful listening and known context.	**X** Speech is generally understandable to familiar and unfamiliar listeners.	Speech pronunciation is similar to that of a native speaker. **X**

another (e.g., "Write a letter to Joe about your book, and then we'll make it into a book report."). These tools can also be adapted to rate a student's writing ability in his or her primary language, as long as there are available personnel who are trained with the matrix and are both fluent and literate in the student's home language.

Narrative Assessment

The conditions in which a student produces a sample of oral language can significantly affect how well this language sample represents his or her actual language competence. Many linguists contrast a person's language competence—what she or he knows or can do—with language performance, or how this knowledge is used in a particular circumstance (Fromkin & Rodman, 1983; Freeman & Freeman, 2001). The best measures of language proficiency elicit student performance that genuinely reflects language competence. In nearly all cases, this involves going beyond standardized assessments to demonstrate how students use language in authentic, real-life situations. Such opportunities, which are easily found in the home with family and in unstructured social situations, can also exist at school when we create the right conditions. Narrative assessments often provide teachers with such opportunities.

The ability to develop cohesive narratives (storytelling structures) is a critical component of second language acquisition for several reasons. Of primary interest to educators, this skill is essential for literacy development that goes beyond associating sounds with symbols or letters and decoding words out of context. An underlying knowledge of narrative forms and structures helps students better understand both written passages and orally presented material. This knowledge enables the reader to skim text for essential content, as well as comprehend narrative formats used for informing or persuading.

There are many ways to look at and sample narrative language. Assessing a CLD student's ability to produce narratives in the primary language can provide

---

close-up *on Assessment 5.6*

Pitfalls of narrative assessment:

- Examiners may not be familiar with the discourse patterns of the CLD student's culture.
- Unfamiliar material used as a prompt may not be meaningful to the CLD student and may not generate a valid response.

Teacher tips for the successful elicitation of samples for narrative assessment:

- Give students a sample of what "telling a story" means.
- Use picture books or photos as narrative prompts.
- Focus on topics that students will readily understand or that hold great relevance for them.

valuable insights into foundational knowledge and skills. As mentioned earlier, this information can greatly aid instructional planning, especially when paired with measures of narrative development in the second language.

Activities and techniques for eliciting student narratives can yield especially rich samples of language. However, the type and quality of sample a student creates depends on a variety of variables. For example, teachers who are not fluent in the CLD student's language or comfortable with the discourse patterns of that culture often begin by encouraging L1 narratives using prompts that rely on simplified grammar and vocabulary. Students perceive the teacher's limitations and naturally respond by simplifying their vocabulary and sentence structures to better communicate with the teacher. Unfortunately, these efforts to facilitate communication may then be perceived as limitations of the student rather than the teacher. Such misperceptions can negatively affect a student's education, as the teacher who believes L1 skills are limited may fail to draw on the student's prior linguistic knowledge as a learning asset.

Because we so often use language to assess language, it is important to always consider how the teacher's own language skills, speaking style, choice of wording, and subject of conversation may influence a student's response. Not all classroom communication breakdowns are student-driven.

The material a teacher uses to stimulate a response should be meaningful to the student. The importance of this was underscored during a professional development exercise when teachers from the dominant culture were asked to write narratives about photographs of familiar (e.g., Statue of Liberty) and unfamiliar (e.g., India's Red Fort) cultural icons. These teachers demonstrated significant difficulty and frustration while writing about the unfamiliar icon. The following was excerpted from a participating teacher's reflection journal about the exercise.

When we began this assignment, I thought it was an interesting way to involve students in a group writing activity and something I might like to use in class. It seemed easy to think of words to describe the Statue of Liberty because I was so familiar with it and visited it last summer. Our group had fun brainstorming words and then writing the paragraph. I thought everyone was very proud of the symbolism the Statue of Liberty provides to the United States—a place of freedom, equality, beauty, diversity, opportunity and patriotism. I thought the paragraphs that each group wrote were extremely creative and enjoyable to hear.

As we looked at the second picture of the large stone building (India's Red Fort), I had a hard time thinking of descriptive words because I was unfamiliar with the building. Looking at it brought up no past experiences or memories, no feelings or ideas. I wondered why this picture had been chosen for the activity, as it seemed no one in the group knew what it was. I thought it was more difficult to compose the paragraph and did not feel the excitement to read it or hear others read as I had felt about the first picture. When we were told that the second picture was an important patriotic symbol for another country, I thought this must be how ELL students feel when given similar assignments related to U.S. culture.

During another group's discussion following this activity, one teacher mentioned that although she and other African Americans understood and appreciated the symbolism, not all would associate the Statue of Liberty with the idea of unequivocal freedom that was expressed by others. This comment enabled other teachers to see that perceptions and cultural experiences influence a student's ability to respond authentically (or as predicted by a teacher) to a given prompt.

There are many tips that classroom teachers should keep in mind when eliciting narratives from CLD students. In some cases, asking students to "tell me a story" is far too vague, unless the teacher provides the CLD student enough examples of the expected type of response. Examiners can provide samples or do a "walk through" (joint production) of an example story before expecting students to generate their own original narratives from a prompt. Other sources of inspiration for stories can include wordless picture books, videos or computer stories with no audio, news or magazine stories or photos, photos of class activities, and family photos. Topics might include recently viewed movies, television shows (Spanish language *novelas,* for example, have clearer story lines than English language soap operas), current events (especially dramatic ones), field trips, or significant events such as a recent fight between students. Although unpleasant, events such as fights can elicit excellent examples of settings and characters with unique attention to sequence, antecedent, consequence, problem, solution, and alternate ending. Wherever possible, it is worthwhile to document spontaneous narrative activities such as these, as they are often the best evidence of student skills.

Story Retelling Assessment

Story retelling is an alternative method of eliciting oral or written narratives from CLD students and is a common component of language proficiency assessments. For some students, story retelling facilitates language production. The opportunity to hear a story first provides a model that students can use for retelling the story and can reveal much about individual proficiency levels. Nonetheless, issues such as auditory memory, cultural norms, and task familiarity can confound the ability of other students to perform this essentially expressive task. Because factors other than targeted skills can have such a strong influence, some researchers argue against story retelling as a means of assessing linguistic ability (Gutierrez-Clellan & Quinn, 1993). This contention is supported by the research of MacSwan, Rolstad, and Glass (2002), who found that 20 percent of the 38,887 Spanish-speaking students sampled for their study (students who took the Spanish version of the IDEA Proficiency Test Preschool [IPT-P]) did not respond at all when prompted to retell a story. The inordinately high percentage of students who did not respond on this subtest suggests that teachers or examiners should consider alternative methods of eliciting narratives for students who don't "perform" under structured conditions.

In practice, there may be a number of reasons why students do not respond at all or with the desired detail when asked to retell a story they have just heard.

---

assessment *FREEZE FRAME* 5.9

Story retelling abilities among CLD students may be negatively affected by a variety of complicated factors other than the students' linguistic skills.

For instance, it is highly artificial and pragmatically inappropriate for the student to retell a story that the evaluator has just related. The evaluator can overcome this obstacle by asking the student to retell the story to another person, a puppet, or an audiotape. A student may also have an unclear understanding of the expected response, or the conditions, situation, or narrative format may be culturally unfamiliar or uncomfortable for the student. Teachers should be attuned to and inquire about evidence of narrative skills (e.g., telling jokes or stories, sharing anecdotes, describing movie plots) and proficiencies in other contexts, especially when assessing a relatively unschooled student. For example, the following vignette about Domingo illustrates how valuable home visits can be for assessing a CLD student's linguistic strengths and needs.

Domingo recently moved with his family from a rural part of Mexico where he received most of his schooling from itinerant teachers who periodically came through town to instruct various grade levels together for two to three months at a time. On entering the fifth grade in the United States, he had probably received fewer than two years of academic instruction in his primary language and had experienced this instruction inconsistently over a five-year period.

Domingo's ESL teacher found that he did poorly on the school's tests of native language ability. The counselor cautioned that, although they can raise language concerns, tests comprising academic vocabulary may not be fair indicators of Domingo's actual linguistic abilities. Domingo also performed poorly on assessments of Spanish achievement and was unable to retell the stories he had listened to on audiotape. Mr. Weiss, the classroom teacher, wondered whether Domingo's cognition and memory were too poor for him to participate in the full grade-level classroom curriculum, even with ESL support. In essence, Mr. Weiss became increasingly concerned that Domingo might be a candidate for special education. A bilingual social worker accompanied Mr. Weiss to Domingo's home to gather background information and prepare his parents for the anticipated evaluation of this apparently slow child.

During the interview, the school personnel were surprised to learn that Domingo was actually considered quite bright by his family. He had quickly learned to use the map that guided their move from Mexico and reliably estimated how far they could travel each day before needing more gas. By the time they reached Dallas, Domingo knew that ten dimes, four quarters, or twenty nickels equaled a dollar, and he spent the rest of the trip amusing himself with the number of combinations he could create with this new currency. According to his mom, Domingo still enjoyed mapping and planning fantasy trips on the well-worn map of their journey.

As Mr. Weiss listened to the mother's translated musings, he recognized the wry tone he used occasionally as he spoke of his own son's inclination toward "nerdiness." This was not, however, the Domingo he saw in school. As they wrapped up the interview, laughter erupted from Domingo, his father, and his uncle in the other room. Mom shook her head. "That Domingo knows so many jokes; every day he tells us another. One night he told my brother twenty-eight Pepito stories in a row," quickly adding, "He also knows the Bible stories; ask him any one." Mr. Weiss was dumbfounded but assured Domingo's mother that he would love to hear her son share similar talents in school. By the time they left, Domingo no longer seemed slow. Instead, he seemed to be a child with both significant educational needs and promise.

In a familiar and comfortable setting, CLD students who are acquiring English can often demonstrate skills and abilities they are unable, for whatever reason, to demonstrate in school. Students who have relatively little experience with the expectations and norms of the classroom setting—and who are at the same time learning another language—are doubly disadvantaged. Teachers of CLD students must often be quite creative to discover their students' true proficiencies and needs.

Written and Oral Cloze Assessments

Written and oral cloze assessments can also be used in a variety of ways to gather information about the student's progress in language acquisition and content-area learning. According to Ortiz (2004), the elements of most languages are remarkably redundant. As a result, we can comprehend messages that are distorted or missing a number of elements by accessing our prior knowledge and applying our understanding of the system for that language. Oral or written cloze tasks are often employed as components of language assessment on the premise that a student's knowledge of this language redundancy correlates highly with her or his overall proficiency in that language. There are multiple ways to construct oral and written cloze assessments. When a fixed ratio format is used, every *nth* (e.g., seventh) word is deleted throughout the passage. This is generally used to sample a student's more holistic knowledge of the language. However, teachers can choose to omit certain types of words, such as pronouns or past-tense verbs, to measure particular aspects of morphologic and syntactic development. Figure 5.11 is an example of a teacher-created, fixed ratio cloze assessment in which every eighth word is deleted.

Oral cloze tasks are constructed in much the same way as written cloze tasks but must be administered in person or with a recorded voice. Oral cloze assessments are powerful and highly adaptable ways to gather information about a student's emerging language acquisition and mastery of skills. They can help a student bridge simple recognition of language patterns with more accomplished linguistic skills and can facilitate the emergence of new skills. For example, such a process played out in Mrs. Wesley's class when Mrs. Moran, the ESL teacher, modeled semantic and auditory cues to a group of CLD students. As she increased group awareness of language patterns, Mrs. Moran also gained an enhanced sense of overall student progress in this area, as illustrated in the following vignette:

> Mrs. Moran, the ESL teacher, combined pull-out and in-class inclusion models to meet her students' needs. Mrs. Wesley, the first-grade teacher, asked Mrs. Moran for help teaching students to rhyme. She had tried *everything* to encourage them, but most just "didn't get it." Mrs. Moran was happy to plan her next whole-class lesson around this challenge and started by reading the rhyme-laden book *If You Give a Mouse a Cookie* (Numeroff, 1985). She read the first line of each rhyme and showed the correspond-

■ figure 5.11 Assessment Artifact: Written Cloze

Word Bank				
was	zoo	zebras	and	to
and	and	little	feet	elephants
they	with	monkeys	to	

On a hot and sunny day, Letica _____ her mother decided to go to the _____. They brought sunglasses, bottles of drinking water, _____ a camera. The first exhibit they saw _____ the home of two gray elephants. The _____ were enormous! They had huge ears, big _____, and very long trunks. Next they went _____ the building where the monkeys lived. Some _____ were busy eating and others were playing _____ old tires. Letica's favorite monkey was the _____ baby monkey. Letica and her mother continued _____ visit the many animals in the zoo. _____ took pictures of the lions, tigers, and _____. At the end of the trip, Letica _____ her mother were both very tired.

---

ing picture. Then, paying very close attention to cadence, she read the second line and paused ever so slightly before saying the final rhyming word.

By the fourth rhyme, some of the students were calling out the rhyming words. Mrs. Moran nodded and continued without breaking the gentle flow of the poem's meter. To close the lesson, students used props to retell the story together as Mrs. Moran probed other language skills, such as sequence and vocabulary.

Mrs. Wesley took notes as Mrs. Moran started a new activity by laying four of the props from the story in a row. The broom, comb, bed, and chair provided a limited range of familiar responses from which the students could choose their rhymes.

> **Mrs. Moran:** I like the way rhymes sound. Let's see if we can make some of our own. *Wake up, wake up you sleepy head, it's time to get up out of _____.*
> **Class:** Bed!
> **Mrs. Moran:** *If you're hungry, grab a pear, and then come sit down on a _____.*
> **Class:** Chair!
> **Mrs. Moran:** *But looking at this dirty room makes me want to use a _____.*
> **Class:** Broom!

The students responded well to this oral cloze format. It provided semantic cues as well as auditory patterns and limited choices. By the end of the session, students were also having fun completing oral cloze rhymes *without* visible choices (e.g., *My little brother likes to eat. His favorite food to eat is _____*). Mrs. Wesley was pleased to learn that 90 percent of the spontaneous and sometimes silly responses produced actually rhymed. After listening to one another's choices, the students developed a word bank of possible answers (*meat, wheat, feet, seat, beet,* and so forth), some of which they were now generating without the scaffold of an oral cloze prompt. By using this approach, Mrs. Wesley determined which students demonstrated language proficiency levels insufficient to support this skill and which students were indeed developmentally ready to recognize these auditory patterns, given appropriate methods and supports.

Oral cloze methods also work well in combination with story retelling. For example, Mrs. Moran knew that CLD students often provide limited initial responses when prompted to "retell a story." Therefore, when this occurred, she followed up by asking students to "help *me* with the story," which she began to retell using an oral cloze format with regularly spaced pauses. As she arrived at each of these pauses in the story, she gestured to students, asking them to fill in the missing word, and then continued. Pacing is important for maintaining a natural flow and aiding comprehension of the narrative context. Mrs. Moran knew from her experiences that most initially unresponsive students do well with this approach. In this case, most of the students provided appropriate answers, demonstrating both comprehension and retention of the original material. In this way, Mrs. Moran obtained important assessment information, as well as insights about those students unable to comprehend the task.

Mrs. Moran's oral cloze activities provided uniquely scaffolded instruction, allowing students to learn and practice new skills in story retelling. Many of the CLD students were then able to listen to a new story and retell it with sufficient attention to sequence and detail for the exercise to prove a valuable diagnostic assessment. As with all assessments, familiarity with the tasks involved is essential if story retelling assessments are to yield information that teachers can use to appropriately differentiate instruction.

Listening Skills Assessments

Listening skills can be assessed in a variety of contexts, but observers should be acutely aware of environmental cues that can facilitate a student's comprehension. When CLD students are unable to adequately comprehend the language of instruction, direction, or assessment, they more keenly attend to available physical, interpersonal, and nonverbal cues. Although this serves as a testament to their resourcefulness, it can also prompt the teacher to overestimate a student's second language comprehension and subsequently misinterpret his or her academic struggles. In other words, a student's excellent *overall* comprehension strategies could easily mislead a teacher to think that the student has better language skills than he or she actually has.

---

assessment *FREEZE FRAME* 5.10

A student's excellent *overall* comprehension strategies could easily mislead a teacher to think that the student has better language skills than he or she actually has.

Wherever possible, teachers should require CLD students to demonstrate listening skills in ways that do not involve spoken language (e.g., perform a task or make a physical signal of understanding). If, for example, a student's understanding of a story is evaluated solely on his or her ability to retell it or to answer questions about it (especially in L2), the teacher will likely find it virtually impossible to distinguish between the student's language skills and his or her comprehension. This is especially important when students are verbally limited in L2 but also applies to the performance of seemingly fluent CLD students and native English speakers as well. Although students may be talkative, it can be difficult to determine whether these students really understood the targeted material. Therefore, careful evaluation of CLD students' listening skills includes tasks that do not combine performance and skills in other domains, as well as those that do. The specifics of these tasks will, of course, vary greatly by grade level but may include:

1. Following oral instructions:
   —Give students simple one-step directions such as, "Get out a crayon."
   —Add modifiers such as, "Get out a *blue* crayon."
   —Increase the number of steps such as, "Open your health book and turn to page 14."
   —Gradually incorporate linguistic concepts (*of, unless, however, whether,* and so on) such as, "*Unless* you brought your lunch today, please line up at the door."
   —Direct students to perform an experiment or create a product while checking to see how students respond to step-by-step instructions. This process better assesses listening skills than does providing detailed instructions all at once (the latter is often a memory issue versus a language issue).
   —Ask students to relay instructions to a peer in the L2, or separate L2 listening skills from L2 verbal skills by having the CLD student relay his or her understanding of L2 instructions to a peer in the L1.
2. Responding to questions:
   —Students answer yes/no questions orally, with a head shake or nod, or thumbs up/thumbs down.
   —Provide the CLD student with a closed set of responses from which to orally or physically select an answer (e.g., pictures, words, or sentences from which to choose; questions phrased with modeled choices such as, "Who invented the light bulb, Edison or Einstein?").
3. Demonstrating curricular learning:
   —Have students identify main characters, story sequence, problem/resolution, or content-area answers by pointing to or otherwise nonverbally selecting depictions of the appropriate response.
   —Direct students to create a picture or product representing a core concept.
   —Have students use graphic organizers to display pictorial or written understanding of concepts or relationships.

Among the more authentic ways to assess the listening skills of a CLD student are situations in which the student's ability to perform a task requires him or her to effectively integrate listening skills and clarification strategies. These barrier activities involve one student giving another student directions to perform a task or to replicate a design, despite a physical barrier (e.g., open file folder, piece of cardboard) that prevents one student from seeing the other's referent. Barrier

Accommodative Assessment Practices 5.1

Mrs. Falcon enjoys differentiating her science lessons for a diverse class of CLD and special education learners. She carefully reviews all available records and intentionally observes how each student responds to her multilevel lessons. Within a single week, she learns that Karina understands concepts better when they are explained verbally. On the other hand, Jared is far more visual. He has already amazed the class by doodling impressively accurate replicas of the plant and animal cells that they had seen only briefly on an overhead slide. Mrs. Falcon has also noted that despite Lissette's blank stare when called on to answer questions during the lesson, Lissette excitedly pointed to everything that Jared named during a discussion of his drawing.

■ *How might these observations inform the way Mrs. Falcon teaches and assesses Karina, Jared, and Lissette? In what ways might she adapt her classroom instruction to best accommodate the needs and assets these students bring to the classroom?*

activities compel students to draw on and value active listening skills that are not commonly addressed in traditional classrooms. Some teachers may actually de-emphasize these skills during classroom instruction or assessment. One of the most powerful features of barrier activities is that, after initial training and modeling, such activities promote engagement and skill building with very little input or interference from the teacher.

In the following example, Josue and Abram work as a team to help their sophomore ESL class win a pizza party—but the students only win pizza when everyone in the class successfully completes the task. The students are highly motivated as each person in each pair takes turns as either the player or the observer.

Josue and Abram's first attempt to identically arrange five geometric shapes ended in surprise disaster. As they worked together, they felt sure they would win. However, they didn't realize until the final moment that failure to clarify had led to fundamental misunderstandings neither had recognized while they had been working together. Their teacher, Mr. Sing, loved it when students discovered this for themselves. He had often wondered how frequently these miscommunications occur in teaching and learning. Over the years, Mr. Sing had noted with concern how many CLD students did not actively listen or seek clarification regarding unfamiliar, ambiguous, or confusing material. He had begun to speculate on whether the students had become accustomed to simply "getting the gist," even though their language skills had developed sufficiently for deeper comprehension.

As a rule, Mr. Sing praised those students who asked for definitions of unfamiliar words as he taught, and he had been known to intentionally use nonsensical terms just to see who was listening. He encouraged all his students to ask clarifying questions because he believed it was the students' job to listen with their *mind* as well as *ears*—to listen to understand, recognize when they did not comprehend, and do something about it.

Josue and Abram had been watching other teams win and lose just as they had, but they were ready to try again. Josue considered the twenty shapes of varied form, size, and color. He only needed to use five. It seemed so easy.

Josue: Take the big yellow rectangle and put it in the middle.

Abram: The one that looks like a box or a French fry?

Josue: The rectangle. It's long from top to bottom and skinny side to side. Yeah, it looks kinda like a French fry.

Abram: Okay, I got it. Put it in the middle?

Josue: Yeah. (*Remembering another team's problem*) Make it vertical.

Abram: Vertical?

Josue: Vertical is up and down like a basketball pole.

Abram: Okay, I put the big, yellow rectangle up and down, vertical . . . in the middle.

Josue: Take the medium-sized purple circle and put it on top.

Abram: On top of what? The paper?

Josue: Put the purple circle on top of the yellow rectangle.

Abram: On top . . . in the middle?

Josue: No, not touching it . . . on top . . . *above* it, like a lollipop.

By the time all five pieces were in place, Abram and Josue had practiced academic listening and natural clarification skills, with repetition that was natural to the context of the activity. Mr. Sing assessed Abram as having grown so much in clarification ability that he planned to pair Abram next with Saul, who still did not recognize communication breakdowns. The students were becoming more aware of their own learning as they were motivated to earn the pizza party. Mr. Sing planned to later add a sphere, rhombus, cylinder, cube, and cone to their list of choices for this exercise.

Like Mr. Sing, many teachers find it easier to plan language assessment when they identify the linguistic demands of their curriculum. These insightful teachers also look at the activities they already use and determine how they might also be used as a means of assessment.

■ Formal Assessment of Language Proficiency

The formal assessment of CLD students whose primary language is not English has become a recurrent focus of policymaking, research, reform, and debate in education. Educational reform initiatives, especially those at the federal level, are often the impetus behind these trends in education. The most recent of these reform initiatives have advocated standardized formal assessments, the results of which are thought to be comparable across school districts and across states. Consequently, the emphasis of language programming for CLD students is increasingly grounded in standardized assessments of language proficiency. Linn and Miller (2005) have distinguished standardized formal assessments as those that are designed by specialists and then administered, scored, and interpreted for relevant stakeholders under standard conditions.

Accordingly, this chapter first summarizes the nature of those standardized formal assessments that tend to be the most widely used in U.S. public schools. Related discussion explores key issues surrounding the use of these standardized language proficiency assessments in professional practice with CLD students.

Standardized Formal Assessments of Language Proficiency

Federal legislation often stipulates that schools must meet certain requirements in assessing the English language proficiency of CLD students who are acquiring English. These criteria seek to enhance the alignment of instruction, learning, and assessment while increasing school and district accountability for student success. Standardized tests are usually a key component of recommended guidelines. This can move the focus of language assessment from communicative authenticity (informal assessments) to the type of validity attributed to well-developed standardized assessments (formal assessments). However, both types of assessment provide important information for identification, placement, monitoring, and exit from alternative language programs.

A variety of formal assessments are available and have been used to assess different aspects of language proficiency. These generally include specific tasks designed to measure students' listening, speaking, reading, and writing capabilities. Most formal assessments are not conducted by classroom teachers and are, therefore, beyond the scope of this text. However, intuitive teachers of CLD students use the results of such assessments in planning and delivering accommodative classroom instruction. Accordingly, these teachers learn about the nature of formal assessments used by their school district, as well as general guidelines for interpreting the student outcome reports (results) generated by these assessments. Table 5.1 provides examples of formal assessments of language proficiency. Classroom teachers are encouraged to visit the testing agency's website or contact the agency's commercial or institutional representative for more specific information about particular versions of formal standardized assessments.

Formal standardized attempts to measure the language proficiency of CLD students often involve administering essentially monolingual tests in two or more languages. Although this does provide significant information about separate language skills, these assessments may not tell us much about the differential language use and skills that influence effective communication for bilingual speakers in either language. In addition, although some of these assessments are available in languages other than Spanish or English, most standardization and comparability instruments are constructed around these two languages.

Some formal language assessments have been developed to permit bilingual CLD students to demonstrate more holistic language knowledge and competency. Generally, this means that students are assessed in one language and are either simultaneously or sequentially prompted to provide missing or incorrect information in the alternate language. These approaches are based largely on Cummins's (1984, 1996) conceptualization of a bilingual person's common underlying proficiency. They operate on the theory that a CLD student's structural and communicative language knowledge is best demonstrated through assessment in contexts in which

■ table 5.1   Formal Assessments of Language Proficiency

Language Assessment	Key Characteristics
Preschool Language Assessment Scale (Pre-LAS 2000) (Duncan & DeAvila, 1998)	This assessment is designed to measure the developing language and preliteracy skills of preschool-age children in order to inform the placement of these young language learners into the most appropriate classroom settings. It is available in English and Spanish.
Language Assessment Scale—Oral (LAS—O) (Duncan & DeAvila, 1990)	This assessment measures the listening and speaking skills of students in grades 1 through 6 and 7 through 12. Like the Pre-LAS, it is available in English or Spanish and is useful in assessing primary language development or to identify students for placement in, and exit from, bilingual/ESL programs. The LAS—O contains an optional observation form that can be completed by another examiner to further support or triangulate findings used to determine whether a student is be ready for redesignation.
Language Assessment Scale—Reading/Writing (LAS—R/W) (Duncan & DeAvila, 1990)	This assessment measures reading and writing skills in English or Spanish L1 ability levels. It may be used to identify students for placement in, and exit from, bilingual or ESL programs. The test combines selected response and writing sample evaluations to assess vocabulary, fluency, reading comprehension, mechanics, and usage.
IDEA Proficiency Test (IPT) (Ballard & Tighe, 2004)	This assessment offers oral, reading, and writing versions available in Spanish and English. It is also designed to assess both social and academic language. Like other assessments of this type, the IPT may be used to measure primary language skills but is most often employed for the identification, placement, and (re)classification of CLD students who are acquiring English in appropriate classroom contexts.
Woodcock-Muñoz Language Survey Revised (WMLS-R) (Woodcock, Muñoz-Sandoval, Ruef, & Alvaredo, 2005)	This assessment is another popular measure of Spanish and English that comes with a computerized scoring program. This scoring program generates a narrative that describes the student's cognitive academic language proficiency (CALP) in English or Spanish, or the relative proficiency between languages if both versions of the test are administered.
Maculaitis Assessment of Competencies II (MAC II) (Touchstone Applied Science, 2001)	This assessment evaluates the English proficiency of K–12 students through a variety of subtests designed to measure speaking, listening, reading, and writing. A ten-minute screening test can be used to assist schools with the placement of CLD students in any grade.
Stanford English Language Proficiency (SELP) assessment (Harcourt Assessment, 2003)	This assessment was developed to measure and align the reading, writing, listening, and speaking skills of CLD students with curricular standards. This assessment measures both the academic and social language of students in grades K–12. A five-minute screening version of the SELP also exists for students who lack sufficient English skills to take the full assessment. This version can be used to support decisions to appropriately exempt particular students from certain assessments, or as a quick placement screen pending more comprehensive assessment.

both languages are accessed, even though one language may be dominant. These assessments are standardized and have been normed using performances of similar bilingual students under similar conditions. Such norming better accounts for relevant linguistic and cultural factors. Two assessments of this kind are the Dos Amigos Verbal Language Scale and the Bilingual Verbal Ability Tests Normative Update.

The Dos Amigos Verbal Language Scale (Critchlow, 1996) is easily administered and uses eighty-five pairs of opposites in Spanish and English to measure conceptual linguistic knowledge. Qualitative results provide information about relative proficiency in each language. The provision for qualitative interpretation also facilitates a more holistic picture of proficiency levels in the two languages as they are demonstrated separately and in unison. This is significant because bilingual students often exhibit a home and community vocabulary in the primary language that is broader than the academic vocabulary they can demonstrate in English. Therefore, assessing language proficiency in one language alone can provide misleading information about the student's overall vocabulary knowledge.

Analyzing response differences and performance can also demonstrate whether the student is accessing L1 knowledge to help him or her process concepts in L2. For instance, a student may correctly respond that "*blanco*" is the opposite of "*negro*." However, the same student may respond to the English prompt that the opposite of "*black*" is "*brown*." Such responses indicate that the student can use words to make the targeted conceptual connection in the L1 but does not yet grasp L2 words in ways that demonstrate a similar level of processing.

The Bilingual Verbal Ability Tests Normative Update (BVAT-NU) (Muñoz-Sandoval, Cummins, Alvaredo, Ruef, & Schrank, 2005) also takes into consideration both the native and second language and comprises three subtests from the Woodcock-Johnson III Tests of Achievement (Woodcock, McGrew, & Mather, 2001) that have been translated into eighteen languages (now including Hmong and Navajo). The BVAT scoring software generates a report that differentiates among the student's bilingual verbal ability, CALP skills, and relative language proficiency in languages assessed.

For some CLD students who are acquiring a second language or are using their first language less, there may be a significant difference between their expressive and their receptive skills. This disparity may not show up on assessments that measure all language competencies with tasks requiring a verbal response. Being aware of this disparity can help the classroom teacher plan lessons that are comprehensible at higher levels and still provide necessary supports and modifications for verbal participation.

Examples of assessments developed to separate the receptive and expressive domains are the Receptive One-Word Picture Vocabulary Test (ROWPVT) (Brownell, 2000b) and its companion, the Expressive One-Word Picture Vocabulary Test (EOWPVT) (Brownell, 2000a). These assessments, originally developed for English speakers, have been translated into Spanish and are normed on bilingual students in the United States. Like the BVAT, these assessments score students' relative proficiency and comparable skills in both Spanish and English.

State-Developed or State-Adopted Variations of Standardized Formal Assessments

In response to state and federal accountability requirements, as well as historic inconsistency in state testing practices, there is a growing trend among states to develop (or subcontract the development of) their own assessments for CLD students who are acquiring English. The following discussion highlights the efforts of selected states.

The California English Language Development Test (CELDT) (California Department of Education, Revised annually) is one example of a state test designed to assess the English language proficiency of students whose home language is not English. Before the CELDT, districts in California were free to choose from a variety of state-approved assessments of language proficiency, most of which were commercially produced. However, as in other states with such policies, California experienced problems arising from a lack of uniform assessment criteria and the inability to compare results of dissimilar assessments across districts. Like the assessments it replaces, the primary purpose of the CELDT is to identify students whose first language is not English, monitor their progress, serve as one criterion for redesignation, and provide informative data for gauging program effectiveness.

The state of Washington responded similarly by adopting the Washington Language Proficiency Test (WLPT) (MetriTech, 2002) as its statewide reading and writing assessment. This test serves as a companion to the state's oral language proficiency test. Although the WLPT assesses English language proficiency, the instructions for the assessment may be presented more comprehensibly in the student's primary language. This is a commonly recommended practice for ensuring that the results more genuinely reflect language proficiency, as opposed to reflecting student confusion about testing procedures and expectations.

In 2005 the state of Kansas adopted the Kansas English Language Proficiency Assessment (KELPA), developed by the Center for Educational Testing and Evaluation (CETE), which is affiliated with the University of Kansas. The KELPA was normed on CLD, English-language-acquiring students from across the state and was reviewed by a council of non-native-English-speaking adults from diverse cultural and linguistic backgrounds. The purpose of these reviews was to identify and eliminate culturally biased items. The KELPA is aligned with English for Speakers of Other Languages (ESOL) standards for Kansas and assesses proficiency in listening, speaking, reading, and writing.

Interpreting the Results of Standardized Language Proficiency Assessments

Formal standardized assessments of second language proficiency generally measure a CLD student's competency with targeted skills such as reading, writing, speaking, or listening. The results are reasonably assumed to represent new learning and are used to compare individual or group growth toward the standard on which it is based. In best practice, second language proficiency assessments should rarely be interpreted to infer anything about a student's innate linguistic or cognitive abilities.

Unfortunately, the results of language proficiency assessments are not always interpreted cautiously, especially when the assessment is administered in the student's primary language. Although there are certainly reasons to gather information about a CLD student's primary language, relying on formal assessments or inappropriate testing procedures can lead to erroneous findings, inaccurate assumptions, and the potentially harmful placement of CLD students.

For example, it is not uncommon for students who were raised in bilingual U.S. communities to perform poorly on language proficiency assessments (for languages other than English) that were developed and normed in countries outside the United States. This is especially true if these students received classroom instruction only in English. When combined with apparent evidence of a student's limited English proficiency, these results are sometimes misinterpreted to indicate innate language or learning problems. In reality, the results more often reflect cross-cultural discontinuities or differing expectations and norms across educational systems. Educators should carefully examine the normative basis of such assessments to ensure that they are valid for the population of students served. By giving serious consideration to the appropriateness of assessments and by being knowledgeable about language acquisition variables, we help ensure that results actually lead to unbiased instructional decisions and practices.

Not all standardized assessments of language proficiency are created equal. Some may be designed with vocabulary or constructs seemingly unrelated to classroom goals and objectives. For example, a newly ESL-endorsed elementary teacher was dismayed after closely reviewing a common language proficiency test:

> My husband . . . and I and several other teachers in my building didn't have a clue what several of the [English] vocabulary words mean. If the students I tested got less than half of these words right and adults don't have a clue what many of the words are either, what is this test really testing?

Other problematic content or stimuli include culturally or experientially narrow items (e.g., picture prompts of men panning for gold), which inevitably measure content-area knowledge as well as language.

Effective teachers of CLD students are also concerned with the currency of language proficiency assessments. They check to ensure that the pictures and references in an assessment are relevant to modern-day life. For example, classroom teachers often report that many students misidentify pictures of televisions and typewriters as computers. Others do not recognize pictures of bar soap. Similarly, CLD students often arrive with varied experiences and provide alternate answers that make sense to them (and indeed demonstrate the targeted skills), only to have these answers marked incorrect on the assessment. Examiners should scrutinize both the assessment and the student's performance. It is critical to reflect on what each assessment actually measures, as well as on student skills the assessment may fail to take into account.

Additional Complicating Variables in Standardized Formal Assessment

Standardized assessments should be administered in a consistent manner to promote reliable comparisons between students and groups. Teachers and test administrators should be aware of variables that affect the reliability of formal assessments. These variables include, but are not limited to:

Variables of Administration:

- Effective professional development in proper and unbiased assessment administration
- Fluency in the language of assessment
- Rapport with students (to decrease their anxiety and build confidence)

Variables of Situation:

- Deficiencies in the setting (such as a room that is noisy or distracting, too warm or cold, etc.)
- Unfavorable assessment times (such as during normal recess period, rest time, or immediately before or after a holiday)
- Linguistic climate (such as whether students have positive and "comfortable" feelings about using the targeted language)

Although this list is not exhaustive, it does exemplify influences that can skew assessment results. Accordingly, teachers and other educators should always consider the context of assessments before making decisions based on them.

■ Further Considerations

The purpose of increased accountability is to ensure that all children have a legitimate opportunity to succeed in school and that their educational needs are not brushed aside. Educational reform efforts attempt to target inequities in student learning through measures that hold schools and school districts accountable for student academic success. Nevertheless, this drive for accountability, in turn, fosters an increased emphasis on standardized testing—an effort that often fails to measure relevant progress or achieve intended results. Consequently, reflective teachers are increasingly uncomfortable with accountability and assessment measures that have questionable validity with CLD students.

As this chapter discusses, language can be defined in so many ways and along so many continua that there is no one agreed-upon set of skills that truly reflects this amazing human gift. Therefore, it is not uncommon to find that different language assessment developers have chosen radically different tasks to measure the same skill (for example, language comprehension). This, along with the fact that many language assessment developers customize their assessments to align with individual state standards, reminds us that we must always critically analyze and reflect on assessment results. The best way to know what our language proficiency assessments are—and *are not*—telling us, as well as how reliably they inform us about CLD student learning, is to consistently align their findings with other assessments of language performance and achievement.

Programming-Related Issues: Language Proficiency Assessment

Necessarily, issues of placement and programming for CLD students who are acquiring English as a second language are topics beyond the scope of this text. Nonetheless, the results of assessing acculturation, content-area skills and knowledge, and, in particular, language proficiency can aid decision making associated with these issues. Therefore, the following discussion highlights salient, grade-level issues of language proficiency assessment that are relevant to the identification, placement, monitoring, and exit of CLD students. This discussion is by no means exhaustive but provides a synopsis of issues that should be considered.

Identification

Assessing English language proficiency is critical in determining whether a CLD student can participate in the curriculum without additional supports. This determination should be, but is not always, based on a combination of factors, including standardized assessment results, informal assessment outcomes, observation, and parent and teacher input. Students whose English language proficiency does not meet stated criteria are often identified as limited English proficient and are, as a result, entitled to instructional modifications and access to alternative language programs designed to alleviate language issues in content-area learning.

Placement

Careful consideration of language proficiency data and academic skills, combined with knowledge of available programs (e.g., transitional bilingual, dual language, content-based ESL), is necessary for identifying the setting that will provide the CLD student maximum access to the curriculum. The appropriateness of student placement is determined through ongoing assessment of language acquisition, social adjustment, and curricular learning.

Monitoring

Alternate versions of formal assessments that can be readministered at midyear provide a useful update on student progress and can help determine whether to reassign a student to grade-level classes. Informal assessment approaches and other forms of data gathering discussed earlier are also vital in helping teachers monitor student status and progress relative to changing curricular demands.

Exit

The redesignation of CLD English-language-learning students has the potential to affect perceived student or program success. Students must typically meet language

Teachers can use a portfolio to clearly document a CLD student's BICS and CALP development in all four language domains (i.e., listening, speaking, reading, and writing). A portfolio is the most comprehensive method of understanding both the assets and the needs of these students. The following checklist can be used in the ongoing assessment and monitoring of language skills.

Portfolio/Cumulative Folder Checklist

Items to be included:			Date
Interview or Parent Survey on Language Use			
Home Language Survey			
Initial LAS Test			
Subsequent LAS Tests	Grade	Score	
	K	/	
	1st	/	
	2nd	/	
	3rd	/	
	4th	/	
	5th	/	
CLD Student Background Survey			
BICS Evaluation (L1 & L2)			
CALP Evaluation (L1 & L2)			
Native Language:			
Literacy Screening (grades K–5)			
Reading Benchmark (grades 3–5)			
Writing Sample (grades 3–5)			
English Language:			
Literacy Screening (grades K–5)			
Reading Levels (grades 3–5)			
Early Writing Assessment			
Cognitive Learning Strategy Use			

proficiency and academic criteria to be exited from the ELL (or LEP) designation. Because higher-performing students who exit a language program are continually replaced by lower-proficiency students entering the program, it is nearly impossible for this group as a whole to demonstrate the type of adequate yearly progress required by state or federal mandates. In response to this issue, some states are enacting policies to keep redesignated students in this ELL category for up to two years (Abedi, 2004). However, other states may simply delay the redesignation of qualified students. This practice effectively denies otherwise capable students access to a more appropriate and challenging curriculum (Abedi & Dietel, 2004).

In California the passage of Proposition 227, which mandates English-only education, was promoted as a means to more rapid attainment of English language proficiency (Unz & Tuchman, n.d.). Supporters of this initiative anticipated faster acquisition of English and one- to two-year transitions of students to English-only classroom instruction. However, in a study of emerging data on the reclassification of ELL students, Grissom (2004) has noted, "State law asserts that ELL designation should not normally exceed one year, but after four or five years of schooling, only 30 percent of ELL students had been reclassified" (p. 10). These findings are consistent with those of Thomas and Collier (2002), who found no significant changes in California's English achievement among students designated as ELL following the implementation of Proposition 227. In fact, the indications are that this initiative has not resulted in the quick transitions to English-only instruction anticipated by its proponents.

The complexities of English language acquisition have proved relatively unresponsive to methods or techniques to accelerate the process (Thomas & Collier, 2002; Hakuta, Butler, & Witt, 2000). Therefore, educators are well advised to consider multilevel educational and linguistic criteria, rather than political agendas, to determine when students are ready to participate in the full curriculum of an English-only classroom environment. To effectively improve education for CLD students, these decisions must be based on student needs and current best practices.

■ key concepts

Anecdotal logs	First language proficiency	Parent interviews
Barrier activities	Formal language assessment	Phonology
Basic interpersonal communication skills (BICS)	Home language surveys	Pragmatics
	Informal language assessment	Rubrics
Cloze assessments	Language competence	Second language proficiency
Cognitive academic language proficiency (CALP)	Language performance	Semantics
	Listening skills assessment	Silent period
Common underlying proficiency (CUP)	Matrices	Story retelling assessment
	Morphology	Style shifting
Communicative competence	Narrative assessment	Syntax

■ professional conversations on practice

1. Discuss rationales for assessing primary language proficiencies of CLD students whose first language is not English. How does the notion of CUP underscore the need to assess these proficiencies?

2. Discuss why structural knowledge of a second language is necessary, but not sufficient, for proficiency in that language.

3. Discuss why classroom teachers of CLD students whose first language is not English should know how to interpret and implement the findings of formal standardized language proficiency assessments.

4. Discuss why classroom teachers of CLD students should use home visits and the valuable information gleaned from them. Are there advantages for CLD parents or guardians as well? If so, what are some of these advantages?

5. Discuss types of formal standardized language proficiency assessments and the importance of ensuring that these assessments have been normed on similar bilingual students assessed under similar conditions.

■ questions for review and reflection

1. What are at least two rationales for assessing native language proficiency of CLD students whose first language is not English?

2. How is CUP involved in the transfer of knowledge and language skills from the CLD student's primary language to a second language?

3. How can assessing the English language (L2) proficiency of a CLD student benefit the teacher in planning and delivering classroom instruction?

4. What are the five subsystems of language? List and describe each.

5. How can minor phonemic distinctions between English and other languages cause problems when assessing CLD students whose first language is not English?

6. Which language subsytem may require a lifetime of ongoing development and refinement? Why?

7. How can the pragmatics of languages make it difficult to assess CLD students in English?

8. What are the similarities and differences between structural and communicative knowledge of a language?

9. Why is it difficult to rely on a single sample of a CLD student's second language proficiency? How do cross-cultural differences contribute to these difficulties?

10. What are the strengths and weaknesses of home language surveys for data collection? List and describe each.

11. What are at least three advantages of a home visit for collecting data about the background experiences and language proficiency of a CLD student whose first language is not English? List and describe each.

12. What are at least three advantages of parent or guardian interviews as informal assessments of language proficiency? List and describe each.

13. What are the advantages of matrices or rubrics for informally collecting data about language proficiency?

14. What are at least two reasons why the ability to develop cohesive narratives is critical to second language acquisition? List and describe each.

15. What are potential problems with story retelling as a means for informally assessing language proficiencies of CLD students whose first language is not English? What can classroom teachers do to avoid these pitfalls?

16. What factors may prompt classroom teachers to overestimate the second language abilities of CLD students whose first language is not English? (Be specific.) What are the implications for assessing listening skills?

17. What are at least three formal standardized assessments of language proficiency? List and briefly describe each.

18. Why have some states developed their own formal standardized assessments of English language proficiency?

19. What are at least three variables that may influence the reliability of formal language proficiency assessments? List and describe each.

objectives

- Discuss why content-area assessments are often underemphasized in classroom practices for CLD students.
- Differentiate between formative and summative content-area assessments.
- Discuss types of informal formative assessments available to grade-level teachers of CLD students.
- Describe the advantages of self-assessment for CLD students.
- Discuss the merits and concerns of using technology-based assessments with CLD students.
- Discuss types of portfolios that grade-level teachers can use for informally and summatively assessing content-area learning of CLD students.
- Describe how grade-level teachers and CLD students can collaborate on the organization and content of an assessment portfolio.
- Discuss the types of formal formative assessments available to grade-level teachers of CLD students.
- List questions grade-level teachers should consider while interpreting formal formative assessment results of content-area learning.
- Discuss the influence of high-stakes tests on the types of formal summative assessment teachers conduct in the classroom.
- Discuss the merits and concerns of using high-stakes tests to formally and summatively assess content-area learning.

Assessment of Content-Area Learning

When students' language, culture and experience are ignored or excluded in classroom interactions, students are immediately starting from a disadvantage. Everything they have learned about life and the world up to this point is being dismissed as irrelevant to school learning; there are few points of connection to curriculum materials or instruction and so students are expected to learn in an experiential vacuum. Students' silence and nonparticipation under these conditions have frequently been interpreted as lack of academic ability or effort; and teachers' interactions with student have reflected their low expectations for these students, a pattern that becomes self-fulfilling.

Jim Cummins, *Negotiating Identities: Education for Empowerment in a Diverse Society*

chapter outline

Formative Content-Area Assessment
Informal Formative Assessment
Formal Formative Assessment

Summative Content-Area Assessment
Informal Summative Assessment:
Portfolios as Authentic Assessments
Formal Summative Assessment:
High-Stakes Tests

The Role of Language in Content-Area Assessment

Bias in Classroom-Based Content-Area Assessments

Programming-Related Issues: Content-Area Assessment
Identification
Placement
Monitoring
Exit

---

critical standards *Guiding Chapter Content*

TESOL/NCATE teacher standards reflect professional consensus on standards for the quality teaching of PreK–12 CLD students. Additionally, the CEEE Guiding Principles and their accompanying indicators serve as a framework to assist practitioners, policymakers, and clients as they collaborate to enhance academic enrichment and language acquisition among CLD students. Therefore, to help educators understand how they might appropriately target and address national professional teaching standards in practice, we have designed the content of this chapter to reflect the following standards.

TESOL/NCATE Standards for P–12 Teacher Education Programs

Domain 4: Assessment. Candidates understand issues of assessment and use standards-based assessment measures with ESOL students.

- **Standard 4.b.** Language Proficiency Assessment. Candidates know and can use a variety of standards-based language proficiency instruments to inform their instruction, and understand their uses for identification, placement, and demonstration of language growth of ESOL students.

    4.b.1. Understand and implement national and state requirements for identification, reclassification, and exit of ESOL students from language support programs.

    4.b.3. Understand, develop, and use criterion-referenced assessments appropriately with ESOL learners.

    4.b.4. Understand, construct, and use assessment measures for a variety of purposes for ESOL students.

    4.b.5. Assess ESOL learners' language skills and communicative competence using multiple sources of information.

Note: All TESOL/NCATE Standards are cited from TESOL (2003). All Guiding Principles are cited from Center for Equity and Excellence in Education (CEEE) (2005). Reprinted by permission.

- **Standard 4.c.** Classroom-Based Assessment for ESL. Candidates know and use a variety of classroom and performance-based assessment tools that are standards-based to inform instruction.

  4.c.2. Use various instruments and techniques to assess content-area learning (e.g., math, science, social studies) for ESOL learners at varying levels of language and literacy development.

CEEE Guiding Principles

Principle #5: English language learners are evaluated with appropriate and valid assessments that are aligned to state and local standards and that take into account the language development stages and cultural backgrounds of the students.

5.1 **Assess** English language learners on the same content and according to the same performance standards as all students, varying the assessment as needed to accommodate the individual characteristics of the learner, including, but not limited to, the student's level of English language proficiency.

5.45 **Employ** culturally and developmentally appropriate, authentic, criterion-referenced, and other alternative assessment instruments that are capable of measuring gains in content-area academic knowledge and English language proficiency.

5.10 **Use** a variety of formal and authentic assessment techniques to enhance classroom knowledge of English language learners and to evaluate their academic and linguistic progress.

Professional organizations as well as state and local education agencies have responded to legislative initiatives that target public education (e.g., NCLB) with the development of overarching standards of achievement, which are used to measure student progress and align instruction. Such standards are intended to provide guidance, consistency, and accountability for what is taught in U.S. classrooms, regardless of the setting, teaching style, and student demographics. As a result of such initiatives, teachers are held accountable for the achievement of *all* students, including historically excluded groups such as CLD students whose first language is not English and those with disabilities (Herrera & Murry, 2004; Lara & August, 1996). The initial reaction of many educators is one of dismay followed by resistance. Others try to embrace the challenge of creating learning environments that actively involve and enrich all students.

Although content-area assessments are essential to the teacher's monitoring of CLD student progress toward the mastery of academic standards, they are, nonetheless, sometimes underemphasized and underestimated in their particular value for these students. In many cases, this is because there is a sense that language is the paramount issue that must be addressed before academic knowledge can or should be measured in the classroom. Most teachers readily recognize the difficulties that language can present to student achievement. However, in their efforts to address these challenges, teachers may create an imbalance in their instruction. That is, they may tend to follow either an inadvertent or an intentional focus on language development opportunities and objectives they deem prerequisite. In the process, these teachers may overlook the importance of the acquisition of core, grade-level concepts among CLD students. Although teachers may have the best of intentions, such actions and emphases may actually widen the learning gap for CLD students (Thomas & Collier, 2002; Ramírez, Yuen, Ramey, & Pasta, 1991).

An examination of what we know about first language acquisition reveals that there is a developmental time line to the process that cannot be significantly accelerated, regardless of our best efforts (Chomsky, 1968; Owens, 2001). There has yet to be found any form of intervention or degree of stimulation that will dramatically hasten the process of first language acquisition for our children. Although the level of L2 acquisition positively correlates with academic success, we also know that it generally requires a minimum of five to seven years for students to learn a second language to the level necessary for full academic application. Those without opportunities for L1 instructional support may require eight to ten years to reach that level of readiness (Thomas & Collier, 1997, 2002). If teachers withhold content instruction until students gain this level of English fluency, CLD students will find it extremely difficult to catch up to their native-English-speaking peers.

> **assessment FREEZE FRAME 6.1**
>
> Postponing content-area instruction until CLD students gain academic language skills widens the achievement gap between these learners and their native-English-speaking peers.

Content-area assessment is essential to inform us about how well CLD students are learning academic material during the period in which they are also acquiring English. Given the myriad languages, cultures, and backgrounds of our students, a great deal of reflection and planning is needed as teachers find ways to access, uncover, and maximize the content-area skills and knowledge that CLD students already bring to the learning environment. In their discussion of these and related issues, Eaker, DuFour, and Burnette (2002, p. 41) have suggested the following, relevant questions:

> What do we want students to learn?
> How will we know if they have learned it?
> What are we going to do if they do not learn it?

Such questions help guide and align our standards-based instruction, but the answers may not be nearly as instructive for CLD students unless we also ask:

> Under what conditions (levels of support) does each particular student learn?
> What can the students do with what they have learned?

Stiggins (2002, p. 758) acknowledges the learner's ability to drive his or her own instruction and asks us to further consider:

> How can we use assessment to help all our students *want* to learn?
> How can we help them feel *able* to learn?

Assessments that are (a) aligned with standards and curricula; (b) chosen, developed, or accommodated to be reliable indicators of learning; and (c) valued by students and teachers for their authenticity will illuminate the answers to these types of questions. This chapter focuses on the measurement of content-area learning of CLD students. Content-area assessments are usually described as either formative or summative, and may in either case be informal or formal. We explore the value of using different types of assessments in different ways, and at different times, to better understand the dynamic relationship between teaching and learning while also preparing students to demonstrate their knowledge and skills on high-stakes tests.

■ Formative Content-Area Assessment

Formative assessments are tools and strategies employed by grade-level and other teachers to determine what and how their students are learning so that instruction can be modified accordingly while it is still in progress. Black and Wiliam (1998) refer to this as assessing what is happening "inside the black box" as opposed to simply measuring its inputs and outputs. In this manner, *formative* assessments contrast with *summative* assessments, which only measure knowledge or skills on termination of instruction.

Like summative assessments, formative assessments are based on standards and indicators of curricular learning, but unlike summative assessments, they tell us what is currently happening so we can make needed adaptations along the way. This process is somewhat like referring to a compass every few miles to check your direction rather than waiting until you have reached the end of the line (or not) to realize you were on the wrong track. There are many ways to formatively assess student learning, and Shavelson and the SEAL Group (2003) describe these assessments as existing along a continuum from informal unplanned ("on-the-fly") to formal planned ("embedded") (p. 4). The following sections include sample vignettes of what effective formative assessment can look like in practice.

---

close-up *on Assessment 6.1*

Formative assessment:

- Is most effective when based on standards and indicators of curricular learning
- May be effectively used to adapt and accommodate classroom instruction
- Takes place during instruction

Summative assessment:

- Is most effective when based on standards and indicators of curricular learning
- May be effectively used to measure the end results of instruction
- Takes place after instruction

Informal Formative Assessment

Perhaps no single form of assessment is as effectual for the teacher or as beneficial for the CLD student as informal formative assessment. This is because the tools that are typically associated with this type of assessment hold the capacity to reveal the nature and strength of *incremental* academic progress among CLD students. For the teacher, the assessment of incremental progress often provides a more realistic, authentic portrait of the student's capacities as well as her or his strides in both language acquisition and content-area learning. The knowledge gained from these assessments both reduces the potential frustration of many teachers and keeps their instructional accommodations focused on incremental, but ongoing, progress.

Ms. Schuette, a music teacher who works with CLD students, realizes the daily challenges her students face as they participate in the grade-level curriculum. Therefore, she designed a rubric that could be used to assess the progress of her students from one grading period to another. The rubric, which is depicted in Figure 6.1 (and related appendix resource), has four levels. Level 4 is the highest level of student performance, and there is no time restriction for reaching this level. This assessment tool is designed to address issues of (a) placement of students, (b) accountability of student performance, (c) demonstration of authentic progress, and (d) measurement of school effectiveness. In addition to helping a teacher know which skills to build or focus on, this rubric can be shared with students and parents in discussions of student performance.

For CLD students, the assessment and documentation of these incremental gains tend to both lower the affective filter and enhance motivation for new learning. Too often, formal assessment measures fail to provide these students with any sense of progress and accomplishment. In contrast, informal formative assessments are an opportunity to encourage, motivate, and challenge these students to higher levels of academic achievement and language acquisition.

Inquiry Assessment

One of the most common types of informal formative assessment occurs in the dialogue of teaching. Research demonstrates that teachers who recognize and differentially respond to student learning behaviors during spontaneous interaction positively influence student learning (Ruiz-Primo & Furtak, 2004). For some teachers, this begins rather intuitively, is reinforced through experience, and is best validated by the success of their students. It becomes a natural part of how they teach. These teachers catch those "on-the-fly" moments in which clarification, connection with prior learning, and probes of higher-order thinking keep all learners' wheels engaged with the curriculum and continuing to move forward. The example to follow is illustrative:

> Before reading *Bob the Snowman* (Loretan & Lenica, 1993) to her kindergarten class, Ms. Lam asks if anyone has ever seen a snowman. Most have not, but several volunteer that they have indeed seen a *real* one on TV or in a movie. Ms. Lam begins reading the

■ figure 6.1 Assessment Artifact: Student Progress Rubric

Music Assessment Rubric

Level 1:

- Observes class activities with little participation
- Begins to hum certain parts of songs as class sings
- Appears to understand little or no English instructions given in class
- Very little attempt to do actions and movements
- Does not yet try to tap simple rhythms

Level 2:

- Continues to mostly just observe the class
- Sings some words and phrases of songs in class (sheltered English)
- Follows simple classroom instructions with repetition
- Begins to repeat movements to various songs
- Begins to try to tap simple rhythms

Level 3:

- Is willing to actively participate in class activities
- Sings entire songs with class
- Follows simple classroom instructions
- Performs simple movements with class
- Can tap simple rhythms

Level 4:

- Fully participates in class activities
- Sings songs fluently
- Follows most classroom instructions without difficulty
- Masters movements or motions to various songs
- Can tap complex rhythms

story of a snowman living up North who is told by a migrating bird how beautiful everything is, and how much more fun it is, in the South. Bob decides he'd like to go there too. Ms. Lam draws the students' attention to the picture of Bob in the snowy North and the bird in the sunny South and asks the class if Bob should go. They respond with a resounding "Yes!"

Ms. Lam: Look at where Bob lives now. Is it hot or cold?
Several voices: Cold!
Ms. Lam: How can you tell it's cold?
Juan: (He raises his hand and then points to the picture of a boy in a coat.)
Ms. Lam: Good thinking! I wear a coat when it's cold too. Who wore a coat to
   school today? (Several heads shake "No.")

Ms. Lam: Why didn't you wear a coat, Marisa?

Marisa: It's too hot!

Ms. Lam: What's it like in the South? Is it hot or cold? (The picture shows the bird in a palm tree on a sunny beach.)

Class: Hot! (Ms. Lam turns the page as Bob begins his journey.)

Ms. Lam: As Bob heads for the train station . . .

Marco (in an apparent non sequitur): Bob's got a snow cone head!

Ms. Lam: Yes, his head and body are made of snow like a snow cone. How many of you have ever had a snow cone? (Eight hands fly into the air.) What happens to snow cones on a really hot day?

Julia: My snow cone melted in the park.

Juan: It gets water.

Marisa: Bob's going to melt!

With this revelation, the class revises their advice to Bob, although he travels anyway. Eventually, he does melt, turns into a puddle, evaporates, becomes a fluffy cloud, blows north, gets heavier, and returns home in the form of new-fallen snow. This wonderful story has different levels of concepts that range from basic vocabulary and emotions to prediction, sequencing, weather, states of matter, life cycles, cause and effect patterns, and story format. Ms. Lam had used this book easily in her previous school but never had encountered a group like this, in which no one had experience with snow. She was ill prepared for the initial inability of her students to see a problem with Bob's plan. By relating Bob's head to a snow cone, Marco provided a context that bridged others' prior learning with unfamiliar concepts and allowed the students to work at higher levels of understanding throughout the remainder of the story. Ms. Lam decided, and noted in her reflection journal, that when she introduces *Bob the Snowman* next year, she'll remember not to limit prior learning connections to the snows of her New England past but also include the snow cones of her students' Laredo, Texas, present.

Ms. Lam used documentation and reflection to isolate the particulars of lesson dynamics. Such professional practices better ensure that evidence of learning and critical relationships between teaching and learning do not become blurred into a generalized perception of a lesson that simply did or did not go well. There is also great potential for teachers to glean assessment information from these types of interactions by noting the specifics of *who* responded *how* to *what* and then consider that information in future planning. To get a reliable window into students' content-area learning, teachers particularly need to carefully structure the types of questions posed when using conversation or inquiry assessment techniques with CLD students.

Newcomers like Juan, for example, can often demonstrate comprehension of targeted information by pointing to an object, word, or picture or by responding "yes," "no," thumbs up, or thumbs down to simple questions. Teachers can accommodate students' language levels by using basic "wh" questions, and then "how" and "why" questions, before they attempt more abstract prompts or complex questions. Sample prompts and questions in a discussion about *Bob the Snowman* might include:

- "Show me the snowman."
- "Where is it cold?"
- "Who spoke to Bob?"
- "Should Bob go south?"
- "Why not?" (Students with limited proficiency in English can demonstrate advanced thinking by pointing to the sun, just as Juan pointed to a jacketed child to answer the inferential question, "How can you tell it's cold?")

Inquiry assessment can also take the form of a whole-class inclusion activity. For example, prompts like the following could be used for an activity in which each student has a sheet with pictured objects and animals:

- "Point to the cheese."
- "Who ate the cheese?"
- "Point to all the animals."
- "Which animal is bigger, the dog or the horse?" (answer embedded)
- "Which animal [vehicle, dinosaur, etc.] do you like best?"
- "Raise your hand to tell me *why* you like it best."

In a science conversation about plants, questions might include:

- "Does our plant need water?" (thumbs up, thumbs down)
- "Does our plant need soil, or dirt?"
- "Does our plant need ice cream?"
- "Does our plant need sun?"
- "Does our plant need snow?"
- "Raise your hand to tell me *why* you think it does or does not need snow."
- "Raise your hand to tell me how you think the plant gets food."

Open-ended questions are more difficult but have value as a modeled and anticipated form of query that can be answered by others until CLD students are ready. Figure 6.2 summarizes types of questions and prompts that are appropriate for students in different stages of second language acquisition.

In all cases, visual referents provide much-needed support until a student's performance suggests that she or he no longer needs the assistance. Thinking of instructional questions as keys rather than probes is helpful. Each is uniquely shaped to open a specific door, inviting a student to bring his or her knowledge into the learning zone. In constructive classroom environments, this door remains open for access to prior knowledge and experiences that are the bricks and mortar of each student's ability to construct new knowledge.

assessment *FREEZE FRAME* 6.2

Thinking of instructional questions as keys rather than probes is helpful. Each is uniquely shaped to open a specific door, inviting a student to bring his or her knowledge into the learning zone.

■ **figure 6.2** Questions and Prompts According to Stage of SLA

Preproduction	Early Production

Questions or directives that students can respond to or follow before they are ready to speak
 	
• Where is _____?
• Show me the _____.
• Bring me the _____.
• Point to the _____.
• Touch your _____.
• Is this a _____?
• Are you wearing _____?
• Who is wearing _____?
• Put the _____ on the _____.
• Give _____ the _____.
• Who wants _____?
	Yes/no questions
	  • Do you have scissors?
	  • Is a spider an insect?
	Either/or questions
	  • Did Billy go to a store or park?
	  • Is this food or clothing?
	One- to two-word response questions
	  • Who is the line leader today?
	  • What is Kenya riding?
	Questions that elicit naming items from groups or categories
	  • What animals did we see at the zoo?
	  • Which of these were marsupials?

Speech Emergence	**Intermediate Fluency**

Questions that require elaboration
  • *Why* did Will miss the bus?
  • *How* did he get to school?
  • *What happened* when he got to school?
Questions that ask for more information
  • *Tell me about* your vacation.
  • *Describe* your favorite place.
	Questions that inspire/probe higher-order thinking skills
	  • What will happen if . . .
	  • How are _____ and _____ alike?
	  • How are they different?
	  • What would you do if . . .
	  • What do you think about . . .
	  • How did you vote and why?

Source: Adapted from Alaska Department of Education and Early Development. (n.d.). *Sample assessment instruments*. Curriculum Frameworks Project. Author.

When classroom teachers use predictable patterns of conversation assessment, students begin to anticipate questions and think about the material in terms of inquiry. This can only occur, however, when adequate time is provided for responses. It is not uncommon for teachers to wait less than one second for a response after they pose a question. If no student response is provided in that time, they are likely to either ask another question or answer the question themselves (Black & Wiliam, 1998; Echevarria, Vogt, & Short, 2004; Rowe, 1974). This practice excludes the CLD student, who requires more time to process language. In addition, the only kinds of questions a student can answer within such a short time are generally those requiring very little thought or formulation. Rather than facilitating or assessing higher-level thinking, these types of questions merely probe the efficiency with which students memorize facts.

Wiliam (2004) promotes questioning as one of the four realms of formative assessment and feedback most likely to improve student performance on achievement measures, including standardized tests. Teachers who effectively use questioning strategies with CLD students:

- Adapt the language of the question for maximum comprehension
- Formulate questions that elicit deeper levels of thought but can be answered without complex language
- Allow adequate time for responding
- Affirm "I don't know" answers as opportunities to engage the class in brainstorming alternate ways to make sense of the material

As students' language proficiencies increase, their attention to the higher-level language or cognitive prompts and responses of others may encourage their own processing of the concepts at more advanced levels. The objective of this type of assessment approach is to determine what the student has learned from the lesson and what that implies for instruction.

Observation Assessment

Observation assessment is another type of informal formative assessment that is particularly useful in the accommodation of CLD students. Teacher observations made during instruction can provide information that may be crucial to determining the crux of a student's difficulties with content-area material. Such observations also enable teachers to provide students with opportunities to build their confidence and readiness to attempt higher levels of classroom involvement. The following scenario illustrates the use of observation assessment in practice:

> José struggles self-consciously and quits prematurely when called on to read in class. It seems he is still a nonreader. One day Mrs. Kay notes that he follows along well with his fingers as other students read aloud, pausing precisely where they do. In that moment, she makes a preliminary assessment that he may in fact be reading silently but is not yet able or ready to read aloud unsupported. She alters her instruction by having the whole class read the next paragraph together. Mrs. Kay watches as José reads the entire paragraph aloud with the class and makes a note in her anecdotal log. She excitedly decides to have students do this again tomorrow, alternating choral reading with student-read sentences to see if José will be more comfortable or capable reading smaller segments by himself.

Through cycles of observation and modification, teachers such as Mrs. Kay are informally assessing their students throughout the day. The advantage Mrs. Kay has is that she also documents these instances of informal assessment and uses the new information to alter her instruction according to the learning responses of her students. This ongoing refinement allows her to zero in on the zones in which her students are capable of maximal growth as she adjusts her teaching to those levels.

A potential drawback to a reliance on unplanned informal assessment is that even highly significant observations that occur in the course of instruction are likely to remain unrecorded. The primary reason for this is that in a dynamic classroom, there is just too much happening. That's one reason that ready-made or teacher-created observation checklists are popular. These can take many forms, limited only by the teacher's creativity, preferences, and time. One method, adaptable to any setting, involves listing all or selected students along the left side of a single page and targeted curricular behaviors along the top. As illustrated in Figure 6.3 (and related appendix resource), a teacher can easily note with narrative detail or a simple check mark the occurrence of observed behaviors during specified or unspecified activities. Checklists are especially helpful when educators observe students in action, working collaboratively, or exhibiting unpredicted or spontaneous evidence of skills (e.g., correctly counting change for the pop machine). Documentation of the conditions in which a behavior occurs, as well as those in which it does not, can be instructive in the design of future learning environments and activities.

Informal observation assessment can also look at how well the students learn through their own observations. Many of us can cite examples of students learning negative behaviors by watching others, but this natural tendency to learn by example can also be drawn on positively during classroom instruction. Children have been found to learn just as effectively through intently observed activities as those experienced hands-on. This is particularly potent for CLD students who are going through periods of relative silence or acculturation (as discussed in Chapter 4) but who may be able to learn well through scaffolded observation and instructional accommodations. Central to the concept is that the observed activity is understandable and that there is an anticipation of imminent or eventual participation (Rogoff, Paradise, Mejía Arauz, Correa-Chávez, Angelillo, 2003). Effective use of scaffolded observation is demonstrated in the following vignette:

> Ms. Reyes looks out on eight kindergarten students circled in front of her on the carpet. They excitedly eye her plain brown bag. They've seen it before. It always holds something different . . . but it's always something fun! Ms. Reyes carefully removes each item, labeling, describing, and discussing its use. There are two cans of frosting (vanilla and chocolate), several toppings (shredded coconut, yellow candy stars, and red sprinkles), plastic knives, spoons, paper napkins, plates, and two kinds of cookies. Ms. Reyes intentionally calls on those with the strongest language and academic skills first. All eyes are riveted on the cookies.
>
> **Ms. Reyes:** Josh, would you like a cookie?
> **Josh:** Yes, please.
> **Ms. Reyes:** Which kind would you like, a white sugar cookie or a brown chocolate cookie?
> **Josh:** A brown chocolate cookie.
> **Ms. Reyes:** Let's put your cookie on a plate. How would you like me to decorate it? I have . . . (she points while naming all the options).
> **Josh:** Chocolate frosting.
> **Ms. Reyes:** Here's the chocolate frosting. What should I do with it?
> **Josh:** Put it on the cookie. (Ms. Reyes puts the can of frosting on the cookie. There is silence and then the students laugh.)
> **Josh:** No, you have to open it. (She opens the can.)

figure 6.3 Observation Checklist

Student Name	Follows directions without a model	Uses nonverbals to communicate understanding or express needs	Uses single words to answer questions or express needs	Uses simple sentence structures for social purposes	Uses simple sentence structures for curricular purposes	Other comments or observations
Ahmed A.	X	X	X	X		Said, "I play too?" on playground
Feliciana G.		X				Hasn't cried all week
Mindy H.		X	X	X		Needs to watch before doing
Luciano L.	X	X	X			Words just now emerging
Ghassem M.	X	X				Joins play during recess
Van N.	X	X	X	X	X	Volunteers during whole group
Sara N.	X	X	X	X		Talkative in Housekeeping Ctr.
John (Kang) V.	X	X	X			Asks for help/chooses snack

Josh: Put it on the cookie... please. (She begins to set the can on the cookie a second time.)

Josh: Not the can; put the *frosting* on the cookie! (Ms. Reyes looks into the can, puzzled.)

Josh: Put the knife in. (She puts the knife in and leaves it.)

Josh (laughing): Scoop it out and put it, no, *spread* it on the cookie!

This pattern of scaffolding, modeling, and self-expansion continues through all phases of decoration. The finished cookies are set aside until all are completed, and the process becomes more efficient with successive student turns even though several students face communicative challenges. The language use of CLD students is notice-ably more specific and complex under these conditions than during regular classroom discourse. The students enjoy the humor of the lesson but also realize Ms. Reyes will fol-low their instructions explicitly, attending to words such as *in, on, more, as much, enough, spread, shake, sprinkle,* and so forth. Academic vocabulary pertaining to color, size, posi-tion, and quantity concepts also becomes meaningful in this context.

Ms. Reyes observes when students are unable to produce the targeted structures and modifies her prompts accordingly. For example, Nahla has been in school two months and has little prior exposure to English. Observation checklists reveal she uses mostly single words and gestures to communicate in the classroom. By the time her turn arrives, Nahla has been watching intently. She knows what she wants and has grasped the most significant words that will make that happen. With every classmate's previous turn, she has very likely rehearsed her own requests.

Nahla: Cookie... chocolate!

Ms. Reyes: You want a chocolate cookie? Here's a chocolate cookie. Do you want frosting?

Nahla: Chocolate frosting... please. (Nahla does not wait for a prompt.)

Nahla: Put knife... frosting on cookie.

Later, in response to Ms. Reyes's sprinkling of only a tiny amount of red candy on top, Nahla shakes her head and before a model can be provided says, "Not enough... more candy, please."

Although the lesson seems simple, in a very short time Ms. Reyes has added another important dimension to her knowledge about how Nahla and the other stu-dents learn. This informal yet deliberate assessment has indicated that several students not previously thought to have acquired many kindergarten concepts did indeed have the cognitive ability to learn curricular material in a highly communicative les-son that maximized the learning potential of anticipatory observation. Given other indicators, Nahla was only expected to use single words and perhaps demonstrate recognition of one or two colors. Instead, after observing others work, she responded at multiple levels by using expanded utterances and grasping unanticipated curricular concepts.

As illustrated, one of the most exciting aspects of differentiated instruction is that it also allows for differentiated assessment. Such purposeful differentiation can occur in a variety of contexts at all academic levels.

Accommodative Assessment Practices 6.1

Mr. Gruber's history class is studying the chapter on major forms of government. He has taught this material many times but never before with such a diverse class. He has general education students who read at the fifth- to twelfth-grade levels and two special education students. The district's new inclusion model also mandates that students with limited English skills remain in their core curricular classes (with support offered last period in the ESL seminar). This was a challenge at first, but the ESL teacher, Mrs. Tran, has been providing great ideas to make lessons more comprehensible and is able to reinforce or preteach some of the more abstract concepts during the seminar. Mr. Gruber has noticed that the students as a whole seem more involved when they work with one another than in more traditional, teacher-led formats. However, he wonders how he can determine whether they are really learning the material.

Classes that Mr. Gruber has taught in the past have tended to enjoy game show formats like that of *Jeopardy!* Yet Mr. Gruber is concerned that unless he intentionally stacks the deck or limits play, the academically struggling students and limited English speakers will not experience success. The last thing he wants is for any of them, even the leaders, to find the activity a stratifying experience. He reflects on his favorite cooperative education strategies and decides to play Quiz Quiz Trade (Kagan, 1994). The activity begins with all students reading a section of the text. Mr. Gruber is focused on knowledge of content rather than on language, so he encourages a willing bilingual student to interpret the text for newcomer Miguel. Maria and Thuy have fairly good BICS and are able to read in English but may get only the gist of each section. He hopes the activity will help them flesh out the content material in a dynamic way.

After reading the passage, each student thinks of a question that focuses on a basic understanding or vocabulary word from the text and writes it, along with the answer, on a 3" x 5" card. The students understand that these questions are "right there" questions they can pull from the text, because Mr. Gruber often refers to his chart on higher-order thinking skills. Students then pose their question to a partner, who in turn asks his or her own question. At this point, partners trade cards and find another partner. With each successive exchange, the student draws from the thought processes of other students, incorporates them into his or her own understanding of the material, poses those questions, and hears another's perspective on the answer.

In subsequent rounds, the students are asked to expand on the established concepts and develop questions that are progressively more analytical. The questions evolve to elicit inferences, comparisons, and explanations. By the time Sandy asks Maria to explain the difference between *theocracy* and *dictatorship*, Maria has been able to hear those terms explained in several different ways and has formed her own concept of their meaning. Maria states: "In theocracy, God tells people the rules. In a dictatorship, a man, one man, tells people the rules." Despite working in her less fluent language, Maria's response reveals synthesized comprehension of a complex curricular concept. In the final round, students ask one another to apply the content and ideas in real-life scenarios. Mr. Gruber discovers that this approach is far more powerful than a textual scavenger hunt because students deeply contemplate the text content as they develop questions and prompts for the facts or ideas they have discovered. The process engenders natural scaffolds as students make and share meaning together.

Near the end of class time, Mr. Gruber uses a few questions from the collected cards for a quick verbal quiz. They talk about the responses and how they came up with, found, or reasoned out the answers. He also guides his students to think more metacognitively about their learning. Mr. Gruber will use the rest of the questions to create a more formal formative test for the next class that includes traditional sections such as multiple choice, true or false, fill-in-the-blank, and short-answer essay. Those results will be analyzed differentially for content knowledge and the students' abilities to handle different test formats; in this way, Mr. Gruber knows what to emphasize next. He wants to ensure that all students learn the content-area material and that they are able to demonstrate that learning on high-stakes tests.

■ *In what additional ways might Mr. Gruber collect data and document student learning during this activity?*

■ *What variations could Mr. Gruber add to the activity to keep the attention of the students and enhance their motivation to learn?*

Structured Authentic Assessments

Although educators occasionally are fortunate to observe related behaviors in unplanned situations, most of the time the saliency and richness of the skills demonstrated by students will depend on the opportunities inherent in the educational activities that teachers plan. As illustrated in the following examples, the design of structured authentic assessments reflects the efforts of teachers to combine creativity and targeted curricular concepts.

Ms. McKinley knows that CLD students in the early stages of second language acquisition might have difficulty comprehending a science unit on plant parts. Therefore, she and some of her fellow teachers designed a science activity with language modifications that would enable the participation of all students in the class. The activity involves having students work in heterogeneous (Spanish and English) pairs to identify the parts of an illustrated plant. As one modification (see Figure 6.4), the students are given an unlabeled diagram of the plant along with word cards in Spanish and English for the different plant parts. The partners take turns placing the Spanish and English words in the appropriate blanks. Students check their work using a plant diagram that is labeled with terms in both languages.

When the activity is used as an individual assessment, each student is given an unlabeled diagram and a set of the Spanish and English word cards. The student then glues the word cards in (or near) the blanks. Alternative assessments such as this provide CLD students the opportunity to demonstrate conceptual knowledge without being hindered by language challenges.

> **assessment FREEZE FRAME 6.3**
>
> The design of structured authentic assessments reflects the efforts of teachers to combine creativity and targeted curricular concepts.

Another of the many ways to assess students in authentic contexts is to develop situations or scenarios in which students exhibit targeted skills while working toward the creation of a product or project of interest. In such situations, students are fully engaged and motivated to draw on all their skills and resources to achieve an identified goal. The following scenario illustrates the effective use of an authentic, cooperative group assessment with CLD students.

Mrs. William's second-grade class is studying living creatures and their environments. They recently had the opportunity to visit the local zoo and see many animals. The zoo guide was interesting but talked much too fast for some of the students who were acquiring a second language. Fortunately, Mrs. William had made sure that L2 peers were included in each group of students to facilitate understanding among the CLD students. She knew that using the native language helps students learn, but some of the English-speaking students also do a very nice job of retelling information in creatively comprehensible English.

During the zoo visit, the students were encouraged to take notes or draw pictures to remind themselves of the most interesting things about the animals or places they saw. Later, each group used this information to develop questions for the other students. The questions often required that students give detailed descriptions of the animals

■ **figure 6.4** Assessment
Artifact: Plant Part
Identification

Label these parts of this plant:

flower	flor
flowers	flores
stem	tallo
leaf	hoja
root	raíz

or their environment. A checklist guided the students to develop at least one question each about an animal classification (e.g., Turtles and snakes belong to what group?), a geographical region (e.g., Name three animals that live in the jungle.), animal eating habits (e.g., What do ducks eat?), and a predatory relationship (e.g., What animal likes to

Accommodative Assessment Practices 6.2

Ms. Lewis also tries to incorporate authentic activities and assessments into her classroom assessment practices. To help her students learn the parts of a cell, Ms. Lewis has students build models that include various cell parts and descriptions of their corresponding functions. The Assessment Artifact below depicts the work of a CLD student who labeled her animal cell model in both her native language and English. In a reflection about this activity, Ms. Lewis wrote:

student engagement often have to "step out on a limb." As they try activities they have never previously used, effective teachers reflect on ways in which the lessons and associated assessments succeeded or require further refinement.

■ *Ms. Lewis believes that the model representation helped her CLD students remember the parts of the cell. What specific supports to student learning and benefits to authentic assessment does such a model provide?*

I have taught this science lesson for three years, and this is the first year that I had students make a model of the cell. Usually, we cover the lesson and do some worksheets. I think the model representation helped [CLD and other students] to remember the parts of the cell. We also viewed a video on cells this year, so students could visually see movement of live cells as well as different cell types and structures. I feel that I am growing professionally because I am now incorporating language support into my lessons, and I am focusing more on the needs and learning styles of all of my students. The cell model offers an alternative form for assessing students.

Teachers such as Ms. Lewis who adapt and modify lessons to increase

■ **Assessment Artifact: Animal Cell Model**

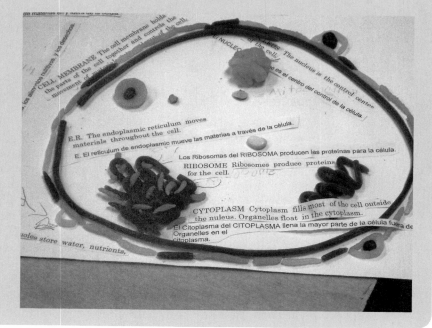

eat ducks?). As students quizzed one another, they noticed how many different correct answers were elicited from each group.

The next day, students continued to work in groups to design their own zoos. Mrs. William informed them that the zoo would be located just outside of town, so they needed to consider the region's weather conditions and determine each animal's appropriateness for the zoo or need for shelter. Students were asked to include at least one type of animal that did not live in the zoo they had visited the previous day. The plan of the new zoo was to have more animals living together in realistic habitats than in the current zoo. The primary assignment or test for students was to create three habitats where at least fifteen animals (five in each habitat) could live safely.

As they worked together, the students pooled their previously learned (but still fresh) knowledge. Jesse wanted the zoo to have chickens but knew from experience that chickens shouldn't live anywhere near foxes or snakes. Linda wanted prairie dogs in the farm habitat because cows, goats, and horses don't eat them. However, Sam knew that prairie dog burrows could break the horses' legs. When they finally finished, each group prepared to present its zoo to the class.

The class checked the ideas of each group by using a rubric to determine whether the group could (a) describe each habitat, (b) explain the reason for its plants, shelter, and boundary type, (c) describe each animal's main traits, and (d) explain why each animal was chosen. When Mrs. William heard the groups share their final presentations, she was confident that all the students in her class had gained a far greater and more durable understanding of the curricular concepts (as well as greater ability to generalize them) than if she had just spent an entire week on verbal lessons followed by a paper-and-pencil test.

Teachers can also follow this type of collaborative activity with individual tests, a group test in which all members work together to discuss and record the answers, or a combination of both.

Teacher-Made Tests

Teacher-made tests can complement all other forms of assessment, but the development of classroom tests that are appropriate for CLD students requires the careful consideration of several factors. The content tested should, of course, reflect what has been taught and should be probed in the manner best suited for students' demonstration of knowledge. Task analysis skills should be separated into their component parts so that mastery of subskills can be determined. Factual or memorized material can be assessed via objective formats that have pictures or mastered vocabulary presented in a familiar test design (e.g., matching, multiple choice). The correct answer should be easily distinguished from incorrect answers, given an understanding of the concepts being measured. Vague or ambiguous prompts are essentially meaningless and sometimes punitive because they tell us only about a student's language and testing finesse rather than the student's content-area comprehension. Assessment in Action 6.1 provides additional guidelines for creating effective prompts.

Although objective tests might seem less complicated for CLD students, these learners may actually find it easier to tackle questions that require synthesis, explanation, or analysis through short-answer essays if they are supported with access to graphic organizers and bilingual dictionaries (if applicable). When teachers grade the essays of CLD students, they may choose to focus solely on content rather than on literacy criteria, or teachers can generate separate scores for each.

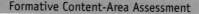

■ Assessment in Action 6.1: Creating Prompts for Teacher-Made Tests

The following guidelines better ensure that teacher-made tests are accommodative:

1. Carefully design prompts and foils so as to not unduly advantage or disadvantage students with varying linguistic skills. For example, although some students may automatically know the answers to the following fill-in-the-blank questions, others (who may or may not be sufficiently familiar with the content material) might be cued by grammar structures that indicate the correct answers:

   _____ eat a variety of vegetation, including tree bark.

   a. Moose
   b. Walrus
   c. Penguin
   d. Arctic wolf

A person who explores caves is called a _____.

   a. entomologist
   b. ethnographer
   c. agronomist
   d. spelunker

2. Consider the range of responses that may be elicited from items. For example, "Tyrannosaurus rex was a _____." (possible responses include dinosaur, meat-eater, GoBot, etc.). Determine whether to accept all logical responses or revise the prompt to more specifically probe the targeted content. For instance, this item can be rewritten, "Tyrannosaurus rex ate only _____."

3. Avoid using words such as *always, never, all,* and *none* when designing multiple-choice assessments to gather information about content knowledge. These words tend to favor students with greater linguistic experience.

Additional tips for the development of teacher-made tests (Educational Testing Service, 2003; Salend, 2005) include:

- Identify the purpose of the test.
- Determine what type of test would be most appropriate based on the material, student variables, and what you want to measure.
- Control the language level of the test unless that is the curricular area being assessed. Avoid ambiguous or vague prompts. Linguistically complex forms (e.g., *unless, although*), clausal constructions, and negatives often lead to misinterpretation of the question.
- Keep questions short and specific to lessen the impact that differences in reading speed and fluency have on indices of content learning.
- Consider the element of time when developing a test. Inadequate time or time pressure injects several biasing elements into the testing situation that detract from a teacher's ability to distinguish results based on knowledge from those resulting from testing conditions.

Educators who develop effective teacher-made tests remember that it is essential to give students mediated opportunities to work with these formats so they are better equipped to interpret them in high-stakes tests.

> ### close-up *on Assessment* 6.2
>
> Among guidelines for the creation of teacher-made assessments are the following:
>
> - Ensure that assessment items specifically probe the targeted material.
> - Avoid syntax or grammar structures that may direct students to the correct answers or assess language proficiency versus content-area learning.
> - Minimize the use of words such as *always, never, all,* and *none* that favor students with more extensive linguistic experience.

Students are not born savvy test takers. They develop testing competence through ongoing attention to characteristics of question formats they encounter in testing situations. It is important for students to understand that test taking, just like playing video games or basketball, requires a set of skills and involves not only subject knowledge but also heightened awareness and practice. The tips provided in Figure 6.5 (and related appendix resource) offer educators guidance for teaching students how to strategically approach test formats such as multiple choice, matching, true or false, sentence completion, and essay questions. However, when sharing these tips with CLD students, it is essential that teachers incorporate appropriate examples and scaffolding, depending on the academic and language proficiency levels of their students. For example, a teacher might introduce approaches to multiple-choice testing at very early levels by using strategies such as those demonstrated by Mr. Jin in the following vignette:

Mr. Jin places on the floor three pictures (covered, or pasted inside down-turned paper plates), which will serve as the possible answers to a question. He then explains to the class that one of these is the correct answer to the question he is going to ask, but rather than focusing on the choices, they should first try to see if the answer pops into their heads. He reads the story-based question from the board:

Mr. Jin: What was the main setting for *Charlotte's Web*? (As he nods to their raised hands, the students volunteer "a farm" and "a fair.")

Mr. Jin: Are those names for the same place, or were there different settings in this story?

Class: Different settings.

Mr. Jin: Yes, let's reread the question together.

All: What was the main setting for *Charlotte's Web*?

Mr. Jin: The question asks for the *main* setting. What does that mean?

Sara: Where they were most of the time.

Mr. Jin: Do you all agree?

Class: Yes!

Mr. Jin: What do you think was the main setting for most of the book?

Class: The farm.

■ **figure 6.5** Test-Taking Tips for Students

Testing Tips

Multiple Choice

- Read the question and think of the answer before reading the selections.
- Eliminate choices that are obviously incorrect or unrelated to the content.
- Carefully analyze and choose from among the remaining options.
- Look for grammatical clues.

Matching

- Make sure you know the rules and understand the directions well (e.g., whether items can be used more than once).
- Read the first item in column one and then all possible matches before answering.
- First answer items that appear less difficult; skip (and note) difficult items to reconsider when the answer field has narrowed (if one answer per item).
- As you proceed, mark out or highlight choices that have been used in order to focus your attention on remaining responses for review.

True or False

- Words that qualify statements, such as *rarely, sometimes, most,* and *usually,* are more likely associated with correct answers than words that make the statement 100 percent true or false, such as *always, never,* and *every.*
- Read each item carefully; mark it false if any part of it is not correct or true.
- Highlight prefixes and negative words, and consider their power to change meaning.

Sentence Completion

- To help determine the answers, convert these items into questions.
- Pay attention to grammatical clues as well as length or number of blanks to identify targeted responses.

Essay

- Highlight key words related to directions, such as *explain, compare,* and *describe.*
- Read the question, note important points to address, and outline your response before beginning to write.
- Rephrase the question as the first sentence of the answer, detail your response accordingly with transitions between ideas, and summarize main points in your closing statement(s).
- If unable to complete an item, note its key points and create an outline.
- Proofread your response for legibility, spelling, grammar, and style.

Source: Adapted from Salend (2005), pp. 503–504.

Mr. Jin: Let's see if the farm is among our answers. (He reveals a picture of a school.)
Class: No, that's a school.
Mr. Jin: (Reveals the next picture of a market.)
Class: No!
Kenji: (laughing) That's where Wilbur was gonna end up!

Mr. Jin (impressed with Kenji's inferential thinking but keeping the class on track): If we know for sure that the school and the market were not the main setting, what can we guess about the last choice?

Class: It's a farm.

Mr. Jin: Yes, since we knew the answer without looking, it should be a farm. Let's look. (Reveals the third picture.)

Class: It's a farm!

Mr. Jin: What if our last choice was a picture or word we didn't recognize (he replaces the farm with a word written in Chinese), but we knew the other two answers were wrong? Would this be a good guess?

Sara: Yes, I bet that says *farm*!

Mr. Jin: If you guessed this was the right answer because you knew the other two answers were wrong, that would be a good guess. And you are right . . . it does say *farm*!

Students who have been exposed early in their education to mediated examples of test-taking strategies in formats that continually adapt to their skills and curricula will, by later years, be able to benefit from a modified tips list of their own and eventually employ these strategies independently across test-taking contexts.

Point-in-Time Assessments

Point-in-time assessments are those quizzes or tests that a teacher employs to gather immediate quantitative feedback about student learning. Often, but not always, such assessments involve the measurement of skills that are acquired hierarchically. Some skills in mathematics are acquired in this way. For example, it is clearly important to check the ability of a given student to add single digits before moving on to double digits and regrouping. Spelling tests and vocabulary quizzes are also among the more common point-in-time classroom assessments.

Many teachers who use ongoing assessments such as portfolios or projects also find value in regular quizzes to check for understanding. Assessments that are capable of measuring incremental progress are especially valuable for CLD students. The teacher can subsequently revise instruction or implement interventions at the most salient and opportune time rather than waiting until the student is significantly behind. According to Salend (2005), "Shorter and more frequent tests of specific content rather than fewer, longer, and more comprehensive tests can help students who have difficulty remembering large amounts of information" (p. 515). Although performance-based assessments have tremendous value in the measurement of classroom learning and skills, students have actually been found to perform better in areas such as math and science when their teachers also frequently used point-in-time assessments (Wenglingsky, 2000).

assessment FREEZE FRAME 6.4

Point-in-time assessments are those quizzes or tests that a teacher employs to gather immediate quantitative feedback about student learning.

Curriculum-Based Measurement

Another approach to measuring the incremental progress of learners involves the growing field of curriculum-based measurement. Like criterion-referenced tests (which are discussed in a subsequent section), teacher-made tests, and point-in-time assessments, curriculum-based measurements (CBMs) are designed to directly measure the acquisition of curricular skills. However, although each is a form of broader curriculum-based assessment, there are some significant distinctions.

To design criterion-referenced and teacher-made tests, long-range objectives are broken down into skills and subskills that are taught and measured sequentially throughout the year. Although it stands to reason that mastery of these distinct hierarchical components will inevitably result in broader core-area knowledge, this cannot always be assumed. For example, a student might be able to demonstrate mastery of addition with and without regrouping during those respective lessons but perform poorly when required to differentially determine and apply those same processes in more global assessments (or when problems requiring these separate processes are presented together) (Fuchs, 2004). Fuchs and Deno (1991) contrast this model of *mastery* measurement with *general outcome* measurement.

CBMs are best characterized as general outcome measurements. Instead of measuring the mastery of incremental steps to an academic goal, CBMs repeatedly sample global skills from which a growing mastery of subskills can be inferred. This is similar in principle to what is sometimes referred to as informal differentiated assessment but differs in that CBMs can be standardized in their administration for an entire class or group.

In a process described by Hosp and Hosp (2003), a teacher using curriculum-based measurement first identifies academic goals and objectives the student is expected to master over the course of the school year or semester. The teacher then uses

---

close-up on Assessment 6.3

Mastery and general outcome measurements can be compared and contrasted as follows:

- Mastery measurement (used with criterion-referenced and teacher-made assessments):
  —Long-range objectives are broken down.
  —Skills and subskills are taught and measured sequentially over time.
  —Mastery of hierarchical components is presumed to result in broader core-area knowledge.
- General outcome measurement (used with curriculum-based measurements):
  —Academic goals and objectives for a year or semester are identified.
  —Mini-tests or probes are created and used to gauge student progression toward global goals.
  —Knowledge of subskills and holistic applications is documented through growth in the number of correct items or correct steps per item.

these outcomes to develop mini-tests called CBM probes, which can be administered at regular intervals throughout the year. These CBM probes gauge student progress toward the terminal goal. An advantage to such probes is that teachers can create graphic representations of the data that are easy to maintain and comprehensible to parents. Using our math example, CBM probes might comprise twenty-five items that draw on a range of skills expected to be mastered during the year (e.g., one, two, and three place-value addition and subtraction, with and without regrouping). Student progress with subskills as well as holistic applications will be demonstrated by growth in the number of correct items or correct steps per item.

A number of studies indicate that CBMs demonstrate good reliability and validity as measures of ongoing student learning (Marston, 1989; Fuchs & Fuchs, 1992, 2003). CBMs also tend to be quality indicators of student performance on certain high-stakes reading assessments (McGlinchey & Hixson, 2004). However, additional research is needed in areas related to CLD learners and the contexts of their instruction. It seems reasonable, for example, that CLD students learning to read in their primary language will demonstrate a different slope of skill mastery than those who either receive highly accommodated or essentially unaccommodated instruction that is delivered only in English. CBMs can also be used effectively to determine when students schooled in L1 have developed sufficient native language skills to support the transition to English academic instruction (Shinn, Baker, Habedank, & Good, 1993) and to monitor the progress of CLD students on reintegration or designation into grade-level education classrooms (Shinn, Powell-Smith, Good, & Baker, 1997).

Because CBMs provide consistent curriculum-based feedback on student progress, these assessments are useful to classroom teachers as they determine and measure the efficacy of their curriculum-based instructional accommodations for CLD students. In addition, teachers who reflect on and self-monitor their use of CBMs tend to demonstrate a noticeably broader range of instructional modifications than those who do not self-monitor or those who do not use CBMs. Self-monitoring of CBM use has also been correlated with significantly greater student progress, particularly in math (Allinder, Bolling, Oats, & Gagnon, 2000).

Self-Assessment

In most classrooms, teachers continue to be primarily responsible for rating and evaluating student work. Traditional grading systems are supported for a variety of reasons, which include simple formats for informing parents and the presumed capacity to motivate students. Although the results are not entirely consistent, some researchers have correlated an emphasis on grades with increased incidence of cheating (Anderman, Griesinger, & Westerfield, 1998) and attitudinal shifts from a learning to a grade orientation (Farr & Trumbull, 1997). Grade-oriented learning environments are particularly harmful to CLD students. Typically in such environments, less attention is paid to the process, or construction, of learning than to the result, the quality of which is generally determined by someone other than the learner. For many CLD students, such practices reinforce an external locus of control and further reduce their sense of self-efficacy in learning.

The promise of self-assessment extends well beyond the ability to provide information about achievement. Indeed, this promise may speak to core aspects of a student's motivation and perspective on learning (Stiggins, 2002). Self-evaluation systems engage students in their learning and foster relationships with teachers as mentors and guides rather than as omnipotent evaluators.

One of the reasons self-assessment practices are so potent is that proper implementation necessitates that students are provided a clear grasp of the target objectives and criteria. Highly effective teachers share their vision of student learning by informing students of the outcomes that are expected from classroom work and study. Objectives might be explained in the form of rubrics with examples, delineation of specific skills, discussion of criteria, or the ideal of a real-world application (authenticity). Although it is always important for students to understand how they will be assessed, there is significant data suggesting that practicing self-assessment according to such criteria leads to improved academic learning and performance (Stiggins, 1997).

In their review of research, Black and Wiliam (1998) found support for the argument that formative self-assessments among students tend to enhance achievement: "far from being a luxury, [student self-assessment] is in fact *an essential component of formative assessment*" (p. 143). Stiggins (2002) also describes regular self-assessment as a fundamental component of assessment for learning through which "students can watch themselves grow over time and thus feel in charge of their own success" (p. 5). Students who self-assess become more confident learners willing to work hard, make decisions, and take risks to achieve their own learning goals.

Self-assessment charts or graphs can function in a variety of ways depending on grade level and content. Simple formats, such as the one depicted in Figure 6.6 (and related appendix resource), might involve listing tasks, skill competencies, or knowledge areas along one axis and descriptors of comfort or success along the other. These descriptors might correlate directly with objective indices of mastery such as percentage correct in multiplication tables (ones, twos, threes, etc.), qualitative terminology (e.g., lost, uncomfortable, getting it, comfortable, super), or pictorial representations (e.g., sad, confused, curious, or happy faces; red, yellow, or green stoplights) (Wiliam, 2004). Students are taught to plot and recognize their own progress as they assess themselves along targeted parameters of learning. As with other forms of assessment, it is important to emphasize what has been accomplished and to promote the mutual discussion of ways to address what has not. Innovative educators might also elect to model self-assessment of their own learning of curricular material or a recently undertaken hobby.

Self-assessment practices also enhance the student's ability to explain and describe his or her thinking processes and responses in testing situations. Such information can provide a teacher with valuable insights into the student's depth of content understanding or reveal alternate interpretations of a particular prompt. Such opportunities for explanation are extremely important with CLD students, who may bring different frames of reference to a task or lesson.

> **assessment *FREEZE FRAME* 6.5**
>
> Self-assessment practices also enhance the student's ability to explain and describe his or her thinking processes and responses in testing situations.

■ **figure 6.6** Assessment Artifact: Self-Assessment Rubric

Literature Circle Presentation Preparation
Self-Assessment Rubric

Student Name:

Title of Book:

Presentation Preparation Activities	Please circle the most appropriate response to each statement. 1 = Never 4 = Frequently 2 = Rarely 5 = Always 3 = Sometimes				
1. I came to group meetings prepared (on time and ready to make an honest effort to understand the material).	1	2	3	4	5
2. I willingly read from the book when it was my turn.	1	2	3	4	5
3. I actively participated in discussions.	1	2	3	4	5
4. I listened attentively while members shared thoughts.	1	2	3	4	5
5. I respected the ideas and opinions of other members.	1	2	3	4	5
6. I helped my group discuss the general questions.	1	2	3	4	5
7. I helped discuss the questions specific to our book.	1	2	3	4	5
8. I identified at least one question that needed to be addressed.	1	2	3	4	5
9. I helped define presentation responsibilities.	1	2	3	4	5
10. I prepared for my presentation responsibilities (gathered materials, rehearsed part, asked for advice when necessary, etc.).	1	2	3	4	5

With which group members did you work most effectively?

Additional Comments:

Accommodative Assessment Practices 6.3

Mr. Piña decided to model self-assessment by using his experiences with playing an accordion. He shares with the class that he has always wanted to learn how to play the accordion and that he recently found one at a garage sale. His fifth-grade class is intrigued by the accordion's buttons and bellows but oddly surprised at Mr. Piña's inability to produce anything that sounds like music. Carla volunteers that her uncle plays the accordion, and he agrees to give Mr. Piña lessons. The students are doubtful that Mr. Piña will learn to play a song by Christmas. He posts a small chart on the wall on which he will plot how he feels each week about his progress (i.e., lost, uncomfortable, getting it, comfortable, or super). The students want to be involved too, so together they develop their own additional rubric to rate his eventual success:

1. No one can recognize the song.
2. A few recognize the song; there are too many errors; it is way too slow or fast.
3. Many recognize the song; there are some errors; it is a little too slow or fast.
4. Nearly everyone recognizes the song and can sing along.

During the first two weeks, Mr. Piña's chart shows that he does not feel at all like a learner, but by week three he's moved from *lost* to *uncomfortable* along his own rubric. The class applauds. In October he brings the accordion back into class and demonstrates his learning. The students rate his performance a 2 according to their rubric, and Gaby laughs, "He probably started as a 0 rather than a 1." Mr. Piña feels that he's now *getting it*. By Christmas his averaged rubric rating from the class is 3.6, but even so everyone enjoys singing along.

Technology-Based Assessment

In the information age, technology drives our society. In addition to technological applications for everything from household management to entertainment and citizenship (news, consumerism, voting), technology is also uniquely suited to meet some of the critical needs of CLD learners. Carefully chosen technologies can facilitate the CLD student's comprehension and demonstration of content-area learning by providing:

1. Access to native language supports or resources that enhance student comprehension
2. Contextual supports such as pictures, videos, and audio clips, as well as more authentic learning opportunities through simulations and so forth
3. One-on-one instruction that provides immediate feedback at the student's learning level
4. Programmed adjustment of content and complexity that adapts to student responses, scaffolds new knowledge, and engenders a sense of success
5. Added dimensions to cooperative and project-based learning activities, including communication with, and access to, outside resources
6. Opportunities to access and enhance higher-order thinking skills as the student connects new and prior learning through self-directed inquiry

Accommodative Assessment Practices 6.4

On a sentence completion test with picture cues of a cookie, spoon, apple, and cup, Adan circled the cookie as the best response to: "I eat beans with a _____." It seems clear to Mr. Rossi that Adan is either unable to read or did not adequately comprehend the prompt, but he's not sure which. Mr. Rossi hoped this format would give him insights into this student's skills but realizes he won't know much more about Adan's learning if he simply marks the test item wrong. He reads the item again. Perhaps the problem is the preposition *with*. Mr. Rossi had not thought of it when he created the test, but the question could be interpreted as meaning what you eat along with your beans, rather than what you use to eat beans. Nevertheless, it is possible that Adan just couldn't read or understand the words. Mr. Rossi calls Adan to his desk and asks him to read the response to the item aloud. Adan smiles, "I eat beans with a tortilla."

- *What factors contributed to Adan's "incorrect" answer?*
- *Given the skill being assessed, was his answer actually wrong?*
- *What might Mr. Rossi do differently as a result of this experience?*

Accordingly, technological applications can augment our repertoire of performance and project-based assessments, but they also offer a range of modifications to more traditional tests that were not previously possible or practical for the typical teacher.

Some programs allow teachers or students to choose the assessment design, modifications, and response format that is most likely to yield valid information about students' abilities in content areas. Options may include audio presentation, verbal or written response, first language translation, use of bilingual online dictionaries, extended time, and so forth. For many teachers, these modifications are actually easier to provide via technology than through adaptations, materials, or personnel currently available to them on site.

Another strength of technology-assisted assessments is that they can be designed (or purchased with the design) to respond dynamically to the performance patterns of a single student. For example, computer-assisted tests (CATs) are now available to differentially assess students who are performing above or below assigned grade level on their mastery of targeted knowledge and skills. These out-of-grade-level assessments are structured so that items answered correctly are followed by more complex or difficult prompts, whereas those answered in error lead to more simplified branches of the material or content. This reduces the number of superfluous items and provides generally equivalent data in far less time. If the overall pool of test items is large, students are unlikely to take the same test twice. Therefore, CATs can usually be readministered more frequently than traditional forms of standardized assessment. In this way, CATs provide teachers and students with critically important *en route* information as they progress toward annual goals (Van Horn, 2003).

When considering the use of technology-assisted assessments, Salend (2005) recommends the following:

1. Scrutinize items or the structure of computer-assisted assessments for cultural or linguistic bias.
2. Carefully evaluate these tools for language demands that may unfairly affect the CLD student's demonstration of knowledge and skills.
3. Consider student familiarity and comfort with technology in general when determining the appropriateness of test use.
4. Think about the extent to which the format precludes accommodations (e.g., highlighting) that may be particularly relevant and useful for the CLD student.

Among other technology-based assessments of content-area learning are observational tools such as the Ecobehavioral System for the Contextual Recording of Interactional Bilingual Environments (ESCRIBE) (Arreaga-Mayer, Tapia, & Carta, 1993). This assessment system was specifically developed to provide insights as to what is actually going on in the "black box" of teaching and learning with CLD students. This technology supports direct contextual, observational measurement of ecological (pertaining to the environment), teacher, and student behaviors in culturally and linguistically diverse classrooms. ESCRIBE allows us to better quantify and correlate those factors that most affect CLD student achievement, refine our instructional accommodations with greater specificity, and gather critical data to support further studies and practice (Arreaga-Mayer, 1992).

The Internet can also prove extremely beneficial to our work with CLD students and families. Innovative opportunities (Salend, 2005) include, but certainly are not limited to:

- Ongoing assessment formats such as electronic portfolios and interactive journals
- Teacher-made assessments to be used as self-assessments and point-in-time measures (www.funbrain.com; www.quia.com)
- Test-taking resources, practice tests, or computer-assisted tests (www.edutest.com; www.homeroom.com)
- Resources for creating, designing, and interpreting surveys
- Online web pages to inform parents and students about assignments, deadlines, and instructional goals
- Electronic mail to inform parents of grades, absences, concerns, celebrations, and accomplishments. (Note: These should be scrutinized for cross-cultural sensitivity and cross-linguistic comprehensibility.)

When use of the Internet is involved in any aspect of instruction or assessment, responsible teachers address the need for students to understand issues of digital citizenship, which include plagiarism, acceptable access, and general matters of e-conduct.

Formal Formative Assessment

Formal assessments encompass more than the periodic high-stakes assessments that tend to dominate conversations in staff meetings and lounges. Like informal

close-up *on Assessment 6.4*

Formal formative assessments should be scrutinized for their validity with the classroom population of CLD students to be assessed. Among the variety of these assessments that may be available to teachers are the following:

- Norm-referenced or criterion-referenced tests that are designed for (or permit) periodic updating
- Formal assessments that accompany a standardized program of instruction (e.g., SRI)
- Assessments that are part of district curricular units
- Some assessments that are facilitated by computer (e.g., Advantage Learning, MAP, STAR)

assessments, formal assessments are tools that teachers can use effectively to gather data about instruction and learning in their classrooms. Data made available from these tests not only help teachers modify and revise instruction for their students but can also lead to the development of specific intervention strategies for students with differential needs (Charles & Mertler, 2002). Teachers may consider their high-stakes "look–alike" tests as formal formative assessments, but many districts identify formal formative assessments as the centrally developed or adopted tools used as a barometer of student learning across settings such as classes, schools, or districts. Such assessments include (a) norm-referenced or criterion-referenced tests designed for (or permitting) periodic update, (b) formal assessments that accompany a standardized program of instruction (e.g., SRI), (c) assessments that are part of district curricular units, and (d) some assessments that are facilitated by computer (e.g., Advantage Learning, MAP, STAR).

Norm-Referenced and Criterion-Referenced Tests

This section of the chapter discusses those formal formative assessments that are specifically applicable to classroom teachers of CLD students. Norm-referenced and criterion-referenced tests are each useful as formal formative assessments. The differences between these two kinds of tests usually have more to do with their purpose than their content or form (Boehm, 1973; Bond, 1996). Norm-referenced assessments are designed and used to measure differences among students. Items mastered or failed by a majority are discarded in favor of those deemed most likely to distinguish among test takers. Often this results in a test with fewer, more heavily weighted items per skill. On the other hand, criterion-referenced tests provide information on the acquisition or demonstration of selected components and target instructional skills among students without regard to the relationship between one student's performance and the achievement of others.

In general, reliance on tests that sample skills through a limited number of items is less informative to our teaching than is the use of assessments that include multiple opportunities to probe or elicit demonstration of content-area knowledge. If the primary purpose of formative assessment is to enlighten our understanding of how well a student is learning (and how well the teacher is teaching) the targeted material, there may be particular merit in using criterion-referenced rather than norm-referenced assessments of content-area learning. Regardless of the type used, the assessment should measure what we intend to measure and provide reliable information that is useful. To this end, well-designed criterion-referenced tests not only provide formal formative information about student mastery of specified skills but also give us insight into the levels of prerequisite knowledge necessary to perform the tasks.

> **assessment FREEZE FRAME 6.6**
>
> In general, reliance on tests that sample skills through a limited number of items is less informative to our teaching than is the use of assessments that include multiple opportunities to probe or elicit demonstration of content-area knowledge.

Commercially Produced Assessments

The growing population of CLD students in public schools has resulted in an expanding market for assessment tools that aid our understanding of these students and enhance our ability to assess their learning. Marketed tests can be very attractive, as the majority offer formative numerical indices of student skills, and some are developed for use in other languages. A sole reliance on such tests in the belief that they allow us to easily identify and address discrete areas of student need can result, however, in inappropriate placement and instructional practices for CLD students. Readers are cautioned to review discussions in Chapter 5 regarding the validity of any "normed" tests for diverse populations. Used judiciously, however, some of these tools can indeed provide auxiliary pieces of information that may augment a school's more authentic and dynamic picture of student progress in content-area learning.

The Snapshot Assessment System (Rangel & Bansberg, 1999) is an example of a marketed tool that can be used to ascertain information about the content-area learning of CLD students. It is designed to assess the student's related knowledge in Spanish or English but can be administered as a formal formative assessment by teachers who speak only English. In roughly twenty minutes, reading, writing, science, and math can be sampled sufficiently to obtain an overview of a student's L1 or L2 knowledge and skills in core academic areas. One reason the Snapshot is popular among classroom teachers is that it does not simply compare CLD students with an artificial norm in order to derive a statistic that does little to inform instruction. Instead, this assessment provides tangible evidence of standards-based skills in order to aid the teacher in the development of appropriate instructional plans (see Chapter 3 for additional details).

Interpreting Assessment Results

In all cases, the usefulness of assessment data hinges on our ability to knowledgeably interpret the results. When professional teachers are familiar with the formats, implications, and limitations of assessments, they can begin to identify factors in results that lead them to further examine the source of the data or individual student variables before determining success or failure of student learning. Questions to consider include:

- Where and how is the content of the assessment represented in the school's curriculum?
- Have the skills and concepts assessed been taught in a comprehensible manner?
- Is there classroom evidence of content learning that contradicts the results of the assessment? If so, why do the discrepancies exist?
- Were sufficient assessment accommodations provided to mediate the linguistic complexity of the assessment?
- How might a student's level of acculturation or task familiarity have affected her or his performance on the assessment?

The answers to these questions should prove extremely informative, especially when combined with knowledge of language acquisition processes and an awareness of the sociocultural contexts of the instruction and assessment being examined.

Although necessary for accountability and statistical applications, formal assessments can and should coexist effectively with ongoing informal assessment processes. Coltrane (2002) argues that alternative assessments, which he terms performance-based assessments, tend to better mirror the actual instruction that students receive in the classroom. Moreover, he maintains that such assessments help to provide a clearer picture of students' skills, knowledge levels, and academic progress than any single test score. Similar arguments are prevalent in the literature of assessment and best practices for CLD students (Herrera, 2001; Herrera, Trujillo, & Cano, 2005; O'Malley & Pierce, 1996).

■ Summative Content-Area Assessment

Summative content-area assessments are designed to measure student understanding following a sustained period of instruction or participation in a series of instructional sequences. These assessments emphasize the level of student mastery attained and the efficacy of instruction or schooling patterns. From a student perspective, summative assessments are about quantifying performance and determining either grades or sufficient performance to pass to the next level of education or career. From an educator perspective, summative assessments can be used to refine instruction but are more often associated with issues of accountability. From a policy perspective, summative assessments of content-area learning are increasingly about politics, accountability, and rationales for funding decisions.

Informal Summative Assessment: Portfolios as Authentic Assessments

Student assessment portfolios can be used for either formative or summative purposes. However, summative portfolios focus on learning outcomes and provide evidence of the range and extent of a student's skills and knowledge in the content areas. Cooper (1999) summarizes three distinct forms of summative, content-area portfolios. Competency-based or outcomes-based portfolios are constructed in conjunction with a curriculum framework or set of standards for content-area skills and knowledge to be attained. Negotiated learning portfolios provide evidence of learning in relation to a learning contract, which is negotiated between the student and the teacher and specifies goals, objectives, and methods for learning as well as assessment tools for measuring learning outcomes. This type of portfolio emphasizes not only the *what* of learning but also the *why*. Bibliographic portfolios are typically arranged chronologically according to the sequence of learning opportunities to which the student was exposed.

For each of these types of summative portfolios, teachers and students may collaborate to determine the evidence that is chosen for inclusion in the portfolio. For example, they may elect to include artifacts that are indicative of the students' best work. Teachers and students may also decide to include certain process folders in a portfolio. Such folders demonstrate more of the incremental gains (and setbacks) through which the students progressed in order to arrive at the artifacts highlighted in the portfolio.

Finally, students and teachers may decide to build a portfolio around a combination of teacher assessments and student self-assessments that are variously indicative of both process and product learning. The best competency-based portfolios are developed in this manner and emphasize both the effectiveness of the teacher's instruction and the student's self-directedness in skill development and self-assessment. Increasingly, the literature of best practices for CLD students advocates the use of such competency-based portfolios for informal summative assessment (Baca & Cervantes, 1998; Hall, Griffiths, Haslam, & Wilkin, 2001; Herrera, 2001; O'Malley & Pierce, 1996).

Cooper (1999) describes a more or less general process for the development of such portfolios. This six-step portfolio-building process (as adapted for teacher and student purposes) can be summarized as follows:

Step 1: Identify the skills and content-area knowledge the student should develop.

Step 2: Based on the results of step 1, develop specific learning outcomes the student is to attain.

Step 3: Plan classroom instruction and activities through which students will develop those learning strategies that will better enable them to achieve the target outcomes.

Step 4: Identify performance indicators that students and the teacher will use to assess progress toward the target outcomes.

Step 5: Use classroom activities, teacher assessments, and student self-assessments to assemble evidence that the performance indicators have been met.

Step 6: With the student, negotiate the organization of this evidence so that the portfolio and student performance are easily understood by key stakeholders, including other assessors, administrators, and parents.

Because a single item of evidence may be applicable to more than one performance indicator or learning outcome, it is often necessary for the teacher to develop an appropriate cross-referencing system for the student portfolio. In some cases, commentary or a caption may also be needed to explain the relevance of an item of evidence.

E-Portfolios

Although funding issues at the state and local levels have inhibited the progression of this trend, some schools and some classrooms are beginning to use e-portfolios. An e-portfolio is an electronic version of a formative or summative content-area assessment in the form of a portfolio. Such portfolios are variously referred to in the literature as online portfolios, digital portfolios, or webfolios. Although there are slight differences in the ways that each is conceptualized, the differences among them tend to prove nominal.

Of the advantages of e-portfolios, at least two are noteworthy. First, such portfolios are *efficient* in that they reduce the number of resources necessary to manage the portfolio assessment process. Second, such portfolios are *effective* because they build on the many advantages already associated with the portfolio-based assessment of CLD and other students. Various templates, electronic guides, and resources are available on the Internet for teachers who wish to capitalize on this trend. However, most effective conversions to such portfolios require economies of scale and schoolwide participation and funding. For more information about e-portfolios, teachers should consult Barrett (2000), who categorizes five levels of technological sophistication necessary for the use of online portfolios.

Formal Summative Assessment: High-Stakes Tests

Formal summative assessments of content-area learning are increasingly at the heart of school reform and educational funding debates as well as educator accountability arguments. Because the outcomes or results of these assessments have ramifications for the future education, careers, and life paths of students, such assessments are now synonymous with terms such as *high-stakes tests* and *pivotal assessments*. Now more than ever, teachers live and breathe the air of high-stakes tests. It permeates their planning, instruction, and relationships with students and their feelings about their careers. In many places, the results of these tests hold stakes that are just as high for teachers as they are for students and schools. This emphasis on scores has actually prompted some teachers to intentionally disregard administration protocol or to directly teach to the test (Goodnough, 1999). However, the more common response is to focus more intensely on skills and drills in preparation for these tests.

Although such a narrow focus of instruction on the content and constructs of the test has some degree of merit, triangulated studies (e.g., Amrein & Berliner, 2002; Volante, 2004) suggest that the potential for detrimental trade-offs is high and that such trade-offs often result in reductionistic, skills-bound learning, an inability to demonstrate higher-order thinking, and low student motivation. These effects have been noted by other researchers as well who contest the predictive ability of standardized tests and their power to provide informative data about actual student learning (e.g., Burger & Krueger, 2003).

What, then, can teachers do to promote the success of CLD students on high-stakes tests? First, effective educators recognize the power of both formative and summative assessments to guide them as they facilitate students' construction of knowledge. Second, these teachers strive to:

1. Align learning goals with state and local standards
2. Define and describe the desired academic outcomes
3. Ensure the equitable access of all students to educational content and learning opportunities
4. Knowledgeably interpret and respond to student learning behaviors in context
5. Ensure that students enter testing situations with the tools necessary to reduce their affective filters and maximize their performances (e.g., test-taking strategies and skills, experience with modifications, confidence)

In this way, teachers actively promote the classroom engagement and academic success of CLD students in grade-level learning environments. Students who are thus engaged and successful in their learning are, in turn, increasingly self-motivated and prepared to demonstrate their skills and knowledge on high-stakes tests.

■ The Role of Language in Content-Area Assessment

Unfortunately, many schools and districts opt to "prepare" their CLD students for high-stakes tests in English by denying them classroom opportunities to learn, and to demonstrate their learning, through the native language or appropriately modified instructional techniques and assessments. These practices significantly compromise not only the education of CLD students but also the ability of teachers to understand and differentially respond to the students' learning processes. Moreover, validity issues arise when linguistic and presentation modifications that were not used during instruction are then used to assess CLD learning on high-stakes tests. For example, most schools and districts that attempt to accommodate students' first language needs either use personnel of varying qualifications to provide written or verbal translation or purchase marketed translations of English-based tests. However, simply translating tests from English to the student's native language does not significantly improve performance unless the student actually received instruction in his or her native language. This concern holds true even for tests (e.g., Supera, Logramos, Aprenda, SABE, Woodcock–Muñoz) that are designed for use with specific CLD populations. If students have not been exposed to the content-area curriculum in their native language or do not possess sufficient literacy skills in the native language, the tests will not yield valid results (Abedi, 2001; Abedi, Lord, & Hoffstetter, 1998; August & Hakuta, 1997).

Because a large number of languages spoken by CLD students cannot be supported by existing materials or testing personnel, and because the majority of CLD students in this country receive their academic instruction in English, it becomes more appropriate for many students to be assessed in English, their nondominant language. For others, the decision is systemic rather than individualized. However, in either case, one must strongly consider the impact that language may have on a CLD student's capacity to comprehend what is being asked and to demonstrate acquired knowledge by means of language-loaded assessment formats.

Mr. Loucks, a fifth-grade teacher, understands the potential benefits of allowing CLD students to use their native language to demonstrate academic capacities. In the following passage, he reflects on his instructional practices to enhance the writing skills of one particular Spanish-speaking student. Figure 6.7 depicts a sample of this student's writing. For purposes of anonymity, the student's name has been changed to Enrique.

> The practice of having one of my ELL students occasionally complete his Weekend Write-up in Spanish was a highlight for both him and the class. At the beginning Enrique was not a willing writer. When I asked him to write about his weekend, I'd get maybe two or three sentences at best. As time progressed, I realized that Enrique indeed was a fairly fluent writer in Spanish, his L1. Although at first he was hesitant to write in much detail in Spanish, his writing really blossomed when I allowed him to share his writing with the class. Probably the highlight for Enrique and the class was the time I made an overhead transparency of what he was reading and they could follow along. Not only was this an opportunity for my class to realize that it was indeed a gift to be bilingual, but it also helped them realize that there were things they didn't know—like Spanish. Enrique's credibility in the class skyrocketed when he started sharing and claiming his Spanish language, instead of trying to hide it.
>
> As time went on, Enrique's writing continued to flourish. That isn't to say it was perfect. As you can see . . . Enrique didn't believe in punctuation. ☺ This was a continual struggle for him. Once he got writing, he wanted to just write, not punctuate. I know he still struggles with this in 6th grade, but at least he was writing. I'd rather allow him to be fluent in writing his L1 than be so preoccupied with the mechanics that he loses his interest in writing.
>
> Enrique was also allowed to write his State Writing Assessment in Spanish. . . . We had already started our first day of prewriting during the State Assessment when Enrique approached me and wanted to know if he could write in Spanish. When I asked him why he wanted to do this, he said it was because he could do a better job in Spanish. Our curriculum director called the . . . [State] Department of Education and was told that as long as there was a qualified scorer available, [Enrique] could write in Spanish. As you might suspect, Enrique got hammered in Conventions and Fluency, but scored well in Ideas and Content, Organization, and fair in Voice and Word Choice.

Mr. Loucks's professional and accommodative practices were pivotal in the appropriate assessment of this student. Because he had previously allowed Enrique to write in his native language, Mr. Loucks saw the validity of Enrique's request to complete the state writing assessment in Spanish. Cross-culturally competent teachers such as Mr. Loucks advocate on behalf of CLD students for assessment accommodations that enable these students to best demonstrate their abilities.

Teachers and administrators who share an inclusive vision of student learning understand that the purpose of assessment, at all levels, is to inform and guide the instruction of students. This can only occur when the manner and the content of student instruction and assessment are aligned. Therefore, classroom teachers

■ **figure 6.7** Assessment Artifact: L1 Writing Sample

■ Page 1

ARTIFACT 1.1 {11-16-03}

Fin De Semana!

El Sabado fui a patinar con
Los alumnos de La escuela y
anduvimos patinando y tambien
jugamos limbo y tambien nos
pusimos a jugar quen podia ir
mas recio y cuando acabamos
patinamos despacio y Luego yo
Yva dando La Buelta pero ai
venia Mr. Rhodes con una linia
de estudiantes y cuando me fige
uy venia y Luego chocamos y
con el patin medio en Lacintura
y Luego me Levante y mediso
que si estava bien y yo Le dise
que si y me sali a comprar
comida para comer y Luego fui a
jugar Los juegos y despoesque
avia terminado de jugar fui a
patinar por 5 minutos y despues
de 5 minutos fui por mis zapatos
y despues yo y mis amigos nos subimos
al camion y empezamos a platicar
sobre que fue lo que se les hiso
mas divertido y tambien platicamos
sobre lo que aciamos en La

■ Page 2

escuela el lunes y despues
yegamos a La escuela y nos
bajamos de el camion y despues
me fui a mi casa y cuando llegue
a mi casa Les conte a mis padres
y a my ermana todo lo que
ocurio en el fin de patinaje.

De Parte De

are encouraged to implement appropriate assessment accommodations. This will not only facilitate learning but also significantly increase the alignment and accuracy of high-stakes tests to validly measure CLD students' content-area knowledge and skills.

To reduce test anxiety and provide CLD students with appropriate language support, Mr. Wille synthesized the input of fellow teachers to create a test vocabulary handbook, an excerpt of which is pictured in Figure 6.8. The teachers identified vocabulary terms and phrases frequently found in the instructions of standardized tests. Then they provided an explanation for the testing vocabulary as well as a visual to enhance comprehensibility. The definitions were translated into Arabic, Chinese, Korean, and Spanish. This tool enabled teachers within the school system to use consistent testing language as they prepared students to take standardized assessments. The handbook was beneficial for *all* students because the instructions were simple and precise. Moreover, the testing language the students used during classroom instruction was the same language they encountered in formal assessment.

> **assessment *FREEZE FRAME* 6.7**
>
> Cross-culturally competent teachers advocate on behalf of CLD students for assessment accommodations that enable these students to best demonstrate their abilities.

■ Bias in Classroom-Based Content-Area Assessments

Multidimensional assessment is critical for CLD learners because such assessment is based on concepts of learning and intelligence that go beyond those emphasized by cultures that value logic, linearity, and verbal skills as the primary indicators of innate ability. When visual, tactile, kinesthetic, intrapersonal, and interpersonal skills are equally recognized avenues of learning and intellect, CLD students have increased access to the curriculum and opportunities to demonstrate authentically internalized knowledge. It is not enough, however, to simply provide hands-on activities. Differences in language, past experiences (personal and educational), sociocultural precepts, and approaches to novel tasks may continue to preempt the access of CLD students to the learning goals of traditionally designed projects or multimodal activity (Westby, Dezale, Fradd, & Lee, 1999).

> **assessment *FREEZE FRAME* 6.8**
>
> When visual, tactile, kinesthetic, intrapersonal, and interpersonal skills are equally recognized avenues of learning and intellect, CLD students have increased access to the curriculum and opportunities to demonstrate authentically internalized knowledge.

The absolute certainty with which we contend that our views and experiences are universal becomes especially problematic when we consider issues of assessment. One of the reasons bias may be difficult to address is that it is not always easy to recognize. The following vignette illustrates this dilemma:

> As she reviewed her students' scores on a district math assessment, a Kansas teacher was mystified as to why so many of her CLD students did poorly on a particular item. The question involved having the students calculate how many checkerboards would

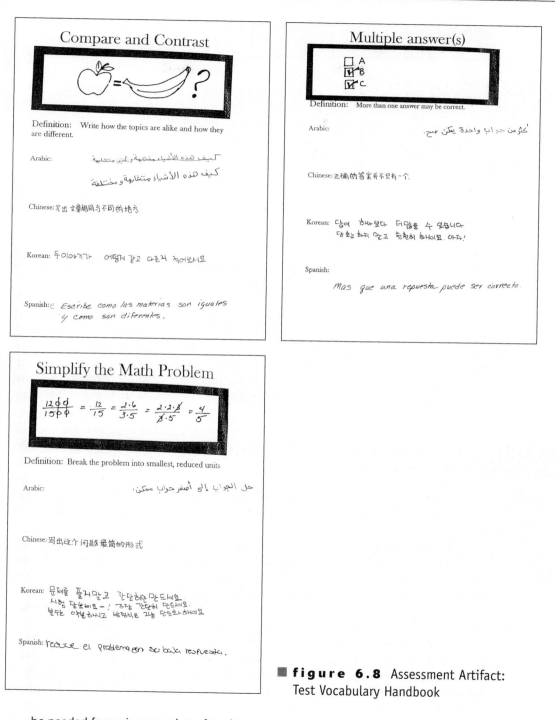

figure 6.8 Assessment Artifact: Test Vocabulary Handbook

be needed for a given number of students to play checkers. Students were required to show their work in mathematical and pictorial form. To her surprise, the teacher noted that most of the CLD students depicted three to four students at a game. Although their

close-up *on Assessment 6.5*

Effective school leaders:

- Involve staff in ongoing professional development, discussion, and reflection related to student assessment
- Directly address and share examples of unwitting bias in assessments
- Recommend guiding questions to direct the development of assessments that reduce bias

related calculations were correct, the students' answers were graded as incorrect. According to the teacher:

> Even though this test question was about something as insignificant as checkers, it served to separate the "haves" from the "have-nots" and the "knows" from the "know-nots," but not in the area of math. To me this is just a tiny example of how entire groups of people can be held back, be it inadvertently or intentionally.

As this example demonstrates, test items that require cultural knowledge as well as content-area knowledge may hinder appropriate interpretation of assessment results.

Although it is a recognized concern that tests designed for large groups of students must be scrutinized in terms of their appropriateness for all students, similar biases may also exist in teacher-made tests. In the following example, Principal Richard Wirtz poses the following questions as he reflects on his role as an assessment leader:

> When assessments are designed to test content or prior knowledge, are they free from cultural bias? Do I plan staff development that considers assessment training? Are examples of test items shared that display test bias and some that don't? Do I outline the requirements that make up quality test items . . . guidelines . . . if you will? Are teachers expected to reflect on questions they should ask themselves before attempting to write test items that display cognitive skills without compromising the background of the student?

These are excellent questions. Effective learning leaders involve staff in ongoing training, discussion, and reflection related to assessment. They directly address and share examples of unwitting bias in tests. They recommend guiding questions for teachers to consider as they work to reduce bias in their assessments. It is difficult to produce test items and tasks that are equally free of bias for all students in today's diverse classrooms. However, our objective in all cases is to identify and rectify, to the greatest extent possible, controllable elements of bias in our assessment tools and procedures.

Astute teachers recognize that a potential for bias exists in all forms of assessment. In some classes, particular students may be perceived as more capable or diligent based on factors such as race, language proficiency, dialect, affiliations, or the teacher's previous experience with similar or related students. Teachers may inadvertently provide differing amounts of support and feedback during ongoing assessments such as portfolios, or allow unrelated opinions or political concerns to influence their subjective ratings of student work. Although these issues can cloud or corrupt the validity of nonstandardized assessments, the capacity of such assessments to positively influence student learning and contribute significantly to what we know about how students learn compels us to improve our control of bias rather than diminish the role of these valuable tools. The following questions may help educators identify bias within a variety of assessment tools and approaches (Hamayan & Damico, 1991; Ovando, Collier, & Combs, 2003):

1. Is the content of the assessment linked to known student experiences?
2. Does the assessment take into account the impact of prior school experiences?
3. Have cultural values and practices (e.g., cooperation versus competition, role of time) been considered for their impact on student responses?
4. Is the task appropriate to the developmental level(s) of the students?
5. Have the language demands of the task been adjusted for the language proficiency level(s) of the students?
6. What are the prerequisite skills or knowledge assumed by the task?
   —Are they related to the target being measured?
   —If not, are they known (not assumed) to be familiar to the students?
   —How can this item be modified to reduce the potential for bias?
7. Are assessment accommodations employed during assessment consistent with those used during content-area instruction?
8. Has the assessment process and product been reviewed by others for sources of potential bias?
9. Are the criteria for responses or goal attainment clearly defined?
10. How has rater and inter-rater reliability been addressed (e.g., "blind" grading and exchanges)?

Some teachers who have begun to embrace the promise of better assessment practices now ask, "Will an increase in authenticity and reduction of bias in assessments result in higher demonstrated achievement of CLD students?" The answer is, "Not necessarily . . . but they certainly can." Because the goal of content-area assessment is to measure academic learning, effective assessment practices simply provide a clearer picture of instructional efficacy with a given student or group. Therefore, students who are not receiving accommodative instruction that fosters engaged participation in the curriculum will continue to perform poorly. If bias and inequity are not recognized at the instructional level, even the least biased assessments will yield inherently biased results.

■ Programming-Related Issues: Content-Area Assessment

Necessarily, issues of placement and programming for CLD students who are acquiring English as a second language are topics beyond the scope of this text. Nonetheless, the results of assessing acculturation, content-area skills and knowledge, and, in particular, language proficiency can aid decision making associated with these issues. Therefore, the following discussion highlights salient, grade-level issues of content-area assessment that are relevant to the identification, placement, monitoring, and exit of CLD students. This discussion is by no means exhaustive but provides a synopsis of issues that should be considered.

Identification

Ideally, the identification of CLD students for differential instruction is not based solely on a single measure or limited sampling of literacy domains (listening, speaking, reading, and writing). Within each of these domains are innumerable factors that render otherwise identical scores fundamentally inequivalent. Many protocols to identify CLD students who are not yet proficient in English gather little, if any, information about content-area knowledge and skills. However, the determination of whether students have a history of prior L1 education or have been exposed to cognitively rich experiences and conversation in L2 is essential to appropriate placement.

Placement

Creative and individualized placement may be needed for CLD students who would benefit in many ways from a newcomer program but who have skills that would not be capitalized on in this environment. Unfortunately, it is common to discover CLD students placed, for example, in remedial math despite mastery of calculus in a prior country or setting. Teachers are encouraged to discover the facets of each student's learning background that expose strengths or resources that can be drawn on in accommodative classrooms.

Monitoring

Ongoing and varied formative assessments provide teachers with (a) information needed to monitor and document student progress, (b) input for appropriate instructional modifications, (c) indicators that a student may need enhanced levels of differential support, and (d) evidence of a student's readiness for redesignation. Unless teachers monitor to maintain a comprehensible level of instructional and intellectual rigor, students may become so accustomed to added support that they doubt their abilities to be successful on their own. Attention to student empowerment and confidence are, therefore, encouraged at all times but become especially important as readiness for exit approaches.

Exit

Student performance on content-area assignments and assessments are part of the body of evidence necessary to consider a student's redesignation from differential programming designed to support English language acquisition. Teachers are encouraged to review multiple sources of data when making recommendations about the best instructional situation for a CLD student. When educators closely monitor student learning in various contexts, it is generally apparent when a CLD student is ready to be exited from a program. Although subjective input from teachers can be extremely valuable to the process, there are occasions when teachers are either inclined to underestimate student readiness or desire to shield students from the accommodated experience. Such resistance to redesignation without sufficient (especially data-driven) rationales can inhibit educational opportunities and growth potentials among CLD students.

■ key concepts

Bibliographic portfolio
Commercially produced assessment
Competency-based portfolio
Criterion-referenced test
Curriculum-based measurement
E-portfolio
Formal formative assessment
Formal summative assessment

Formative assessment
General outcome measurement
High-stakes tests
Informal formative assessment
Informal summative assessment
Inquiry assessment
Mastery measurement
Negotiated learning portfolio
Norm-referenced test

Observation assessment
Outcomes-based portfolio
Point-in-time assessment
Self-assessment
Summative assessment
Teacher-made test
Technology-based assessment

■ professional conversations on practice

1. Discuss the purpose of assessment and ways that high-stakes tests are consistent and inconsistent with this purpose.
2. Discuss why formative content-area assessments might be better than summative assessments for accommodating instruction and promoting learning for CLD students.
3. Discuss how content-area assessments may be culturally or linguistically loaded, measuring knowledge of the dominant culture or language rather than content-area learning.
4. Discuss why self-assessment strategies may prove particularly beneficial to CLD students.

■ questions for review and reflection

1. Why are content-area assessments sometimes underemphasized with CLD students?
2. How much time does second language acquisition typically take for CLD students who receive no native language support?
3. What assessment-related problems occur when translating tests from English to a CLD student's native language?
4. What are similarities and differences between formative and summative content-area assessments?
5. How does limited wait time in conversation-based instructional assessment (inquiry assessment) negatively affect content-area learning for CLD students?
6. What are key features of informal observation assessments?
7. What concerns should teachers have when developing their own informal content-area assessments for CLD students? Explore at least two.
8. What is the difference between point-in-time and observational assessments?
9. Why is it critical to measure incremental gains in content-area learning and second language acquisition with CLD students?
10. What are similarities and differences between mastery and general outcome measurement?
11. What are CBMs designed to measure?
12. What steps should teachers follow as they develop curriculum-based measures for assessing content-area learning of CLD students?
13. How are student self-assessments consistent with the idea of a constructivist learning environment?
14. Why should teachers carefully consider the use of technology-based assessments with CLD students? Explore at least three reasons.
15. What types of informal formative assessments have teachers successfully used with CLD students to measure content-area learning? Explore four or more.
16. What is the difference between criterion-referenced and norm-referenced assessments?
17. What are useful steps to follow when developing criterion-referenced tests for CLD students?
18. What concerns should teachers have as they interpret formal formative assessments of content-area learning?
19. What questions should teachers explore in determining whether bias exists in content-area assessments? Discuss at least three.

objectives

- Explain the terms *exceptionality* and *disproportionality*.

- Describe the significance of the phrase "opportunity to learn" in classroom assessment practices for CLD students.

- Discuss the classroom assessment implications of the term *least restrictive environment*.

- Discuss the academic, attention, and behavior difficulties of CLD students that classroom teachers may erroneously interpret as indicators of a learning disability.

- Detail the types of constructive data a classroom teacher can provide to a teacher assistance team regarding a CLD student who is having difficulties with classroom material.

- Differentiate between preassessment for general education and preassessment for special education.

- Explain why a classroom teacher should not refer a CLD student to special education before attempting scaffolded or mediated instruction.

- Defend why assessment modifications for CLD students and potential biases in assessments should be reported as critical aspects of assessment findings pertinent to a referral.

- Explain why CLD parents, guardians, and extended family members (as pertinent) should participate in the referral and assessment processes for special education.

- Discuss factors that may explain why CLD students are consistently overrepresented in special education and underrepresented in gifted and talented programs.

- Define and discuss SLAAP, as well as the most significant implications of SLAAP for classroom teachers of CLD students.

- Discuss questions classroom teachers should ask during the preassessment process and before referring a CLD student to special education.

Special Education Issues in the Assessment of CLD Students

When I moved to [a SPED classroom in a new school], my class was again filled with Spanish students. Many of them were labeled "borderline," which I soon discovered meant that they could have functioned in a regular class if [appropriate] interventions had been used. . . . I often felt my class was a dumping ground for students the teachers could not handle. More than once a teacher would remark that the student just did not "fit" in her classroom.

Shirley Wilson
PreK Teacher

critical standards *Guiding Chapter Content*

TESOL/NCATE teacher standards reflect professional consensus on standards for the quality teaching of PreK–12 CLD students. Additionally, the CEEE Guiding Principles and their accompanying indicators serve as a framework to assist practitioners, policymakers, and clients as they collaborate to enhance academic enrichment and language acquisition among CLD students. Therefore, to help educators understand how they might appropriately target and address national professional teaching standards in practice, we have designed the content of this chapter to reflect the following standards.

TESOL/NCATE Standards for P–12 Teacher Education Programs

Domain 3: Planning, Implementing, and Managing Instruction Candidates know, understand, and use standards-based practices and strategies related to planning, implementing, and managing ESL and content instruction, including classroom organization, teaching strategies for developing and integrating language skills, and choosing and adapting classroom resources.

- **Standard 3.a. Planning for Standards-Based ESL and Content Instruction.** Candidates know, understand, and apply concepts, research, and best practices to plan classroom instruction in a supportive learning environment for ESOL students. Candidates serve as effective English-language models, as they plan for multilevel classrooms with learners from diverse backgrounds using standards-based ESL and content curriculum.

  3.a.3. Plan students' learning experiences based on assessment of language proficiency and prior knowledge.

Domain 4: Assessment. Candidates understand issues of assessment and use standards-based assessment measures with ESOL students

- **Standard 4.a. Issues of Assessment for ESL.** Candidates understand various issues of assessment (e.g., cultural and linguistic bias; political, social, and psychological factors) in assessment, IQ, and special education testing (including gifted and talented), the importance of standards-based assessment, and the difference between language proficiency and other types of assessment (e.g., standardized achievement tests of overall mastery), as they affect ESOL student learning.

Note: All TESOL/NCATE standards are cited from TESOL (2003). All Guiding Principles are cited from Center for Equity and Excellence in Education (CEEE) (2005). Reprinted by permission.

4.a.4. Distinguish between a language difference, gifted and talented, and special education needs for ESOL students.

- **Standard 4.b. Language Proficiency Assessment.** Candidates know and use a variety of standards-based language proficiency instruments to inform their instruction and understand their uses for identification, placement, and demonstration of language growth of ESOL students.

   4.b.1. Understand and implement national and state requirements for identification, reclassification, and exit of ESOL students from language support programs.

   4.b.4. Understand, construct, and use assessment measures for a variety of purposes for ESOL students.

CEEE Guiding Principles

Principle #3: English language learners are taught academic content that enables them to meet challenging performance standards in all content areas, consistent with those for all students.

3.7 **Use** appropriate multiple assessment tools and techniques to measure English language learners' progress in achieving academic standards and in acquiring English proficiency; use assessment results to inform classroom teaching and learning, and communicate these results to families in a meaningful and accessible manner.

Principle #4: English language learners receive instruction that builds on their prior knowledge and cognitive abilities and is responsive to their language proficiency levels and cultural backgrounds.

4.1 **Consider** the whole student, including English language proficiency, language/cultural background, native language literacy, and appropriate and valid student assessment data when making decisions about placement and provision of services for English language learners.

Principle #5: English language learners are evaluated with appropriate and valid assessments that are aligned to state and local standards and that take into account the language development stages and cultural backgrounds of the students.

5.1 **Assess** English language learners on the same content and according to the same performance standards as all students, varying the assessment as needed to accommodate the individual characteristics of the learner, including, but not limited to, the student's level of English language proficiency.

5.6 **Review** on a regular basis whether assessments administered are being used appropriately (e.g., for purposes for which the tests have been validated) for English language learners.

5.10 **Use** a variety of formal and authentic assessment techniques to enhance classroom knowledge of English language learners and to evaluate their academic and linguistic progress.

One of the most challenging dilemmas teachers face is wondering *if* and *when* to consider special education for CLD students. Unless educators have substantial knowledge of, and are responsive to, the unique sociolinguistic needs of CLD students, these students are at greater risk of being misidentified, mislabeled, and consequently miseducated in our schools. Paolo may be one such student.

close-up *on Assessment* **7.1**

One of the most challenging dilemmas teachers face is wondering *if* and *when* to consider special education for CLD students. Unless educators have substantial knowledge of, and are responsive to, the unique sociolinguistic needs of CLD students, these students are at greater risk of being misidentified, mislabeled, and consequently miseducated in our schools.

When Paolo entered prekindergarten speaking no English, his parents were advised that the best way to help him succeed in school would be to stop speaking Portuguese at home. Respectful of the teachers' expertise, Mr. and Mrs. Souza tried their best to comply with this recommendation, but it proved particularly difficult for Paolo's mother, who had not yet acquired much English. As a result of their efforts to minimize Paolo's exposure to Portuguese, the dynamics of the Souza home changed considerably. The spontaneity and descriptive richness of previous interactions was replaced by awkwardly simplistic discourse. Those times when Paolo's parents did "slip" or "regress" to Portuguese were accompanied by oddly mixed feelings of relief and guilt.

By the middle of his kindergarten year, Paolo spoke English well enough to get along with friends and communicate basic needs at school. He also began to show a rejection of the Portuguese language at home, reminding his parents to "speak English," or simply ignoring their comments in the native tongue. Paolo's teachers interpreted this preference as a positive step in the acquisition of English but began to notice the onset of academic concerns. By the year's end, Paolo was the only student who had not fully memorized the alphabet. His teacher provided Mrs. Souza with flash cards to practice over the summer and recommended she read to him daily in English.

Unfortunately, despite the additional practice and exposure to English, the initial first-grade assessment revealed that Paolo had actually lost ground over the summer, naming fewer letters in September than had been mastered the previous May. As an intervention, Paolo worked with a tutor on his letters and phonics while the rest of the class read and discussed stories during language arts. By mid-year, Paolo had a basic command of phonics but could only blend sounds to form words with a picture referent. Without visual choices, he often said the wrong word even after correctly sounding out the letters. The reading specialist suggested that memory or a very limited vocabulary might be factors in his performance. Having learned the essentials of phonics, Paolo rejoined his class for language arts but lacked many of the skills and experiences assumed for these lessons. Although Paolo's teacher knew he was technically an "ESL" student, she was not sure whether this was really an issue because even Paolo's parents described him as English-dominant. However, his English comprehension and expression were noticeably poor when compared to other English speakers. Paolo's teacher considered retention but reluctantly advanced him on to second grade.

This type of case prompts reflective teachers to consider the following questions:

- Does Paolo demonstrate any characteristics of a learning disability?
- Does he demonstrate characteristics of a language disability? In English? In his primary language?
- What experiences or phenomena other than disability might account for his lack of full proficiency in either language?

In the case of Paolo's academic difficulties, such teachers would also examine the potential role of the following:

- Paolo's language acquisition history
- The sociolinguistic environment at his home and school
- Paolo's educational opportunities
- The particular instructional practices used with Paolo

Those involved with the education of CLD students often discover that thoughtful exploration of these questions and possibilities not only helps them mediate the multiple issues surrounding CLD students and special education but also profoundly informs their understanding of the students' regular education needs.

■ What Is Special Education?

Special education is the term given to a range of programs and supports, to which exceptional students are entitled by law, that ensure each student receives a free and appropriate public education. This assurance, commonly referred to as FAPE, is described in Part B and Appendix C of the Individuals with Disabilities Education Act (IDEA) (Public Law 105–117, reauthorized in 2004). To be eligible for special education services, students must be identified as having one or more cognitive, linguistic, or physical exceptionalities that require such students to receive special instructional approaches or supports in order to participate in and benefit from the curriculum. Such exceptionalities include speech or language impairments, behavioral disorders, specific learning difficulties, physical impairments

close-up *on Assessment 7.2*

Special education is the term given to a range of programs and supports, to which exceptional students are entitled by law, that ensure each student receives a free and appropriate public education. This assurance, commonly referred to as FAPE, is described in Part B and Appendix C of the Individuals with Disabilities Education Act (IDEA) (Public Law 105–117, reauthorized in 2004).

(e.g., mobility, vision, hearing), or cognitive skills that are significantly higher or lower than the average range of a student's peers. In the case of students with severe cognitive impairments, academic goals may represent the general curriculum in the broader sense of helping these students develop the life skills necessary to function as independently as possible in society.

Although there is variation in the criteria required by each state to meet the definition of exceptionality, special education eligibility is generally understood to exclude achievement discrepancies that are the result of external variables such as language, experience, cultural difference, socioeconomic status, attendance, mobility, and family crises. Because intrinsic or natural exceptionalities can be assumed to occur in all populations at similar rates, we would expect all groups to be represented in special education in numbers proportional to their representation in a given population. No group would be significantly more or less likely to be placed in special education than another group (Artiles & Harry, 2004).

> **assessment FREEZE FRAME 7.1**
>
> Although there is variation in the criteria required by each state to meet the definition of exceptionality, special education eligibility is generally understood to exclude achievement discrepancies that are the result of external variables such as language, experience, cultural difference, attendance, mobility, and family crises.

For example, a school district with 35 percent Caucasian, 20 percent African American, 25 percent Hispanic, 10 percent Asian, 5 percent American Indian, and 5 percent Biracial or Other would expect to see similar demographic patterns in all its special education programs, including those for the gifted and talented. Consider the implications for such a district that has the following special education demographics:

	American Indian	Asian	African American	Caucasian	Hispanic	Biracial / Other
School District Population	5%	10%	20%	35%	25%	5%
Gifted/Talented		16 %	4%	75%	4%	1%
Learning Disabilities		4%	27%	36%	33%	
Speech/Language Impaired	3%	14%	19%	30%	33%	1%
Behavior Disorders			34%	28%	31%	7%
Visually Impaired	6%	8%	22%	37%	24%	3%

As this table illustrates, students from different ethnic backgrounds are represented disproportionately in this district's special education programs. For example, although 10 percent of the student population is Asian, 16 percent of students in gifted and talented programs are Asian, and no Asian students have been identified as having behavior disorders. By contrast, African American students make up 20 percent of the student population, yet only 4 percent of students in gifted and talented programs are African American, and African Americans represent 34 percent of students identified as having behavior disorders.

Further examination of these data reveals "visually impaired" is the exceptionality that most closely reflects the overall representation of students in the district. Why might this be the case? For which exceptionalities might language acquisition or cultural mismatch be factors in the disproportional representation of CLD students? What other potentially informative demographic information is missing from this table?

Is Disproportionality Really an Issue?

Yes. Data included in the twenty-fourth annual report to Congress on IDEA implementation in 2002 revealed that despite the fact that the percentage of the general population that did not speak English in the home increased by only 2.5 percent between 1987 and 2001, there was a nearly 11 percent increase in special education placements for students from those homes during the same period. When this type of data is disaggregated further, interesting patterns become clear. Hispanic students, for example, continue to be overrepresented in special education programs for learning disabilities, hearing, and orthopedic impairments (U.S. Department of Education, 2002b). African American and American Indian students, especially males, are often overrepresented in programs for learning disabilities, mental retardation, and behavioral disorders (Yates, 1998). African American, Hispanic, and American Indian students are also typically underrepresented in programs for the gifted and talented (Ford, 1998). This is a situation that continues despite training efforts to improve identification of CLD students (Bernal, 2003). In addition, "although Asian American students are often underrepresented in special education, recent studies have highlighted concerns about the cultural and linguistic appropriateness of the identification and placement process" (Poon-McBrayer & Garcia, 2000).

Researchers have identified a number of factors that appear to contribute to the disproportionate consideration of CLD students for special education. Those most commonly noted include:

- Racial and ethnic minorities are more likely to experience poverty, which is a factor in special education referrals and placements (Oswald, Coutinho, Best, & Singh, 1999; Proctor & Dalaker, 2002).

close-up *on Assessment 7.3*

Hispanic students, for example, continue to be overrepresented in special education programs for learning disabilities, hearing, and orthopedic impairments. African American and American Indian students, especially males, are often overrepresented in programs for learning disabilities, mental retardation, and behavioral disorders. African American, Hispanic, and American Indian students are also typically underrepresented in programs for the gifted and talented. This is a situation that continues despite training efforts to improve identification of CLD students.

- Economic status and immigration issues, which are more prevalent among CLD students than the general population, are associated with higher student mobility, which can significantly affect a student's opportunity to learn. The U.S. Department of Education (2002a) found that schools serving large proportions of migrant students had lower academic expectations, less consistent content and performance standards, and less experienced teachers than other schools.
- A historic lack of school accountability for practices and instances of disproportionality may actually perpetuate existing imbalances (Townsend, 2000). Inappropriate special education placements and actions locate achievement or behavior problems within the student population and enable the educational system to avoid taking necessary measures to identify and accommodate the general education needs of diverse students (Baca & Cervantes, 2004).
- Low-income students as a group, which includes the majority of CLD students, typically have less access to a quality education provided by highly qualified teachers who use techniques and materials known to be effective for diverse learners (Biddle & Berliner, 2002).
- Low school achievement is found to be a significant factor in the determination of disability (Hosp & Reschly, 2004; MacMillan, Gresham, & Bocian, 1998); therefore, educational practices that result in achievement gaps between CLD and dominant-culture students may contribute to the overrepresentation of CLD students in special education.
- Despite concerns regarding the influence of culture, language acquisition, and prior educational experiences, many schools continue to rely on discrepancy models that interpret achievement gaps as indicators of learning disability (Smith Bailey, 2003; Ortiz, 2004; Baca & Cervantes, 2004).
- Despite the range of considerations necessary to determine genuine educational disability, assessment teams often make decisions based on insufficient information (Overton, Fielding & Simonsson, 2004) or use of standardized assessments that are not developed, normed, or administered appropriately for CLD students (Reynolds, Lowe, Saenz, 1999). Furthermore, teachers tend to rely on oral language proficiency as an indicator of academic performance (Limbos & Geva, 2001).
- Teachers may misinterpret culturally different behaviors as indicators of learning or behavioral disability (Salend, 2005).
- Students acquiring a second language often exhibit academic, attention, and behavior difficulties that are similar to those of students with a learning disability (Collier, 2004; Fradd & McGee, 1994).

assessment FREEZE FRAME 7.2

Inappropriate special education placements and actions locate achievement or behavior problems within the student population and enable the educational system to avoid taking necessary measures to identify and accommodate the general education needs of diverse students.

Although most teachers recognize that CLD students may have difficulty with skills such as vocabulary, pronunciation, and grammar, many have never considered the numerous other characteristics associated with students with learning disabilities that are also typical of students acquiring a second language or experiencing acculturation (see Figure 7.1).

Why Should We Be Concerned?

For a number of reasons, disproportional representation in special education is a matter of concern for administrators, teachers, parents, and other stakeholders. One overriding reason is the realization that disproportionality can be a strong indicator that students are not being identified for, or placed in, the most appropriate programs. By appropriate, we mean *least restrictive;* that is, the program or setting in which students can maximally participate in and be challenged by the curriculum. For most students, the least restrictive environment is regular education. However, the unaccommodative regular classroom may actually be very restrictive to the CLD student who is either overwhelmed or underchallenged in that setting. In this situation, it is most likely the level of instructional accommodation rather than the presence or absence of student exceptionality that should be addressed first.

When nondisabled students are misidentified and placed in special education settings, they are disenfranchised from the broader offerings and opportunities of the grade-level classroom. For these students, the special education setting or classroom is a more restrictive setting that may constrain their learning. In contrast, the student with a genuine disability is often better able to learn when provided the type of structure and supports that would typically restrict other learners. Fortunately, many schools have begun implementing practices based on the understanding that least restrictive environments are not the same for all students. Increasing numbers are moving away from pull-out programs toward inclusive classrooms where purposeful collaboration between grade-level, ESL, and special education teachers fosters optimal learning environments for students.

The other side of disproportional representation is underrepresentation. In some cases, truly exceptional students may be denied consideration for services because all their difficulties are attributed to language, or because schools lack the confidence or experience to distinguish between language acquisition phenomena and learning disabilities. Whenever students are being over- or underidentified

---

close-up *on Assessment 7.4*

When nondisabled students are misidentified and placed in special education settings, they are disenfranchised from the broader offerings and opportunities of the grade-level classroom. For these students, the special education setting or classroom is a more restrictive setting that may constrain their learning. In contrast, the student with a genuine disability is often better able to learn when provided the type of structure and supports that would typically restrict other learners.

figure 7.1

Typical Characteristics of Both English Speakers with a Learning Disability and Second Language Learners without a Disability

Sources: Collier (2004), Fradd and McGee (1994), and Baca and Cervantes (2004).

LITERACY

Difficulty with sound–symbol association

Sounds out words but unable to blend

Poor orientation to page and text

Below grade-level reading

Struggles in content areas

Unusual spelling errors

Letter reversals

Difficulty with grammar structures

Trouble remembering
- Words/text read
- Syllable sequences
- Letters/numbers seen

SOCIAL/VOCATIONAL

Anxious or emotional

Distracted or withdrawn

Limited attention span

Frustrates or angers easily

Appears to lack motivation

Exhibits disorderly behavior

Poor-quality work

Poor social skills with peers

Oral class participation
- Limited
- Off-topic

LANGUAGE

Appears delayed compared to peers

Articulation and grammar errors

Limited vocabulary

Difficulty following directions

Forgets easily
- What was just said/heard/read
- Previously learned information

Poor phonemic awareness skills
- Unable to rhyme
- Struggles with auditory sound blending

Misunderstands pragmatics—body language

Narratives lack details/sequence

Comprehension problems

SCIENCE/MATH

Overreliance on fingers or manipulatives

Poor performance on timed tests

Difficulty remembering
- Content-area vocabulary
- Processes and procedures

Poor comprehension

Difficulty with orally presented materials
- Story problem formats
- Abstract concepts

assessment FREEZE FRAME 7.3

When CLD students are more likely than others to be removed from the grade-level classroom for special programming, those left behind are denied the richness of diverse perspectives and experiences that complement their own learning.

for special education services, students are being effectively disenfranchised from their maximal participation in the curriculum. In addition, there are more subtle consequences of disproportionality that affect all students. When CLD students are more likely than others to be removed from the grade-level classroom for special programming, those left behind are denied the richness of diverse perspectives and experiences that complement their own learning.

Implications for Classroom Teachers

According to Brown (2004), a teacher's professional development in the critical role that language acquisition and acculturation play in student performance is "the first step in reducing the over-referral of CLD students for special education" (p. 226). Brown has proposed the term *second language acquisition-associated phenomena* (SLAAP) to describe the set of issues that confound the determination of disability with CLD students. These phenomena can include factors such as culture shock, first language loss, inconsistent education, and reduced opportunities to learn stemming from inappropriate instructional models, low teacher expectations, mobility, and so forth.

Students who are in the process of learning within another language and culture typically exhibit many of the same characteristics seen in the dominant-culture students with genuine language or learning disorders. To determine whether a perceived difference is, in fact, a disability, educators need to carefully assess the context in which the concern occurs and the history of its development. Unfortunately, these critical steps are most often overlooked, omitted, or downplayed in the referral of CLD students to special education.

Occasionally, a particular student will stand out as having an atypical level of difficulty learning classroom material. Concerned teachers modify their lessons and the manner of delivery to find "keys" to teaching the child, but they may also need to consult others for assistance in planning further interventions. Sometimes the ideas and recommendations provided reflect common approaches for all students and are not appropriately tailored to the specific needs of the CLD student. This is less likely to occur when individuals knowledgeable about language acquisition and cultural diversity are included on teams that assemble periodically to facilitate the intervention planning process. Although the names for these teams (e.g., prereferral, student intervention, teacher assistance) and their specific functions may vary, they commonly provide teachers with important guidance and opportunities to reflect on the nature of presented student concerns. Consider the following scenario:

> Jaime is currently in the seventh grade. He came to the United States and entered school in the middle of last year, but teachers have become concerned that, despite occasional translation support from a Spanish-speaking paraprofessional, he is still nowhere near

grade level. Jaime is not even able to successfully work with his peers on third- and fourth-grade-level material used by the remedial reading and ESL teachers.

The reading teacher has expressed the concern that Jaime should be in special education, but the ESL teacher, Mrs. Jaeger, thinks that he is "bright." She has observed him during his unstructured time with the other Spanish-speaking students and has noticed that Jaime usually takes the lead in organizing games and is quick with responses that make his friends laugh. Tension has developed between these teachers because of their different perspectives on Jaime's inherent abilities. However, each agrees that Jaime is not able to work anywhere near grade level in either Spanish or English and neither is sure why.

The school's bilingual social worker accompanies Mrs. Jaeger to Jaime's home to find out more about Jaime's school history. His mother reports they had lived in a rural part of Mexico where access to education was inconsistent and offered to all children simultaneously, regardless of educational level. When asked, his mother estimates that Jaime had been in school about a total of ten or twelve months before coming to the United States. Her answers to additional questions and the perceptions she shares of her child indicate that she does not see him as very different from other children his age that she had known in Mexico.

This information helps the intervention team in addressing Jaime's case. It explains many of the perceived problems, even his difficulties with learning material in Spanish. They now know much of the prior instruction provided had not been at Jaime's learning level, regardless of language, so his lack of achievement is not conclusive evidence of an innate learning problem.

An informal probe of Spanish literacy skills reveals Jaime does have the critical foundations of literacy in his primary language. These and other assessment results indicate that Jaime is able to read and comprehend in Spanish at the early second-grade level. Although consistent with his educational history, these skills are not enough for him to benefit from the higher-level translated texts and supports used with other newcomers. Had teachers known this information sooner, they would have better understood his inability to perform academic tasks, despite what were initially considered adequate supports.

A student interview also reveals Jaime has developed functional literacy from environmental print and is proud of his ability to write words such as *Walmart, Wendy's, open,* and *closed* without a visual model. Using an early elementary probe of English reading, teachers also discover Jaime is beginning to transfer Spanish literacy skills to his new language by phonetically spelling *knife, fork,* and *spoon.* Given this more detailed description of Jaime's skills, which includes statements about what he has mastered and can demonstrate, the team is able to develop much more appropriate interventions to better promote his learning and language acquisition.

Staff should have identified the information revealed at this point in the intervention process within the first few weeks of Jaime's enrollment. Had the staff implemented and adhered to a protocol for prereferral of new CLD students (see Figure 7.2), the following proactive measures might have been taken:

- Data from Jaime's educational history would have prompted academic probes and revealed the inappropriateness of standard newcomer materials for him.

■ **figure 7.2** Prereferral Approaches to CLD Student Concerns

- Use methods such as those described in Chapter 3 (e.g., records review, interview, observation) to gather preinstructional assessment information in the following areas:
    - Educational history (e.g., type, language, and consistency of instruction)
    - Primary language proficiency (e.g., developmental milestones, language use patterns within the home, current use/proficiency levels, evidence of L1 loss)
    - English proficiency (e.g., amount/type of prior exposure, current use/proficiency levels, academic performance in language-laden settings)
    - Acculturation (e.g., time in country, learning style, cultural norms)
    - Medical history (e.g., vision, hearing, chronic mental or physical illness)
- Develop a profile of student skills based on information and evidence obtained through preinstructional assessment.
- Accommodate the delivery of instruction (e.g., first language support, sheltered English, modified instructional level) to maximize the student's ability to participate and engage in the curriculum.
- Monitor the student's response to comprehensible instruction provided:
    - At appropriate learning levels (regardless of age/grade)
    - With attention to learning style differences
    - Under individual and collaborative conditions
- Employ varied means to assess student learning in context. Identify the conditions in which the student does learn. Seek evidence of applied skills and learning in other contexts. Use this information to continually inform and adapt instruction so the student can experience both success and challenge with the curriculum
- If academic or behavioral concerns persist, consider referral to the intervention team, which may include the parent(s), an advocate of their choosing, a well-trained interpreter, affective or academic specialists knowledgeable in the issues related to CLD students, and, whenever possible, a specialist in bilingual special education.

- Information about Jaime's skills and interests would have informed the development of relevant, engaging tasks that were at his learning level (e.g., Wendy's menu mathematics).
- Bilingual paraprofessional support might have been used to bridge Jaime's prior knowledge and new concepts.
- Jaime's Spanish proficiency would have enabled him to orally participate in higher-level discussions with heterogeneous cooperative groups that included at least one other bilingual student.
- Formative assessment to monitor Jaime's participation in and success with modified and accommodated instruction would have more accurately revealed his learning capacities.

As with virtually all aspects of special education referral, the ability to make appropriate and valid decisions is highly dependent on the validity and quantity of information provided by the classroom teacher about the student's prior and current educational experiences. Such information is crucial to determining whether the student's learning (or lack thereof) is consistent with his or her opportunity to learn.

The Importance of Information: Review and Request

There are actually many reasons why a CLD student might appear to have learning problems or a learning disability. The most predominant is that the classroom environment or instruction does not allow the CLD student to participate at his or her level of potential. This often occurs because school educators perceive the student's language to be a barrier rather than an asset to learning. Such perceptions can lead to practices that reduce *learning opportunity* by either watering down the curriculum or preventing the student's access to it through unaccommodated instruction. In addition, some teachers may not understand that factors such as prior educational experiences, learning style, and acculturation may also be contributors to situations that interfere with student learning.

To determine whether a student's difficulties are the result of instructional mismatch, inconsistent educational experiences, or an innate language or learning disability, teachers and others must begin by gathering a complete, detailed history. (This subject, including the importance of biopsychosocial, education, and language histories, is thoroughly discussed in Chapter 3 of this text.) To avoid inappropriate assumptions about the CLD student's abilities and prevent an inappropriate referral, this preassessment and baseline information must be collected early in the school year, or on the arrival of the student, and used as a guide to appropriate instructional adaptations or accommodations.

Once information is overlooked, there is no guarantee the missing pieces will be identified and addressed in the course of a special education referral process. This phenomenon is recurrent in the field and was the focus of a study that examined the decision-making practices of assessment personnel with regard to CLD students (Overton et al., 2004). In this study, experienced professionals were asked to consider the special education eligibility of four hypothetical cases involving CLD students. The referral information provided for each student referenced important factors related to language proficiency, culture, and environment, but insufficient information was provided to properly consider the potential role of such factors in each student's learning or behavior concerns. Despite the complex issues involved, 83 percent of the assessment personnel involved in this study proceeded to make special education eligibility decisions based on the blatantly inadequate data provided.

Such studies reveal the type of practices that continue to result in inappropriate educational programming for CLD students. Accordingly, thorough and knowledgeable review of all referrals is necessary to:

- Understand the role of personal and educational experience in achievement
- Determine and distinguish between a student's innate versus situational needs
- Address the instructional methods or cultural climate that may be contributing to a student's difficulties in a particular setting

The implementation of practices that carefully examine the entirety of a student's history invariably leads to improved recognition of, and responsiveness to, the need for attitudinal, instructional, or organizational change.

■ Preassessment for Special Education

Although previously discussed as best practice for all CLD students, *preassessment* is also a term that can be used in special education to denote the process of gathering the specific information needed to decide whether special education considerations, including evaluation, are warranted. Whereas general education preassessment strives to gather information to inform *forthcoming* placement and instruction, special education preassessment, or prereferral, looks at similar data for its ability to shed light on *current* learning or behavioral concerns. In other words, the goal of special education prereferral is to determine what the student knows and can do and whether knowledge and performance are consistent with what one would expect based on that student's educational and experiential history.

If, for example, a student such as Jaime has received limited education in his native country, he may be very unlikely to experience classroom success even when instructed using lower grade-level content and when provided native language support. Without an awareness of the student's experiential, educational, and language acquisition history, a teacher might easily compare this student with cultural and linguistic peers who are performing well under the same conditions and mistakenly suspect the presence of an innate learning disability. It is, therefore, extremely important to examine all aspects of a student's past and present language, learning, and social experiences for their ability to explain or nullify current assumptions about learning and language acquisition abilities. As teachers explore a CLD student's history, the following questions may yield information that proves particularly relevant to this prereferral process:

> **assessment FREEZE FRAME 7.4**
>
> Without an awareness of a student's experiential, educational, and language acquisition history, a teacher might easily compare the student with cultural and linguistic peers who are performing well under the same conditions and mistakenly suspect the presence of an innate learning disability.

- How is the "behavior" or perceived "delay" exhibited in the primary language or home environment? In general, genuine behavioral, language, and some learning disabilities are also evident to family members, who note differences in this child as compared with her or his siblings and peers. When parents or guardians are consulted (e.g., through home visits), they often provide wonderful insights into their children's learning patterns, knowledge bases, and background experiences. Such insights greatly enhance a teacher's capacity to check potentially inaccurate assumptions about learning and language acquisition capacities.
- Is English achievement at an expected level given the student's stage of English acquisition? A student's ability to participate in and benefit from instruction is invariably affected by his or her proficiency in the language of instruction, especially if accommodations are not consistently used to increase content comprehensibility.
- Does the student's language acquisition history appear to account for strengths or weaknesses in the primary language? If a student's opportunities to use and maintain her or his first language have diminished due to English exposure, she or he may experience some degree of first language loss before fully ac-

quiring the second language. When such a student is assessed in both languages, neither language may appear strong, and this can be misinterpreted as an indication of an innate language delay or a learning disorder.

- Is L1 achievement consistent with the amount and time period of L1 academic instruction? Careful consideration of the amount and type of native language instruction is necessary to determine whether the student's current learning patterns are consistent with prior academic experiences.

- How does the student respond to scaffolded or mediated learning? One of the most critical sources of prereferral information is anecdotal and product evidence of how the student responds to sheltered or other forms of accommodative classroom instruction provided at a level consistent with the student's previous academic and linguistic experiences. CLD students who demonstrate grade-level or expected learning under these conditions may indeed have significant academic needs but are unlikely to prove to have a learning disability. Many students, however, have not been given an opportunity to learn and benefit from sheltered or accommodative instruction. When such needs-based instruction has not yet been attempted, teachers and other educators must carefully guard against erroneous assumptions about the students' learning capacities.

- Is the teacher assistance team, which facilitates interpretation and processing of information provided, made up of or informed by diverse individuals, parents or guardians, and family and community members who understand the student's language and culture?

A well-developed prereferral intervention process that includes consideration of these questions may reveal that a student's current difficulties can reasonably be explained or accounted for on the basis of her or his prior opportunities to learn (see Figure 7.3). Although the referral process ends, the volume of gathered data is available to significantly inform the classroom teacher's enhanced instructional modifications that enable the student to progress with academic material in the context of a grade-level classroom. If, however, the student's background experiences and other preassessment information (e.g., responsiveness to interventions) do not seem to account for the noted learning concerns, a full and individual evaluation of language, cognition, achievement, and social skills may be the next recommendation.

> **assessment FREEZE FRAME 7.5**
>
> One of the most critical sources of prereferral information is anecdotal and product evidence of how the student responds to sheltered or other forms of accommodative classroom instruction provided at a level consistent with the student's previous academic and linguistic experiences.

Attention to the Assessment Process

Federal regulations require the use of nonbiased assessment measures and techniques when serving the differential needs of CLD students (U.S. Congress, 1999). Because of long-standing concerns in this area, the Individuals with Disabilities Education Improvement Act (2004) includes notable amendments and language to

■ **figure 7.3** Prereferral Flowchart: Questions Every Teacher Should Answer *Before* Referring a CLD Student for Special Education

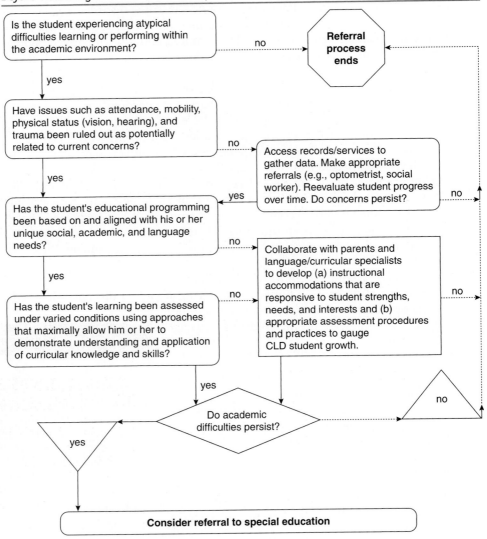

address issues related to CLD students. Among these amendments are the following from section 602.10–13 of the act:

(10)(A) The Federal Government must be responsive to the growing needs of an increasingly diverse society.

(11)(A) The limited English proficient population is the fastest growing in our nation, and the growth is occurring in many parts of our nation.

(B) Studies have documented apparent discrepancies in the levels of referral and placement of limited English proficient children in special education.

(C) Such discrepancies pose a special challenge for special education in the referral of, assessment of, and provision of services for our nation's students from non-English language backgrounds.

(12)(A) Greater efforts are needed to prevent the intensification of problems connected with mislabeling and high dropout rates among minority children with disabilities.

(B) More minority children continue to be served in special education than would be expected from the percentage of minority students in the general school population.

These amendments strengthen the original law that stipulates a number of protections to ensure that all students, including those with limited English proficiency, receive appropriate special education evaluations. IDEA requirements state that eligible CLD students who demonstrate need are placed in least restrictive learning environments that also take into account these students' unique language acquisition needs. Teachers and other evaluating personnel are encouraged to review the law in detail, noting in particular stipulations and recommendations such as the following that address communication with parents and the language of assessment.

- Parents should be notified on their child's initial referral to special education and their consent obtained for special education actions, including evaluation or changes to an existing placement. Although documents of notification and consent must be written in a language that is understandable to the general public, it must also be appropriately and accurately translated orally, in writing, or by other means (e.g., sign language) as necessary to ensure that CLD parents understand the content and intent of the proposed action(s).

- Students should be assessed "in the language and form most likely to yield accurate information on what the child knows and can do academically, developmentally, and functionally, unless it is not feasible to so provide or administer" (IDEIA, 2004, section 614.[a](3)[ii], p. 59). In accordance with this requirement, schools should make every effort to assess students in their home or dominant language using instruments and administration procedures that are valid and reliable for that population. Caution is recommended in any efforts to interpret bilingual student performance based exclusively or primarily on language or academic tests that are normed on, or compare the students with, monolingual students of either language.

- Academic knowledge, skills, and capacities among students should be assessed in the language in which these students are receiving instruction. When this language of instruction is not the student's primary or dominant language, appropriate modifications should be employed to reduce the degree to

> **assessment *FREEZE FRAME* 7.6**
>
> IDEA requirements state that eligible CLD students who demonstrate need are placed in least restrictive learning environments that also take into account these students' unique language acquisition needs.

which culture and language may interfere with their demonstration of academic knowledge, skills, and capacities.

- When reporting results, the evaluator should describe any modifications that were used to reduce the effect of potential bias in assessments. For example, the evaluator might mention "a translator was used to administer the assessment in the student's primary language" or "an interpreter translated and modified the assessment questions in a manner consistent with the student's culture and local dialect." Note that these statements are not synonymous. The second reflects greater control for potential bias.

- If an assessment is used or administered in a manner different from the conditions under which it was standardized, it is preferable to qualitatively describe student performance and correlate that with other forms of data than to cite potentially misleading scores. Such a statement might read, "As this assessment is normed on monolingual Spanish speakers receiving consistent educational instruction in their primary language, comparison of this student to that group is inappropriate. However, analysis of student performance reveals (e.g., mastery of the following skills . . . difficulties with . . .)."

Assessment information gathered through formal evaluation is best used to augment and illuminate rather than replace or override information gathered in more contextual and authentic contexts. For this reason, references to specific diagnostic instruments are omitted here in favor of an emphasis on the knowledge bases necessary for all educators to select among, and interpret the results of, a multitude of available tools. When a detailed understanding of a student's prior life, language, and learning experiences is compared with his or her current ability to demonstrate skills in varied contexts, it is possible to make well-informed decisions about whether the student should receive special education services or more accommodative levels of sheltered instruction in the classroom.

close-up *on Assessment 7.5*

Assessment information gathered through formal evaluation is best used to augment and illuminate rather than replace or override information gathered in more contextual and authentic contexts. For this reason, references to specific diagnostic instruments are omitted here in favor of an emphasis on the knowledge bases necessary for all educators to select among, and interpret the results of, a multitude of available tools. When a detailed understanding of a student's prior life, language, and learning experiences is compared with his or her current ability to demonstrate skills in varied contexts, it is possible to make well-informed decisions about whether the student should receive special education services or more accommodative levels of sheltered instruction in the classroom.

The following vignette illustrates many of the assessment dynamics that have been discussed up to this point in the chapter:

Asusena was in the third grade when she was referred by her teacher to the student intervention team at her school. This team was composed of Asusena's ESL and classroom teachers, two other teachers esteemed for their knowledge and effectiveness with diverse learners, a counselor familiar with the community, a bilingual interpreter trained in special education issues and terminology, and Asusena's mother, the recognized expert on this child.

The team began by reviewing pertinent school records. According to the home language survey, Spanish was the language of the home. Asusena's mother nodded as this was reported and translated for her participation. Preassessment of L1 proficiency indicated Asusena began school with well-developed primary language skills. Asusena also demonstrated a history of consistent school attendance and ESL services. In this particular school, the majority of students were provided ESL support by classroom teachers who modified instruction in accordance with knowledge gained through an ESL endorsement or specialized training in sheltered instruction. Spanish- and Vietnamese-speaking paraprofessionals were used in the lower grades as well as with older newcomers to provide pre- and postinstructional content support in the primary language. All other instruction, including literacy development, was provided in English only.

Recent language proficiency assessments revealed that Asusena demonstrated intermediate English oral fluency. Her reading and writing skills, however, were found to be well below those of her CLD peers (even lower than those of the students who did not perform as well on oral tests). These findings were supported by the anecdotal and observational logs of Mrs. Karas, the classroom teacher. Although Asusena was able to participate well in most aspects of her accommodative classroom, writing was indeed among the academic and behavioral concerns Mrs. Karas had for Asusena.

In discussing Asusena's strengths, Mrs. Karas noted that Asusena participated well in class during group time and always appeared to have understood the story or lesson presented through activities or lecture. Considering Asusena's apparent ability to learn, Mrs. Karas did not understand why Asusena was unable to transfer her skills and motivation to seatwork. More perplexing was Asusena's recent tendency to act up in certain situations.

Counselor (to Mrs. Karas): Can you describe one of these situations?

Mrs. Karas: In general, Asusena gets along well with others, but she can become very irritable with classmates during indoor recess. At first, I thought she was just having a bad day, but this has happened on several occasions and is affecting the desire of other students to let her join their play.

Counselor: Does this occur during outside recess?

Mrs. Karas: No, never. She's actually somewhat of a leader and very popular. So I've become concerned that something may be going on. It's just not like her to get so angry with friends.

As she listened to the translated comments, Asusena's mother looked puzzled. She shared that Asusena always seemed to play well at home with siblings or cousins, whether indoors or out, rain or shine.

Consulting Teacher 1 (to mother): What type of activities or games does she like to play at home?

Mother: Mostly they like to play Barbies, marbles, and jacks. She's really good at jacks. She already knows she can pick up three sets of three with one left over, and two sets of four with two left over. . . . She knows all the patterns.

Mrs. Karas: Wow, I don't see that skill in math. In fact, she rarely finishes two-digit addition pages without help. She seems to know the facts in her head but has trouble putting them on paper. Most everyone finishes before her. Lately, I've given her fewer problems, more widely spaced. This helps a little but she is still making lots of errors. One day I asked her to say everything out loud as she worked the problem. I noticed she was not only misreading some of the numbers, like 2 for 5, but she also had trouble staying in the same column while adding.

Consulting Teacher 1 (to Mrs. Karas): Despite her paperwork, I'm hearing you and Mom both say that Asusena seems to understand the facts and concepts in her head. Is that correct?

(Mrs. Karas looked at Asusena's mother and nodded.)

Asesena's mother (smiling): Yes.

Consulting Teacher 2: Getting back to the conflicts with peers, what type of activities are students doing during indoor recess?

Mrs. Karas: Well, I like to make everything a learning opportunity, so most of my games involve some use of reading, writing, or math skills. There are several game boards that require students to solve math problems, follow directions, or answer questions on cards.

ESL Teacher: What about your students who have yet to acquire enough English for those demands?

Mrs. Karas: Every one of my students is aware of who may need more support, and they always offer to help read or translate so everyone can play.

Consulting Teacher 1: Do they offer to help Asusena?

Mrs. Karas: They really don't offer to help Asusena because she speaks English better than many. In fact, that can be a problem in our cooperative groups because she always wants to be the person who reports. I've heard some of the students call her a *sabelotodo* [know-it-all].

Consulting Teacher 2: What is happening in the games when Asusena gets upset?

Mrs. Karas: Now that I think of it, they complain about how she reads the cards. Some students even accuse her of cheating because she holds the cards very close, gets mad when the others ask to see them, and then decides she doesn't want to play.

Consulting Teacher 1: Tell me again—how are her reading and writing skills?

ESL Teacher: Although we know oral skills develop before reading and writing skills, Asusena is having more trouble in those areas than I would expect, given her oral English proficiency. Mrs. Karas and I have been collaborating on a few interventions, but it really doesn't appear her difficulties are related to language.

Mrs. Karas: Yes, I've allowed Asusena to buddy with a partner. Although she often contributes her share or more to the content of the discussion, she always prefers the buddy to write. At first I discouraged this, but Asusena's written work never got done or was completely indecipherable. Now I allow Asusena to copy her partner's notes of their collaborative responses, but there are still significant errors in letter recognition and orientation, even while copying.

By the time the team had met for a second and third time, all members, including Asusena's mother, had concluded Asusena was exhibiting difficulties that could not be explained solely on the basis of her socialization, language acquisition, or academic experiences. Asusena was then referred to a multidisciplinary assessment team comprising experienced professionals with keen understandings of the informal and formal approaches (as covered in Chapters 2–6) that would be least biased and most effective in the assessment of Asusena's situation. These multidimensional analyses were interpreted in light of their ability to explain or account for the volume of authentic and dynamic information that had already been compiled. In this case, multiple sources of evidence revealed that Asusena demonstrated a specific learning disability characterized by atypical difficulties with visual processing that were significantly affecting her ability to read and write.

The Bilingual Special Education Student

Special education is typically not effective for grade-level learners but is appropriate for genuinely exceptional CLD students if adapted to meet the unique language acquisition needs of those whose first language is not English (Maldonado, 1994; Wilkinson & Ortiz, 1986). Students such as Asusena who demonstrate both eligibility and need for special education services may also continue to be eligible for special alternative language programming. Neither program is mutually exclusive, and a student does not become less in need of language support because of his or her eligibility for other services.

In these cases, the multidisciplinary assessment team, including the parents or guardians, develops a culturally and linguistically appropriate individualized education program (IEP) that, among other things, stipulates the languages, strategies, and settings of instruction that best minimize barriers to student achievement. Among recommended accommodations of this IEP, the multidisciplinary team is likely to incorporate a combination of accommodations that relate to the biopsychsocial and language histories of the student, as well as her or his general education needs. A sample range of potential accommodations is detailed in Figure 7.4. This figure compares and contrasts the pedagogical and logistical accommodations that are specific to CLD or special education (SPED) students and those that are common to both.

Unfortunately, the instructional programs and recommendations for CLD students with learning disabilities are all too often the same as those recommended for their native-English-speaking peers, with little or no consideration given to their unique language needs (Chang, Lai, & Shimizu, 1995; Ortiz & Wilkinson, 1989). Whether the result of inexperience or a disinclination to expend the time and resources necessary, the tendency to simplify the needs and complexities of CLD students can compromise every stage of the education process. One study that looked at the profiles of Asian students identified with learning disabilities (Poon-McBrayer & Garcia, 2000) revealed:

- Although twenty-four of the twenty-six students had been considered limited English proficient according to their language records, only twenty-one were so identified in their special education folders.
- The students' levels of native language proficiency had been assessed only through, and based on, parent opinion.

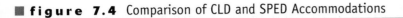

■ **figure 7.4** Comparison of CLD and SPED Accommodations

CLD Accommodations

Create print-rich classroom
Teach integrated skills lessons
Provide lesson outlines in L1
Encourage L1 development
Use age-appropriate reading
Monitor BICS skills (L2)
Monitor CALP skills (L2)
Monitor acculturation process
Send home notes in L1
Value students' cultural heritage

Model skills for student
Provide extra wait time
Post tips in work area
Reduce ambient noise
Use multisensory approaches
Teach test-taking skills
Build lessons on familiar topics
Highlight and color-code text
Follow predictable daily routine
Reduce amount of text on page
Preteach vocabulary, concepts
Use visual aids/realia
Use cooperative learning
Use graphic organizers
Use student-authored stories
Encourage self-reflection

SPED Accommodations

Grade on progress or effort
Access assistive technology
Provide access to large print
Establish quiet space to de-escalate
Use developmentally appropriate reading materials
Arrange seating for sensory needs
Remove from distractions
Provide amplification

- Despite no real assessment of L1 and the fact that the majority of the students scored below average on English language proficiency tests, English was determined to be the dominant language of twenty-one of the twenty-six students.
- Interpreters were actually involved in assessing the language skills of only five students from this group.
- Most students qualified for services based on a discrepancy between their performance on a IQ test and their achievement in the second language.
- ESL services were recommended (but not detailed) for only two students.
- No evidence was found to justify the fact that twelve students were exited simultaneously from ESL on placement in special education.

close-up *on Assessment* **7.6**

Unfortunately, the instructional programs and recommendations for CLD students with learning disabilities are all too often the same as those recommended for their native-English-speaking peers, with little or no consideration given to their unique language needs.

Accommodative Assessment Practices 7.1

Given that the most powerful use of assessment is to inform instruction, how might the assessment practices discussed in previous chapters of this text enable classroom teachers to proactively address the following situations that contribute to overreferral?

- **Insufficient background information often leads to inappropriate placement and expectations.** Assumptions made about a student's prior educational experiences can lead to placement in classes that, although below grade level, are nevertheless well above the level at which the student can be expected to learn most effectively, given his or her history. The reverse of this scenario is also sometimes a recurrent problem.
- **Teachers who do not identify or draw on a student's funds of knowledge overlook linkages that would otherwise facilitate the student's participation in and understanding of the curriculum.** The potential for students to maximally benefit from instruction is diminished if their learning is limited to the relationships they can draw between unfamiliar referents and the new material.
- **Pressure on teachers to prepare students to take high-stakes tests often prompts teachers to** provide *grade-level,* rather than *differentiated,* instruction. By presenting new information at levels at which students lack the prerequisite skills and, therefore, cannot participate, teachers effectively preclude CLD students from learning. The ironic result is that instead of being better prepared for the test, these students fall further and further behind in the curriculum.
- **Instruction that is not accommodated for the language proficiency of a student disenfranchises the student from content-area learning.** When instruction is presented through language that is not made comprehensible by scaffolding or sheltering, CLD students are unlikely to learn content-area material at expected levels.
- **Classroom instruction and assessment practices that do not account for acculturation frequently yield results that are misinterpreted.** Teachers who do not understand the impact of acculturation on CLD students are more likely to misinterpret these students' difficulties as indications of learning or behavior problems rather than as predictable reactions to the significant social, linguistic, and academic demands of their lives.

- There were no references to modifications or recommendations regarding continued English language needs or development for these students.

The practices revealed in this study reflect common failures to regard language proficiency as critical to all aspects of learning and assessment.

■ Reevaluation Considerations

Many of the CLD students featured in the vignettes of this text might easily have been referred for and placed in special education had their teachers not understood and responded to the critical information that was gathered through multiple types of assessment. Moreover, knowledgeable teachers using innovative methods of assessment may find themselves questioning the status of CLD students in their class who have already been placed in special education. It is not at all unusual to hear recurrent comments such as:

- "I can tell Hien is a bright student. Everything he demonstrates is what we'd expect of a CLD student with his background. Hien learns just as well as the others when given the chance to learn and show what he knows in other ways."
- "When I asked why Sonia goes to special education, I was told she has a language problem that affects learning. Then I found out she wasn't even tested in her own language."

Under IDEA, teachers and parents with concerns about the appropriateness of a student's existing placement or services can request a reevaluation at any time. During this process, the teacher will want to present evidence of current student skills that demonstrate the student's ability to learn when provided with supports known to be effective with CLD students. In some settings, a teacher with greater experience and knowledge about CLD students may need to serve as a resource to student intervention or child study teams that lack this area of expertise. This resource person may even find it necessary to advocate for best practices that are not yet familiar to diagnostic personnel. Examples of such practices include:

- Comprehensive assessment that does not rely on previous data gathered using potentially biased assessments or methods
- Inclusion of authentic assessment data and informal indicators of student achievement
- Assessment of the current instructional setting for its facilitation of and differentiated responsiveness to student learning
- Careful consideration of the student's achievement in light of her or his educational history (e.g., consistency of schooling, language supports)
- Inclusion of parent information regarding related skills or learning as it occurs within the context of the home and community

> **assessment *FREEZE FRAME* 7.8**
>
> Under IDEA, teachers and parents with concerns about the appropriateness of a student's existing placement or services can request a reevaluation at any time. During this process, the teacher will want to present evidence of current student skills that demonstrate the student's ability to learn when provided with supports known to be effective with CLD students.

As illustrated throughout this chapter, the vast majority of the issues related to the over- and underreferral of CLD students to special education can be addressed through appropriate instruction and assessment in all phases of their academic, acculturation, and language acquisition processes.

▪ key concepts

Achievement discrepancies
Bilingual special education student
Disproportionality
Exceptionality
General education preassessment

Individualized education program (IEP)
Learning disability
Least restrictive environment
Overrepresentation
Reevaluation

Special education preassessment
Student intervention team
Teacher assistance team
Underrepresentation

1. CLD students are overrepresented in special education and underrepresented in gifted and talented programs. Discuss factors contributing to this discrepancy. Which of these factors do you consider most important?

2. Define and discuss SLAAP. What are the most significant implications of SLAAP for classroom teachers of CLD students? Explain.

3. Discuss why classroom environments and practices that accommodate CLD student needs and assets are essential for reducing the over-referral problem for CLD students. What sorts of classroom assessment practices are mutually accommodative?

4. Discuss questions teachers should ask during the preassessment process before determining that a special education referral is necessary for a CLD student. Discuss three to five questions.

5. It is not uncommon for educators to assume that a CLD student is unable to function in either language (L1 or L2). How can effective preassessment test such an assumption?

6. Unfortunately, instructional programs and recommendations for CLD students with learning disabilities are all too often the same as those recommended for grade-level native-English-speaking peers—and reflect little or no consideration for the language needs of these students. Discuss why this problem is recurrent in education. What can teachers, as advocates, do to change these practices?

1. What are three types of exceptionality that may qualify a student for special education services?

2. Do eligibility requirements for special education typically exclude achievement discrepancies resulting from such external variables as language, experience, and cultural differences? Why or why not?

3. Why would we expect demographic subgroups of students to be represented in special education in the same proportion they are represented in the population at large?

4. How would you explain the term *disproportionality*?

5. How would you explain the term *exceptionality*?

6. CLD students continue to be overrepresented in special education programs. What factors contribute to this persistent problem?

7. How does relying too heavily on oral language proficiency as an indicator of academic capacity contribute to the overrepresentation of CLD students in special education?

8. CLD students whose first language is not English sometimes exhibit academic, attention, and behavioral difficulties that teachers misinterpret as indicators of a learning disability. What are at least three examples of such difficulties?

9. What is a least restrictive environment? Explain.

10. What are consequences for other grade-level students when CLD students are overrepresented in special education? Explain.

11. What types of constructive data can a classroom teacher provide a teacher assistance team regarding a CLD student who is struggling with classroom material?

12. How can preassessment be differentiated for general education and special education? Be specific.

13. Should a classroom teacher refer a CLD student to special education before attempting scaffolded or mediated instruction? Why or why not?

14. According to IDEA, CLD students whose first language is not the language of instruction should be assessed in their first or native language. How would you defend this stipulation? What are valid concerns about such assessments?

15. Why must assessment modifications for CLD students and potential biases in assessments be reported as critical aspects of assessment findings? How might translator use be reported? Explain.

16. Does a CLD student's eligibility for special education services eliminate the need for ongoing language programming? Explain your answer.

17. What is the relationship between the acronym IEP and the term *least restrictive environment*? Explain your answer.

18. What differentiates a CLD special education student from other students in special education? Explain your answer.

19. Why should parents, guardians, and extended family members participate in special education referral and assessment processes? Explain your response.

Postinstructional Assessment

When learning 5 posture rules [of keyboarding], I use games. We write the rules, practice the rules, repeat the rules, and then I have contests. Actually it was quite cool because I put [students] on teams so they can train each other. Everyone on his or her team would compete at some point and the team wins. I see kids helping each other and learning social skills. We model how to encourage one another and what is good sportsmanship. One of my ESL [CLD] students, who were only here for a week, came to check out and I met his mother. He had a lot of trouble speaking English so pronouncing the rules was hard for him. He stumbled when he was saying the rules at first but we practiced and he was actually a finalist in one of the contests. He gave me a hug and said I was his most favorite teacher and he was going to miss me.

Donna Villegas
Middle School Teacher

critical standards *Guiding Chapter Content*

TESOL/NCATE teacher standards reflect professional consensus on standards for the quality teaching of PreK–12 CLD students. Additionally, the CEEE Guiding Principles and their accompanying indicators serve as a framework to assist practitioners, policymakers, and clients as they collaborate to enhance academic enrichment and language acquisition among CLD students. Therefore, to help educators understand how they might appropriately target and address national professional teaching standards in practice, we have designed the content of this chapter to reflect the following standards.

TESOL/NCATE Standards for P–12 Teacher Education Programs

Domain 1: Language. Candidates know, understand, and use the major concepts, theories, and research related to the nature and acquisition of language to construct learning environments that support ESOL students' language and literacy development and content area achievement.

- **Standard 1.b. Language Acquisition and Development.** Candidates understand and apply concepts, theories, research, and practice to facilitate the acquisition of a primary and a new language in and out of classroom settings.
    - **1.b.5.** Understand and apply current theories and research in language and literacy development.
    - **1.b.12.** Help ESOL students develop academic language proficiency.
    - **1.b.13.** Help ESOL students develop effective language learning strategies.

Domain 3: Planning, Implementing, and Managing Instruction. Candidates know, understand, and use standards-based practices and strategies related to planning, implementing, and managing ESL and content instruction, including classroom organization, teaching strategies for developing and integrating language skills, and choosing and adapting classroom resources.

- **Standard 3.a. Planning for Standards-Based ESL and Content Instruction.** Candidates know, understand, and apply concepts, research, and best practices to plan classroom instruction in a supportive learning environment for ESOL students. Candidates serve as

Note: All TESOL/NCATE Standards are cited from TESOL (2003). All Guiding Principles are cited from Center for Equity and Excellence in Education (CEEE) (2005). Reprinted by permission.

effective English-language models, as they plan for multilevel classrooms with learners from diverse backgrounds using standards-based ESL and content curriculum.

3.a.3. Plan students' learning experiences based on assessment of language proficiency and prior knowledge.

Domain 4: Assessment. Candidates understand issues of assessment and use standards-based assessment measures with ESOL students.

- **Standard 4.b. Language Proficiency Assessment.** Candidates know and use a variety of standards-based language proficiency instruments to inform their instruction and understand their uses for identification, placement, and demonstration of language growth of ESOL students.

    4.b.4. Understand, construct, and use assessment measures for a variety of purposes for ESOL students.

    4.b.5. Assess ESOL learners' language skills and communicative competence using multiple sources of information.

CEEE Guiding Principles

Principle #3: English language learners are taught academic content that enables them to meet challenging performance standards in all content areas, consistent with those for all students.

3.7 Use appropriate multiple assessment tools and techniques to measure English language learners' progress in achieving academic standards and in acquiring English proficiency; use assessment results to inform classroom teaching and learning, and communicate these results to families in a meaningful and accessible manner.

Principle #4: English language learners receive instruction that builds on their prior knowledge and cognitive abilities and is responsive to their language proficiency levels and cultural backgrounds.

4.11 Understand and value the linguistic backgrounds and cultural heritages of their English language learners' families and use this information to enrich classroom instruction and to support their students' learning of academic content.

Principle #5: English language learners are evaluated with appropriate and valid assessments that are aligned to state and local standards and that take into account the language development stages and cultural backgrounds of the students.

5.10 Use a variety of formal and authentic assessment techniques to enhance classroom knowledge of English language learners and to evaluate their academic and linguistic progress.

■ Teacher-Driven Postinstructional Assessment

In postinstructional assessment, the teacher's role is to elicit and document the mental representations (Bruer, 1993) that students have created during the lesson. The responsibility lies in determining, in multiple ways, how the learner has organized the new vocabulary (language objectives) and concepts (content objectives) that have been taught and the degree to which the student is able to articulate his or her knowledge. When beginning to think about postinstructional assessments (PIAs), effective teachers recognize and plan for assessing both procedural (skills-based) and declarative (fact-based) knowledge. To accomplish this, they use multiple techniques and strategies that have been aligned with standards for expected outcomes or products with regard to both content and language. These assessments provide the teacher with opportunities to assess linguistic and academic growth as well as cognitive learning processes and sociocultural skills. Among the questions that may be answered through the classroom teacher's postinstructional assessment of the CLD student are the following:

- Stage of second language acquisition
- Use of academic language (e.g., target vocabulary) in multiple contexts
- Depth of conceptual or content understanding and knowledge
- Level of application of learning strategies taught
- Level of motivation in relation to the various content-area tasks
- Level of collaborative and social skills to meet academic needs

Table 8.1 gives a brief sample of assessment techniques and strategies appropriate for each of these areas. A more in-depth exploration is given later in this chapter.

Effective postinstructional assessment is driven by the educator's desire to determine and document whether both types of lesson objectives—content and language—have been met. The documentation might then be used for the following: (a) to set expectations; (b) to monitor growth in the four dimensions of the CLD student biography; (c) to inform the teacher of interventions that may be required to maximize student engagement, motivation, and learning; (d) to review material the student may not have grasped during instruction; and ultimately (e) to assign grades for individual accountability.

Linguistic Postinstructional Assessment

The ability of CLD students to fully participate in daily classroom activities is highly dependent on their ability to process the language of the classroom. Knowing a

close-up *on Assessment* 8.1

Effective postinstructional assessment is driven by the thoughtful educator's desire to determine and document whether both types of lesson objectives—content and language—have been met. The documentation might then be used for the following:

- To set expectations
- To monitor growth in the four dimensions of the CLD student biography
- To inform the teacher of interventions that may be needed during instruction to maximize student engagement, motivation, and learning
- To review material the student may not have grasped during instruction
- To assign grades for individual accountability

■ **table 8.1**   Postinstructional Assessment Techniques and Strategies

Assessment Area	Techniques
Stage of Second Language Acquisition (SLA)	• Teacher ratings and checklists • Language rubrics • Anecdotal records • Unplanned observations • Planned observations • Student self-ratings • Oral interviews • Role-play
Academic Language Use and Vocabulary	• Teacher ratings and checklists • Dialogue journals • Oral interviews • Role-play • Planned observations • Think-pair-share • Word sorts
Depth of Conceptual/ Content Knowledge	• Text to self connections • Tests • Rubrics • Essay writing
Level of Learning Strategy Application	• Observation checklists • Time lines • Mind maps • Flowcharts • Problem solving • Drawings • Outlines • Narrative analysis
Level of Motivation for Content-Area Tasks	• Student checklists • Informal observations • Student interviews • Engagement and motivation logs
Level of Collaborative and Social Skills	• Oral interviews • Informal observations • Self-assessment checklists • Peer response sheets • Collaborative skills checklists • Narrative summary of collaborative skills • Rating scales

student's language abilities provides the teacher with information needed for scaffolding instruction, asking appropriate questions, and making decisions about group configurations. Moreover, classrooms that do not provide for or allow language and intellectual risk taking, because of real or perceived language proficiencies, do not use the linguistic assets that students bring to the classroom to accelerate academic achievement. Therefore, it is imperative that teachers monitor and document the linguistic abilities of their CLD students.

Language assessment must encompass the following four areas to be effective:

- Student listening capabilities
- Student oral language development
- Student reading comprehension
- Student writing skills

Assessment of these four areas requires the teacher to embed techniques for both informal and formal documentation throughout the instructional process. To provide meaningful information for the documentation of growth, the assessments must be purposeful, ongoing, and timely.

There are many ways to postinstructionally assess the language capacities of CLD students. One of the more informative yet easily implemented of these is to track a student's language development along an adapted or adopted continuum of skills. In the example presented in Figure 8.1 (and related appendix resource), benchmarks of language acquisition in the areas of listening, speaking, reading, and writing are arranged in the order of the stages commonly associated with second language acquisition (i.e., preproduction, early production, speech emergence, intermediate fluency, and advanced fluency). Teachers who understand the skills involved in, and potentially elicited by, particular curricular activities find it much easier to postinstructionally assess whether students have demonstrated these skills, given appropriate opportunities and facilitation. Even in the absence of deliberate preplanning, it is often not difficult to note whether and when the hallmark skills of language development have been attained.

In addition to evaluating language skills in terms of assessment continua, some schools find great value in applying a similar pattern of notation to their continua of academic skills. At one such school, all student progress in reading and writing is measured along a literacy continuum that begins with preemergent behaviors such as "enjoys listening to stories" or "uses writing tools (e.g., crayons, paintbrushes) to make purposeful marks." Students advance hierarchically to skills such as "interprets technical manuals" and "writes appropriately annotated research reports."

Many classroom teachers also have discovered that such continua can enhance both their communications with parents regarding the student's achievements in L2, and the parents' understanding of primary language skills as being fundamental to the student's classroom success. Even in schools where first languages are not routinely assessed, observations of student language use during whole-group

figure 8.1 Continua for the Assessment of English Language Development

Student Name: _____

	Preproduction	Early Production	Speech Emergence	Intermediate Fluency	Advanced Fluency
Date					
Listening	• Cannot yet understand simple expressions or statements in English.	• Understands previously learned expressions. • Understands new vocabulary in context.	• Understands sentence-length speech. • Participates in conversation about simple information. • Understands a simple message. • Understands basic directions and instructions.	• Understands academic content. • Understands more complex directions and instructions. • Comprehends main idea. • Effectively participates in classroom discussions.	• Understands most of what is heard. • Understands and retells main idea and most details from oral presentations and conversations.
Date					
Speaking	• Is not yet able to make any statements in English.	• Uses isolated words and learned phrases. • Uses vocabulary for classroom situations. • Expresses basic courtesies. • Asks very simple questions. • Makes statements using learned materials. • Asks and answers questions about basic needs.	• Asks and answers simple questions about academic content. • Talks about familiar topics. • Responds to simple statements. • Expresses self in simple situations (e.g., ordering a meal, introducing oneself, asking directions).	• Initiates, sustains, and closes a conversation. • Effectively participates in classroom discussions. • Gives reasons for agreeing or disagreeing. • Retells a story or event. • Compares and contrasts a variety of topics.	• Communicates facts and talks casually about topics of general interest using specific vocabulary. • Participates in age-appropriate academic, technical, and social conversations using English correctly.

	Preproduction	Early Production	Speech Emergence	Intermediate Fluency	Advanced Fluency
Date					
Reading	• Is not yet able to read any words in English. • Is not yet able to identify the letters of the Roman alphabet. • Is not yet able to decode sounds of written English.	• Reads common messages, phrases, and/or expressions. • Identifies the letters of the Roman alphabet. • Decodes most sounds of written English. • Identifies learned words and phrases.	• Reads and comprehends main ideas and/or facts from simple materials.	• Understands main ideas and details from a variety of sources.	• Reads authentic text materials for comprehension. • Understands most of what is read in authentic texts.
Date					
Writing	• Is not yet able to write any words in English. • Is not yet able to write the letters of the Roman alphabet.	• Copies or transcribes familiar words or phrases. • Writes the letters from memory and/or dictation. • Writes simple expressions from memory. • Writes simple autobiographical information as well as some short phrases and simple lists. • Composes short sentences with guidance.	• Creates basic statements and questions. • Writes simple letters and messages. • Writes simple narratives.	• Writes more complex narratives. • Composes age-appropriate original materials using present, past, and future tenses. • Writes about a variety of topics for a variety of purposes.	• Write summaries. • Takes notes. • Compares and contrasts familiar topics. • Uses vivid, specific language in writing.

Source: Wichita Public Schools, Wichita, Kansas. Reprinted by permission.

instruction, pair sharing, differentiated group instruction, and informal conversational probes can provide important insight into the student's level of skills in the native language.

CLD parents are also critical sources of key language information. When, for example, a parent reports that his or her child is able to retell events or discussions that have occurred at school, state and support opinions, read with comprehension, or demonstrate other strong academic and linguistic behaviors in the primary language, the teacher can note these insights in a different color pen (or otherwise differentiated manner) on the language development continuum. Such simple techniques can provide powerful information that allows effective teachers to recognize new skills that emerge first, or preexist, in the primary language and to optimize these in the course of second language and content-area instruction.

Postinstructional assessment that truly affects academic learning is well thought out and implemented throughout the lesson. It provides a representative sample of all four literacy domains—listening, speaking, reading, and writing. To maximize the value of this kind of assessment, effective educators ensure that CLD students are afforded opportunities to develop their language skills during lesson delivery. Activities are organized in meaningful ways that allow opportunities for teacher observations. The following are key questions to consider when planning for the assessment of language:

- Has a purpose been set for the observation (i.e., will it be used to assess growth/progress or academic achievement)?
- Do the tasks allow for language use that is authentic?
- Have the checklists, rubrics, and so forth been aligned with the objectives?
- Is the reading material at the CLD student's reading level?
- Is the writing task connected to the objectives?
- Does the student have the necessary background knowledge to be able to respond to the writing task?

Documenting and systematically analyzing language growth throughout the school year provides the teacher with student information that is vital to making decisions about practice.

Academic Postinstructional Assessment

One can frequently walk into a classroom where students have finished a unit, topic, or story and observe students passively responding by filling in the bubbles or blanks of a more or less formal assessment. Often the connection between what the student is asked to do on such assessments and the critical concepts or vocabulary of the lesson is scarcely evident. Seldom are students asked to go beyond the rote recall of information in ways that encourage higher-order thinking skills. Such assessments seldom prompt students to evaluate, analyze, and use the information learned in applications that target future learning or events in their daily lives. In other words, students are rarely asked to own the vocabulary and concepts, take them one step beyond the known, and participate in authentic assessments of language development and academic progress.

The purposeful postinstructional assessment of vocabulary and critical concepts arising from a lesson encourages CLD and other students to apply what they have learned to higher-order thinking tasks and problems that involve opportunities for both collaborative and independent evaluations. The following strategies and techniques are embedded in the assumption that, as teachers, we want to move beyond the rote recitation of facts toward authentic opportunities for students to actually *think* about the information learned. We strive to create postinstructional assessments that provide relevant and useful feedback, for both the teacher and the student. Such assessments set the stage for ensuring that students reach Bloom's (1956) highest levels of understanding (see Table 8.2 for an overview of these levels). According to Tombari and Borich (1999), postinstructional assessment should:

- Include strategic thinking—the ability to draw on one's prior knowledge and use specific learning strategies to respond to the postinstructional assessment task
- Provide a clear opportunity for students to communicate deep understanding of the topic through a resulting end product, which allows the teacher to assess beyond superficial conceptual knowledge
- Have meaning for the student beyond merely earning a grade

> **assessment *FREEZE FRAME* 8.3**
>
> The purposeful postinstructional assessment of vocabulary and critical concepts arising from a lesson encourages CLD and other students to apply what they have learned to higher-order thinking tasks and problems that involve opportunities for both collaborative and independent evaluations.

Conceptualizing postinstructional assessment in these terms promotes the sort of CLD student engagement, motivation, and application that we often fail to observe in our increasingly diverse classrooms.

PIA Strategies for Assessing Student Progress against Language and Content Objectives

The following are a variety of strategies for the postinstructional assessment of academic knowledge among CLD and other students. Many of these strategies also enable the classroom teacher to simultaneously assess content-specific language development among students.

Concept Maps   There are multiple types of concept maps that teachers can use to assess and document the vocabulary and concepts students have learned from a lesson. A concept map provides the opportunity for students to portray the learning that has taken place during the lesson through visual representations of the terms and concepts, the appropriate relationships among concepts, and the meaningful interpretations CLD students made regarding the new information. The type of concept map selected by the teacher is highly dependent on the assessment task.

■ **table 8.2** Overview of Student Characteristics According to Bloom's Taxonomy

Knowledge	Students at Level I of Bloom's taxonomy tend to respond according to the simple recall of information gleaned from instruction or classroom activities. This includes the recall of facts, definitions, rules, and basic concepts.
Comprehension	Students at Level II of Bloom's taxonomy tend to demonstrate an understanding of facts, as well as the skills of organizing, comparing, translating, interpreting, and giving descriptions. Students at this level not only recall information but are also able to restate that information in their own words.
Application	Students at Level III of Bloom's taxonomy are able to solve problems in new and variant situations by applying acquired knowledge, facts, techniques, and rules in different ways. Students at this level are able to take what has been learned in one context and solve problems with that learning in another.
Analysis	Students at Level IV of Bloom's taxonomy are able to examine, categorize, and analyze information (including the identification of motives or causes). Students at this level make inferences and find evidence to support generalizations. They are able to locate themes in readings and identify the main ideas in narrative text.
Synthesis	Students at Level V of Bloom's taxonomy are capable of compiling information in variant ways, combining elements in new patterns. Therefore, students at this level are capable of synthesizing alternative solutions to problems. They are comfortable taking information and creating something new.
Evaluation	Students at Level VI of Bloom's taxonomy are able to present and defend opinions by making judgments about information by assessing the validity of ideas, or by evaluating the quality of a work based on a set of criteria. Students at this level (a) are comfortable in relying on their own refined judgment and are capable of justifying their decisions, and (b) demonstrate a higher level of thinking and information processing.

The following are types of concept maps that can be used to assess the conceptual understanding of CLD students in the content areas.

- P-W-L-L maps support CLD students as these students: **P**—articulate the *prior* academic and experiential knowledge they had regarding the topic; **W**—pose questions regarding *what* may still be unknown; L—relate what was *learned*; and L—take the learning to the next level by linking it to their daily *life* experiences and/or potential applications. Although similar to K-W-L and K-W-L-H charts, these concept maps (see Figure 8.2) can be used to better accommodate instruction for CLD students with limited English proficiency. Before information is charted, the teacher uses visuals to aid comprehension of the topic, and students discuss with one another ideas to share with the teacher. After the lesson, students make explicit connections between the content concepts and their daily lives. This opportunity encourages CLD students to *own* what they have learned.

- Venn diagrams provide CLD students with opportunities to think about similarities and differences between concepts presented. Students must be able to think critically about what has been learned in order to categorize the information appropriately.
- Plot diagrams are used in reading to support the CLD student's identification of critical points in the story or novel. This type of concept map (see Figure 8.3) is often used with complex reading and provides a visual representation of what the student has read and learned.
- Cultural literary response maps are used for organizing and classifying the main ideas in a story or novel. The student then connects the story or novel

■ figure 8.2 P-W-L-L Map

P (Prior academic and experiential knowledge)	**W** (Questions about the unknown or what students want to know)	**L** (What was learned)	**L** (Link to daily life experiences and/or potential applications)

■ **figure 8.3** Plot Diagram

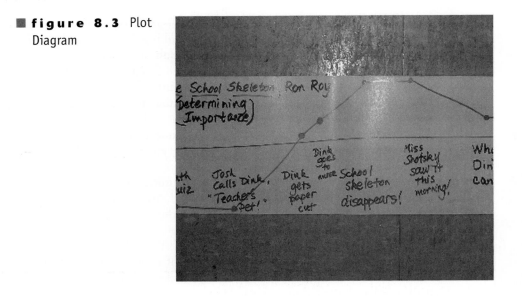

to his or her life experiences and home culture. A cultural literary response map reduces the language demands on CLD students as their understanding of critical aspects of the story is assessed. This type of concept map may also serve as a great organization tool for writing stories that incorporate connections to the student's cultural and experiential background. Figure 8.4 (and related appendix resource) illustrates one example of a cultural literacy response map.

Postinstructional Reflection Journals Reflection journal writing can be an effective tool for assessing student learning and capacity building. The written response provides an opportunity for CLD students to connect the objectives of the lesson with past and future learning. A structured response format that asks the student to respond to the content objective by describing both what was learned and the ways the new knowledge is meaningful to future learning increases the probability that the information will become part of the student's permanent memory.

For CLD students whose first language is not English, such journals also provide writing opportunities for language development and assessment. Insightful teachers sometimes allow CLD students who are in the early stages of second language acquisition to write the journal in their native language. Paraprofessionals, volunteer parents, or community members may then be used to assist with translation as needed.

So What! Now What? This assessment activity requires CLD students to write down as many of the critical lesson concepts as they are able. The students are then asked to evaluate why it is important to learn the information. This activity is great for assessing learning in the content areas. After the individual work is completed,

■ **figure 8.4** Cultural Literacy Response Map

Title of Story: _____	Name: _____

Story Elements

Setting:	
Main characters:	
Problem in the story:	
Main events in the story:	

My Cultural Connections

1. When I read this story, I thought about how in my culture . . .

2. The character I could relate to most was _____.
   I could relate to this character because:

3. The experience(s) from my own background that helped me understand the story included:

4. Other cultural connections I made included:

What do you think?

1. What do you think would have happened if the main character had done something different?	
2. How do you think the main character felt? Why?	
3. How would you have felt if you were the main character? Why?	

students are asked to compare with a partner. Finally, the class (as a group) compiles the information into a chart that is available for future reference.

Mind Mapping   Mind maps emphasize conceptual relationships and allow CLD students to demonstrate learning through both linguistic and nonlinguistic representations, thus providing a natural scaffold for students with varying linguistic and academic backgrounds. Mind maps lead students to focus on the most important information that was learned about the topic. Through the representations, the teacher is able to assess the student's organization of the content concepts as well as her or his overall level of comprehension. Mind maps take a variety of forms depending on the student and the assignment (see Chapter 4 for additional uses of mind mapping).

These are but a few of the many postinstructional strategies that can be used to assess academic learning and capacity building (beyond simple recall of information) and, at the same time, guide students to make connections between the new knowledge and their future or daily lives. Postinstructional assessment for CLD students that is interactive and challenging yields more information about the content and language learning that students have achieved during the lesson.

Cognitive Postinstructional Assessment

Recently, literature in the field has focused on teaching and assessing cognitive and metacognitive learning strategies, and the role these strategies play in CLD student academic achievement (Anderson, 2002; Bialystok, 2001; Chamot & El-Dinary, 2000; Chamot & O'Malley, 1994; Montes, 2002). Cognitive learning strategies enable the learner to approach a problem with a set of tools for solving the problem in a logical, effective manner. Metacognitive learning strategies, on the other hand, provide the learner with the critical thinking skills needed to monitor her or his own learning (e.g., choice and implementation of cognitive learning strategies). Teaching, modeling, practicing, and assessing cognitive and metacognitive learning strategies set the stage for CLD students to take responsibility for their own thinking and learning.

CLD students who have cognitive and metacognitive learning strategies available to them are more likely to think critically, problem solve, make decisions, and question their own thinking about a task (Chamot & O'Malley, 1994). It is not within the scope of this chapter or text to discuss the immense variety of learning strategies available for each of the content areas. However, the following are some recommended strategies for assessing a student's use of cognitive and metacognitive processes to comprehend and manipulate concepts that have been taught during a specific lesson, unit, or theme.

> **assessment *FREEZE FRAME* 8.4**
>
> Teaching, modeling, practicing, and assessing cognitive and metacognitive learning strategies set the stage for CLD students to take responsibility for their own thinking and learning.

PIA Strategies for Assessing Cognitive and Metacognitive Processes

CLD and other students who are encouraged to think about both the processes of their own thinking and the effectiveness of those processes tend to enhance their own academic performance across content areas (Chamot & O'Malley, 1994; Marzano, 2004; Marzano, Pickering, & Pollock, 2001; Herrera & Murry, 2005). At the same time, teachers who encourage such thinking are afforded authentic opportunities for the assessment of cognitive and metacognitive development among their CLD students. The following strategies provide teachers with authentic assessment opportunities.

Analyze Draw Decide (ADD) Student are guided to think about the "presenting problem" and analyze what is happening in the story, problem statement, or event. Students then draw a visual representation of the "schema" the situation presents based on his or her prior knowledge, experience, or learning. Using the visual representation, students make a decision about the best course of action to pursue and rationalize their decision.

Prediction Time Line A problem related to one or more critical concepts of the lesson is posed for students to solve. As the lesson evolves, the teacher stops at critical points and asks students to document their predictions about what will happen next. Students draw or write what is leading them to their predictions. Students check their answers as the teacher proceeds with the lesson. After the lesson, students (in pairs) discuss and analyze the accuracy of their predictions. Students then reflect on and write about the factors or information that accurately or inaccurately led them to each prediction.

Pen Pal Flowcharts. Students are asked to document the planning process for their writing task or project. As each student completes his or her flowchart, the teacher poses questions that prompt the student to think about his or her thinking and make any necessary adjustments. Providing this feedback guides the CLD student to rethink his or her plan and provides the teacher with insights into the learning strategies that the student is using to accomplish the task.

Observing students and questioning students' thought processes is central to the assessment of students' use of learning strategies. Monitoring the problem-solving and reasoning strategies of a student as he or she approaches different types of tasks and assignments provides opportunities for the teacher to document the student's use of, and effectiveness with, both cognitive and metacognitive learning strategies. Observation rubrics used for this purpose can be scored or anecdotal. Subsequently, observation outcomes should be periodically shared with students as PIA feedback. When a student has mastered a cognitive or metacognitive strategy, he or she can then draw on this strategy in problem solving and higher-order analyses across a variety of content areas. Figure 8.5 (and related

■ **figure 8.5**   Rubric for the Assessment of Cognitive and Metacognitive Strategy Use

Criterion	Student Performance			Score
	Limited	Some Exploration	Extensive Analysis	
	1 Point	*3 Points*	*5 Points*	
1. Student identifies the problem or the task he or she is being asked to do.				
2. Student thinks about the identified problem and reasons out strategy to use.				
3. Student applies the strategy and evaluates effectiveness.				
4. Student evaluates his or her answer.				
5. Student evaluates the strengths and weaknesses of his or her learning processes.				
Total Score:				

appendix resource) depicts a rubric that can be used to document student use of cognitive and metacognitive learning strategies.

Sociocultural Postinstructional Assessment

At some point, most people have had to pick up a phone to call someone when they could not determine an answer to a problem, or have studied with others in groups to pass a difficult exam. In these instances, the sociocultural strategies learned from parents, teachers, and friends often guide individuals to contact those with whom they have successfully interacted or collaborated with before. That is, these skills lead people to contact their *lifelines* when they need to discuss a difficulty or ask questions for clarification.

The intentional development of sociocultural skills is often as important to the academic achievement of CLD students as any other form of scaffold teachers may put into place during instruction. In fact, it has been effectively argued that CLD and other students often have as much to learn from purposeful interactions and collaborations with more capable peers as they do from the classroom teacher (Herrera & Murry, 2005; Herrera, Perez, & Murry, in press; Moll et al., 1992; Vygotsky, 1962). When teachers of CLD students explicitly develop these socio-

Accommodative Assessment Practices 8.1

Miss Jackson uses narrative assessment in her ninth-grade science class. After each lesson and throughout the school year, students visit the school library. There, they locate a newspaper or periodical article, a DVD or video, an article from the Internet, or a book chapter that relates to the topic of the most recent science lesson. The students are encouraged to select their topic-related artifact according to what is of interest to them and has real-world applications. Students are then asked to read or watch their library artifact and to write a story about the topic based on what they have learned from either the lesson or their library artifact or both. CLD students are free to write their narrative in either their native language or English. Miss Jackson uses bilingual paraprofessionals within the school or parent volunteers to translate native language narratives as needed.

Since the beginning of the school year, the students of Miss Jackson's class have been gradually introduced to her preferred format for science narratives. However, students are encouraged to adapt that format as consistent with writing in the science genre. Such narrative assessments provide Miss Jackson with the following sorts of information, including indications of students':

- Comprehension of the science lesson
- Capacities to read scientific narratives/ discourse
- Abilities to synthesize multiple perspectives on a science topic
- Capacities to apply what they have learned
- Abilities to write coherent narratives related to science
- Capacities to use appropriate syntax in narrative construction

Additionally, such narratives provide authentic information about CLD students' emergent proficiencies in the English language, the native language, or both.

■ *Of the aforementioned types of information that can be gathered using this postinstructional assessment, which are related to the linguistic dimension of the CLD student biography? The cognitive dimension? The academic dimension?*

cultural skills among their students, these skills become useful tools students can use as they master the critical concepts and vocabulary of a lesson.

Resourceful classroom teachers often use these sociocultural interactions and collaborations to postinstructionally assess their students. For example, the interactions of cooperative learning activities often facilitate the teacher's postinstructional assessment of CLD students' sociocultural skills, including asking for help, actively listening for information, initiating collaborative conversations, giving directions, and negotiating differing cultural perspectives on problem solving and collaboration.

Contrary to some perspectives, such skills are not necessarily learned automatically. In fact, the acquisition of these sociocultural skills can be especially difficult for CLD students, whose ways of communicating, comprehending, and

assessment *FREEZE FRAME 8.5*

The intentional development of sociocultural skills is often as important to the academic achievement of CLD students as any other form of scaffold teachers may put into place during instruction.

expressing themselves may differ from those of the culture of the school. CLD students who receive assessment feedback on their progress in developing these skills (a) learn to recognize the potential value of these skills in learning, (b) are afforded opportunities to develop these skills in a monitored context, and (c) recognize which skills require further development and refinement.

For example, some CLD students, in the context of curriculum-based learning, do not know which questions to ask or are timid about asking questions in front of the entire class. Cooperative learning activities can be intentionally structured in ways that specifically target the development of appropriate questioning skills in a low-risk environment. At the same time, it is possible to structure these activities so that the development of these sociocultural skills can be informally monitored and assessed.

A cooperative learning structure that promotes the development and assessment of sociocultural skills in group learning intentionally accounts for the following:

- Linguistic demands of the task(s)
- Levels of acculturation demonstrated by the students
- Purpose of the grouping
- Opportunities for peer clarification, elaboration, or repetition of information that may have been missed or not understood during the lesson
- Cooperative group activities that occur in a low-risk and natural setting

For assessment purposes, some teachers may use observations and mental notes that they discuss with students at a later date. Others may decide to use skill checklists that are returned to the students for review. Still others may re-

close-up *on Assessment 8.2*

A cooperative learning structure that promotes the development and assessment of sociocultural skills in group learning intentionally accounts for the following:

- Linguistic demands of the task(s)
- Levels of acculturation demonstrated by the students
- Purpose of the grouping
- Opportunities for peer clarification, elaboration, or repetition of information that may have been missed or not understood during the lesson
- Cooperative group activities that occur in a low-risk and natural setting

For assessment purposes, some teachers may use observations and mental notes that they discuss with students at a later date. Others may decide to use skill checklists that are returned to the students for review. Still others may record anecdotal notes that are more or less immediately discussed with the students. Ultimately, CLD and other students are encouraged to use feedback from these informal assessments in the purposeful refinement of their sociocultural skills.

cord anecdotal notes that are more or less immediately discussed with the students. Ultimately, CLD and other students are encouraged to use feedback from these informal assessments in the purposeful refinement of their sociocultural skills.

PIA Strategies for Assessing Sociocultural Processes

The following strategies are representative of a variety of postinstructional strategies that classroom teachers can use to assess sociocultural skills development among their CLD students. Although the list of possible strategies is by no means exhaustive, it is intended to provide examples for teachers as they develop similar strategies that are particular to their site-specific student populations and community dynamics.

Partner Sticky Notes As students engage in content-area reading, the teacher asks them to pose questions about words or concepts they do not understand. These questions are recorded on sticky notes. After the assigned passage is read, students work in pairs, with each student posing his or her questions(s) to a partner. If the partner does not know an answer, the partner has the right to pass on the question. If the partner does answer, the student then asks how the partner derived the answer. Once one student's questions are addressed, the students switch roles and proceed again.

The pair then moves to a group setting and uses the same process to pose any unanswered questions to the class. If necessary (and at the end), the class poses any remaining unanswered questions to the teacher. The teacher answers the questions and provides the strategy or strategies he or she used to respond appropriately. Throughout the question-and-answer sessions, the teacher observes and makes anecdotal notes on the ability of students to question, listen, collaborate in a cross-cultural environment, and respond to the questions posed. The teacher also models these social and communication skills as he or she assesses and listens to the groups and partners.

Triad Interview Students write interview questions related to the critical concepts of the lesson. Then students select a partner to interview and record his or her answers. The partners then switch roles and repeat the interviewing process. After the students have interviewed each other, the recorded information is paraphrased and combined. The partners either agree on the information or they disagree and the necessary changes are made. The final interview results are then presented to a group or the class. During the activity, the teacher watches for types of questions posed, active listening, the effectiveness of sociocultural interactions and collaborations, and comfort with paraphrasing.

Quiz Quiz Trade In this strategy (adapted from Kagan [1994]), all students read the same selection of curriculum-based text (allow more English proficient peers to translate the text for less proficient peers in the native language, if possible). After reading the passage, each student thinks of a question that addresses a basic understanding or vocabulary word from the text and writes that question (along with the answer) on a 3" × 5" card. Then students pose their question to a partner, who will in turn pose his or her own question. Next, the partners trade cards and find another partner. With each successive exchange, the student is taking someone else's thought processes, incorporating them into his or her own schema, posing those questions, and hearing yet another's perspective on the answer. In subsequent rounds, the teacher asks the students to expand on the established concepts as they develop questions that become progressively more analytical. By the fifth round, students are encouraged to apply the content and expanded ideas to real-life scenarios.

The postinstructional strategies and activities presented in this chapter represent only a fraction of possible authentic assessments of student learning. Limitations exist only when teachers begin to box themselves in with concerns about time and where these ideas can be incorporated within existing programs, which often are so prescriptive and restrictive that they have limited the ability of teachers to create appropriate assessments. In such instances, we educators must remember that authentic postinstructional assessment provides the most meaningful information for planning instruction and meeting the needs of CLD students.

But What about the Grade?

At this point, teachers may be thinking, "These strategies for authentic assessment are all well and good, but how do I determine a grade for the content of the lesson?" This is one of the most common questions asked by educators who must document a letter or percentage grade for all students in the classroom. Ultimately, teachers are responsible for reporting whether a student has met the goals set by the curriculum and guiding standards.

Our education system has a history of limiting teachers' views of grading and the potential of the reported results to enhance the student's motivation to engage, aspire, and take risks during learning endeavors. So much is determined by policies that reflect the unquestioned and unreflective values, norms, and traditions that have been part of school systems for decades. Grading systems were decided long before the changing demographics and diversity in classrooms became the norm rather than the exception. It is not within the scope of this chapter to address the many complexities of fairness issues and the grading policies of school districts across the United States. Instead, the focus of this chapter is on the need to (a) assess, for each lesson, the extent to which students (especially CLD students) achieved the intended objectives of the lesson, and (b) document progress in student motivation, engagement, thinking processes, and social collaboration toward academic achievement and linguistic development.

Therefore, the chapter is less concerned with drawing conclusions about the grade and the meaning of the grade than with implications of assessment results to support future learning and to inform the teacher about appropriate accommoda-

close-up *on Assessment 8.3*

Our education system has a history of limiting teachers' views of grading and the potential of the reported results to enhance the student's motivation to engage, aspire, and take risks during learning endeavors. So much is determined by policies that reflect the unquestioned and unreflective values, norms, and traditions that have been part of school systems for decades. Grading systems were decided long before the changing demographics and diversity in classrooms became the norm rather than the exception.

tions for the student population served. The goal of postinstructional assessment, then, is to move beyond a grade and the grading system. This system conveys limited information about the knowledge and skills that were learned and the degree to which they were learned (superficial versus deep). By contrast, reflective teachers are concerned with *understanding* in assessment. Such teachers strive to determine how well students were able to:

- Construct meaning from the unknown
- Incorporate new content and concepts into their preexisting foundations of knowledge
- Build new skills that transcend the content areas
- Collaborate with diverse peers to share, learn, and articulate new information

At first glance, this alternative perspective on appropriate postinstructional assessment may appear to rely on a comparatively subjective foundation. However, this perspective does not eliminate the need to plan for the assignment of a less subjective grade that can be shared with parents and policymakers. Rather, it asks that educators consider ways to provide multiple and varied opportunities for CLD students to enhance their linguistic, academic, cognitive, and sociocultural skills and knowledge *before* using the norms of the grade level to assign a permanent grade. Only through authentic learning experiences and activities, opportunities for student practice, and ongoing process-focused assessments can a teacher appropriately scaffold instruction and provide timely feedback in order to enhance the product focus of grade-level-appropriate achievement and learning.

As educators embark on the journey toward equitable decisions about grading and the CLD student, they consider the multitude of variables concerning the learner's growth and achievement that might be shared with students, parents, future teachers, and administrators. They also determine the subset of

assessment *FREEZE FRAME 8.6*

Reflective teachers realize that perhaps the most desirable goal of postinstructional assessment is to move beyond a grade toward useful information about what knowledge has been gained, what capacities have been maximized, and what skills have been developed.

variables they will use to make decisions about the student's grade. The following questions can guide a teacher's decisions about what to include in the final grade for a lesson or unit:

- What are the objectives of this lesson or unit regarding both knowledge (content/concepts) and language (listening, speaking, reading, and writing) skills?
- Will percentage or symbol grades be given to indicate achievement of the selected objectives?
- What are the purposes of the grades or observations that will be recorded?
- In what ways will opportunities for practice and feedback (to incrementally assess progress and growth) be provided?
- Which activities will be assigned a grade for product assessment, and which activities will be used as process assessments to ensure ongoing progress?
- Will there be a homework grade?
- Will there be a cooperative learning grade?
- What checklists, rubrics, or anecdotal notes will be used to document progress and achievement?
- What weight will be given to each piece of the final reported achievement score?

The following additional questions can guide decisions about a student's final grade for the instructional term or year:

- What information will be used to calculate the final grade?
- Will the grade be an absolute measure of achievement?
- Will the grade be reflective of linguistic, academic, cognitive, and sociocultural aspects of learning and academic performance?
- Will some aspects of the practice and application be weighted more than others?
- What roles will attitude, motivation, and cooperation play in the final grade?

Among classroom teachers of CLD students, the assignment of final grades should reflect thorough consideration of these and related questions. Above all, teachers should reflect on whether the assessments used, and grades assigned, provide a multifaceted picture of the potential that CLD students are capable of demonstrating.

■ Conclusion

We began this text by discussing the changing demographics of our society and the growing diversity of our students. We noted that these last few decades have been a particular challenge for teachers whose own professional training and prior socialization may not have prepared them well for so many differences among their students. Yet, because teaching is a caring and reaching profession, teachers are adapting to and, in many cases, already meeting this formidable challenge. In this text, we share information and insights relevant to assessment and critical to the efforts of educators to address this challenge—that is, to appropriately accommodate the assets and needs of CLD students and families. We encourage readers, as teachers and as adaptive professionals, to apply what they know and have learned, to share their best practices and enthusiasm for teaching, and to advocate for the many contributions that diversity can bring to our classrooms and to our society.

■ key concepts

Analyze Draw Decide [ADD]

Assessment continua

Cognitive learning strategies

Concept maps

Content objectives

Cultural literacy response maps

Language objectives

Metacognitive learning strategies

Mind mapping

Partner sticky notes

Pen pal flowcharts

Plot diagrams

Postinstructional assessments

Postinstructional reflection journals

Prediction time line

P-W-L-L maps

Quiz Quiz Trade

Sociocultural learning strategies

So What! Now What?

Strategic thinking

Triad interview

Venn diagrams

■ professional conversations on practice

1. Discuss the importance of both language and content objectives for the appropriate instruction of CLD students.

2. The ability of many CLD students to participate in daily classroom activities depends on their capacity to process the language of the classroom. Discuss specific ways that teacher-driven PIAs in the linguistic dimension of the CLD student biography provide teachers critical information for scaffolding instruction for students whose first language is not English. How might instruction be scaffolded for a CLD student whose proficiency is in the preproduction stage of second language acquisition?

3. Discuss critical differences between K–W–L charts and P-W-L-L maps.

4. Discuss whether classroom teachers should incorporate postinstructional assessments that emphasize (a) process (graded and nongraded assessments that build capacity), (b) product (graded assessments that evaluate capacity related to grade-level expectations), or (c) both

product and process. Discuss from all four perspectives of the CLD student biography.

5. Although it can be fairly easy to determine from classroom observations and informal assessments whether a student adequately uses metacognitive learning strategies, it is often more difficult to actually guide the student to more advanced levels of self-monitoring. Discuss at least two additional strategies not already mentioned in this text for enhancing the use of metacognitive learning strategies with CLD students.

6. Creating a community of learners in the classroom requires that each member be equally appreciated, accepted, and valued. However, CLD students often face innumerable challenges in demonstrating to peers the linguistic, academic, cognitive, and sociocultural skills and knowledge they possess. Discuss specific ways that CLD students can teach or model these skills for their native-English-speaking peers.

■ questions for review and reflection

1. What two or more types of knowledge and skills are typically assessed by effective PIAs?

2. What are at least three typical questions answered by teacher-driven PIAs, as discussed in this chapter?

3. The fulfillment of what two types of lesson objectives are best documented with PIAs?

4. The effective use of teacher-driven PIAs serves what purposes? (List at least three.)

5. Appropriate PIAs for students whose first language is not English must encompass what four literacy areas?

6. What questions must one consider when planning for language assessment?

7. What language behaviors are associated with speech emergence in the English language development continua discussed in this chapter?

8. How can parents contribute to a CLD student's language development progress?

9. What is strategic thinking, and how can a classroom teacher develop this with CLD students?

10. How do postinstructional reflection journals allow CLD students to demonstrate achievement in relation to the content and language objectives of a lesson or unit?

11. What is the difference between cognitive and metacognitive learning strategies, and what is the importance of assessing how students use them?

12. How does a prediction time line promote higher-order thinking with CLD students?

13. Why are sociocultural learning strategies crucial to the academic achievement of CLD students?

14. What is the value of cooperative learning activities in developing sociocultural learning strategies?

appendix

Resource List

Name: _____   Date: _____

Assignment/Project: _____

Effort & Achievement Comparison Rubric	
Effort	**Achievement**
5 = I put maximum effort into this task. I stretched myself to complete this task despite its difficulty. I approached task difficulties as challenges to be overcome. I built new capacities as a result of confronting these challenges.	5 = I exceeded the objectives of this task.
4 = I put exceptional effort into this task. I stretched myself to complete this task despite its difficulty. I approached task difficulties as challenges to be overcome.	4 = I met all of the objectives of this task.
3 = I put moderate effort into this task. I stretched myself to complete this task despite its difficulty. I approached task difficulties as challenges to be overcome.	3 = I met at least half of the objectives of this task.
2 = I put average effort into this task. I stretched myself to complete this task despite its difficulty.	2 = I met less than half of the objectives of this task.
1 = I put limited effort into this task.	1 = I did not meet the objectives of this task.
Scale: 5 = Excellent 4 = Outstanding 3 = Good 2 = Improvement Needed 1 = Unacceptable	

Lifeline Hook: A Peer Assessment

Content Area: ✎ Writing   📖 Reading   ✳ Science   🖩 Math

❑ Other Content Area

(Peer 1 Name) _____. I like the way (Peer 2 Name) _____ ❑ thought out, ❑ reasoned, ❑ worked, ❑ explored, ❑ documented, ❑ visualized, ❑ described, _____ (another word you could use to give your peer feedback) _____ (e.g., problem, challenge, assignment).

I can tell that you (my peer) understood the objective(s) by:

1.

2.

3.

I have questions about:

1.

2.

3.

What questions do you (my peer) have?

1.

2.

3.

Questions and comments **WE** (as peers) have for the teacher.

1.

2.

3.

Comments:

A summary of what we learned from each other:

Student Self-Assessment of Content Concepts and Vocabulary

Content Area: ❑ Reading ❑ Writing ❑ Science ❑ Math ❑ Social Studies
 ❑ Other: _____

Content Objectives:

Language Objectives:

Key Vocabulary:

I have knowledge of the concept from the last school or classroom I attended:
 ❑ Not at all ❑ Some ❑ A lot

What I remember includes:

I have knowledge of the key vocabulary from the last school or classroom I attended:
 ❑ Not at all ❑ Some ❑ A lot

I used the key vocabulary for:
 ❑ Reading ❑ Discussion ❑ Writing

To better understand the vocabulary, it would help me if:
 1.
 2.
 3.

My home experiences support my understanding of the vocabulary/concept in the following ways.
 1.
 2.
 3.

For this topic, I can contribute the following:

Skills Development Chart—Home Survey

Dear Parent,

Although _____ has not been in school very long, we know that some children have already been learning important academic concepts at home. Please review the types of skills listed on this page. Circle the skills that you can answer now and then post the chart on your refrigerator for a few days while you check your child's responses to a few more. This information will help us spend more time teaching new skills rather than working on those skills your child already knows.

Student's Name: _____   Grade: _____   Teacher: _____

Academic Skills Demonstrated with Clothes/Laundry

Can your child:

				Comments
Yes	No	Unsure	Sort laundry by *color?*	
Yes	No	Unsure	Locate items that *match* (e.g., socks)?	
Yes	No	Unsure	Tell you which shirt or sock is *bigger/smaller?*	

Academic Skills Demonstrated in the Kitchen

Can your child:

				Comments
Yes	No	Unsure	Sort items by *color* or *shape?*	
Yes	No	Unsure	Sort boxes or cans by *size* (e.g., large cans/small cans)?	
Yes	No	Unsure	Sort items *in order* from smallest to largest?	
Yes	No	Unsure	Show you which cup is *empty* and which is *full?*	
Yes	No	Unsure	Identify items from the same *group* (e.g., fruits, vegetables, desserts)?	
Yes	No	Unsure	Pick out foods having a particular *characteristic* (e.g., sweet, smooth)?	
Yes	No	Unsure	Tell you which bowl has *more* (e.g., ice cream, beans)?	
Yes	No	Unsure	Tell you which container has the *most* or *least* (e.g., grapes, chips)?	
Yes	No	Unsure	Tell you which foods he or she *does* or *does not* like?	
Yes	No	Unsure	Demonstrate that he or she knows *where* to find or put things in the kitchen?	
Yes	No	Unsure	Demonstrate that he or she understands that the refrigerator is *cold* and the stove is *hot?*	
Yes	No	Unsure	Select the correct *number* of spoons or napkins to help set the table for a family meal?	

Parent Signature: _____   Date: _____

Skills Development Chart—Home Survey (Spanish)

Estimado Padre,

Aunque _____ no ha atendido a la escuela mucho tiempo, sabemos que los niños aprenden conceptos importantes en casa. Repase por favor los tipos de destrezas enumeradas en esta hoja. Marque las destrezas que pueda contestar ahora. Ponga esta hoja en su refrigerador, y después de observar por algunos días, responda las preguntas faltantes. Esta información nos ayudará a tomar más tiempo en la enseñanza de nuevas destrezas y no en las que ya son conocidas por el niño.

Nombre del estudiante _____   Grado: _____   Maestra/o: _____

Destrezas académicas demostradas con la ropa

Comentarios

Puede su hijo/a:

				Comentarios
Sí	No	No sé	¿Clasificar ropa por *color*?	
Sí	No	No sé	¿Localizar los artículos que *emparejan*? (calcetines)	
Sí	No	No sé	¿Decirle cual camisa o calcetín es *más grande o más chico*?	

Destrezas académicas demostradas con la cocina

Comentarios

Puede su hijo/a:

				Comentarios
Sí	No	No sé	¿Clasificar artículos por *color o forma*?	
Sí	No	No sé	¿Clasificar cajas o botes por *tamaño*? (bote grande, bote chico)	
Sí	No	No sé	¿Clasificar artículos *en orden* de más chico a más grande?	
Sí	No	No sé	¿Enseñarle cual vaso está vacío y cual está *lleno*?	
Sí	No	No sé	¿Identificar artículos del mismo *grupo*? (frutas, vegetales, postres)	
Sí	No	No sé	¿Escoger comidas con *características* particulares? (dulces, lisas)	
Sí	No	No sé	¿Decirle cual plato hondo tiene *más*? (helado, frijoles)	
Sí	No	No sé	¿Decirle cual envase contiene *lo más o menos*? (uvas, papitas)	
Sí	No	No sé	¿Decirle cuales comidas *le gustan o no le gustan*?	
Sí	No	No sé	¿Sabe *donde* encontrar o poner cosas en la cocina?	
Sí	No	No sé	¿Entiende que el refrigerador es *frió* y la estufa es *caliente*?	
Sí	No	No sé	¿Seleccionar correctamente *el número* de cucharas y servilletas para la hora de la comida?	

Firma del Padre: _____   Fecha: _____

Cultural Profile from Home Visit

Student Name:

_____

Ethnicity:

_____

Country of Birth:

_____

Native Language/Other Languages Spoken at Home:

_____

Second Language Proficiency (LAS score/Information on parent questionnaire or survey):

_____

Family Specifics:

_____

Cultural Characteristics:

_____

_____

_____

_____

Other Information:

_____

_____

_____

_____

LOA* Observation Rubric

Student:			
Date of Observation		Time of Observation	
Criterion	**Range & Rating**	**Anecdotal Notes**	**Monitor Status****
Level of affect	5 Upbeat 0 Sullen and/or Angry		
Data:	5 - 4 - 3 - 2 - 1 - 0		
Level of interaction with peers of a similar culture and/or language	5 Highly Interactive 0 Withdrawn		
Data:	5 - 4 - 3 - 2 - 1 - 0		
Level of interaction with peers of a different culture and/or language	5 Highly Interactive 0 Withdrawn		
Data:	5 - 4 - 3 - 2 - 1 - 0		
Communication effectiveness with peers of a different culture and/or language	5 Highly Effective 0 Ineffective		
Data:	5 - 4 - 3 - 2 - 1 - 0		
Level of participation in group learning	5 Highly Participative 0 Nonparticipative		
Data:	5 - 4 - 3 - 2 - 1 - 0		
Level of student engagement with classroom learning activities	5 Highly Engaged 0 Not Engaged		
Data:	5 - 4 - 3 - 2 - 1 - 0		
Legend:	* LOA = Level of Acculturation ** Status Range = Enhance, Maintain, or Reduce Monitoring of LOA		

Communication Functions Checklist

Please indicate whether the following communicative behaviors are:

Observed (+)   Reported (R)   Not Observed (–)

Student Name: _____

	L1	L2
1. Student comments on actions of self or others.		
2. Student initiates conversations.		
3. Student maintains a topic in conversation.		
4. Student follows multipart directions.		
5. Student uses language to request (action/object, assistance, information, clarification, etc.).		
6. Student uses language to tell (needs, feelings, thoughts, answers to questions).		
7. Student describes experiences (retells events).		
8. Student predicts outcomes or describes solutions.		
9. Student expresses and supports opinions.		
10. Student uses language to express imaginative and creative thinking.		

Basic Interpersonal Communication Skill (BICS)

L1	L2	Listening
○	○	Understands school/classroom routines
○	○	Responds, with little hesitation, when asked to perform a nonverbal task
○	○	Follows oral directions at the end of lesson (with familiarity and modeling)
○	○	Listens to peers when process is provided
○	○	Becomes distracted when lesson is not differentiated
○	○	Distinguishes sameness or difference between English sounds

L1	L2	Speaking
○	○	Is comfortable with groups speaking English
○	○	Communicates with peers in social settings
○	○	Responds to questions in class when the question is context embedded or the teacher provides scaffolding
○	○	Is able to retell a pictured, cued, or scaffolded story
○	○	Can describe the topic of the lesson using limited vocabulary
○	○	Struggles with concept retelling when topic is not contextualized
○	○	Withdraws when group discussions go beyond known vocabulary
○	○	Is eager to participate when language demands are supported

L1	L2	Reading
○	○	Recognizes common language of school
○	○	Recognizes environmental print (e.g., signs, logos, McDonald's)
○	○	Can match or read basic sight words
○	○	Reads best when material is contextualized
○	○	Demonstrates limited use of reading strategies
○	○	Volunteers to read when material is known

L1	L2	Writing
○	○	Writes personal information (e.g., name, address, phone number)
○	○	Writes with contextual and/or instructional scaffolding
○	○	Writes with some spelling errors
○	○	Writes with many spelling errors
○	○	Writes with moderate to high levels of syntax errors

Source: Adapted from: B. Bernhard & B. Loera (1992). Checklist of language skills for use with limited English proficient students. *Word of Mouth Newsletter*, 4(1). San Antonio, TX: Lauren Newton.

Cognitive Academic Language Proficiency (CALP)

L1	L2	**Listening**
O	O	Is able to carry out academic tasks without language support
O	O	Understands vocabulary in different content areas (e.g., *sum* in math vs. *some* in science)
O	O	Understands process/sequence across content areas
O	O	Uses selective attention when taking notes
O	O	Understands teacher idioms and humor
O	O	Understands English language functions
O	O	Comprehends teacher lecture, movies, and audiovisual presentations

L1	L2	**Speaking**
O	O	Asks/answers specific questions about topic of discussion
O	O	Uses temporal concepts (e.g., first, next, after) appropriately
O	O	Recognizes the need for, and seeks, clarification of academic tasks or discussion
O	O	Expresses rationale for opinion
O	O	Poses thoughtful questions
O	O	Actively participates in class activities and discussions
O	O	Volunteers to answer subject-matter questions of varying difficulty

L1	L2	**Reading**
O	O	Demonstrates knowledge and application of sound–symbol association
O	O	Demonstrates phonemic awareness skills such as sound blending, elision, and rhyming
O	O	Regards print with appropriate spatial skills and orientation (e.g., left to right, top to bottom)
O	O	Interprets written words and text as the print representation of speech
O	O	Understands differential use of text components (e.g., table of contents, glossary)
O	O	Reads for information and understanding
O	O	Reads independently to gather information of interest

L1	L2	**Writing**
O	O	Performs written tasks at levels required by the curriculum
O	O	Uses complex sentences appropriate for grade level
O	O	Writes from dictation
O	O	Writes for audience and purpose
O	O	Understands purposes and application of writing conventions
O	O	Uses writing as a tool for personal means (e.g., correspondence, notation, journaling)
O	O	Writes compellingly or creatively (e.g., editorials, poetry, lyrics, stories)

Source: Adapted from: B. Bernhard & B. Loera (1992). Checklist of language skills for use with limited English proficient students. *Word of Mouth Newsletter,* 4(1). San Antonio, TX: Lauren Newton.

Student Oral Language Observation Matrix: SOLOM

Student Name _____ Grade _____ School _____ Date _____

Language of Student _____ Rater Name _____ Total Score _____

	1	2	3	4	5	Score
Comprehension	Cannot understand even simple conversation.	Has great difficulty following everyday social conversation, even when words are spoken slowly and repeated.	Understands most of what is said at slower than normal speed with some repetitions.	Understands nearly everything at normal speed, although occasional repetition may be necessary.	Understands everyday conversation and normal classroom discussion without difficulty.	
Fluency	Speech is so halting and fragmentary that conversation is virtually impossible.	Usually hesitant, often forced into silence because of language limitations.	Everyday conversation and classroom discussion frequently disrupted by student's search for correct manner of expression.	Everyday conversation and classroom discussion generally fluent, with occasional lapses while student searches for the correct manner of expression.	Everyday conversation and classroom discussion fluent and effortless; approximately those of a native speaker.	
Vocabulary	Vocabulary limitations so severe that conversation is virtually impossible.	Difficult to understand because of misuse of words and very limited vocabulary.	Frequent use of wrong words; conversation somewhat limited because of inadequate vocabulary.	Occasional use of inappropriate terms and/or rephrasing of the ideas because of limited vocabulary.	Vocabulary and idioms approximately those of a native speaker.	
Pronunciation	Pronunciation problems so severe that speech is virtually unintelligible.	Difficult to understand because of pronunciation problems; must frequently repeat in order to be understood.	Concentration required of listener; occasional misunderstandings caused by pronunciation problems.	Always intelligible, although listener conscious of a definite accent and occasional inappropriate intonation pattern.	Pronunciation and intonation approximately those of a native speaker.	
Grammar	Errors in grammar and word order so severe that speech is virtually unintelligible.	Difficult to understand because of errors in grammar and word order; must often rephrase or restrict speech to basic patterns.	Frequent errors in grammar and word order; meaning occasionally obscured.	Occasional errors in grammar or word order; meaning not obscured.	Grammar and word order approximately those of a native speaker.	

Expressive Communication Rubric

Student Name: _____

Date(s) Completed   X above_____   X below_____

	Level 1	Level 2	Level 3	Level 4
Message effectiveness	Unable to understand intent/meaning.	Difficult to understand.	Able to understand most but not all of message.	Message is easily understood.
Language structure	Multiple errors with word order and grammar.	Noticeable errors but student able to convey aspects of the message.	Uses mostly correct structures with some errors.	Use of language structures is similar to that of a native speaker.
Vocabulary	Incorrect word choices and/or limited vocabulary hinder social and academic communication.	Relies on a limited range of vocabulary to communicate.	Vocabulary is not usually conspicuous but is rarely specific or elaborate.	Varied types of words, including idioms, are used with facility.
Pronunciation	Speech is often unintelligible.	Speech is understandable with careful listening and known context.	Speech is generally understandable to familiar and unfamiliar listeners.	Speech pronunciation is similar to that of a native speaker.

Portfolio/Cumulative Folder Checklist

Items to be included:			Date
Interview or Parent Survey on Language Use			
Home Language Survey			
Initial LAS Test			
Subsequent LAS Tests	Grade	Score	
	K	/	
	1st	/	
	2nd	/	
	3rd	/	
	4th	/	
	5th	/	
CLD Student Background Survey			
BICS Evaluation (L1 & L2)			
CALP Evaluation (L1 & L2)			
Native Language:			
Literacy Screening (grades K–5)			
Reading Benchmark (grades 3–5)			
Writing Sample (grades 3–5)			
English Language:			
Literacy Screening (grades K–5)			
Reading Levels (grades 3–5)			
Early Writing Assessment			
Cognitive Learning Strategy Use			

Music Assessment Rubric

Level 1:

- Observes class activities with little participation
- Begins to hum certain parts of songs as class sings
- Appears to understand little or no English instructions given in class
- Very little attempt to do actions and movements
- Does not yet try to tap simple rhythms

Level 2:

- Continues to mostly just observe the class
- Sings some words and phrases of songs in class (sheltered English)
- Follows simple classroom instructions with repetition
- Begins to repeat movements to various songs
- Begins to try to tap simple rhythms

Level 3:

- Is willing to actively participate in class activities
- Sings entire songs with class
- Follows simple classroom instructions
- Performs simple movements with class
- Can tap simple rhythms

Level 4:

- Fully participates in class activities
- Sings songs fluently
- Follows most classroom instructions without difficulty
- Masters movements or motions to various songs
- Can tap complex rhythms

Teacher Observation Checklist

Student Name	Follows directions without a model	Uses nonverbals to communicate understanding or express needs	Uses single words to answer questions or express needs	Uses simple sentence structures for social purposes	Uses simple sentence structures for curricular purposes	Other comments or observations

Testing Tips

Multiple Choice

- Read the question and think of the answer before reading the selections.
- Eliminate choices that are obviously incorrect or unrelated to the content.
- Carefully analyze and choose from among the remaining options.
- Look for grammatical clues.

Matching

- Make sure you know the rules and understand the directions well (e.g., whether items can be used more than once).
- Read the first item in column one and then all possible matches before answering.
- First answer items that appear less difficult; skip (and note) difficult items to reconsider when the answer field has narrowed (if one answer per item).
- As you proceed, mark out or highlight choices that have been used in order to focus your attention on remaining responses for review.

True or False

- Words that qualify statements, such as *rarely, sometimes, most,* and *usually,* are more likely associated with correct answers than words that make the statement 100 percent true or false, such as *always, never,* and *every.*
- Read each item carefully; mark it false if any part of it is not correct or true.
- Highlight prefixes and negative words, and consider their power to change meaning.

Sentence Completion

- To help determine the answers, convert these items into questions.
- Pay attention to grammatical clues as well as length or number of blanks to identify targeted responses.

Essay

- Highlight key words related to directions, such as *explain, compare,* and *describe.*
- Read the question, note important points to address, and outline your response before beginning to write.
- Rephrase the question as the first sentence of the answer, detail your response accordingly with transitions between ideas, and summarize main points in your closing statement(s).
- If unable to complete an item, note its key points and create an outline.
- Proofread your response for legibility, spelling, grammar, and style.

Source: Adapted from Salend (2005), pp. 503–504.

Literature Circle Presentation Preparation
Self-Assessment Rubric

Student Name:

Title of Book:

Presentation Preparation Activities	Please circle the most appropriate response to each statement. 1 = Never 4 = Frequently 2 = Rarely 5 = Always 3 = Sometimes				
1. I came to group meetings prepared (on time and ready to make an honest effort to understand the material).	1	2	3	4	5
2. I willingly read from the book when it was my turn.	1	2	3	4	5
3. I actively participated in discussions.	1	2	3	4	5
4. I listened attentively while members shared thoughts.	1	2	3	4	5
5. I respected the ideas and opinions of other members.	1	2	3	4	5
6. I helped my group discuss the general questions.	1	2	3	4	5
7. I helped discuss the questions specific to our book.	1	2	3	4	5
8. I identified at least one question that needed to be addressed.	1	2	3	4	5
9. I helped define presentation responsibilities.	1	2	3	4	5
10. I prepared for my presentation responsibilities (gathered materials, rehearsed part, asked for advice when necessary, etc.).	1	2	3	4	5

With which group members did you work most effectively?

Additional Comments:

Student Name: _____

Continua for the Assessment of English Language Development

	Preproduction	Early Production	Speech Emergence	Intermediate Fluency	Advanced Fluency
Date					
Listening	• Cannot yet understand simple expressions or statements in English.	• Understands previously learned expressions. • Understands new vocabulary in context.	• Understands sentence-length speech. • Participates in conversation about simple information. • Understands a simple message. • Understands basic directions and instructions.	• Understands academic content. • Understands more complex directions and instructions. • Comprehends main idea. • Effectively participates in classroom discussions.	• Understands most of what is heard. • Understands and retells main idea and most details from oral presentations and conversations.
Date					
Speaking	• Is not yet able to make any statements in English.	• Uses isolated words and learned phrases. • Uses vocabulary for classroom situations. • Expresses basic courtesies. • Asks very simple questions. • Makes statements using learned materials. • Asks and answers questions about basic needs.	• Asks and answers simple questions about academic content. • Talks about familiar topics. • Responds to simple statements. • Expresses self in simple situations (e.g., ordering a meal, introducing oneself, asking directions).	• Initiates, sustains, and closes a conversation. • Effectively participates in classroom discussions. • Gives reasons for agreeing or disagreeing. • Retells a story or event. • Compares and contrasts a variety of topics.	• Communicates facts and talks casually about topics of general interest using specific vocabulary. • Participates in age-appropriate academic, technical, and social conversations using English correctly.

(continued)

Student Name: _____

	Preproduction	Early Production	Speech Emergence	Intermediate Fluency	Advanced Fluency
Date					
Reading	• Is not yet able to read any words in English. • Is not yet able to identify the letters of the Roman alphabet. • Is not yet able to decode sounds of written English.	• Reads common messages, phrases, and/or expressions. • Identifies the letters of the Roman alphabet. • Decodes most sounds of written English. • Identifies learned words and phrases.	• Reads and comprehends main ideas and/or facts from simple materials.	• Understands main ideas and details from a variety of sources.	• Reads authentic text materials for comprehension. • Understands most of what is read in authentic texts.
Date					
Writing	• Is not yet able to write any words in English. • Is not yet able to write the letters of the Roman alphabet.	• Copies or transcribes familiar words or phrases. • Writes the letters from memory and/or dictation. • Writes simple expressions from memory. • Writes simple autobiographical information as well as some short phrases and simple lists. • Composes short sentences with guidance.	• Creates basic statements and questions. • Writes simple letters and messages. • Writes simple narratives.	• Writes more complex narratives. • Composes age-appropriate original materials using present, past, and future tenses. • Writes about a variety of topics for a variety of purposes.	• Write summaries. • Takes notes. • Compares and contrasts familiar topics. • Uses vivid, specific language in writing.

Source: Wichita Public Schools, Wichita, Kansas. Reprinted by permission.

Cultural Literacy Response Map

Title of Story: _____   Name: _____

Story Elements

Setting	
Main characters	
Problem in the story	
Main events in the story	

My Cultural Connections

1. *When I read this story, I thought about how in my culture . . .*

2. *The character I could relate to most was* _____.
   I could relate to this character because:

3. *The experience(s) from my own background that helped me understand the story included:*

4. *Other cultural connections I made included:*

What do you think?

1. What do you think would have happened if the main character had done something different?	
2. How do you think the main character felt? Why?	
3. How would you have felt if you were the main character? Why?	

Rubric for the Assessment of Cognitive and Metacognitive Strategy Use

Criterion	Student Performance			Score
	Limited	Some Exploration	Extensive Analysis	
	1 Point	*3 Points*	*5 Points*	
1. Student identifies the problem or the task he or she is being asked to do.				
2. Student thinks about the identified problem and reasons out strategy to use.				
3. Student applies the strategy and evaluates effectiveness.				
4. Student evaluates his or her answer.				
5. Student evaluates the strengths and weaknesses of his or her learning processes.				
Total Score:				

accommodation   See *mutual accommodation.*

acculturation   The process of adjusting to a new culture that is different from one's home culture.

affective filter   Controls the extent to which an individual internalizes input by converting it into learning. It has been compared to a defense mechanism because if it is raised it may negatively influence language acquisition, academic success, and classroom behavior and action.

assessment accommodation   A measure that is taken to ensure that the results of a typically formal student assessment reflect only measurement of the targeted skills or knowledge rather than the student's language ability, level of acculturation, or testing finesse.

authentic assessment   Refers to assessments that are generally developed directly from classroom instruction, group work, or related classroom activities and that provide an alternative to traditional assessments. Authentic assessments emphasize real-world problems, tasks, or applications that are relevant to the student and his or her community.

basic interpersonal communication skills (BICS)   The language ability needed for casual conversation. This usually applies to the interpersonal conversation skills of CLD students (e.g., playground language).

cognitive academic language proficiency (CALP)   The language ability needed for learning academic skills and concepts in situations in which contextual clues are not present and an abstract use of language is required.

common underlying proficiency (CUP)   Refers to the conceptual knowledge that acts as the foundation on which new skills are built. Both L1 and L2 facilitate the development of such fundamental cognitive patterns within individuals. The language biographies serve as a bridge, connecting new information with previously acquired knowledge.

culturally and linguistically diverse (CLD)   Preferred term for an individual or group of individuals whose culture or language differs from that of the dominant group.

English language learner (ELL)   Individuals who are in the process of transitioning from a home or native language to English. However, *CLD* is the preferred term because *CLD* emphasizes both the cultural and linguistic assets a student brings to the classroom.

English submersion   Describes the "sink-or-swim" programmatic notion that no language services or accommodations should be provided to second language learners. Rather, students are expected to rapidly acquire the English language skills needed for full participation in the grade-level classroom, with no additional language support.

formative assessment   A tool or strategy employed by grade-level and other teachers to determine what and how their students are learning so that instruction can be modified accordingly while it is still in progress.

funds of knowledge   The knowledge, skills, and background experiences students and families have gained through prior socialization in a particular culture and as speakers of particular languages.

limited English proficient (LEP)   A person who is in the process of acquiring English as an additional language. This term is frequently used in government documents. However, because *LEP* emphasizes inadequacies rather than abilities, *CLD* is the preferred term.

mutual accommodation   The collaborative interactions between a CLD student and an educator that maximize the resources and learning strategies each brings to the school or classroom environment.

opportunity to learn   The degree to which potential barriers to learning are addressed such that all students have equitable access to the curriculum. Conditions that may affect a student's opportunity to learn include the (in)appropriateness of curricula, instructional strategies, materials, and facilities, as well as the skills and commitment of educational personnel (e.g., teachers, administrators, superintendents) to ensure the academic success of all students.

rebus cue   The use of a rebus picture to aid in the generation or interpretation of text (see *rebus picture*).

rebus picture   A picture or symbol used to represent a syllable or word in text or puzzles.

redesignation   Also referred to as reclassification, this term describes the process of determining the transitional need of a student for additional or continuing participation in language services.

reliability   The power of an assessment to gather consistent evidence of skills, regardless of the examiner, time, place, or other variables related to its administration.

scaffolding   The use of supporting aids and activities that enable a student to perform tasks that would otherwise be too complex for his or her abilities.

schema   (pl. schemata) A memory framework that enables one to store declarative knowledge as interrelated concepts and ideas that can be recalled as isolated facts or as structured associations.

silent period   The first stage, or preproduction stage, of the second language acquisition process. During this period, a CLD student may communicate in only nonverbal ways as he or she primarily listens to the new language and tries to understand its patterns and rules before attempting production in that language.

summative assessment   A tool or strategy employed by grade-level and other teachers to measure the knowledge or skills of students upon the completion of an instructional lesson, theme, or unit.

validity   The ability of an assessment, process, or product to measure the knowledge or skills it is intended to measure.

Abedi, J. (2001, Summer). Assessment and accommodations for English language learners: Issues, concerns, and recommendations. *National Center for Research on Evaluation, Standards, and Student Testing (CRESST) Policy Brief, 4.*

Abedi, J. (2004). The No Child Left Behind Act and English language learners: Assessment and accountability issues. *Educational Researcher, 33*(1), 4–14.

Abedi, J., & Dietel, R. (2004). Challenges in the No Child Left Behind Act for English-language learners. *Phi Delta Kappan, 85*(10), 782–785.

Abedi, J., Lord, C., & Hoffstetter, C. (1998). *Impact of selected background variables on students' NAEP math performance* (CSE Tech. Rep. No. 478). Los Angeles: University of California, National Center for Research on Evaluation, Standards, and Student Testing.

Alcala, A. L. (2000). *The preliterate student: A framework for developing an effective instructional program. ERIC Digest.* College Park, MD: ERIC Clearinghouse on Assessment and Evaluation. (ERIC Document Reproduction Service No. ED447148)

Allinder, R. M., Bolling, R. M., Oats, R. G., & Gagnon, W. A. (2000). Effects of teacher self-monitoring implementation of curriculum-based measurement and mathematics computation achievement of students with disabilities. *Remedial and Special Education, 21*(4), 219–226.

Amrein, A. L., & Berliner, D.C. (2002). High-stakes testing, uncertainty, and student learning. *Education Policy Analysis Archives, 10*(18). Retrieved August 28, 2004, from http://epaa.asu.edu/epaa/v10n18

Anderman, E. M., Griesinger, T., & Westerfield, G. (1998). Motivation and cheating during early adolescence. *Journal of Educational Psychology, 90*(1), 84–93.

Anderson, J., Moeschberger, M., Chen, M. S., Jr., Kunn, P., Wewers, M. E., & Guthrie, R. (1993). An acculturation scale for Southeast Asians. *Social Psychiatry and Psychiatric Epidemiology, 28,* 134–141.

Anderson, N. J. (2002). *The role of metacognition in second language teaching and learning.* Washington, DC: ERIC Clearinghouse on Languages and Linguistics. (ERIC Digest No. EDO-FL-01–10)

Anthony, J. L., & Lonigan, C. J. (2004). The nature of phonological awareness: Converging evidence from four studies of preschool and early grade school children. *Journal of Educational Psychology, 96*(1), 43–55.

Arreaga-Mayer, C. (1992). *Ecobehavioral assessment of exceptional culturally and linguistically diverse students: Evaluating effective bilingual special education programs.* Paper presented at the Third National Research Symposium on Limited English Proficient Student Issues: Focus on Middle and High School Issues, Washington, DC. Retrieved April 21, 2005, from www.ncela.gwu.edu/pubs/symposia/third/mayer.htm

Arreaga-Mayer, C., Tapia, Y., & Carta, J. J. (1993). Ecobehavioral System for the Contextual Recording of Interactional Bilingual Environments: ESCRIBE [Software system]. Lawrence: Biobehavioral Measurement Core, University of Kansas.

Artiles, A. J., & Harry, B. (2004). *Addressing culturally and linguistically diverse student overrepresentation in special education: Guidelines for parents.* Practitioner Brief Series. Denver, CO: National Center for Culturally Responsive Educational Systems.

August, D., & Hakuta, K. (Eds.). (1997). *Improving schooling for language-minority children: A research agenda.* Washington, DC: National Academy Press.

Baca, L., & Cervantes, H. (1998). *The bilingual special education interface.* Upper Saddle River, NJ: Merrill.

Baca, L. M., & Cervantes, H. T. (2004). *The bilingual special education interface* (4th ed.). Upper Saddle River, NJ: Prentice Hall.

Ballard & Tighe. (2004). *IDEA Proficiency Test (IPT)*. Brea, CA: Author.

Barona, A., & Miller, J. A. (1994). Short Acculturation Scale for Hispanic Youth (SASH-Y): A preliminary report. *Hispanic Journal of Behavioral Sciences, 16*(2), 155–162.

Barrett, H. C. (2000). *How to create your own electronic portfolio*. Retrieved April 20, 2005, from http://electronicportfolios.com/portfolios/howto

Berkowitz, A. J., Desmarais, K. H., Hogan, K., & Moorcroft, T. A. (2000). Authentic assessment in the informal setting: How it can work for you. *The Journal of Environmental Education, 31*(3), 20–24.

Bernal, E. (2003). Evaluating progress toward equitable representation of historically underserved groups in gifted and talented programs. In J. A. Castellano, *Special populations in gifted education: Working with diverse gifted learners* (pp. 177–186). Boston: Pearson Education.

Berry, J. W. (1992). Cross-cultural psychology: Research and applications. New York: Cambridge University Press.

Berry, J. W., Kim, U., Power, S., Young, M., & Bujaki, M. (1989). Acculturation attitudes in plural societies. *Applied Psychology: An International Review, 38*, 185–206.

Berube, M. S., et al. (2001). *Webster's II new college dictionary*. Boston: Houghton Mifflin.

Bialystok, E. (2001). *Bilingualism in development: Language, literacy, & cognition*. New York: Cambridge University Press.

Biddle, B. J., & Berliner, D.C. (2002). Unequal school funding in the United States. *Educational Leadership, 59*(8), 48–59.

Black, P., & Wiliam, D. (1998). Inside the black box: Raising standards through classroom assessment. *Phi Delta Kappan, 80*(2), 139–144, 146–148. Retrieved August 13, 2004, from www.pdkintl.org/kappan/kbla9810.htm

Bloom, B. S. (Ed.). (1956). *Taxonomy of educational objectives: Book 1, cognitive domain*. New York: Longman.

Bloom, L., & Lahey, M. (1978). *Language development and language disorders*. New York: Wiley.

Boehm, A. E. (1973). Criterion-referenced assessment for the teacher. *Teachers College Record, 75*(1), 117–126.

Bond, L. A. (1996). Norm- and criterion-referenced testing. *Practical Assessment, Research & Evaluation, 5*(2). Retrieved March 22, 2005, from http://PAREonline.net/getvn.asp?v=5&n=2

Brown, C. L. (2004). Reducing the over-referral of culturally and linguistically diverse students (CLD) for language disabilities. *NABE Journal of Research and Practice, 2*(1), 225–234.

Brownell, R. (Ed.). (2000a). Expressive One-Word Picture Vocabulary Test. Novato, CA: Academic Therapy Publications.

Brownell, R. (Ed.). (2000b). *Receptive One-Word Picture Vocabulary Test*. Novato, CA: Academic Therapy Publications.

Bruer, J. T. (1993). *Schools for thought: A science of learning in the classroom*. Cambridge, MA: MIT Press.

Burger, J. M., & Krueger, M. (2003). A balanced approach to high-stakes achievement testing: An analysis of the literature with policy implications. *International Electronic Journal for Leadership in Learning, 7*(4). Retrieved April 5, 2005, from www.ucalgary.ca/~iejll

Buriel, R., & Rueschenberg, E. (1989). Mexican American family functioning and acculturation: A family systems perspective. *Hispanic Journal of Behavioral Sciences, 11*(3), 232–244.

Buxton, C. (1999). Designing a model-based methodology for science instruction: Lessons from a bilingual classroom [Electronic version]. *Bilingual Research Journal, 23*(2–3). Retrieved November 12, 2002, from http://brj.asu.edu/v2323/articles/art4.html

Buzan, T. (1983). *Use both sides of your brain: New techniques to help you read efficiently, study effectively, solve problems, remember more, think clearly*. New York: E. P. Dutton.

Caldwell, L. D., & Siwatu, K. O. (2003). Promoting academic persistence in African American and Latino high school students: The educational navigation skills seminar in an Upward Bound program. *The High School Journal, 87*(1), 30–38.

California Department of Education. (n.d.). *Student oral language observation matrix (SOLOM)*. Unpublished instrument. Sacramento: Author.

California Department of Education. (n.d.). *Student written language observation matrix (SWLOM)*. Unpublished instrument. Sacramento: Author.

California Department of Education. (Revised annually). *California English Language Development Test (CELDT)*. Sacramento: Author.

Center for Educational Testing and Evaluation (CETE). (2005). *Kansas English Language Proficiency Assessment*. Lawrence: Author.

Center for Equity and Excellence in Education (CEEE). (2005). *Promoting excellence principles and indicators*. Arlington, VA: Author.

Chamot, A. U., & El-Dinary, P. B. (2000). *Children's learning strategies in language immersion classrooms*. Washington, DC: National Capital Language Resource Center. (ERIC Document Reproduction Service No. ED445518)

Chamot, A. U., & O'Malley, J. M. (1994). *The CALLA handbook: Implementing the cognitive academic language learning approach*. Reading, MA: Addison-Wesley.

Chamot, A., & O'Malley, J. (1996). The cognitive academic language learning approach: A model for linguistically diverse classrooms. *The Elementary School Journal, 96*, 259–273.

Chang, J. M., Lai, A., & Shimizu, W. (1995). LEP, LD, poor, and missed learning opportunities: A case of inner-city Chinese American children. In L. L. Cheng (Ed.), *Integrating language and learning for inclusion: An Asian/Pacific focus* (pp. 265–290). San Diego, CA: Singular Publishing Group.

Chappuis, S., & Stiggins, R. J. (2002). Classroom assessment for learning. *Educational Leadership, 60*(1), 40–43.

Charles, C. M., & Mertler, C. A. (2002). *Introduction to educational research* (4th ed.). Boston: Allyn and Bacon.

Chomsky, N. (1968). *Language and mind*. New York: Harcourt, Brace & World.

Cisero, C. A., & Royer, J. M. (1995). The development and cross-language transfer of phonological awareness. *Contemporary Educational Psychology, 20*, 275–303.

Coerr, E. (1986). *The Josefina story quilt*. New York: HarperCollins.

Collier, C. (2004). The assessment of acculturation. In *Handbook of Multicultural School Psychology* (in press). Retrieved May 5, 2005, from www.crosscultured.com/articles.asp?category=158

Coltrane, B. (2002). *English language learners and high-stakes tests: An overview of the issues*. Retrieved March 22, 2005, from www.cal.org/resources/digest/0207coltrane.html

Coohey, C. (2001). The relationship between familism and child maltreatment in Latino and Anglo families. *Child Maltreatment, 6*(2), 130–142.

Cooper, T. (1999). *Portfolio assessment: A guide for lecturers, teachers, and course designers*. Perth, WA: Praxis Education.

Cortez, A. (2003, January). The emerging majority: The growth of the Latino population and Latino student enrollments [Electronic version]. *IDRA Newsletter*. Retrieved May 17, 2005, from www.idra.org/Newslttr/2003/Jan/Albert.htm

Cosentino de Cohen, C. (with Deterding, N.). (2005). *Adult learners/instructional aides initiative: Survey of states and districts*. Washington, DC: The Urban Institute.

Crawford, J., & Impara, J. C. (2001). Critical issues, current trends, and possible futures in quantitative methods. In V. Richardson (Ed.), *Handbook of research on teaching* (4th ed., pp. 133–173). Washington, DC: American Educational Research Association.

Critchlow, D. E. (1996). *Dos Amigos verbal language scales*. Novato, CA: Academic Therapy Publications.

Cuéllar, I., Arnold, B., & Maldonado, R. (1995). Acculturation Rating Scale for Mexican Americans–II: A revision of the original ARSMA scale. *Hispanic Journal of Behavioral Sciences, 17*(3), 275–304.

Cummins, J. (1981). The role of primary language development in promoting educational success for language minority students. In C. F. Leyba (Ed.), *Schooling and language minority students:*

A theoretical framework (pp. 3–49). Los Angeles: Evaluation, Dissemination and Assessment Center, CSULA.

Cummins, J. (1984). *Bilingualism and special education: Issues in assessment and pedagogy.* Clevedon, UK: Multilingual Matters.

Cummins, J. (1996). *Negotiating identities: Education for empowerment in a diverse society.* Los Angeles: California Association for Bilingual Education.

Cummins, J. (2001). *Language, power, and pedagogy: Bilingual children in the crossfire.* Philadelphia: Multicultural Matters.

Cushner, K., McClelland, A., & Safford, P. (2006). *Human diversity in education: An integrative approach* (5th ed.). Boston: McGraw-Hill.

Diaz-Rico, L. T., & Weed, K. Z. (2006). *The cross-cultural, language, and academic development handbook: A complete K–12 reference guide* (3rd ed.). Boston: Allyn and Bacon.

Dixon Rayle, A., & Myers, J. E. (2004). Wellness in adolescence: The roles of ethnic identity, acculturation, and mattering. *Professional School Counseling, 8,* 81–90.

Duncan, S. E., & DeAvila, E. A. (1990). *Language Assessment Scales.* Monterey, CA: CTB/McGraw-Hill.

Duncan, S. E., & DeAvila, E. A. (1998). *Pre-Language Assessment Scale 2000.* Monterey, CA: CTB/McGraw-Hill.

Durgunoglu, A. Y., Nagy, W. E., & Hancin-Bhatt, B. J. (1993). Cross-language transfer of phonological awareness. *Journal of Educational Psychology, 85*(3), 453–465.

Durkheim, E. (1951). *Suicide* (J. A. Spaulding & G. Simpson, Trans.). New York: Free Press. (Original work published 1897)

Eaker, R., DuFour, R., & Burnette, R. (2002). *Getting started: Reculturing schools to become professional learning communities.* Bloomington, IN: National Educational Service.

Echevarria, J., Vogt, M., & Short, D. J. (2004). *Making content comprehensible for English language learners: The SIOP model* (2nd ed.). Boston: Allyn and Bacon.

Educational Testing Service (ETS). (2003). *Linking classroom assessment with student learning.* Princeton, NJ: Author.

Edwards, J. R. (1989). *Language and disadvantage* (2nd ed.). London: Cole and Whurr.

Engel, G. (1977). The need for a new medical model: A challenge to biomedicine. *Science, 196*(4286), 129–136.

Escamilla, K. (1999). The false dichotomy between ESL and transitional bilingual education programs: Issues that challenge all of us. *Educational Considerations, 26*(2), 1–6.

Farr, B. P., & Trumbull, E. (1997). *Assessment alternatives for diverse classrooms.* Clevedon, UK: Multilingual Matters.

Firestone, W. A., & Mayrowetz, D. (2000). Rethinking "high stakes": Lessons from the United States and England and Wales. *Teachers College Record, 102*(4), 724–749.

Fix, M., Passel, J. S., & Ruiz-de-Velasco, J. (2004). *School reform: The demographic imperative and challenge.* Paper presented at the IZA/Urban Institute Workshop on Migration, Washington, DC. Retrieved May 18, 2005, from www.iza.org/conference_files/iza_ui_2004/fix.pdf

Ford, D. Y. (1998). The underrepresentation of minority students in gifted education: Problems and promises in recruitment and retention. *The Journal of Special Education, 32*(1), 4–14.

Fradd, S., & McGee, P. (with Wilen, D.). (1994). *Instructional assessment: An integrative approach to evaluating student performance.* Reading, MA: Addison-Wesley.

Franco, J. N. (1983). An acculturation scale for Mexican-American children. *The Journal of General Psychology, 108,* 175–181.

Freeman, D. E., & Freeman, Y. S. (2001). *Between worlds: Access to second language acquisition* (2nd ed.). Portsmouth, NH: Heinemann.

Fromkin, V., & Rodman, R. (1983). *An introduction to language* (3rd ed.). New York: Holt, Rinehart, & Winston.

Fuchs, L., & Fuchs, D. (2003). Curriculum-based measurement: A best practice guide. *NASP Communiqué, 32*(2). Retrieved April 7, 2005, from www.nasponline.org/publications/cq322cbm insert.html

Fuchs, L. S. (2004). The past, present, and future of curriculum-based measurement research. *School Psychology Review, 33*(2), 188–192.

Fuchs, L. S., & Deno, S. L. (1991). Paradigmatic distinctions between instructionally relevant measurement models. *Exceptional Children, 57*(6), 488–499.

Fuchs, L. S., & Fuchs, D. (1992). Identifying a measure for monitoring student reading progress. *School Psychology Review, 21*(1), 45–58.

Gaines, S. O., Jr., Marelich, W. D., Bledsoe, K. L., Steers, W. N., Henderson, M. C., Granrose, C. S., et al. (1997). Links between race/ethnicity and cultural values as mediated by racial/ethnic identity and moderated by gender. *Journal of Personality and Social Psychology, 72*(6), 1460–1476.

Gates, M. L., & Hutchinson, K. (2005). *Cultural competence education and the need to reject cultural neutrality: The importance of what we teach and do not teach about culture.* Paper presented at the College of Education, Criminal Justice, and Human Services (CECH) Spring Research Conference, University of Cincinnati, OH. Retrieved May 10, 2005, from www.education.uc.edu/SRC2005/abstracts/gates_hutchinson.pdf

Glaser, R., & Silver, E. (1994). *Assessment, testing, and instruction: Retrospect and prospect* (CSE Tech. Rep. No. 379). Los Angeles: University of California, National Center for Research on Evaluation, Standards, and Student Testing. Retrieved May 31, 2005, from www.cse.ucla.edu/products/reports2.htm

Goldman, A. (2003, December). *Inclusion of LEP students in NAEP.* Presentation to the National Center for Educational Statistics, Washington, DC.

Goodnough, A. (1999, December 9). New York City teachers nabbed in school-test cheating scandal. *National Post,* p. B1.

Goodwin, A. L. (2000, March). Honoring ways of knowing. *Equity Resource Center Digest on Education Assessment.* Newton, MA: Women's Educational Equity Act Resource Center.

Goodyear, R. K., Newcomb, M. D., & Locke, T. F. (2002). Pregnant Latina teenagers: Psychosocial and developmental determinants of how they select and perceive the men who father their children. *Journal of Counseling Psychology, 49*(2), 187–201.

Gottardo, A. (2002). The relationship between language and reading skills in bilingual Spanish-English speakers. *Topics in Language Disorders, 22*(5), 46–70.

Grissom, J. (2004). Reclassification of English learners. *Education Policy Analysis Archives, 12*(36). Retrieved April 5, 2005, from http://epaa.asu.edu/epaa/v12n36

Gutierrez-Clellan, V. F., & Quinn, R. (1993). Assessing narratives of children from diverse cultural/linguistic groups. *Language, Speech, and Hearing Services in Schools, 24*(1), 2–9.

Hakuta, K. (1987). Degree of bilingualism and cognitive ability in mainland Puerto Rican children. *Child Development, 58,* 1372–1388.

Hakuta, K. (2001). *The education of language minority students: Testimony of Kenji Hakuta to the United States Commission on Civil Rights.* Retrieved May 17, 2005, from www.stanford.edu/~hakuta/Docs/CivilRightsCommission.htm

Hakuta, K., Butler, Y., & Witt, D. (2000). *How long does it take English learners to attain proficiency?* University of California Linguistic Minority Research Institute, Policy Report 2000–1. Retrieved April 5, 2005, from www.stanford.edu/~hakuta/Docs/HowLong.pdf

Hall, D., Griffiths, D., Haslam, L., & Wilkin, Y. (2001). *Assessing the needs of bilingual pupils: Living in two languages* (2nd ed.). London: David Fulton.

Hamayan, E. V., & Damico, J. S. (Eds.). (1991). *Limiting bias in the assessment of bilingual students.* Austin, TX: PRO-ED.

Hancock, C. R. (1994). Alternative assessment and second language study: What and why? *ERIC Digest.* Retrieved May 20, 2005, from www.cal.org/resources/digest/hancoc01.html

Harcourt Assessment. (2003). *Stanford English Language Proficiency (SELP) Test.* San Antonio, TX: Author.

Hendershot, C. S., MacPherson, L., Myers, M. G., Carr, L. G., & Wall, T. L. (2005). Psychosocial, cultural and genetic influences on alcohol use in Asian American youth. *Journal of Studies on Alcohol, 66*(2), 185–195.

Herrera, S. (2001). *Classroom strategies for the English language learner: A practical guide for accelerating language and literacy development.* Manhattan, KS: The MASTER Teacher.

Herrera, S., & Murry, K. (2004). *Accountability by assumption: Implications of reform agendas for teacher preparation.* Manuscript submitted for publication.

Herrera, S., & Murry, K. (2005). *Mastering ESL and bilingual methods: Differentiated instruction for culturally and linguistically diverse (CLD) students.* Boston: Allyn and Bacon.

Herrera, S., Perez, D., Murry, K. (in press). Transforming hearts and minds. In M. Brisk & R. Mattai (Eds.), *Culturally responsive teacher education: Language, curriculum, and community* (pp. 56–71). Mahwah, NJ: Lawrence Erlbaum.

Herrera, S., Trujillo, L., & Cano, L. (2005). *Preparing migrant preschoolers (and their parents) for success in school.* Paper presented at the National Migrant Education Conference, Burlingame, CA.

Holloway, J. H. (2000). How does the brain learn science? *Educational Leadership, 58*(3), 85–86.

Hosp, J. L., & Reschly, D. J. (2004). Disproportionate representation of minority students in special education: Academic, demographic, and economic predictors. *Exceptional Children, 70*(2), 185–199. Retrieved May 27, 2005, from http://journals.sped.org

Hosp, M. K., & Hosp, J. (2003). Curriculum-based measurement for reading, spelling, and math: How to do it and why. *Preventing School Failure, 48*(1), 10–17.

Indiana Department of Education. (2005). *Best practices: The use of native language during instructional & non-instructional time.* Retrieved August 26, 2005, from www.doe.state.in.us/lmmp/pdf/native_language_use.pdf

Individuals with Disabilities Education Act Amendments of 1997, Pub. L. No. 105–117.

Individuals with Disabilities Education Improvement Act of 2004, Pub. L. No. 108–446, §101.

Retrieved August 23, 2005, from www.vesid.nysed.gov/specialed/idea/home.html

Jensen, E. (2000). *Brain-based learning* (Rev. ed.). San Diego: The Brain Store.

Juffer, K. A. (1983). Culture shock: A theoretical framework for understanding adaptation. In J. Bransford (Ed.), *BUENO Center for Multicultural Education Monograph Series* (Vol. 4, No.1). Boulder: University of Colorado.

Kagan, S. (1994). *Cooperative learning.* San Clemente, CA: Resources for Teachers.

Kameenui, E., & Carnine, D. (1998). *Effective teaching strategies that accommodate diverse learners.* Upper Saddle River, NJ: Prentice Hall.

Kaplan, R. (2005). Contrastive rhetoric. In E. Hinkel (Ed.), *Handbook of research in second language teaching and learning* (pp. 375–391). Mahwah, NJ: Lawrence Erlbaum.

Kayser, H. (1995). *Bilingual speech-language pathology: An Hispanic focus.* San Diego: Singular.

Kirby, J. R., Parrila, R., & Pfeiffer, S. (2003). Naming speed and phonological processing as predictors of reading development. *Journal of Educational Psychology, 95,* 453–464.

Krashen, S. (1982). *Principles and practice in second language acquisition.* Oxford, UK: Pergamon Press.

Krashen, S. (1996). *Under attack: The case against bilingual education.* Culver City, CA: Language Education Associates.

Krashen, S. (2000). *Has whole language failed?* University of Southern California Rossier School of Education. Retrieved November 15, 2002, from www.usc.edu/dept/education/CMMR/text/Krashen_WholeLang.html

Kulis, S., Napoli, M., & Marsiglia, F. F. (2002). Ethnic pride, biculturalism, and drug use norms of urban American Indian adolescents. *Social Work Research, 26*(2), 101–112.

Landrine, H., & Klonoff, E. A. (1994). The African American Acculturation Scale: Development, reliability, and validity. *Journal of Black Psychology, 20*(2), 104–127.

Lara, J., & August, D. (1996). *Systemic reform and limited English proficient students.* Washington,

DC: Council of Chief State School Officers, and Stanford, CA: Stanford Working Group.

Lau v. Nichols, 414 U.S. 563 (1974).

LeDoux, J. (1996). *The emotional brain.* New York: Touchstone.

Lewis, T. J., & Jungman, R. E. (Eds.). (1986). *On being foreign: Culture shock in short fiction, an international anthology.* Yarmouth, ME: Intercultural Press.

Limbos, M. M., & Geva, E. (2001). Accuracy of teacher assessments of second-language students at risk for reading disability. *Journal of Learning Disabilities, 34*(2), 136–151.

Linn, R. L., & Miller, M. D. (2005). *Measurement and assessment in teaching* (9th ed.). Upper Saddle River, NJ: Prentice Hall.

Loretan, S., & Lenica, J. (1993). *Bob the snowman.* New York: Scholastic.

Lurie, N. O. (1991). The American Indian: Historical background. In N. R. Yetman (Ed.), *Majority and minority: The dynamics of race and ethnicity in American life* (pp. 132–145). Boston: Allyn and Bacon.

MacMillan, D. L., Gresham, F. M., & Bocian, K. M. (1998). Discrepancy between definitions of learning disabilities and school practices: An empirical investigation. *Journal of Learning Disabilities, 31,* 314–326.

MacSwan, J., Rolstad, K., & Glass, G. V. (2002). Do some school-age children have no language? Some problems of construct validity in the Pre-LAS Español. *Bilingual Research Journal, 26*(2), 213–238.

Madaus, G., West, M. M., Harmon, M. C., Lomax, R. G., & Viator, K. A. (1992). *The influence of testing on teaching math and science in grades 4–12* (NSF Rep. No. SPA8954759). Chestnut Hill, MA: Boston College, Center for the Study of Testing, Evaluation, and Educational Policy.

Maldonado, J. A. (1994). Bilingual special education: Specific learning disabilities in language and reading. *Journal of Educational Issues of Language Minority Students, 14,* 127–148. Retrieved May 27, 2005, from www.ncela.gwu.edu/pubs/jeilms/vol14/maldonad.htm

Marston, D. B. (1989). A curriculum-based measurement approach to assessing academic performance: What it is and why do it? In M. R. Shinn (Ed.), *Curriculum-based measurement: Assessing special children* (pp. 18–78). New York: Guilford Press.

Marzano, R. J. (2004). *Building background knowledge for academic achievement: Research on what works in schools.* Alexandria, VA: Association for Supervision and Curriculum Development.

Marzano, R. J., Pickering, D. J., & Pollock, J. E. (2001). *Classroom instruction that works: Research-based strategies for increasing student achievement.* Alexandria, VA: Association for Supervision and Curriculum Development.

Mattes, L. J., & Nguyen, L. (1996). *Bilingual Language Proficiency Questionnaire: English/Vietnamese edition.* Oceanside, CA: Academic Communication Associates.

Mattes, L. J., & Santiago, G. (1985). *Bilingual Language Proficiency Questionnaire: English/Spanish edition.* Oceanside, CA: Academic Communication Associates.

McGlinchey, M. T., & Hixson, M. D. (2004). Using curriculum-based measurement to predict performance on state assessments in reading. *School Psychology Review, 33,* 193–203.

MetriTech. (2002). *Washington Language Proficiency Test* (WLPT). Champaign, IL: Author.

Moll, L. C., Armanti, C., Neff, D., & Gonzalez, N. (1992). Funds of knowledge for teaching: Using a qualitative approach to connect homes and classrooms. *Theory into Practice, 31*(2), 132–141.

Montes, F. (2002). Enhancing content areas through a cognitive academic language learning collaborative in South Texas. *Bilingual Research Journal, 26*(3), 697–716.

Montgomery, G. T. (1992). Comfort with acculturation status among students from South Texas. *Hispanic Journal of Behavioral Sciences, 14*(2), 201–223.

Moss, M., & Puma, M. (1995). *Prospects: The congressionally mandated study of educational opportunity and growth: Language minority and limited English proficient students.* Washington, DC: U.S. Department of Education.

Muñoz-Sandoval, A. F., Cummins, J., Alvaredo, C. G., Ruef, M., & Schrank, F. A. (2005). *Bilingual Verbal Ability Tests Normative Update (BVAT-NU).* Itasca, IL: Riverside.

Murdock, S. H. (2002, September). *Population change in Texas: Implications for human and socioeconomic resources in the 21st century.* Presentation at the Latino Economic Summit, Austin, TX.

Murry, K., & Herrera, S. (2005a). *Reaching CLD families through differentiated teacher education and practices.* Manuscript submitted for publication.

Murry, K., & Herrera, S. (2005b). *Readiness for accommodation? Teachers and their CLD students.* Paper presented at the annual meeting of the American Educational Research Association, Montreal, Canada.

Murry, K., Herrera, S., & Perez, D. (2005). *CLASSIC/ESL Dual Language Program: Reaching out to educators of English language learners.* Paper presented at the annual meeting of the Association of Teacher Educators (ATE), Chicago, IL.

National Center for Education Statistics (NCES). (2002). *Schools and staffing survey, 1999–2000: Overview of the data for public, private, public charter, and Bureau of Indian Affairs elementary and secondary schools* (NCES 2002–313). Washington, DC: U.S. Department of Education. Retrieved from http://nces.ed.gov/pubsearch/pubsinfo.asp?pubid=2002313

National Immigration Forum. (2003). *Top 10 immigration myths and facts.* Washington, DC: Author. Retrieved May 18, 2005, from www.immigrationforum.org/documents/TheJourney/MythsandFacts.pdf

Nelson-Barber, S. (1999). A better education for every child: The dilemma for teachers of linguistically diverse students. In *Including CLD students in standards-based reform: A report on McREL's diversity roundtable I.* Retrieved September 1, 2004, from www.mcrel.org/PDFConversion/Diversity/rt1chapter2.html

New York State Education Department. (2002). *Key issues in bilingual special education work paper #5.* Retrieved November 12, 2002, from www.vesid.nysed.gov/lsn/bilingual/trainingmodules05rr.pdf

Numeroff, L. (1985). *If you give a mouse a cookie.* New York: HarperCollins Children's Books.

O'Connor, R. E., & Jenkins, J. R. (1999). Prediction of reading disabilities in kindergarten and first grade. *Scientific Studies of Reading, 3*(2), 159–197.

O'Malley, J. M., & Pierce, L. V. (1996). *Authentic assessment for English language learners: Practical approaches for teachers.* Reading, MA: Addison-Wesley.

Ortiz, A. A. (2004, September). *Language acquisition and assessment: Distinguishing differences from disabilities for English language learners.* Session presented at Getting It Right: Improving Education for English Language Learners with Special Needs Workshop, Emporia State University, Emporia, Kansas.

Ortiz, A. A., & Wilkinson, C. Y. (1989). Adapting IEPs for limited English proficient students. *Academic Therapy, 24*(5), 555–568.

Ortiz, S. O. (2004, February). Learning disabilities: A primer for parents about identification. *Communiqué, 32*(5).

Oswald, D. P., Coutinho, M. J., Best, A. M., & Singh, N. N. (1999). Ethnic representation in special education: The influence of school-related economic and demographic variables. *Journal of Special Education, 32*(3), 194–206.

Ovando, C. J., Collier, V. P., Combs, M. C. (2003). *Bilingual and ESL classrooms: Teaching in multicultural contexts* (3rd ed.). New York: McGraw-Hill.

Overton, T., Fielding, C., & Simonsson, M. (2004). Decision making in determining eligibility of culturally and linguistically diverse learners: Reasons given by assessment personnel. *Journal of Learning Disabilities, 37*(4), 319–330.

Owens, R. E. (2001). *Language development: An introduction* (5th ed.). Boston: Allyn and Bacon.

Padilla, A. M. (Ed.). (1980). *Acculturation: The-ory, models, and some new findings.* Boulder, CO: Westview Press.

Paris, S. G., & Ayers, L. R. (1994). *Becoming re-flective students and teachers with portfolios and authentic assessment.* Washington, DC: American Psychological Association.

Pert, C. B. (1997). *Change of mind, molecules of emotion: Why you feel the way you feel.* New York: Scribner.

Phinney, J. S. (1993). A three-stage model of ethnic identity development. In M. E. Bernal & G. P. Knight (Eds.), *Ethnic identity: Formation and transmission among Hispanics and other mi-norities* (pp. 61–79). Albany: State University of New York Press.

Poon-McBrayer, K. F., & Garcia, S. B. (2000). Profiles of Asian American students with LD at initial referral, assessment, and placement in special education. *Journal of Learning Disabili-ties, 33*(1), 61–71.

Proctor, B. D., & Dalaker, J. (2002). *Poverty in the United States: 2001* (Current Population Re-ports P60–219). Washington, DC: U.S. Census Bureau. Retrieved May 27, 2005, from www.census.gov/prod/2002pubs/p60–219.pdf

Quiroga, T., Lemos-Britton, Z., Mostafapour, E., Abbott, R. D., & Berninger, V. W. (2001). Pho-nological awareness and beginning reading in Spanish-speaking ESL first graders: Research into practice. *Journal of School Psychology, 40*(1), 85–109.

Ramírez, J. D., Yuen, S. D., Ramey, D. R., & Pasta, D. J. (1991). *Final report: Longitudinal study of structured English immersion strategy, early-exit and late-exit transitional bilingual education programs for language-minority chil-dren* (Vols. I and II). San Mateo, CA: Aguirre International.

Rangel, R., & Bansberg, B. (1999). *Snapshot As-sessment System: An informal tool for class-room teachers for migrant, language-minority, and mobile students. Grades 1–3, 4–6, 7–8.* Au-rora, CO: McREL Institute.

Reynolds, C. R., Lowe, P. A., & Saenz, A. L. (1999). The problem of bias in psychological assessment. In C. R. Reynolds & T. B. Gutkin (Eds.), *The handbook of school psychology* (3rd ed., pp. 549–595). New York: Wiley.

Rodriguez, D., Parmar, R. S., & Signer, B. R. (2001). Fourth-grade culturally and linguisti-cally diverse exceptional students' concepts of number line. *Exceptional Children, 67*(2), 199–210. Retrieved November 13, 2002, from WilsonSelectPlus database.

Rogoff, B., Paradise, R., Mejía Arauz, R., Correa-Chávez, M., & Angelillo, C. (2003). Firsthand learning through intent participation. *Annual Review of Psychology, 54,* 175–203.

Romero, A. J., Robinson, T. N., Haydel, K. F., Mendoza, F., & Killen, J. D. (2004). Associa-tions among familism, language preference, and education in Mexican-American mothers and their children. *Journal of Developmental & Be-havioral Pediatrics, 25*(1), 34–40.

Roskos, K. A., & Christie, J. F. (2002). "Know-ing in the doing": Observing literacy learning in play. *Young Children, 57*(2), 46–54.

Rosner, J. (1979). Test of auditory analysis skills (TAAS). In *Helping children overcome learn-ing difficulties: A step-by-step guide for parents and teachers* (pp. 77–80). New York: Academic Therapy.

Rowe, M. B. (1974). Wait-time and rewards as instructional variables, their influence on lan-guage, logic, and fate control: Part one—wait time. *Journal of Research in Science Teaching, 11*(2), 81–94.

Ruiz-de-Velasco, J., & Fix, M. (with Clewell, B.). (2000). *Overlooked and underserved: Immi-grant students in U.S. secondary schools.* Wash-ington, DC: Urban Institute Press.

Ruiz-Primo, M. A., & Furtak, E. M. (2004). *In-formal formative assessment of students' under-standing of scientific inquiry.* Paper presented at the annual meeting of the American Educational Research Association, San Diego, CA.

Saleebey, D. (2001). *Human behavior and social environments: A biopsychosocial approach.* New York: Columbia University Press.

Salend, S. J. (2005). *Creating inclusive classrooms: Effective and reflective practices for all students*

(5th ed.). Upper Saddle River, NJ: Prentice Hall.

Sam, D. L., & Oppedal, B. (2002). Acculturation as a developmental pathway. In W. J. Lonner, D. L. Dinnel, S. A. Hayes, & D. N. Sattler (Eds.), *Online readings in psychology and culture* (Unit 8, Chapter 6). Bellingham: Western Washington University, Center for Cross-Cultural Research. Retrieved August 26, 2005, from www.wwu.edu/~culture

Schatschneider, C., Fletcher, J. M., Francis, D. J., Carlson, C. D., & Foorman, B. (2004). Kindergarten prediction of reading skills: A longitudinal comparative analysis. *Journal of Educational Psychology, 96*(2), 264–282.

Searle, W., & Ward, C. (1990). The prediction of psychological and socio-cultural adjustment during cross-cultural transitions. *International Journal of Intercultural Relations, 14*, 449–464.

Shavelson, R. J., & SEAL Group. (2003). *On the integration of formative assessment in teaching and learning with implications for teacher education.* Paper presented at the biannual meeting of the European Association for Research on Learning and Instruction, Padova, Italy. Retrieved September 23, 2004, from www.stanford.edu/dept/SUSE/SEAL/Reports_Papers/Paper.htm

Shinn, M. R., Baker, S., Habedank, L., & Good, R. H. (1993). The effects of classroom reading performance data on general education teachers' and parents' attitudes about reintegration. *Exceptionality, 4*, 205–228.

Shinn, M. R., Powell-Smith, K. A., Good, R. H., III, & Baker, S. (1997). The effects of reintegration into general education reading instruction for students with mild disabilities. *Exceptional Children, 64*(1), 59–79.

Shrake, E. K., & Rhee, S. (2004). Ethnic identity as a predictor of problem behaviors among Korean American adolescents. *Adolescence, 39*, 601–632.

Slavin, R. E. (2006). *Educational psychology: Theory and practice.* Boston: Allyn and Bacon.

Smith Bailey, D. (2003). Who is learning disabled? Psychologists and educators debate over how to identify students with learning disabilities. *Monitor on Psychology, 34*(8), 58.

Spradley, J. P. (1979). *The ethnographic interview.* New York: Holt, Rinehart and Winston.

Sprenger, M. (1999). *Learning and memory: The brain in action.* Alexandria, VA: Association for Supervision and Curriculum Development.

Stiggins, R. J. (1997). *Student-centered classroom assessment* (2nd ed.). Upper Saddle River, NJ: Prentice Hall.

Stiggins, R. J. (2002). Assessment crisis: The absence of assessment *FOR* learning. *Phi Delta Kappan, 83*(10), 758–765. Retrieved October 20, 2004, from www.pdkintl.org/kappan/k0206sti.htm

Suinn, R. M., Richard-Figueroa, K., Lew, S., & Vigil, P. (1987). The Suinn-Lew Asian Self-Identity Acculturation Scale: An initial report. *Educational & Psychological Measurement, 47*(2), 401–407.

Szapocznik, J., & Kurtines, W. (1980). Acculturation, biculturism, and adjustment among Cuban Americans. In A. Padilla (Ed.), *Acculturation, theory, models, and new findings* (pp. 139–159). Boulder, CO: Westview Press.

Teachers of English to Speakers of Other Languages (TESOL). (2003). *TESOL/NCATE program standards: Standards for the accreditation of initial programs in P–12 ESL teacher education.* Retrieved from www.tesol.org

Thanasoulas, D. (2001, August). Language and disadvantage. *ELT Newsletter,* Article 70. Retrieved May 19, 2005, from http://eltnewsletter.com/back/August2001/art702001.htm

The No Child Left Behind Act of 2001, Pub. L. No. 107–110 (2002).

Thomas, W. P., & Collier, V. P. (1997). *School effectiveness for language minority students* (NCBE Resource Collection Series No. 9). Washington, DC: National Clearinghouse for Bilingual Education. Retrieved October 7, 2002, from www.ncela.gwu.edu/ncbepubs/resource/effectiveness

Thomas, W. P., & Collier, V. P. (2002). *A national study of school effectiveness for language mi-*

nority students' long-term academic achievement. Santa Cruz, CA: Center for Research on Education, Diversity & Excellence. Retrieved February 5, 2003, from www.crede.ucsc.edu/research/llaa/1.1_final.html

Thompson, L. W. (2004). *Literacy development for English language learners: Classroom challenges in the NCLB age.* Monterey, CA: CTB/McGraw-Hill.

Tombari, M., & Borich, G. (1999). *Authentic assessment in the classroom: Applications and practice.* Upper Saddle River, NJ: Merrill Prentice Hall.

Touchstone Applied Science. (2001). *Maculaitis Assessment of Competencies II* (MAC II). Brewster, NY: Author.

Townsend, B. L. (2000). The disproportionate discipline of African American learners: Reducing school suspensions and expulsions. *Exceptional Children, 66,* 381–391.

Trifonovitch, G. (1977). Culture learning—culture teaching. *Educational Perspectives, 16*(4), 18–22.

U.S. Congress. (March 12, 1999). IDEA: Rules and regulations. *Federal Register, 64*(8). Washington, DC: Author.

U.S. Department of Education. (2002a). *The same high standards for migrant students: Holding Title I schools accountable.* Washington, DC: Author. Retrieved March 16, 2006, from www.ed.gov/programs/mep/resources.html

U.S. Department of Education. (2002b). *Twenty-fourth annual report to Congress on the implementation of the Individuals with Disabilities Education Act.* Washington, DC: Author. Retrieved June 10, 2005, from www.ed.gov/about/offices/list/osers/osep/research.html

Unger, J. B., Ritt-Olson, A., Teran, L., Huang, T., Hoffman, B. R., & Palmer, P. H. (2002). Cultural values and substance use in a multiethnic sample of California adolescents. *Addiction Research & Theory, 10*(3), 257–279.

Unz, R., & Tuchman, G. M. (n.d.). *English language education for children in public schools.* Retrieved April 15, 2005, from www.humnet. ucla.edu/humnet/linguistics/people/grads/macswan/unztext.htm

Uriarte, M. (2002). The high stakes of high-stakes testing. In Z. F. Beykont (Ed.), *The power of culture: Teaching across language difference* (pp. 1–14). Cambridge, MA: Harvard Education Publishing Group.

Van Hook, J., & Fix, M. (2000). A profile of immigrant students in the U.S. In J. Ruiz-de-Velasco & M. Fix, *Overlooked and underserved: Immigrant students in U.S. secondary schools.* Boston: McGraw-Hill.

Van Horn, R. (2003). Technology: Computer adaptive tests and computer-based tests. *Phi Delta Kappan, 84*(8), 567, 630.

Volante, L. (2004). Teaching to the test: What every educator and policy-maker should know. *Canadian Journal of Educational Administration and Policy, 35.* Retrieved October 12, 2004, from www.umanitoba.ca/publications/cjeap/articles/volante.html

Vygotsky, L. S. (1962). *Thought and language.* Cambridge, MA: MIT Press.

Wangsatorntanakhun, J. A. (1997). *Designing performance assessments: Challenges for the three-story intellect.* Retrieved July 7, 2004, from www.geocities.com/Athens/Parthenon/8658

Wenglingsky, H. (2000). *How teaching matters: Bringing the classroom back into discussions of teacher quality.* Princeton, NJ: Miliken Family Foundation and Educational Testing Service.

Westby, C., Dezale, J., Fradd, S. H., & Lee, O. (1999). Learning to do science: Influences of language and culture. *Communication Disorders Quarterly, 21*(1), 50–65.

Wiliam, D. (2004). Working inside the black box: Assessment for learning in the classroom. *Phi Delta Kappan, 86*(1), 8–21.

Wilkinson, C. Y., & Ortiz, A. A. (1986). *Characteristics of limited English proficient and English proficient learning disabled Hispanic students at initial assessment and at reevaluation.* Austin: University of Texas, Department of Special Education, Handicapped Minority Research Institute on Language Proficiency. (ERIC Document Reproduction Service No. ED283314)

Woodcock, R. W., McGrew, K. S., & Mather, N. (2001). *Woodcock-Johnson III Tests of Achievement.* Itasca, IL: Riverside.

Woodcock, R., Muñoz-Sandoval, A. F., Ruef, M., & Alvaredo, C. G. (2005). *Woodcock-Muñoz Language Survey Revised (WMLS-R).* Itasca, IL: Riverside.

Wright, M. O., & Littleford, L. N. (2002). Experiences and beliefs as predictors of ethnic identity and intergroup relations. *Journal of Multicultural Counseling and Development, 30,* 2–20.

Yates, J. R. (1998, April). *The state of practice in the education of CLD students.* Presentation at the annual meeting of the Council for Exceptional Children, Minneapolis, MN.